W9-CTH-619

DATE DUE

			PRINTED IN U.S.A.

Authors
& Artists
for Young
Adults

ISSN 1040-5682

Authors & Artists for Young Adults

VOLUME 24

Thomas McMahon
Editor

GALE

DETROIT · NEW YORK · TORONTO · LONDON

Thomas McMahon, *Editor*

Joyce Nakamura, *Managing Editor*

Hal May, *Publisher*

Diane Andreassi, Joanne Brod, Ken Cuthbertson, R. Garcia-Johnson,
Marian C. Gonsior, J. Sydney Jones, Irene McKnight-Durham, Nancy Rampson,
C. M. Ratner, Susan Reicha, Jordan Richman, Peggy Saari, Gerard J. Senick,
Kenneth R. Shepherd, Tracy J. Sukraw, Crystal Towns, Kathleen Witman,
Sketchwriters/Contributing Editors

Victoria B. Cariappa, *Research Manager*
Cheryl L. Warnock, *Project Coordinator*
Gary J. Oudersluys and Maureen Richards, *Research Specialists*
Laura C. Bissey and Sean R. Smith, *Research Associates*

Susan M. Trosky, *Permissions Manager*
Maria L. Franklin, *Permissions Specialist*
Michele Lonoconus, *Permissions Associate*
Andrea Rigby, *Permissions Assitant*

Mary Beth Trimper, *Production Director*
Deborah Milliken, *Production Assistant*

Randy Bassett, *Image Database Supervisor*
Mikal Ansari, *Macintosh Artist*
Robert Duncan, *Imaging Specialist*
Pamela A. Reed, *Photography Coordinator*

The paper used in this publication meets the minimum requirements of American National Standard for Information Sciences—Permanence Paper for Printed Library Materials, ANSI Z39.48-1984.

Library of Congress Catalog Card Number 89-641100
ISBN 0-7876-1971-X
ISSN 1040-5682

10 9 8 7 6 5 4 3 2 1

Printed in the United States of America

Contents

Introduction

Authors and Artists for Young Adults is a reference series designed to serve the needs of middle school, junior high, and high school students interested in creative artists. Originally inspired by the need to bridge the gap between Gale's *Something about the Author,* created for children, and *Contemporary Authors,* intended for older students and adults, *Authors and Artists for Young Adults* has been expanded to cover not only an international scope of authors, but also a wide variety of other artists.

Although the emphasis of the series remains on the writer for young adults, we recognize that these readers have diverse interests covering a wide range of reading levels. The series therefore contains not only those creative artists who are of high interest to young adults, including cartoonists, photographers, music composers, bestselling authors of adult novels, media directors, producers, and performers, but also literary and artistic figures studied in academic curricula, such as influential novelists, playwrights, poets, and painters. The goal of *Authors and Artists for Young Adults* is to present this great diversity of creative artists in a format that is entertaining, informative, and understandable to the young adult reader.

Entry Format

Each volume of *Authors and Artists for Young Adults* will furnish in-depth coverage of twenty to twenty-five authors and artists. The typical entry consists of:

—A detailed biographical section that includes date of birth, marriage, children, education, and addresses.

—A comprehensive bibliography or filmography including publishers, producers, and years.

—Adaptations into other media forms.

—Works in progress.

—A distinctive essay featuring comments on an artist's life, career, artistic intentions, world views, and controversies.

—References for further reading.

—Extensive illustrations, photographs, movie stills, cartoons, book covers, and other relevant visual material.

A cumulative index to featured authors and artists appears in each volume.

Compilation Methods

The editors of *Authors and Artists for Young Adults* make every effort to secure information directly from the authors and artists through personal correspondence and interviews. Sketches on living authors and artists are sent to the biographee for review prior to publication. Any sketches not personally reviewed by biographees or their representatives are marked with an asterisk (*).

Highlights of Forthcoming Volumes

Among the authors and artists planned for future volumes are:

Joan Aiken	Lorraine Hansberry	Donna Jo Napoli
Scott Adams	Oscar Hijuelos	Theresa Nelson
Julia Alvarez	Jack Kerouac	James Patterson
Alan Baillie	Ken Kesey	Tamora Pierce
Anthony Burgess	David Klass	Kim Stanley Robinson
Ken Burns	Barry Levinson	Suzanne Fisher Staples
Tim Cahill	Mary E. Lyons	Barry Sonnenfeld
Aidan Chambers	Herman Melville	Marc Talbert
Wes Craven	Claude Monet	Elenora E. Tate
Helen Cresswell	Kyoko Mori	Rob Thomas
Tom Feelings	Michael Moorcock	Edith Wharton
Mel Glenn	Marcia Muller	Oprah Winfrey

Contact the Editor

We encourage our readers to examine the entire *AAYA* series. Please write and tell us if we can make AAYA even more helpful to you. Give your comments and suggestions to the editor:

BY MAIL: The Editor, *Authors and Artists for Young Adults*, Gale Research, 835 Penobscot Building, 645 Griswold St., Detroit, MI 48226-4094.

BY TELEPHONE: (800) 347-GALE

BY FAX: (313) 961-6599

BY E-MAIL: CYA@Gale.com@GALESMTP

Authors & Artists for Young Adults

Tim Allen

■ Personal

Born Timothy Allen Dick, June 13, 1953, in Denver, CO; son of Gerald (a real estate salesperson) and Martha (a community service worker) Dick; married Laura Deibel, 1984; children: Kady (daughter). *Education:* Graduated from Western Michigan University, 1976; studied acting at University of Detroit. *Hobbies and other interests:* Collecting high performance cars.

■ Addresses

Office—Home Improvement, Walt Disney Studios, 500 South Buena Vista St., Burbank, CA 91521.

■ Career

Actor, stand-up comedian, writer. Worked as a creative director at an advertising agency in Detroit, MI.

■ Awards, Honors

Golden Globe Award nomination for best actor in a musical or comedy series, 1993, for *Home Im-*

provement; recipient of several People's Choice Awards.

■ Writings

Don't Stand Too Close to a Naked Man, Hyperion, 1994.
I'm Not Really Here, Hyperion, 1996.

■ Credits

TELEVISION APPEARANCES

Tim Taylor, *Home Improvement,* ABC, 1991—.

Has also appeared on various specials, including *Tim Allen: Men Are Pigs,* Showtime, 1990; *Tim Allen Rewires America,* Showtime, 1991; *Back to School '92* (also known as Education First!) CBS, 1992; *The Ultimate Driving Challenge,* CBS, 1993; *Comedy Club All-Stars VII* (host), Showtime, 1993.

FILM APPEARANCES

Appeared as himself in *Comedy's Dirtiest Dozen,* 1988.

Scott Calvin, *The Santa Clause*, Disney, 1994.
Buzz Lightyear (voice), *Toy Story*, Disney, 1995.
Michael Cromwell, *Jungle 2 Jungle*, Disney, 1997.
For Richer or Poorer, Universal, 1997.

■ Sidelights

When Tim Allen sends out his trademark primal call, "Augh! Augh! Augh!," a sound akin to a gorilla's grunt, he gets attention. The ape call is part of Allen's self-molded brand of humor, which he calls "masculinist," and was first heard in his popular nightclub comedy act. Later he refined his ideas, sold them to Disney, and went on to star in the popular television comedy, *Home Improvement*, about a blustering handyman who hosts a cable television show and is prone to accidents during his fix-up jobs. "Tim is Dagwood [a character from the comic strip *Blondie*] with an attitude, an aggressive goof-up whose masculine pride frequently gets him in trouble with the rest of the family," wrote Ken Tucker in *Entertainment Weekly*. With the help of a group of talented writers, the show shook the TV ratings charts and became a hit almost overnight. Allen became just as popular in print and on the big screen. He was able to master two creative challenges in 1994 when he wrote the best-seller, *Don't Stand Too Close to a Naked Man*, and starred in the Disney film *The Santa Clause*, which some believe is on its way to becoming a Christmas classic. Allen also was the voice of Buzz Lightyear in Disney's 1995 hit *Toy Story*, and in 1997 he starred in the movie *For Richer For Poorer* with Kirstie Alley.

But Allen's life hasn't been all laughs and successful ventures. He was born in 1953 in Denver, Colorado, one of six children in a family of five boys and one girl. (Born Timothy Allen Dick, Allen shortened his name when he entered show business. The butt of a thousand playground jokes because of his family surname, he learned that humor was the best defense to help him through tough times.) His family life laid a strong foundation for his career. "In retrospect it seems that Allen has been preparing for his alter ego since those long-ago Saturday afternoons . . . spent with four brothers and his father, Gerald, a real estate salesman, poring over hardware in the Sears store near their Denver home," according to a *People* magazine article. Allen told Patty Lanoue Sterns in *Friends* that his father would "tinker with cars a lot. He'd always put dual exhaust, different

manifolds on. He made the family wagon loud and fast—my kind of guy."

But Allen's life took an unexpected turn in November 1964 when his father was killed by a drunk driver who smashed into the family's car on the way home from a University of Colorado football game. Though his father had been driving home a carload of people, he was the only one killed; Allen was the only family member who hadn't gone to the game. After Gerald's death, Allen's mother, a community service worker, took her six children and moved back to the family home in Birmingham, Michigan, where she became reacquainted with a man she knew in high school. Widowed with two sons and a daughter of his own, he married Allen's mother and the families were blended.

In school, Allen reveled in his role as the class joker, and his favorite class was, of course, shop. "I loved making stuff and the smell of those places, but I hated the teachers," Allen told *People*. He admitted to Sterns that he didn't want to make teaching shop his career. "It's hard listening to people with no fingers," he joked. After graduating from high school, Allen attended Central Michigan University, then transferred to Western Michigan University where he earned a bachelor's degree in television production in 1976.

Bad Turn With Drugs

About this time, Allen stumbled into trouble for dealing cocaine, though he said he was never more than an occasional recreational user. He told *People* that he didn't know what to do with his life ("I was floundering, actually"), and the money attained by selling drugs was attractive. In 1979 Allen, along with twenty others, was arrested and charged with possession and distribution of narcotics. He spent sixty days in a county holding cell and described it in *People* as being a horrible "caldron of despair." He pleaded guilty at his arraignment. "I knew what I did was wrong," Allen confided to Daniel Cerone in the *Los Angeles Times*. "I did not drag it out in a trial. I knew I made a major mistake. I laid down. Punish me."

Before sentencing he made important choices that ultimately launched his career. Allen took a job at a sporting goods store and went on stage at a Detroit-area nightclub, the Comedy Castle. But the

Allen stars as Tim Taylor, the host of a cable television show, in the hit ABC-TV comedy *Home Improvement*.

laughs would have to wait. Allen was sentenced in November 1980 to eight years in prison at Sandstone Federal Correctional Institution in Minnesota, a minimum security prison. "Allen found humor useful in prison," according to Richard Zoglin in *Time.* "He made the meanest guards laugh by putting pictures of Richard Nixon in the peephole of his cell when they made their rounds." Later he staged comedy shows for the other inmates. While he was in prison, Allen kept ties with his girlfriend, Laura Deibel, who he married in 1984, and with the owner of the Comedy Castle. With time off for good behavior, Allen was released after twenty-eight months. He told Andrew Abrahams in *Ladies' Home Journal:* "I'm glad I paid for it and got straightened out. [It] started this process of deciding what was important. It was like a close call with death."

After he was released, Allen took a job as creative director at a Detroit advertising agency, which he left after he became successful doing commercials for Ford, Chevrolet, and Kmart. True to form, he was also seen in some "Mr. Goodwrench" spots for General Motors. His comedy act took off as he traveled the country performing on the comedy club circuit. Allen went on to become a cable television star, and his TV special *Men Are Pigs* was aired on Showtime in 1990. During that time Allen honed his signature sound, "Augh, Augh, Augh," and grabbed the attention of Disney executives who would forever change his career. His leap into television and movies was ignited in 1990 when Disney Studio executives offered him roles in such projects as a TV sitcom based on the film *Turner and Hooch.* Allen didn't think he was suited for these projects, turned them down, and offered his own idea, which was to become *Home Improvement.*

Character Has Character

Tim Taylor, Allen's character in *Home Improvement,* is a middle-class bread winner living in the Detroit area. He has a wife, Jill, played by Patricia Richardson, and three boys, played by Zachery Ty Bryan, Jonathan Taylor Thomas, and Taran Noah Smith. "Tim Taylor is supposed to be a likable lout, and he is, and not just because Tim Allen is a smart comedian who has proven to be a sly, charming actor," according to Tucker in *Entertainment Weekly.* "Taylor is a vulgar character that viewers can enjoy guilt-free, because his point of

view is balanced—redeemed, even—by Jill's common sense feminism." Taylor's job is hosting a cable television home improvement show called *Tool Time,* and his solution to every problem on the show and at home is to add more power to whatever needs fixing. While everything mechanical he touches usually blows up in his face, he usually comes to terms with his moral dilemmas with more finesse. Tim's *Tool Time* assistant, Al Borland, played by Richard Karn, is the real home improvement expert with all the right answers and techniques. Even though the cable television audience sees this and often applauds Al with much more vigor than Tim, Al always bows to Taylor's lesser abilities and greater charm. Still, Al manages to poke fun at Tim's antics, his catchphrase being, "I don't *think* so, Tim."

Another regular on the show is Wilson, played by Earl Hindman, the next door neighbor who imparts endless nuggets of wisdom from ancient sages and folklore, as well as famous and not-so-famous scribes. In developing the series, Allen envisioned Wilson as a "neighbor who is a man's soul, whom I see only from the eyes up," he told a reporter with the *Washington Post TV Week.* And that's just how the character is seen by the television audiences. Every time Taylor finds himself in a difficult situation with his family or friends, Wilson provides the balm with anecdotal advice. But his identity is always hidden, usually by the backyard fence, but in other scenes behind a plant in the house or some other convenient prop. Several of Wilson's views are derived from author and poet Robert Bly's examination of masculine behavior in the book *Iron John.* Some critics, in fact, speculate that Allen's comedy is merely Bly's wisdom in disguise. As Tucker wrote, Allen's Tim Taylor character "is a comic symbol of the media-hyped 'men's movement'. . . ."

In an interview with Camille Paglia in *Esquire* magazine, Allen made some serious observations about the relationships between men and women in the 1990s. "I don't think feminism is unfair," Allen told Paglia. "I always thought it was just a celebration of what's female or an investigation of such. . . ." He added, "Because of the women in my life, I understand their frustrations in trying to do all of these things: 'I'm supposed to be the corporate woman; I'm supposed to do this; I'm supposed to be the mother.' All the things . . . that are outside the sphere that I created to give myself a buffer so that I could live. You now want

When he accidentally scares Kris Kringle off his roof, rendering the jolly old man incapable of delivering presents, Scott Calvin takes over the reins in *The Santa Clause,* Allen's big-screen debut.

to get me out of that too—you really don't want me to exist. That's how I feel sometimes—you really don't want me to exist."

Tough Audience Tunes In

These male-female issues are often explored on *Home Improvement,* a show that plugged into a large male audience. But it's not only the men watching. In it's first season *Home Improvement* reached number five in the television ratings. Still, the success didn't come without some pain. The brakes were applied, temporarily, on Allen's sky-rocketing success when, as the series was beginning production, rumors circulated about his jail sentence. Allen reluctantly came forward with the news by first telling Disney executives and then the world in a *USA Today* interview. "The audience reacted predictably," Disney's Richard Frank told *TV Guide.* "They said, 'OK, we buy the fact

that someone can make a mistake, and that his life can change for the better.'"

Both Allen and *Home Improvement* have gone on to become fan favorites, winning several People's Choice Awards. Along with this success, Allen taped another cable television special of his stand-up work, *Tim Allen Rewires America.* Allen describes the humor in it as his rendition of feminism for men. He told *TV Time:* "Feminism was never intended to be antimale, so masculinism is not antifemale. It's different than chauvinism—it's a celebration of what is male. And you don't have to be macho to be a masculinist."

His introspective theories about the differences between men and women, his father's death, his family, and the time he spent in prison were the basis of his first book, *Don't Stand Too Close to a Naked Man,* a 1994 best-seller. It was the same year he made his debut on the big screen star-

Allen and co-star Kirstie Alley portray tax-evading New Yorkers who impersonate an Amish couple in *For Richer For Poorer*, a 1997 film.

ring in the Disney film *The Santa Clause*, about a divorced father, Scott Calvin, whose son forces him into the role of Santa when the jolly man from the North Pole falls off their roof on Christmas Eve. "This is the most playfully amusing, inventive new cinematic Christmas fable in several decades," according to Ralph Novak in *People*. In the film, Calvin finds a card in Santa's suit that authorizes anyone who finds it to take Santa's place and finish his rounds should Santa become incapacitated. Calvin grows a huge belly and sprouts white whiskers after learning that he's got the job for life. "Allen is likable (if you like him), and he pulls off plenty of cute bits and sarcastic one-liners," explained Jeff Giles in *Newsweek*.

Two years later his next book, *I'm Not Really Here*, hit the bookstores. In the work, Allen takes a long look at his fame and fatherhood and reveals a serious interest in spiritualism and philosophy. He also gives a not-so-serious glance at ear hair and

flatulence. *People*'s Alex Tresniowski described the work as often self-indulgent, "but Allen deserves points for daring to be dark." Allen's next career adventure was serving as the voice of Buzz Lightyear in the popular Disney cartoon, *Toy Story*, the first full-length film created wholly by computer. The story is about a little boy's toys who are alive and led by a cloth cowboy named Sheriff Woody, whose voice was supplied by Tom Hanks. The boy's new prize toy, space explorer Buzz Lightyear, makes the insecure Woody wonder about his standing in the boy's eyes. This leads to an adversarial relationship between Woody and Buzz until they finally join forces as uneasy partners against Sid, the toy torturer who lives next door. Critics were impressed with the film. David Ansen, writing in *Newsweek*, praised the "cast of voices, led by superbly expressive performances from Hanks and Allen, that brings these computer-generated fantasies to delightfully cantankerous life."

If you enjoy the works of Tim Allen, you may also want to check out the following books and films:

Ellen Degeneres, *My Point—And I Do Have One,* 1996.
Paul Reiser, *Couplehood,* 1994.
Jerry Seinfeld, *Seinlanguage,* 1995.
Mrs. Doubtfire, starring Robin Williams, 1993.

In 1997 Allen starred in *Jungle 2 Jungle,* a film produced by Disney. "Once again, he [Allen]'s an irascible guy's guy who's baffled and exasperated by the mysteries of women and children, yet eminently trainable as a decent human being," Lisa Schwarzbaum explained in *Entertainment Weekly.* Allen plays Michael Cromwell, a New York City commodities broker separated from his wife who is a doctor in an Amazonian village. When Cromwell goes to the jungle to get divorce papers, he learns he has a son and agrees to bring him to New York. This launches the youngster's adjustment to city life, including using a toilet. Adapting to a different lifestyle was also the theme of Allen's next movie, *For Richer For Poorer,* which also featured Kirstie Alley. Allen and Alley play a wealthy New York couple who get caught cheating on their taxes and flee the city. Their escape leads them to Amish country where they desperately try to impersonate an Amish couple, a task they find overwhelming.

Allen lives in the San Fernando Valley with his wife and daughter, but they frequently travel back to Michigan where they have a home in suburban Bloomfield Hills, as well as a lake house in northern Michigan right next door to his in-laws. In his free time Allen has developed a passion for reading books on physics, and he continues to play with his collection of cars, including a 1966 Ferrari and a pair of Mustangs. In fact, Allen was in a fast car in spring of 1997 when he was arrested in Bloomfield Hills for driving under the influence. He was given probation, a restricted driving license, and a $500 fine. "I have been treated fairly by the authorities in my hometown, however, my inexcusable lapse in judgment is a mistake that is embarrassing to myself, my family, and my associates," Allen said through his press agent at the time. "I have learned from this experience, and I am fortunate that my family and associates have forgiven me."

Despite the downfalls and tremendous successes as a stand-up comic, on television, as an author, and finally on the big screen, Allen's longtime friends maintain that he has stayed grounded. "He just never lost perspective," Bruce Economou, an close friend from Michigan, told Zoglin in *Time* magazine. "When he first went to the *Home Improvement* stage, where they were building the sets, and the people from Disney were walking him through, they told him, 'This is for you.' Tim looked at it and said, 'Well, if this show doesn't work, can I have the wood?'"

■ Works Cited

Abrahams, Andrew, *Ladies' Home Journal,* February 22, 1992.
Ansen, David, "Disney's Digital Delight," *Newsweek,* November 27, 1995, p. 89.
Cerone, Daniel, *Los Angeles Times,* September 17, 1991.
Giles, Jeff, "Lumps of Coal," *Newsweek,* November 21, 1994, p. 96.
Novak, Ralph, review of *The Santa Clause, People,* November 21, 1994, pp. 21-22.
Paglia, Camille, "When Camille Met Tim," *Esquire,* February 1995, pp. 68-73.
"Real Men Laugh Last," *People,* July 6, 1992.
Schwarzbaum, Lisa, "Another Vine Mess, Tim Allen," *Entertainment Weekly,* March 21, 1997, p. 53.
Sterns, Patty Lanoue, *Friends,* May/June 1992.
Tresniowski, Alex, review of *I'm Not Really Here, People,* December 2, 1996, p. 32.
Tucker, Ken, "Comforts of 'Home'," *Entertainment Weekly,* May 21, 1993, pp. 36-38.
TV Guide, April 18-24, 1992.
TV Time, November 9-15, 1991.
Washington Post TV Week, December 15-21, 1991.
Zoglin, Richard, "Tim at the Top," *Time,* December 12, 1994.

■ For More Information See

BOOKS

Contemporary Theatre, Film, and Television, Volume 12, Gale, 1994.
Performing Artists, Volume 1, Gale, 1995.

PERIODICALS

Cosmopolitan, September, 1995, p. 242.
Detroit Free Press, June 7, 1991; November 24, 1991; October 5, 1994; November 11, 1994.
Detroit News, December 6, 1997, pp. 1C, 6C.
Entertainment Weekly, October 25, 1991; July 17, 1992; December 30, 1994, p. 20; November 1, 1996, p. 76; November 22, 1996, p. 129; December 20, 1996, p. 61; June 13, 1997, p. 13.
Gentlemen's Quarterly, March, 1994, p. 92.
Ladies' Home Journal, December, 1992, p. 44; December, 1993, p. 112.
People, October 3, 1994, p. 34; November 28, 1994, p. 194; December 26, 1994, p. 46.
Road and Track, June, 1994, p. 96.
TV Guide, September 10, 1994, p. 20; March 4, 1995, p. 37; November 18, 1995, p. 26.*

—Sketch by Diane Andreassi

Greg Bear

nesses, including Microsoft, and to WNET-13 in New York. Science and speculations advisor for pilot episode of *Earth 2*, NBC, 1995. *Member:* Science Fiction Writers of America (former chairman of Grievance Committee and vice-president; president, 1988-90).

■ Personal

Born August 20, 1951, in San Diego, CA; son of Dale Franklin (a naval officer) and Wilma (a secretary and homemaker; maiden name, Merriman) Bear; married Christina Nielsen, January 12, 1975 (divorced August, 1981); married Astrid Anderson, June 18, 1983; children (second marriage): Erik William Anderson Bear, Alexandra Astrid Bear. *Education:* San Diego State College (now University), A.B., 1969.

■ Addresses

Home—506 Lakeview Rd., Alderwood Manor, WA 98037. *Agent*—Richard Curtis, 171 East 74th St., New York, NY 10021.

■ Career

Writer. Has also worked as a bookseller, a freelance journalist, and a teacher in San Diego, CA. Member of the Citizen's Advisory Council on National Space Policy, 1983-90. Consultant to busi-

■ Awards, Honors

Nebula Awards, Science Fiction Writers of America, both 1984, for best novelette "Blood Music" and for best novella "Hardfought"; Hugo Award, 1984, for best novelette "Blood Music"; Prix Apollo, 1986, for *Blood Music;* Nebula and Hugo Awards, 1987, for short story "Tangents"; Nebula Award, 1994, for best novel *Moving Mars.*

■ Writings

NOVELS

Hegira, Dell, 1979.
Psychlone, Ace, 1979, published as *Lost Souls,* Charter, 1982.
Beyond Heaven's River, Dell, 1980, revised edition, Severn House, 1989.
Strength of Stones, Ace, 1981, revised edition, Gollancz, 1988.
Corona: A Star Trek Novel, Pocket Books, 1984.
The Infinity Concerto, Berkeley, 1984.
Eon, Bluejay, 1985.
Blood Music, Arbor House, 1985.

The Serpent Mage, Berkeley, 1986.
The Forge of God, Tor, 1987.
Eternity, Warner, 1988.
Hardfought (bound with *Cascade Point* by Timothy Zahn), Tor, 1988.
Queen of Angels, Easton Press, 1990.
Heads, Legend (London), 1990, St. Martin's Press, 1991.
Anvils of Stars, Warner, 1992.
Songs of Earth and Power (includes *The Infinity Concerto* and *The Serpent Mage*), Legend, 1992, Tor, 1994.
Moving Mars, Tor, 1993.
Legacy, Tor, 1995.
(Editor with Martin Greenberg) *New Legends*, Tor, 1995.
/ [pronounced "Slant"], Tor, 1997.
Dinosaur Summer, Warner Aspect, 1997.

SHORT STORY COLLECTIONS

The Wind From a Burning Woman, Arkham, 1983.
Sleepside Story, Cheap Street, 1988.
Early Harvest, NESFA Press, 1988.
Tangents, Warner, 1989.
Sisters, Pulphouse, 1992.
The Venging, Legend, 1992.
Bear's Fantasies: Six Stories in Old Paradigms, Wildside Press, 1992.

OTHER

Contributor to science fiction periodicals, including *Omni, Analog: Science Fiction and Science Fact,* and *Isaac Asimov's Science Fiction Magazine.* Editor, with wife Astrid, of *Science Fiction Writers Association Forum.* Book reviewer for *San Diego Union Book Review* supplement, 1979-82. Bear's work has been translated into a dozen languages.

■ Adaptations

"Dead Run" was adapted for *The Twilight Zone* television series, 1986; *Blood Music* was broadcast as a radio play, Canadian Broadcasting Company; "The White Horse Child" was adapted for a CD-ROM multimedia presentation, Ebook, 1993.

■ Sidelights

Greg Bear is one of the most important writers in science fiction today. He has won the presti-

gious Nebula Award three times, and he also has two Hugo Awards to his credit. In the *St. James Guide to Science Fiction Writers*, David Brin stated that few SF authors "have been as influential in transforming the genre as Greg Bear, a prolific leader in exploring the concept of *change* as it affects civilization, science, and even human nature. Perhaps no other writer so well typifies one of the hallmarks of science fiction—the belief that ideas are among the most precious things."

Bear was a precocious youngster. His father was an officer in the U.S. Navy, and he was stationed

In this 1985 work, innovative sci-fi author Bear's highly advanced civilization combines space and time travel with an idealized view of man and machine as one, as an asteroid reveals fearful secrets.

at posts around the world. By the time he was twelve years old, Bear had traveled with his parents throughout the continental United States, Alaska, Japan, and the Philippines. It was in Alaska, at the age of nine, that Bear wrote his first short story. By the time he was fourteen, he had begun submitting his stories to magazines, and by the age of fifteen he sold his first short story to Robert Lowndes' *Famous Science Fiction.*

It took Bear five years to sell his next short story, and then his work began to appear in science fiction magazines with some regularity. He first published a novel, *Hegira,* in 1979. (Bear had finished his first novel, entitled *The Infinity Concerto,* when he was nineteen. The book wasn't published until some twelve years later, after Bear had rewritten it.) *Hegira* is the story of a civilization that is trapped in an artificial world. In this world, the only relief from cultural amnesia is found inscribed on the walls of mammoth towers, which stretch above the earth, beyond the sky. Like many of Bear's novels and short stories, *Hegira* combines powerful dream-like images and imaginative concepts to give the reader a new perspective on science and society.

Bear has strong interests in science, particularly astronomy and physics, and history. He has worked as a bookseller and a freelance journalist. On one assignment, he covered the Voyager missions to Jupiter and Saturn for the *San Diego Union.* He has written many articles on film for the *Los Angeles Times,* and he frequently lectures for the San Diego City Schools, acting as a roving teacher and conducting classes on ancient history, the history of science, and science fiction and fantasy.

Bear is also a talented illustrator and a founding member of the Association for Science Fiction Artists (ASFA). His illustrations have appeared in *Galaxy, Fantasy and Science Fiction,* and *Vertex,* as well as on bookcovers. As he remarked on his Website, however, "My last professional work of art was the cover of my own novel, *Psycholone,* in reprint from Tor. I do very little artwork now, devoting myself almost exclusively to writing."

The "Eon" Universe

One of Bear's first works to become a science fiction best-seller, *Eon,* was published in 1985. In the

HUGO AND NEBULA AWARD-WINNING AUTHOR
GREG BEAR
ETERNITY
THE SEQUEL TO EON

Following the highly praised *Eon,* this 1988 novel continues the sci-fi epic of the asteroid-ship Thistledown that stops an inhuman invasion, spans universes and time, and outlives death.

work, a huge, hollowed-out asteroid appears in the solar system and begins to orbit around the earth. Investigators, led by heroine-scientist Patricia Vasquez, discover that this asteroid is actually a spaceship, and that deserted chambers inside the ship, which are filled with forests, lakes, rivers, and hanging cities, are endpoints to "hyperspace tunnels" that reach throughout time and paratime. The asteroid has come from the future of a parallel earth, and as such it holds documents that forecast that nuclear war is only months away. Armed with this information, part of the Earth's population escapes by traveling along a path called the Way. Writing in *Science Fiction Chronicle,* Don D'Ammassa describes *Eon* as "thoroughly readable, with lots of adventure, a complex plot, an interesting mystery, and well resolved characters." On a less favorable note, Gene Deweese, writing in *Science Fiction and Fantasy Book Review,* believed the book to be overlong, and "despite the awesomeness of the setting, there is little mystery. . . ." Alex Raskin, writing in the *Los Angeles Times Book Review,* declares that "This attempt to venture beyond the stylistic frontiers of science fiction isn't wholly successful. . . . Each part, however, is entertaining in itself." In the *Washington Post Book World,* John Clute writes that "the Way has come to represent so complex an image of Future History that it is impossible to grasp it whole. But Bear's own grasp is unfaltering, his control over the ramifying implications of his tale nearly perfect. *Eon* may be the best-constructed hard sf epic yet."

Eternity, which was published in 1988, is a sequel to *Eon.* As the novel begins, Earth has survived a nuclear war, an encounter with a supercivilization, and an alien invasion. The designer of the Way, Pavel Mirsky, appears to warn Earth's inhabitants that the Way, now sealed, must be reopened and then destroyed. In *Science Fiction Chronicle,* Don D'Ammassa credited *Eternity's* "strongly realized characters" and "marvelously inventive setting." Writing in *Publishers Weekly,* Sybil Steinberg called the novel a "slow visionary tale" but noted that Bear's presentation "of the different responses of intricate, interlocking cultures is striking." Reviewing *Eternity* in *Analog: Science Fiction and Science Fact,* Tom Easton remarks, "If you enjoyed the first volume of the duo, you'll enjoy the second. If you didn't, you may still enjoy this one, for it does neatly wrap up the whole ball of string, and the characters do seem better realized."

Legacy is the third volume in the "Eon" series. Twenty-five years after the opening of the Way, Olmy Ap Sennon is sent to spy on 4000 "divaricates" who fled the starship *Thistledown* in order to live in the land of Lamarckia, where they believed they could lead a utopian existence. When he gets there, he finds that they are engaged in a full-blown civil war. Lamarckia is a planet whose ecosystem adapts readily to change; it is populated by organisms that sample and share each other's features and incorporate what they find useful. Sybil Steinberg, writing in *Publishers Weekly,* notes that "This is a stunning SF novel that extrapolates a scientifically complex future from the basic stuff of human nature." In the *New York Times Book Review,* Gerald Jonas notes

Acclaimed for its imaginary universe with artificial intelligence and a boldly conceptualized future, this complex 1990 novel involves a murderous poet and revolutionary family and social structures.

that "Greg Bear, a talented and ambitious writer who never plays it safe, has had his share of successes and failures. *Legacy* . . . is one of his triumphs." In *Booklist,* Roland Green writes that the work "will not disappoint *Eon's* fans and . . . stands well enough to be read on its own."

Blood Music

Blood Music is considered Bear's most influential work. (The novel was based on Bear's short story of the same name. The short story "Blood Music" won both the Hugo and Nebula awards, and the novel won the Prix Apollo Award in France.) The work follows Vergil Ulam, a scientist in California who is attempting to provoke a new form of life. He is determined to tailor a common virus into a computer biochip, but instead he creates an independent microscopic intelligence that breeds, spreads, and mutates. When he is fired from his job because he is caught doing unauthorized experiments, Vergil injects himself with the disease culture in order to smuggle it out of the company. Vergil's cells acquire first the gift of intelligence and then the power to create. Algis Budrys, writing in *Magazine of Fantasy and Science Fiction*, noted that *Blood Music* "is an as yet unaccountably important book; half really real, half painted real, wholly striking." He added that what Bear "has written may be read as a horror novel by some; by dedicated SF readers, it will be read with fascination as we see the classic evolution of the story from its simple initial premise to its fully deployed panoply of eventual consequences." In *Voice of Youth Advocates*, Dolores Maminski believed Bear's "basic idea is an exciting one," but she recommends the short story version. In 1997, *Blood Music* was purchased and optioned for a feature film by Zide Entertainment.

The Forge of God is the first novel in another series by Bear. This complicated end-of-the-world tale is set in 1996, when the Earth is invaded by alien planet eaters. One alien who is found in Death Valley predicts the Earth's destruction, while aliens who arrive in Australia want to welcome the Earth into their galactic community. This creates confusion for scientists and politicians alike, who do not know how to deal with the aliens. Meanwhile, amidst the confusion, the aliens release a device into the Earth's core that will destroy the planet. A network of humans band together to save themselves. In *Voice of Youth Advocates*, Judy Kowalski described the novel as "An interesting speculation on how humans will react to the knowledge of alien invasion. . . ." Faren Miller, writing in *Locus*, noted that in the work, Bear "confirmed his position as one of sf's most skilled and thoughtful Destroyers of Worlds, with a moving, elegiac account of Earth's demolition by the self-replicating machines of alien Planet Killers." John G. Cramer, writing in the *Los Angeles Times Book Review*, noted that Bear's "protagonists are swept along by forces beyond their control, behaving with admirable rationality and doing reasonable and human things in the face of an impossible situation."

In the final pages of *The Forge of God*, young Marty Gordon, who saw the Earth destroyed, begins searching for the aliens who are responsible. In the sequel, *Anvil of Stars*, several children who have been rescued from Earth by a group of alien benefactors are sent on a mission of vengeance to find the planet killers and to destroy their worlds. The children, who live on the spaceship *Dawntreader* and are led by Gordon, grow into young adults who face a moral dilemma—Is it right to eliminate an entire species for revenge? Faren Miller, writing in *Locus*, notes that "Next to *Anvil of Stars*, most novels of space war look like gar-

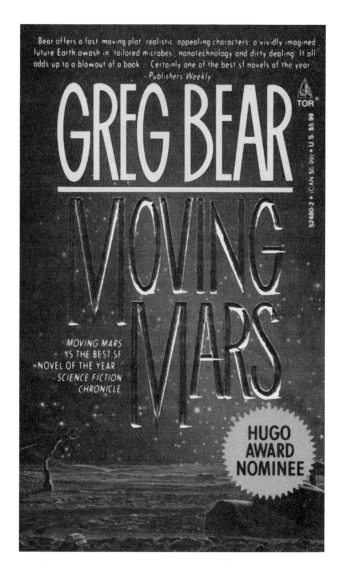

Bear offers a fast-moving plot, realistic, appealing characters: a vividly imagined future Earth awash in tailored microbes, nanotechnology and dirty dealing. It all adds up to a blowout of a book . . . Certainly one of the best sf novels of the year. —*Publishers Weekly*

GREG BEAR

MOVING MARS

"MOVING MARS IS THE BEST SF NOVEL OF THE YEAR" —SCIENCE FICTION CHRONICLE

HUGO AWARD NOMINEE

This 1994 Nebula winner features the intriguing Casseia Majumdar and her former love, the scientist Charles Franklin, who seeks the secrets of time and space at incalculable cost.

ish cartoons. Despite Bear's obvious philosophical/moral agenda, the story feels immensely real." Russell Letson, also writing in *Locus*, notes that "The book's narrative drive is genuinely impressive: I was involved with the characters, I was eager to see the outcome of their engagements with the traps and tricks of the Enemy, and I turned the pages just as fast as I could." In *Booklist*, Roland Green writes that the author is "a master of both technical wizardry and powerful scenes." Reviewing *Anvil of Stars* in *Publishers Weekly*, Sybil Steinberg writes that "Employing plausible new hard-science concepts, Bear fashions an action-packed and often thrilling plot. . . ."

Future Worlds

Queen of Angels is a novel that is set in Los Angeles in 2147. By this time, psychotherapy has become an exact science, creating a rift between the "therapied" and the "untherapied" in society. Many writers and artists choose to remain untherapied because they are afraid that receiving therapy will cause them to become passionless and ruin their creativity. Emanual Goldsmith is a celebrated untherapied poet who has just killed eight of his young disciples, and Mary Choy from the Los Angeles Police Department is assigned to the murder case. As Choy searches for Goldsmith, a team of scientific genius hired by the father of one of the victims is probing Goldsmith's mind to find out why he killed his friends. Laura Staley, reviewing *Queen of Angels* in *Voice of Youth Advocates*, writes that the novel "will provide much entertainment—and food for thought." In *Locus*, reviewer Faren Miller writes "*Queen of Angels* is an ambitious literary novel which forms complex material into a meaningful pattern. . . . It is also science fiction of a high order, filled with the excitement of extraordinary technologies and ideas."

Slant, a sequel to *Queen of Angels*, concerns artificial intelligence and nanotechnology in the twenty-first century. The action revolves around Omphalos, which is reputed to be a cryogenic repository but is actually a huge survival fortress run by Roddy, an artificial intelligence created by a bizarre genius named Seefa Schnee. Omphalos is owned by Artistos, a secret organization made up of a group of wealthy and powerful individuals who want to destroy society, and Schnee has already distributed a virus designed to break down

If you enjoy the works of Greg Bear, you may also want to check out the following books and films:

Isaac Asimov, *The Foundation Trilogy*, 1963.
Ben Bova, *Voyagers*, 1981, *The Alien Within*, 1986, *Star Brothers*, 1990, and *Mars*, 1992.
David Brin, *Startide Rising*, 1983, and *Earth*, 1990.
Arthur C. Clarke, *Childhood's End*, 1953.
2001: A Space Odyssey, a film by Stanley Kubrick, 1968.

the genetic, physical, and mental therapy that holds society together.

The novel *Moving Mars* is set in the same fictional universe as *Queen of Angels*. The novel opens in the year 2171, or Mars Year 53, as the Martian colonists are under pressure to centralize their society of Binding Multiples, or leagues of families. The story is written as a memoir by Casseia Majumbar, a college student who gets caught up in the political conflicts and eventually rises to a diplomatic position. Casseia travels to Earth, where she encounters deep social and cultural divisions between the planets. When Casseia's former lover, Charles Franklin, and his colleagues introduce revolutionary theories in physics that make Mars a threat to Earth, the Earth government disrupts Mars' workings by attacking with computer viruses. Faced with the escalating technological war, Casseia, now vice-president of a newly-elected Martian government, and a few others must decide whether to move their planet—literally.

Writing in *School Library Journal*, Christine C. Menefee notes that *Moving Mars* "is evocative of the *Martian Chronicles* in some winning ways, but its scientific and political content is also rich in contemporary questions." In *Analog: Science Fiction and Science Fact*, Tom Easton writes that Bear "does such a grand job of establishing credibility for a Mars with fossils, a society built on Binding Multiples . . . , realistic politics, and sympathetic characters." In *Locus*, Gary K. Wolfe notes that "the richness of texture with which he [Bear] brings all this off . . . make *Moving Mars* far more than just another entry in the new Mars sweepstakes. . . . Bear's depiction of Martian life and landscapes stands up to the best of them." *Moving Mars* was the winner of the 1994 Nebula Award for best novel.

The hallmark of Bear's stories is his creation of compelling images that stay with the reader long after the story is finished. His work has been compared to that of Robert A. Heinlein and Ursula K. LeGuin because of his ability to reconstruct basic human relationships in plausible ways. As David Brin stated, Bear "applies energy and thorough research to prospecting concepts far beyond today's headlines."

■ Works Cited

Bear, Greg, Website located at http://www.kaiaghok.com/gregbear.

Brin, David, *St. James Guide to Science Fiction Writers*, 4th edition, St. James Press, 1996, pp. 58-59.

Budrys, Algis, review of *Blood Music, Magazine of Fantasy and Science Fiction*, September, 1985, pp. 26-27.

Clute, John, "Asimov's Old-Fashioned Future," *Washington Post Book World*, August 25, 1985.

Cramer, John G., "Self-Reproducing Machines From Another Planet," *Los Angeles Times Book Review*, September 20, 1987.

D'Ammassa, Don, review of *Eon, Science Fiction Chronicle*, December, 1985, p. 42.

D'Ammassa, Don, review of *Eternity, Science Fiction Chronicle*, January, 1989, p. 44.

Deweese, Gene, "Once Over Lightly," review of *Eon, Science Fiction Review*, Summer, 1986, p. 44.

Easton, Tom, review of *Eternity, Analog: Science Fiction and Science Fact*, March, 1989, pp. 181-82.

Easton, Tom, "The Reference Library," *Analog: Science Fiction and Science Fact*, April, 1994, pp. 162-63.

Green, Roland, review of *Anvil of Stars, Booklist*, April 15, 1992, p. 1483.

Green, Roland, review of *Legacy, Booklist*, July, 1995, p. 1865.

Jonas, Gerald, "Science Fiction," *New York Times Book Review*, September 10, 1995, p. 44.

Kowalski, Judy, review of *The Forge of God, Voice of Youth Advocates*, February, 1988, p. 285.

Letson, Russell, review of *Anvil of Stars, Locus*, March, 1992, p. 63.

Maminski, Dolores, review of *Blood Music, Voice of Youth Advocates*, February, 1986, p. 392.

Menefee, Christine C., "Up for Discussion," *School Library Journal*, December, 1994, pp. 38-39.

Miller, Faren, review of *Queen of Angels, Locus*, June, 1990, p. 15.

Miller, Faren, review of *Anvil of Stars, Locus*, March, 1992, p. 19.

Raskin, Alex, review of *Eon, Los Angeles Times Book Review*, July 27, 1986, pp. 8-9.

Staley, Laura, review of *Queen of Angels, Voice of Youth Advocates*, December, 1990, p. 293.

Steinberg, Sybil, review of *Eternity, Publishers Weekly*, September 2, 1988, p. 90.

Steinberg, Sybil, review of *Anvil of Stars, Publishers Weekly*, April 6, 1992, pp. 54-55.

Steinberg, Sybil, review of *Legacy, Publishers Weekly*, May 15, 1995, pp. 58-59.

Wolfe, Gary K., review of *Moving Mars, Locus*, November, 1993, p. 28.

■ For More Information See

PERIODICALS

Booklist, June 15, 1989, p. 1783.

Kirkus Reviews, July 1, 1989, p. 958; June 1, 1997, p. 840; January 1, 1998, p. 27.

Library Journal, March 5, 1997, p. 50.

Locus, November, 1993, pp. 17-18.

New York Times Book Review, September 2, 1990, p. 18; November 14, 1993, p. 74.

Publishers Weekly, July 7, 1989, p. 53; March 10, 1997, p. 23; November 24, 1997, p. 23; December 8, 1997, p. 59.*

—Sketch by Irene Durham

Willa Cather

■ Personal

Given name originally Wilella; born December 7, 1873, in Back Creek Valley, VA; died of a cerebral hemorrhage, April 24, 1947, in New York, NY; daughter of Charles F. (a rancher and insurance salesman) and Mary Virginia (maiden name, Boak) Cather. *Education:* University of Nebraska, A.B., 1895.

■ Career

Newspaper correspondent in Nebraska, c. 1890-1895; *Daily Leader*, Pittsburgh, PA, telegraph editor and drama critic, 1897-1901; traveled in Europe, 1902; Allegheny High School, Pittsburgh, teacher of English and Latin and head of English department, 1902-1905; *McClure's*, New York, NY, managing editor, 1906-1911; full-time writer, 1911-1947. *Member:* American Academy of Arts and Letters.

■ Awards, Honors

Pulitzer Prize for fiction from Columbia University Graduate School of Journalism, 1922, for *One of Ours*; Howells Medal from the American Academy and Institute of Arts and Letters, 1930, for *Death Comes for the Archbishop*; Prix Femina Americaine, 1932, for distinguished literary accomplishment; Gold Medal of the National Institute of Arts and Letters, 1944; honorary degrees from University of Nebraska, University of Michigan, University of California, and Columbia, Yale, Princeton, and Creighton universities.

■ Writings

NOVELS, UNDER NAME WILLA CATHER, EXCEPT AS NOTED

(Under name Willa Sibert Cather) *Alexander's Bridge*, Houghton, 1912, published as *Alexander's Bridges*, Heinemann, 1912, revised edition with preface, Houghton, 1922, reprinted under name Willa Cather with introduction by Sharon O'Brien, New American Library, 1988.

(Under name Willa Sibert Cather) *O Pioneers!*, Houghton, 1913, reprinted under name Willa Cather, Thorndike, 1986.

(Under name Willa Sibert Cather) *The Song of the Lark*, Houghton, 1915, reprinted under name Willa Cather, with a new preface by Cather, J. Cape, 1936, revised edition, with introduction by A. S. Byatt, Virago, 1982, reprinted with foreword by Doris Grumbach, Houghton, 1988.

(Under name Willa Sibert Cather) *My Ántonia*, illustrations by W. T. Bends, Houghton, 1918, reprinted with introduction by Walter Havighurst, 1949, reprinted, Thorndike, 1986.

One of Ours, Knopf, 1922, reprinted with introduction by Stanley T. Williams, 1926.

A Lost Lady, Knopf, 1923, reprinted, 1969.

The Professor's House, Knopf, 1925, reprinted with introduction by A. S. Byatt, Virago, 1981.

My Mortal Enemy, Knopf, 1926, reprinted with introduction by A. S. Byatt, Virago, 1982.

Death Comes for the Archbishop, Knopf, 1927, reprinted with illustrations by Harold Von Schmidt, 1929, reprinted with introduction by A. S. Byatt, Virago, 1981.

Shadows on the Rock, Knopf, 1931, reprinted with introduction by A. S. Byatt, Virago, 1984.

Lucy Gayheart, Knopf, 1935.

Sapphira and the Slave Girl, Knopf, 1940, reprinted, Vintage Books, 1975.

COLLECTIONS, UNDER NAME WILLA CATHER

April Twilights and Other Poems, Knopf, 1923, enlarged, 1933, revised edition edited by Bernice Slote, University of Nebraska Press, 1962.

The Novels and Stories of Willa Cather, thirteen volumes, Houghton, 1937-1941.

Writings From Willa Cather's Campus Years, edited by James R. Shively, University of Nebraska Press, 1950.

Five Stories (includes article by George N. Kates), Vintage Books, 1956.

Early Stories of Willa Cather, edited by Mildred R. Bennett, Dodd, 1957, reprinted, 1983.

Willa Cather's Collected Short Fiction, 1892-1912, edited by Virginia Faulkner, University of Nebraska Press, 1965, revised, 1970.

The Kingdom of Art: Willa Cather's First Principles and Critical Statements, 1893-1896, edited by Bernice Slote, University of Nebraska Press, 1966.

The World and the Parish: Willa Cather's Articles and Reviews, 1893-1902, two volumes, edited by William M. Curtin, University of Nebraska Press, 1970.

Uncle Valentine and Other Stories, edited by Bernice Slote, University of Nebraska Press, 1973.

Willa Cather in Person: Interviews, Speeches, and Letters, selected and edited by L. Brent Bohlke, University of Nebraska Press, 1986.

Willa Cather: Twenty-four Stories, selected with introduction by Sharon O'Brien, New American Library, 1987.

OTHER, UNDER NAME WILLA CATHER

(Under name Willa Sibert Cather) *April Twilights* (poetry), Badger, 1903, revised edition published under name Willa Cather, edited by Bernice Slote, University of Nebraska Press, 1968.

(Under name Willa Sibert Cather) *The Troll Garden* (short stories), McClure, Philips, 1905, reprinted with an afterword by Katherine Anne Porter, New American Library, 1961, definitive edition published under name Willa Cather, edited with introduction and notes by James Woodress, University of Nebraska Press, 1983.

(Editor) *The Life of Mary Baker G. Eddy, and the History of Christian Science,* Doubleday, 1909.

Youth and the Bright Medusa (short stories), Knopf, 1920.

Obscure Destinies (short stories), Knopf, 1932.

(Editor and author of introduction) *The Best Stories of Sarah Orne Jewett,* two volumes, Houghton, 1925.

Not Under Forty (essays and criticism), Knopf, 1936.

The Old Beauty and Others (short stories), Knopf, 1948.

Willa Cather on Writing, Knopf, 1949, reprinted with foreword by Stephen Tennant, University of Nebraska Press, 1988.

Willa Cather in Europe: Her Own Story of the First Journey, edited with introduction and incidental notes by George N. Kates, Knopf, 1956.

Also author, with Dorothy Canfield, of "The Fear That Walks by Noonday." Contributor of short stories, criticism, and articles to *Home Monthly, Ladies' Home Journal, Nebraska Literary Magazine, Nebraska State Journal, Saturday Evening Post,* and *Smart Set.* Though there are no collections of Cather manuscripts, letter collections have been established at the Willa Cather Pioneer Memorial in Red Cloud, Nebraska, and at the University of Nebraska, the Newberry Library in Chicago, and Harvard University, among other locations.

■ Sidelights

"The history of every country begins in the heart of a man or a woman," Willa Cather observed in her second novel, *O Pioneers!,* but the same theme resonates throughout all of her work. Passionately involved with the formative days of the settling of the American Midwest, Cather wrote that story in myriad forms in her dozen novels and three score short stories, but always from the point of view of the individual, not the masses. For Cather, it was the individual heart at work that mattered, whether in love, devoted to family and work, or following the muse of art.

Cather was one of the most influential American writers of the first half of the twentieth century, establishing herself with both novels and short stories as "an American classic," according to Edward A. Bloom and Lillian D. Bloom in their *Willa Cather's Gift of Sympathy*. In her work, Cather both praises the hardy pioneer spirit and mourns the passing of a time in which such a spirit could exist. In novels such as *O Pioneers!*, *The Song of the Lark*, and *My Ántonia*, Cather evokes the prairie of Nebraska where she grew up, and describes the lives of the immigrant settlers of that region in the late nineteenth century, lives which she portrayed nobly yet realistically. "In a sense," James Woodress wrote in *Dictionary of Literary Biography*, "Cather's work is a metaphor for the American westering experience." Later novels such as *The Professor's House* and *A Lost Lady* reverberate with a pessimism born of Cather's reaction to the materialistic culture of the 1920s, while her last novels, including *Death Comes for the Archbishop* and *Shadows on the Rock*, delve into history and explore other regions, the American Southwest and Canada's Quebec.

Though Cather's fame rests primarily on her dozen novels, she was also a master of the short story, writing fifty-eight of them between 1892 and her death in 1947. Her last piece of fiction before she died was a short story, and taken in bulk, the stories account for about a third of her total writing. Though her short story output slowed to a trickle after publication of her first novel in 1912, some of her finest stories appeared in her later period, with "Old Mrs. Harris" and "Neighbor Rosicky" from the 1932 collection, *Obscure Destinies*, considered by many critics and scholars to be among her best pieces of short fiction. Other notable tales are "The Sculptor's Funeral" and "Paul's Case," from her first story collection, *The Troll Garden*, which was published in 1905. The latter was the only story which the fastidious Cather allowed to be anthologized. In her short fiction, Cather explored many of the themes that invest her novels with such passion and meaning: the role of the artist in society, the love of the land, the minute and intricate relations between family members, and the dangers and joys of love. More than in her novels, Cather explored with short fiction a cosmopolitan world, one populated by opera singers, musicians, and artists, yet their quest for self-discovery is, at core, no different from that of her novelistic heroines braving the Nebraska prairie.

"There Was Nothing But Land"

Cather was born in Back Creek Valley, Virginia, on December 7, 1873, the oldest child of what would comprise seven offspring. The importance of family tradition was a signal aspect of Cather's early years; her parents, Charles F. and Mary Virginia Boak Cather, traced their lineage to colonial America. The family sheep farm in Virginia provided at best an uncertain life for the Cathers, and a history of tuberculosis decided them on a radical change of life when Willa was nine. It was decided to move west, to new land opened up on the prairie by the extension of the Burlington Railroad. In 1873 the family packed up their belongings and headed west by train for a homestead on the Nebraska prairie, near the town of Red Cloud in Webster County. Charles Cather's brother and parents had already moved west to Nebraska, and it was hoped such a move would provide a healthier and more lucrative life for the family. Uprooted from the rolling hills of Virginia, the young Cather was thrust into unknown territory, best described by a youthful character in perhaps Cather's most enduring novel, *My Ántonia*. Jostled by the movement of the wagon over the flat country, the young girl in the book muses on the landscape she sees: "There was nothing but land; not a country at all, but the materials out of which countries are made."

It did not take long for the father, Charles, more dreamy than pragmatic, to realize that farming life was not for him. Eighteen months after arriving, he moved his family into Red Cloud, a town of 2,500 inhabitants, where he went into the insurance business. In Red Cloud, Cather resumed her formal schooling, and was also introduced to the bits of culture that such a market town could offer. Around the corner from the Cather's home were the Weiners, educated and transplanted Europeans who opened their library to the curious young girl. Cather took Latin and Greek lessons from a displaced Englishman, and from a Norwegian woman, she learned the delights of music. There were traveling theater companies who periodically came through town, and Cather also took part in amateur theatricals.

Devoted to science as a young girl, Cather planned on a career as a doctor. She often accompanied two of the town's doctors on their rounds, and even assisted once with an amputation, giving the patient chloroform during the operation. In her teen years she also began dressing more like a boy, wearing short hair, and signing herself as "William Cather, M.D." For Cather, this represented a spirited sort of rebellion against the mores of the times, yet some later biographers and critics have read more into such a pose than mere rebellion, raising questions about Cather's sexual orientation. That Cather never married and lived her adult life with a female companion has served to further prompt such conjectures, though Cather herself never commented on her sexuality, either in person or in print.

Cather graduated from high school a young sixteen, and in 1891 entered the freshman class at the University of Nebraska at Lincoln. Her plans still centered on a medical career, but college was to change all that, and very quickly. A freshman English instructor submitted one of Cather's essays, written on Carlyle, to a newspaper in Lincoln, and with its publication, Cather became a writer. It was a course she would not deviate from for the rest of her life. For the next twenty years she would earn her living largely from journalism, turning out an impressive volume of copy as well as short stories. As Woodress pointed out in *Dictionary of Literary Biography,* "Beginning in her junior year at the University of Nebraska, [Cather] supported herself as a journalist." She reviewed books, theater, and music, and wrote as a columnist for the *Nebraska State Journal,* and upon graduation took a position as editor of a new magazine, the *Home Monthly,* in Pittsburgh.

A Writer's Apprenticeship

Cather moved to Pittsburgh in 1895, and remained there until moving to New York in 1906. Her years in Pittsburgh served as a literary apprenticeship for the young writer. In addition to her editing chores, Cather also wrote for Pittsburgh newspapers, and began her poetry and short story endeavors. A friendship with a young woman, Isabelle McClung, provided her with a stable family environment, as she lived in the McClung family mansion from 1901 until she left for New York. A trip to Europe in 1902 opened doors to a larger world, though Cather, unlike many of her generation, would remain firmly rooted in American themes. The last years in Pittsburgh, Cather taught Latin and English at Allegheny High School, and in 1903 she published her first book, a collection of poems, with a vanity publisher.

BANTAM BOOKS

A BANTAM CLASSIC · A BANTAM CLASSIC · A BANTAM CLASSIC · A BANTAM CLASSIC · A BANT

My Ántonia
by Willa Cather

With an Introduction by Stephanie Vaughn

In this celebrated work, a young Czech pioneer faces new challenges when she elopes with a railway conductor and moves to the city.

April Twilights did not make Cather's name. According to JoAnna Lathrop, writing in *Dictionary of Literary Biography,* "Cather's poems can be described as derivative, overintellectual, competent but unexceptional." Yet such early work was valuable for the exploration of themes that would come later, as well as for the development of an epigraphic style in prose, which enabled Cather to use a poetic turn of phrase in her novels. Lathrop concluded that "Willa Cather must be taken seriously as a poet because she must be taken seriously as a literary artist. . . . In Cather's best work, poetry and prose, her struggle between the traditional artistic form and the undisciplined vigor of frontier themes results in literary art." The most popular poem of the collection, often anthologized since, was "Grandmother, Think Not I Forget," but Cather essentially left poetry behind after this initial publication, turning her hand increasingly to the short story form.

Summer vacations as a teacher afforded Cather with unbroken time for this pursuit. Actually, Cather had begun writing short stories during her college years, winning publication from a Boston magazine for the story, "Peter," which later found its way into her novel, *My Ántonia,* as an important episode of that larger work. During her years in Pittsburgh, she worked further on the craft of fiction, experimenting with all sorts of themes, settings, and literary styles. Her avowed model for such early stories was the work of Henry James, but she wrote all manner of stories initially, from ghost stories to fairy tales to historicals and starkly realistic tales. As she began to hone her work, Cather also started to gain publication in national magazines, and by 1905 she published her first collection of stories, *The Troll Garden,* with the help of the New York publisher S. S. McClure, who had read her poems and early journalism and was impressed by the voice of this young writer.

Two of the best tales from this initial volume of short stories, according to most critics, are "The Sculptor's Funeral" and "Paul's Case." In the former, Cather employs the theme of the artist's place in society, a theme which she came back to often in her short stories and sometimes in her novels, as well. The sculptor in question is Harvey Merrick, whose body is brought back to his prairie hometown to be buried. Though a famous sculptor, the locals still have a hard time accepting or understanding Merrick, even in death. Only Merrick's father and his boyhood friend, Jim Laird, now a lawyer, seem to understand the artist's achievement. "Paul's Case" "is the thematic and artistic culmination of *The Troll Garden,*" according to Rosalie Hewitt, writing on Cather's short fiction in *Dictionary of Literary Biography.* Though not an artist, the high school student Paul does have an artistic temperament, and he longs for beauty in a more glamorous environment than that afforded by Pittsburgh. Using stolen money, he escapes to New York, only to end up in disgrace and death. Seduced by art, Paul thinks there is no way for him to achieve his desires once his money runs out.

Many critics, as well as Cather herself, noted the influence of James on this first collection, some panning it for melodramatic license. Bessie Du Bois, for example, writing in the *Bookman,* thought *The Troll Garden* to be a "collection of freak stories that are either lurid, hysterical or unwholesome, and that remind one of nothing so much as the coloured supplement to the Sunday papers." Du Bois, however, singled out "The Sculptor's Funeral" and "Paul's Case" for special merit: stories which had characters that were more than "mere dummies with fancy names, on which to hang epigrams." Cather survived such early reviews, though, to quickly gain a large audience for her tales, and also to develop a thick skin where critics were concerned, listening to the advice of her writing peers instead. Later reviewers have found deeper levels in Cather's short fiction, and "Paul's Case" was reprinted in a second collection, *Youth and the Bright Medusa,* and has been anthologized since. Howard Mumford Jones, an American poet and critic, in a series of lectures delivered at the University of Illinois in 1952, called "Paul's Case" "a memorable study of adolescence, illness, obsession with music, the theater, and luxury, and of moral degeneration and eventual suicide." Another notable tale from this first story collection is "A Wagner Matinee," which chronicles the transformation of an elderly woman as she listens to a Wagner concert.

The year following publication of her short story collection, Cather accepted an editorial position with *McClure's* magazine in New York, a decision which changed her life dramatically. Leaving Pittsburgh behind, as did many of her fictional protagonists, Cather took up her duties of purchasing quality fiction from the likes of Theodore Dreiser, Jack London, and O. Henry, among others. Caught up in the busy world of journalism, Cather had scant time for her own fiction. She continued to write short stories and published these in prominent magazines, such as *Harper's* and *McClure's,* but it was not until 1912 that she published a book-length work again, and this time a novel. *Alexander's Bridge* is the story of a bridge builder from Boston who is building a span across the Saint Lawrence River in Quebec. Married, the engineer, Bartley Alexander, falls in love with an actress, and is ultimately killed while inspecting his own construction. Cather herself later disavowed this early work, noting that she actually had two first novels, for this 1912 work was "very Jamesian in its structure and thematic in treatment," according to Woodress in *Dictionary of Literary Biography*. Valuable in that it showed Cather could go the distance of longer fiction, still the book was not hers; Cather had yet to find her own voice.

"The Best Days Are the First to Flee"

By the time of publication of *Alexander's Bridge*, Cather had left behind the world of journalism to take on writing full time. The advice of friends and fellow writers such as Sarah Orne Jewett, was helpful in this decision. Jewett was also influential in pointing Cather in the direction of her own voice, of her own stories. Slowly Cather began to see that the things that made the best of her short stories live and breathe was the use of Nebraska material, of stories she herself had experienced. A trip to the Southwest in 1912, followed up by a return to her family home in Red Cloud, suddenly allowed Cather to see how she might put two of her shorter fictions together to create a true novel, her actual "first" novel, as Cather saw it.

O Pioneers! is the story of Alexandra Bergson, daughter of Swedish immigrants, who, upon the death of her parents, takes over the family farm and holds it together, sacrificing her youth in the process. In the end, Alexandra is seemingly rewarded by the love of a man who truly deserves her. A major plot digression tells the story of Alexandra's brother Emil, and his illicit love for the married Marie Shebata. The lovers are eventually killed in an orchard by the cuckolded husband. In general, *O Pioneers!* was well received by reviewers and readers alike, and Cather created in Alexandra Bergson "the great earth mother, the pioneer woman," according to Woodress.

Another strong female character is featured in Cather's third novel, *The Song of the Lark*. Here Cather returned to her love of music and also wrote of the Southwest, for which she felt such an affinity. The story of a Swedish girl from Colorado who becomes a great Wagnerian soprano, *The Song of the Lark* is loosely based on the real-life Olive Fremstad, an opera singer from Minnesota, whom Cather had earlier interviewed for an article. In her novel, the protagonist is Thea Kronborg, who grows up in a small Colorado town and early on develops a love for singing. She studies rigorously in Chicago, and during the course of a summer break at Panther Canyon in the Southwest, she reflects on the course of her life and art. Kronborg is influenced by the spirits of the Native American women who once inhabited Panther Canyon and by their unconscious, organic art in pottery. She reflects at one point on the meaning of art: "The stream and the broken pottery: what was art but an effort to make a sheath, a mould in which to imprison for a moment the shining, elusive element which is life itself?" In the end, Kronborg devotes herself to her art, becoming a famous opera star, eschewing the potential joys of a private life for art.

The longest novel of Cather's, *The Song of the Lark* is also a strong statement in favor of women finding their own way in the world, unencumbered by relationships and marriage. Cather, in later years, however, regretted the length of the novel, wishing she had left off with Kronborg just at the doorstep to her success, as Cather herself was in 1915. By the time of publication of *The Song of the Lark*, Cather was busy with the early researches and writing of what would become her most enduring novel, *My Ántonia*. For the opening epigram of that novel, Cather chose a Latin saying, "Optima dies . . . prima fugit," which she translated as "The best days are the first to flee."

My Ántonia

Those "best days" were perhaps the ones spent with the McClung family, to whose home in Pittsburgh Cather still retreated when time allowed. But in 1915, all that changed. With the death of the father, the McClung estate was closed, and the following year, Isabelle McClung, who had been Cather's close friend and possibly her lover, married Jan Hambourg, a concert violinist. Though Cather had already set up a living arrangement with Edith Lewis—an arrangement that lasted until Cather's death in 1947—it appears that the events of 1915 were a turning point for her. Cather traveled to New Mexico and Wyoming in the summer of 1916, needing the renewed vision a change of scenery sometimes provides. It seemed the trick worked, for during her trip, Cather focussed on memories of another Red Cloud inhabitant from her early years, Annie Sadilek, and by the time of her return to New York in the fall of 1916, was ready to start her new novel.

Though Cather began *My Ántonia* in 1916, it is clear that she had been mulling over the use of

Annie Sadilek as a character for many years. By the time she was ready to write, therefore, Cather had already developed a rich program of symbols, allusions, and images with which to relate her story of a Czech immigrant and the rural values she embodies. The novel was laid out in four parts or Books, preceded by an introduction in which an unnamed narrator—perhaps Cather herself—meets an old friend, Jim Burden, who has written a story about a girl, Ántonia Shimerda, both have known since childhood. The novel is thus told through the narrator, Jim Burden, and though in one section, Book III, Ántonia is nowhere present, and only indirectly present in Book IV, the novel is more about Ántonia than Burden.

In Book I, Ántonia is fourteen when Burden first meets her and her family. The culminating event of that first part is the suicide of Ántonia's father, desperately homesick for his native land. In Book II, the Shimerdas move into Black Hawk, a stand-in for Cather's Red Cloud, Nebraska, and Ántonia goes to work for neighbors of the Burden's. Though Burden and Ántonia are in love with each other, neither allows this love to be expressed. Book III follows Burden as he goes to the university where he studies classics and learns of a bigger world, forgetting for the time his youthful infatuation. Book IV takes place twenty years later when Burden learns of Ántonia's scandalous love affair with a railroad worker and of the subsequent birth of an illegitimate child. Abandoned by her lover, Ántonia has married a simple immigrant farmer, Cuzak, and is busy raising her family when Burden, a successful East Coast lawyer, returns to the prairie for a final visit. Through her many struggles, Ántonia remains undefeated and is at peace with her life and many children.

In the writing of this book, Cather employed both a realistic and romantic style. She was working on a theory of writing, later described in "The Novel Demeuble," in the *New Republic* of April 12, 1922, in which prose was stripped bare of unnecessary furnishings and the stage was left in a minimalist spotlight. Cather used this theory to great effect in sections of *My Ántonia*, and also used her organic, episodic style to great advantage. Rather than being a story of plot, the novel, as are many of Cather's, was one of character as elucidated by a myriad of smaller stories. Memorable in *My Ántonia* is one such tale of two Russian brothers, Peter and Pavel, who are haunted by their past: they once threw a bride and groom out of a carriage to save themselves from hungry wolves. As Woodress pointed out in *Dictionary of Literary Biography*, though Ántonia suffers personal tragedy, her ending is essentially happy, a condition denied most other Cather heroines. Twenty years later, Cather could still say that *My Ántonia* was the best thing she had done. "Ántonia is," as Woodress described the character, "the mother of races, the madonna of the wheat fields, a heroic figure in myth and symbol."

Like all great novels, *My Ántonia* has spawned a cottage industry in reviews and critical studies. Critics at the time of publication, as well as more recent ones, have largely agreed with Cather's own assessment of the work. Writing in the *Dial* in 1918, Randolph Bourne noted that *My Ántonia* "lives with the hopefulness of the West. It is poignant and beautiful, but it is not sad." Bourne went on to conclude that with this work Cather "has taken herself out of the rank of provincial writers and given us something we can fairly class with the modern literary art the world over. . . ." The irascible critic and journalist, H. L. Mencken, echoed these praises two years later in *The Borzoi 1920* when he wrote of *My Ántonia*: "Here, at last, an absolutely sound technique began to show itself. Here was a novel planned with the utmost skill, and executed in truly admirable fashion. Here, unless I err gravely, was the best piece of fiction ever done by a woman in America."

Other critics have noted Cather's loving reconstruction of the Nebraska prairie, have commented on her use of a male narrator for the first time, and some, such as Rene Rapin in his *Willa Cather*, have taken her to task for shifting the focus away from Ántonia for large chunks of the novel. "We cannot forget Ántonia," Rapin wrote, "and the book has become out of focus for the sake of two hundred dull pages concerning secondary characters whom we care little about. How could Willa Cather fail to see that with Ántonia's personality and Ántonia's conquest of the soil, her whole book stood and fell?" Yet others, such as E. K. Brown in his *Willa Cather: A Critical Biography*, counter such criticism. "[Willa Cather] always showed impatience at the complaint that *My Ántonia* is not precisely a novel," Brown wrote. "Why should it be? She had never said it was. In this book she was gathering her memories of some persons and places very dear to her, and as she was a writer of stories, the memories had taken a narrative form. . . . Everything in the book is there to convey a feeling, not to tell a story, not to establish a social philosophy, not even to animate a group of characters."

Some critics explain the enduring popularity of the novel by citing Cather's use of the cycles of nature as a cohesive element in the novel, the progress of the book reflecting the cycle of seasons themselves, as James E. Miller, Jr., pointed out in the *American Quarterly*. "My Ántonia closes with the dominant image of the circle, a significant reminder of the general movement of all the structural elements of the book," Miller noted. Feminist critics, on the other hand, often call *My Ántonia* a turning point in Cather's career, something of a sellout from earlier strong female characters who struggled for their art or for the soil, rejecting the comforts of domestic life. Deborah G. Lambert, for example, writing in *American Literature*, observed that the conclusion of the novel "has usually been read as a triumph of the pioneer woman. . . . But in fact . . . Cather and her narrator celebrate one of our most familiar stereotypes, one that distorts and reduces the lives of women." That such divergent opinions could arise over the same novel partly attests to its power. In the end, the important thing is that the novel has endured. Woodress wrote in his *Willa Cather: A Literary Life*, "Few novels are likely to be read longer than *My Ántonia*. In it character, theme, setting, myth, and incident are combined into a narrative of great emotional power. The prose is limpid, evocative, the product of Cather's nearly three decades of learning to master her instrument. For many readers it is her greatest work."

Novels of the Later Period

Between 1918 and 1922, Cather, who always wrote slowly and carefully, published two works, the short story collection, *Youth and the Bright Medusa*, which included reprints of earlier works as well as some new stories, and the war novel, *One of Ours*. Four years in the writing, the novel was sharply criticized, especially for the lack of realism of the final section which takes place on the battlefields of France. However, the work proved to be a best-seller and won the Pulitzer Prize in 1922.

Increasingly in the 1920s, Cather's work took on a more pessimistic turn, reflecting her distaste for the materialistic culture of the age. She wrote in a book of essays, *Not Under Forty*, that "the world broke in two in 1922 or thereabouts," and it was obvious that she felt the life she was familiar with came before this period. In *A Lost Lady* and *The Professor's House*, Cather's own sense of malaise is projected onto her characters. *A Lost Lady* tells the story of Marian Forrester, "a sort of *Madame Bovary* of the plains," according to Woodress in *Dictionary of Literary Biography*. Forrester takes comfort, in alcohol and sexual abandon, from the emptiness of her marriage with a much older man. *The Professor's House* focusses on the materialistic nature of modern life and culture, following the fortunes of Professor Godfrey St. Peter, who after winning a prestigious literary prize suddenly loses focus in his life.

In later novels, Cather turned away from the contemporary world to devote herself to historical fiction. One of her most popular works, *Death Comes for the Archbishop*, is a result of this change of direction. The novel was set in nineteenth-century New Mexico and details the life of an actual historical character, Archbishop Lamy, the first bishop appointed in the territory. Cather took considerable creative license with the particulars of Lamy's life, and created an episodic tapestry of the time, detailing over four decades of the archbishop's life. In this novel, more than any other, she painted a picture of the Southwest as she had earlier done for the Midwest in her fiction. The Canadian critic David Stouck called this novel "her supreme work of art" in *Novel: A Forum on Fiction*. Another historical fiction was *Shadows on the Rock*, which takes seventeenth-century Quebec as its setting, and celebrates, according to Woodress in *Dictionary of Literary Biography*, "the durability of this Canadian outpost of French civilization."

The death of Cather's parents brought her back to family matters and also focussed her attention on her roots, both in Nebraska and Virginia, for her last works. *Obscure Destinies* is a collection of short stories, many of them set in the Midwest. Included in this collection are stories such as "Neighbor Rosicky" and "Old Mrs. Harris," and in total the collection represents, according to Woodress, "perhaps the last great fiction [Cather] wrote." Cather's last novel, *Sapphira and the Slave Girl*, is set in Virginia, and was based on an actual event in which Cather's grandmother helped a slave girl to escape.

If you enjoy the works of Willa Cather, you may also want to check out the following books and films:

Emily Bronte, *Wuthering Heights*, 1847.
Henry James, *The Portrait of a Lady*, 1967.
Edith Wharton, *The House of Mirth*, 1905.
Little Women, starring Katherine Hepburn, 1933.

Cather continued to work until her death in 1947 from a cerebral hemorrhage. Content with her achievements, she lived a quiet life with her companion, Edith Lewis, in a Park Avenue apartment, traveling little and seeing only a close circle of friends. Cather had never been one for publicity, and was more concerned that her publications might go the long haul, that they would endure as true art. Her inclusion in the 1973 *Sixteen Modern American Authors*, as well as in a host of other collections which define the twentieth-century canon of literary greats, would seem to insure that lasting position for Cather, making her a true American classic.

■ **Works Cited**

Bloom, Edward A., and Lillian D. Bloom, *Willa Cather's Gift of Sympathy*, Southern Illinois University Press, 1962.

Bourne, Randolph, "Morals and Art from the West," *Dial*, December 14, 1918, pp. 556-57.

Brown, E. K., *Willa Cather: A Critical Biography*, Knopf, 1953.

Cather, Willa, *O Pioneers!*, Houghton, 1913.

Cather, Willa, *The Song of the Lark*, Houghton, 1915.

Cather, Willa, *My Ántonia*, Houghton, 1918.

Cather, Willa, *Not Under Forty*, Knopf, 1936.

Du Bois, Bessie, "Miss Cather's 'The Troll Garden'," *Bookman*, August, 1905, pp. 612-14.

Hewitt, Rosalie, "Willa Cather," *Dictionary of Literary Biography*, Volume 78: *American Short-Story Writers, 1880-1910*, Gale, 1988, pp. 54-63.

Jones, Howard Mumford, "The Artist," *The Bright Medusa*, University of Illinois Press, 1952, pp. 1-32.

Lambert, Deborah G., "The Defeat of the Hero: Autonomy and Sexuality in 'My Ántonia'," *American Literature*, January, 1982, pp. 676-90.

Lathrop, JoAnna, "Willa Cather," *Dictionary of Literary Biography*, Volume 54: *American Poets, 1880-1945*, Gale, 1987, pp. 21-28.

Mencken, H. L., "Willa Cather," *The Borzoi 1920*, Knopf, 1920, pp. 28-31.

Miller, James E., Jr., "'My Ántonia': A Frontier Drama of Time," *American Quarterly*, Winter, 1958, pp. 476-84.

Rapin, Rene, *Willa Cather*, Robert M. McBride and Company, 1930.

Stouck, David, "Willa Cather's Last Four Books," *Novel: A Forum on Fiction*, Fall, 1973, pp. 41-53.

Woodress, James, "Willa Cather," *Dictionary of Literary Biography*, Volume 9: *American Novelists, 1910-1945*, Gale, 1981, pp. 140-54.

Woodress, James, *Willa Cather: A Literary Life*, University of Nebraska Press, 1987.

■ **For More Information See**

BOOKS

Auchincloss, Louis, *Pioneers and Caretakers: A Study of Nine American Women Novelists*, University of Minnesota Press, 1965.

Cowley, Malcolm, editor, *After the Genteel Tradition: American Writers, 1910-1930*, revised edition, Southern Illinois University Press, 1964.

Daiches, David, *Willa Cather: A Critical Introduction*, Cornell University Press, 1951.

Edel, Leon, *Willa Cather: The Paradox of Success*, Library of Congress, 1960.

Geismar, Maxwell, *The Last of the Provincials: The American Novel, 1915-1925*, Houghton, 1947.

Gerber, Philip, *Willa Cather*, Twayne, 1975.

Hoffman, Frederick J., *The Modern Novel in America, 1900-1950*, Regnery Gateway, 1951.

Kazin, Alfred, *On Native Grounds: An Interpretation of Modern American Prose Literature*, Reynal & Hitchcock, 1942.

O'Brien, Sharon, *Willa Cather: The Emerging Voice*, Oxford University Press, 1987.

Porter, Katherine Anne, *The Collected Essays and Occasional Writings of Katherine Anne Porter*, Delacorte, 1970.

Randall, John H., III, *The Landscape and the Looking Glass: Willa Cather's Search for Meaning*, Houghton, 1960.

Rosowski, Susan J., *The Voyage Perilous: Willa Cather's Romanticism*, University of Nebraska Press, 1986.

Schroeter, James, editor, *Willa Cather and Her Critics*, Cornell University Press, 1967.

Slote, Bernice, and Virginia Faulkner, editors, *The Art of Willa Cather*, University of Nebraska Press, 1974.

Stouck, David, *Willa Cather's Imagination*, University of Nebraska Press, 1975.

Twentieth-Century Literary Criticism, Gale, Volume 1, 1978, Volume 11, 1983, Volume 31, 1988.

Wilson, Edmund, *The Shores of Light: A Literary Chronicle of the Twenties and Thirties*, Farrar, Straus, 1952.

PERIODICALS

Bookman, August, 1913.
English Journal, November, 1933.
Literary Review, December 8, 1923.
Mississippi Quarterly, winter, 1981-82.
Nation, July 27, 1921; December 7, 1932.
New Republic, April 12, 1922; November 27, 1965; July 7, 1973.
New Statesman, August 21, 1981.
North American Review, spring, 1924.
Poetry, July, 1923.
Prairie Schooner, spring, 1972; spring-summer, 1981.
Smart Set, December, 1920.
Studies in the Novel, fall, 1972.
Tribune Books (Chicago), January 4, 1987.*

—*Sketch by J. Sydney Jones*

Marc Chagall

■ Personal

Name originally Moyshe Shagal; born July 7, 1887, in Pestkowatik, Russia (now Belarus); immigrated to France, 1923, naturalized citizen, 1937; died March 28, 1985, in St. Paul-de-Vence, France, buried in St. Paul-de-Vence Roman Catholic cemetery, France; son of Zachar (a laborer) and Feiga-Ita (a grocer; maiden name, Scherlin) Shagal; married Bella Rosenfeld, July 25, 1915 (died September 2, 1944); married Valentina "Vava" Brodsky, July 12, 1952; children: (first marriage) Ida; (with Virginia Haggard) David. *Education:* Studied art with Jehuda Pen, in Vitebsk, Russia (now Belarus), with Nicholas Roerich, Leon Bakst, and others, St. Petersburg, Russia; and in Paris, France.

■ Career

Artist. First solo exhibition in Berlin, Germany, 1914; Commissar for fine arts and founder-director of government art school, Vitebsk, Russia (now Belarus), 1918-20; painter and set designer for Jewish National Theater and art teacher in orphanages, Moscow, Russia, 1920-22; engraver in Ber-lin, Germany, 1923. Visiting lecturer, University of Chicago, 1958. *Wartime service:* Clerk in the Office of War Economy, Petrograd (now St. Petersburg), Russia, c. 1915-17.

Major public commissions include stained glass windows for Metz Cathedral, 1960-68, stained glass windows for synagogue of Hadassah-Hebrew University Medical Center, Jerusalem, 1962, ceiling of Paris Opera House, 1964, and murals for New York Metropolitan Opera House, 1965. Exhibitions of paintings held in numerous cities throughout the world, including Berlin, Paris, New York City, London, and Tokyo. Works represented in permanent collections, including National Museum of Modern Art, Paris; Russian Museum, St. Petersburg; Tate Gallery, London; Los Angeles County Museum of Art; Art Gallery of Toronto and Detroit Institute of Arts.

■ Awards, Honors

Carnegie Prize, 1939; International Prize for Engraving from Venice Biennale, 1948; Erasmus Prize from European Foundation of Culture, 1960; commandeur, 1965, grand officier, 1971, grand-croix, 1977, Legion d'Honneur, Government of France; Wolf Prize from Israeli Parliament, 1982; honorary doctorates from University of Glasgow, 1959, Brandeis University, 1960, University of Notre Dame, 1965, and University of Tel Aviv. Honorary member, American Academy of Arts and Letters, 1959. Made honorary citizen of St. Paul-de-Vence, 1962, City of Jerusalem, 1977.

■ Writings

WITH ILLUSTRATIONS BY CHAGALL

Ma Vie (autobiography), translation from original Russian manuscript into French by wife, Bella Chagall, Stock, 1931; translation from French by Elisabeth Abbott published as *My Life*, Orion Press, 1960; translation from French by Dorothy Williams published as *My Life*, Peter Owen, 1965.

(Author of introduction) Bella Chagall, *Di Ershte Bagegenish*, Book League of the Jewish People's Fraternal Order, I.W.O., 1947.

Poems, translation from original Russian or Yiddish manuscript by Philippe Jaccottet and A. Lassaigne, Cramer (Geneva), 1968, 2nd edition, enlarged, 1975.

Chagall by Chagall (introduction, poetry, and autobiographical remarks), edited by Charles Sorlier, translation from the French by John Shepley, Abrams, 1979.

(Contributor) Sorlier, *Marc Chagall et Ambroise Vollard*, Editions Galerie Matignon, 1981.

Also author of introduction to *Lithographs*, for Braziller.

Contributor of illustrations to editions of numerous works, including the Bible, Homer's *Odyssey*, Jean de la Fontaine's *Fables*, and Nikolai Gogol's *Dead Souls*. Art works featured in numerous exhibition catalogs.

OTHER

Contributor to periodicals, including *Yale Library Magazine, XXe Siecle, Renaissance*, and *Naje Lebn.*

■ Sidelights

When Russian-born artist Marc Chagall died in 1985 at age ninety-seven, he left behind a remarkably prolific and varied body of work. In a career that spanned over three-quarters of a century, Chagall produced paintings, stained glass, mosaics, engravings, and other items in nearly every artistic medium available. Greatly admired for his whimsical images, at his death, according to *Newsweek*'s Jack Kroll, Chagall was "probably the most widely popular artist of the modern era." The magical, child-like quality of his work appealed across cultures and generations. His works were able to transcend both time and culture, as Robert Hughes notes in *Time*, with images from his boyhood and youth that "furnished the unaltering ground of his work for 80 years." While some art critics viewed his later works as almost embarrassingly sentimental, he continued to paint and receive commissions for numerous public art projects even as he approached the end of his life.

Chagall was born in Pestkowatik, Russia on July 7, 1887. He was the oldest of eight children. His father hauled barrels at a herring-pickling plant; his mother ran a small grocery store. When he was ten the family decided to move from their small wooden cabin in Pestkowatik to a larger stone house in Vitebsk, a manufacturing center and one of the most important towns in the region. He obtained his early education at the local Jewish elementary school, where he often dreamed of being a cantor like his grandfather. After he entered the state-run school at age thirteen (his mother had to bribe a professor in order to circumvent the rules excluding Jews from the classrooms), he discovered his love of drawing. Watching a classmate make a sketch of a picture ripped from a magazine, Chagall decided to try it himself. He remembered being thrilled by the experience. In his memoirs, he recalled excitedly rushing home and interrupting his mother's cooking with the words, "Mama . . . I want to be a painter."

Although, like many Jews, Chagall's father felt being an artist was forbidden by the Biblical edict against graven images, he agreed to pay for his son's art lessons. So, Chagall began his formal art instruction at age seventeen. He studied at the Vitebsk studio of Jehuda Pen, a local portrait painter, but for only a few months, quickly absorbing all the artist could teach him. In 1907, Chagall and a friend were determined to go to St. Petersburg, the Russian capital and the one place in their country where the currents of modern European culture could actually be experienced. Again, Chagall came up against the anti-Semitic policies of the Russian State and that almost thwarted his plans, for at the time Jews were only allowed to visit St. Petersburg after obtaining a special permit. Luckily, Chagall's father ar-

Chagall's 1911 masterpiece *I and the Village* was influenced by the cubist movement.

ranged to have an acquaintance tell the authorities that Marc was needed to deliver some items between St. Petersburg and Vitebsk. Once in the capital, Chagall received help from several wealthy Jews who were determined to help young, talented Jewish artists survive. One of his benefactors was a lawyer allowed to have Jewish domestic help as long as they lived in his home. He let Chagall live with him, the artist masquerading as the older man's servant. Chagall made several trips back to his hometown, including one in which he ended up in jail for two weeks for traveling with an expired permit. The bitter reality of being a Jew in Czarist Russia was becoming quite clear to the budding artist.

Leon Bakst, a teacher at the Svanseva School, was the most influential instructor Chagall had in St. Petersburg. When Chagall made his acquaintance, Bakst had just returned from Paris where he had coordinated the set and costume designs for two productions of the Ballets Russes directed by the famous Russian art critic Sergey Diaghilev. The art world of the time was centered in Paris and, through Bakst, Chagall learned of the revolutionary developments in the arts taking place there. Bakst spoke of the works of French founders of impressionism Edouard Manet and Claude Monet, and Dutch expressionist Vincent van Gogh. Like other young artists of his day, Chagall felt their influence as well as that of the fauves, an artistic group led by Henri Matisse with their characteristic bright colors, and of cubism, whose geometric view of the world was championed by Pablo Picasso.

In 1910, when Bakst left Russia to work in Paris, Chagall desperately wished he could accompany him. He had applied for a position as Bakst's assistant, but had failed the exam. Convinced that as an artist he had to live in Paris, he tried unsuccessfully to persuade his father to move the entire family there. Eventually, Maxim Vinaver, a deputy in the Russian *Duma*, or parliament, and one of the first to buy Chagall's paintings, offered to send the artist to Paris and provide him a monthly allowance while he lived there.

Chagall's paintings completed before his arrival in Paris represent the first stage in his development as an artist. From this period are paintings of life in Vitebsk and portraits of the people around him, including his family. *The Dead Man* (1908) shows a dead body surrounded by six funerary candles lying in a dark village street. A woman runs away horrified while a street sweeper works, apparently unaffected by what he sees. Nearby, a fiddler plays on a roof. *Portrait of My Fiancee with Black Gloves* (1909) is the first of many portraits he would paint of Bella Rosenfeld, who later became his wife. While referring to Chagall's earliest works as "dark and melancholy portraits and genre scenes," Hilton Kramer notes in *New Criterion* that they are filled "with a vitality and tenderness that remain irresistible. They are the pictures of a young man for whom painting has become the central experience of his life." These works are more pictorial and less imaginative than his later production. As Louis Lozowick comments in *Menorah Journal,* "He exaggerates both in form and color, but still cleaves to nature with fair fidelity."

Life in Paris

In Paris, Chagall visited the Louvre, the French national art gallery, and frequented the numerous galleries displaying the modern art he had before only seen in poor reproductions. After living for a time in an apartment belonging to a fellow artist, Chagall moved to La Ruche (the Beehive). La Ruche was an area of inexpensive studios dominated by a beehive-like three-story circular building left over from the Parisian Exposition Universelle of 1900. Here, because of his generous allowance, Chagall was able to rent one of the larger, more expensive units, a studio on the top floor of the building. Among his neighbors were artists from a variety of countries, including Chaim Soutine, a Russian painter; Fernand Leger, a French artist who became famous for his compositions made from discarded parts of machines; and Amadeo Modigliani, an Italian painter and sculptor. The Italian-born French poet Guillaume Apollinaire, who would give the surrealist movement its name, was also among those who frequented Chagall's studio. Inspired by the light of Paris, the swirling art world around him, and his own imagination, Chagall painted at a relentless pace. His paintings were brighter, the colors more intense than before. While the subject matter of his paintings often betrayed his homesickness for Vitebsk and those he had left behind there, the change in his works was unmistakable. According to Shona McKay in *Maclean's,* Chagall once remarked, "I brought my objects from Russia—and Paris gave them their light."

Many of Chagall's paintings created during his first stay in Paris are considered by many to be his masterpieces. Despite his denial of being affiliated with any artistic movement, the geometric influence of cubism is apparent. "The hard, crystalline quality of the forms in Chagall's paintings [from this period]," writes Kramer, "together with their transparency—which has the effect of radiating an inner light—and the discipline of their control, all this owes everything to Cubist precedents." Among Chagall's most important works from this period include *Homage a Apollinaire* (1911-12), *I and the Village* (1911-12), *The Poet, or Half-Past Three* (1911-12), *The Soldier Drinks* (1912), and *Paris through the Window* (1913).

Like the avant-garde poetry of Apollinaire in which the poet experiments with the poetic form, in *Homage a Apollinaire* Chagall pushes the representational function of art to its limit. In the middle of the large canvas appears the angular forms of a man and a woman—their bodies joined at the hip. Apparently linking the couple to the Biblical story of the Fall, a hand holding an apple appears at mid-torso. Geometric forms surround the couple and large numbers appear around an outer circle. Near the bottom of the picture is a small shape of a heart pierced by an arrow with the names of Apollinaire and three other literary acquaintances of Chagall's written around it. *The Poet, or Half-Past Three* and *The Soldier Drinks*, while less symbolic than *Homage a Apollinaire*, reveal Cha-gall's cubist tendencies in their geometric construction and their fragmented view of reality.

Chagall borrowed from cubism, but refused to be limited by what he saw as its narrow interpretation of the world. "Chagall was not a supporter of cubism," explains G. Aimee Ergas in *Artists: From Michelangelo to Maya Lin*, "but he used its method of breaking up the parts of a subject or scene to give his paintings their dreamlike quality: animals and people float in the air, depictions of objects are not limited by realistic proportions, and color seems to be applied at random." This is evident in *I and the Village* and in *Paris through the Window*. In the former, the bright green profile of a man gazes lovingly at the head of a white cow and presents her with a sprig of flowers. On the cow's cheek is the figure of a milkmaid milking the same cow, and in the background appears a Russian village and two peasants. One of the peasants and some of the houses

are upside down. *In Paris through the Window*, again, the impossible is presented as natural and normal: a cat with a human face looks out a window at the Eiffel Tower as a parachutist drifts down from an orange-brown sky, a train chugs by upside down, and Chagall himself appears with two faces, one looking forward, one looking back. With his dream-like images Chagall anticipated what would become the surrealist movement, with its emphasis on the subconscious, of the twenties. French art critics of the time seemed unable to understand his art, so the first major exhibit featuring only works by Chagall took place outside of Paris. Apollinaire arranged that a friend of his set up the show in Berlin at the Der Sturm Gallery. Chagall decided to take advantage of the exhibit's location and return home for a while after attending the opening in June, 1914. The outbreak of World War I two months later made travel between countries nearly impossible, preventing his quick return to Paris.

The German exhibit was a critical success. Soon afterwards, in 1915, Chagall's private life took an upwards swing as well when he married Bella Rosenfeld. During the war he worked as a clerk in Petrograd (as St. Petersburg was then called) at the Office of War Economy where Bella's brother, the office director, had managed to find him a position. When he could, he continued painting and exhibited his works in Petrograd and Moscow. In 1916, his wife gave birth to their only child, Ida. Just one year later, the Bolshevik Revolution overthrew the Czar, promising freedom for and an end to discrimination against Jews in Russia.

Although it seemed that Chagall might be named to the prestigious post of Director of Fine Arts in the Ministry of Culture in the new government, he decided to follow his wife's wishes and return to Vitebsk with her and their baby daughter. Soon, however, he was asked by the new Minister of Culture to serve as Commissar for Art in Vitebsk and the surrounding region. He would be in charge of a museum, an art school, and theater production. In 1919, when the first State Exhibition of Revolutionary Art was staged in the former Winter Palace in Petrograd, Chagall was honored by having the first two rooms of the exhibit being devoted entirely to his art. Soon, however, his dreams of bringing art to the people were destroyed as political squabbling caused him to lose his position.

Chagall completed this self-portrait in 1913.

Defying Gravity

Just as it had when he came to Paris, Chagall's artistic style changed again with his return to Russia. His stay in Vitebsk was marked with paintings which seemed to be his attempt at embracing his surroundings in his art. They included a series of landscape paintings and portraits of members of his family. His new wife is included in several of the more important paintings of this period, including *The Birthday* (1915), *Over the Town* (1917-18), *The Promenade* (1917-18), and *Double-Portrait with Wineglass* (1917-18). In these paintings Chagall celebrates his love for Bella; in all of them love seems to make the lovers defy gravity. The first, *The Birthday*, was painted in response to Bella's arrival at his home, a few weeks before their wedding, to celebrate his birthday. She came loaded down with a bouquet of wildflowers, some biscuits and fish, and multi-colored shawls. He was so entranced by her appearance, and her thoughtfulness, that he immediately set up his easel and took out his paints to record the scene. Bella is shown, her feet barely touching the floor, still holding her bouquet, while Marc floats in a lover's swoon above her.

Similar gravity-defying feats are captured in *The Promenade, Over the Town*, and *Double-Portrait with Wineglass*. In *The Promenade* a buoyant Bella is seen floating over a green cubist landscape of geometric houses and hills, kept from floating away only by holding tight to a widely grinning Marc's hand. In *Over the Town*, the couple is seen floating joyfully over Vitebsk, while in *Double-Portrait with Wineglass*, Chagall waves his wineglass in a toast as he balances on Bella's shoulders. Of the latter painting, Sidney Alexander writes in *Marc Chagall: An Intimate Biography*, "This is an entirely fresh invention, and surely one of Chagall's greatest works: full of pictorial brio and remarkably successful in composing a tottering vertical."

In 1920, Chagall and his family moved to Moscow where he designed murals and sets for the new Jewish National Theater. Food was scarce in the Russian capital and, soon, he moved his family to the small town of Malachovska. He also took a position as an art teacher at a colony of about fifty boys orphaned by the war. He realized that in order to provide a better life for his family, he had to leave Russia. In 1922, he succeeded in securing a passport and visa and left Russia for Berlin. There he hoped to reclaim the artwork he had left at the Der Sturm Gallery. Bella, who had a fractured ankle, stayed behind with their daughter and planned on joining him later. In Berlin, Chagall discovered what the rest of the world already knew: he was famous. Rumors of his death in Russia had increased interest in his work and the gallery owner had had no trouble selling all the Chagalls he had. Due to inflation, however, the money offered to Chagall upon his return to Berlin was nearly worthless. Infuriated, the artist filed a lawsuit against the gallery owner, but settled out of court several years later. Soon after arriving in Berlin, Chagall finished writing his memoirs (to be published in English translation as *My Life*) and found a publisher interested in publishing them, illustrated with his own etchings. Chagall went to work immediately studying the art of engraving from a German master and, then, in the space of three weeks, producing twenty prints. Problems with the German translation delayed publication of the text, so the prints were distributed in portfolio form.

In 1923, Chagall received word that a Parisian gallery owner, Ambroise Vollard, wanted to work with him on a book project. Chagall, and his family who had met up with him in Berlin, traveled excitedly to Paris. Upon his return to Paris, Chagall had hoped to reclaim some one hundred fifty paintings that he had left at his studio in La Ruche. Just as his works had disappeared from the Der Sturm Gallery in Berlin, again he turned up empty-handed. In the years ahead, the artist would try to recreate some of his lost paintings, but he had plenty of new work to occupy his time. Vollard wanted Chagall to illustrate a book, and the artist chose Russian author Nikolai Gogol's novel, *Dead Souls*. The next two years were spent producing 107 etchings to accompany Gogol's text. When not working on his illustrations, Chagall and Bella toured the French countryside, inspiring many landscapes and paintings of flowers. With the completion of the Gogol etchings, in 1925, Vollard accepted Chagall's suggestion that he prepare illustrations for the popular *Fables* of French poet Jean de La Fontaine. Chagall was also asked to put together a series of lithographs on the circus. Sometimes accompanied by Ida and Vollard, sometimes alone, Chagall began visiting a nearby circus once a week, or more, for inspiration. In *Art and Culture: Critical Essays*, Clement Greenberg praises Chagall's illustrative works of this period, noting: "Chagall is altogether great in his etchings and drypoints, a master for

The artist seated in front of his painting *Red Roofs* in 1953.

the ages in the way he places his drawings on the page and distributes his darks and lights."

Important Themes

The circus theme appeared not only in the lithographs, but also in many of his paintings. "Throughout his working life," writes Susan Compton in *Chagall*, "Chagall has been fascinated and entranced by the theme." For the artist, she notes, the circus was symbolic of life. Another important theme in Chagall's paintings was intensified by a Vollard commission to illustrate the Bible. In 1931, Chagall and his family traveled to Palestine to research the original locations of biblical events. His experience in the Holy Land deepened his feelings of solidarity with fellow Jews throughout the world. As news of tightening anti-Semitic policies in Germany and elsewhere filtered into France, paintings of grief and sorrow largely replaced the bright, happy paintings of the previous two decades. In 1938, the year marked with the burning of synagogues and the arrest of thousands of Jews in Germany, Chagall painted one of his most highly regarded pictures, *White Crucifixion*. In the painting, Chagall uses the death of Jesus as a symbol of the suffering of all Jews. The figure on the cross in the middle of the painting wears a loincloth made of a Jewish prayer shawl and at his feet lies a seven-branched menorah. Surrounding the figure are various scenes of Jewish persecution: a burning synagogue, a flaming Torah scroll, a group of soldiers storming a village. Even prominent Jews like the Chagalls were not safe from Nazi persecution. In 1941, they were arrested by police and saved only by the quick intervention of an American diplomat. Like so many other artists of the time, they were forced to seek refuge in the United States.

While some critics conclude that by this point Chagall's best work had already been created, the artist spent the rest of his life producing works that would keep his international fame alive. In 1942, he was asked for the first time to design the scenery and costumes for a ballet. The production, *Aleko,* was based on a poem by Russian poet Aleksandr Pushkin and set to the music of Russian composer Peter Tchaikovsky. Performances in Mexico City and New York City were triumphant. Two years later, tragedy struck when Bella died suddenly from an infection while the family was vacationing in upstate New York. Without

If you enjoy the works of Marc Chagall, you may also want to check out the following:

The works of Pablo Picasso, the Spanish artist who helped develop the artistic style called cubism.
The works of Henri Matisse, a French artist known for his fauvist style.

Bella, who had been his model, his inspiration, and his best critic, Chagall felt unable to continue. For nine months he went without painting. Eventually, he returned to his art in an effort to assuage his grief. In 1946, a major retrospective exhibit was held at New York City's Museum of Modern Art. That year he returned briefly to Paris, and again, in 1947, for a retrospective exhibit at that city's Museum of Modern Art. He lived comfortably in High Falls and Sag Harbor, New York, with his companion, Virginia Haggard, and their child, David. Pierre Matisse, an art dealer and son of the famous French painter, paid Chagall a monthly allowance for paintings to be exhibited in his gallery.

In 1948, Chagall decided to return to France permanently. He settled in the south of France, near Nice, where his neighbors included Henri Matisse and Pablo Picasso. A French publisher was found for his illustrated editions of *Dead Souls, Fables,* and the Bible (which Vollard had never printed), and they were finally published over the next eight years. In 1952, Chagall married Valentina Brodsky. He began a series of large paintings based on scenes from the Jewish Scriptures. They would eventually be donated to the country of France which would build the Marc Chagall National Museum of the Biblical Message outside of Nice to display them. For the first time, he worked in clay and stone sculpture; at seventy, he learned the art of stained glass. He compiled an impressive list of important commissions for public works, including stained-glass windows at the Hadassah-Hebrew University Medical Center in Jerusalem, ceiling frescos for the Paris Opera, murals for New York City's Metropolitan Opera House, stained-glass windows at the United Nations headquarters in New York City, and tapestries for Israel's Knesset building in Jerusalem. In

1977, on the occasion of his ninetieth birthday, Chagall received accolades from around the world. He received France's highest honor, the Grand Cross of the Legion of Honor. An exhibition of his works was held in the Louvre in Paris, an honor extended to only two other artists during their lifetime. Although some critics thought his paintings had long lost their vitality, he continued painting until the end of his life. His unique style set him apart from other artists of his time, but his imprint on modern art is indisputable. As Robert Hughes wrote in *Time*, "The best of Chagall remains indispensable to any non-doctrinaire reading of the art of the 20th century."

■ Works Cited

Alexander, Sidney, *Marc Chagall: An Intimate Biography*, Paragon House, 1989.

Chagall, Marc, *My Life*, Orion Press, 1960.

Compton, Susan, *Chagall*, Abrams, 1985.

Ergas, G. Aimee, "Marc Chagall," *Artists: From Michelangelo to Maya Lin*, Volume 1, UXL, 1995, pp. 64-73.

Greenberg, Clement, *Art and Culture: Critical Essays*, Beacon Press, 1961, pp. 91-95.

Hughes, Robert, "Fiddler on the Roof of Modernism," *Time*, April 8, 1985, p. 85.

Kramer, Hilton, "Marc Chagall 1887-1985," *New Criterion*, May, 1987, pp. 1-6.

Kroll, Jack, "Marc Chagall: 1887-1985," *Newsweek*, April 8, 1985, p. 78.

Lozowick, Louis, "Marc Chagall," *Menorah Journal*, August-September, 1924, pp. 343-46.

McKay, Shona, "A Whimsical World of Fantasy," *Maclean's*, April 8, 1985, p. 63.

■ For More Information See

BOOKS

Bober, Natalie S., *Marc Chagall: Painter of Dreams*, Jewish Publication Society, 1991.

Chagall, Bella, *First Encounter*, translated by Barbara Bray, Schocken, 1983.

Crespelle, Jean-Paul, *Chagall*, translated by Benita Eisler, Coward-McCann, 1970.

Haftmann, Werner, *Marc Chagall*, translation by Heinrich Baumann and Alexis Brown, Abrams, 1973.

Haggard, Virginia, *My Life with Chagall: Seven Years of Plenty with the Master as Told by the Woman Who Shared Them*, Donald I. Fine, 1986.

Meyer, Franz, *Marc Chagall*, translation by Robert Allen, Thames & Hudson, 1964.

Modern Arts Criticism, Volume 2, Gale, 1992.

PERIODICALS

Partisan Review, winter, 1944.*

—Sketch by Marian C. Gonsior

C. J. Cherryh

■ Personal

Full name, Carolyn Janice Cherry; born September 1, 1942, in St. Louis, MO; daughter of Basil (a Social Security Department representative) and Lois (Van Deventer) Cherry. *Education:* University of Oklahoma, B.A., 1964; Johns Hopkins University, M.A., 1965.

■ Addresses

Home—Edmond, OK. *Agent*—Matt Bialer, William Morris Agency, 1325 5th Ave., New York, NY 10019.

■ Career

Writer. Oklahoma City Public Schools, Oklahoma City, OK, teacher of Latin and ancient history, 1965-77; freelance writer, 1977—. Artist-in-residence and teacher, Central State University, 1980-81. *Member:* Science Fiction Writers of America (vice-president, 1993-94), Space Studies Institute, L-5 Society (life member, member of board), Phi Beta Kappa.

■ Awards, Honors

Woodrow Wilson fellow, 1965-66; John W. Campbell Award, 1977; Hugo Awards, World Science Fiction Convention, 1978, for short story "Cassandra," 1982, for *Downbelow Station*, and 1988, for *Cyteen*; Balrog Award, 1982, for short story "A Thief in Korianth"; *Locus* award, 1988.

■ Writings

SCIENCE FICTION NOVELS

Brothers of Earth, DAW (New York City), 1976.
Hunter of Worlds, DAW, 1976.
Hestia, DAW, 1979.
Serpent's Reach, DAW, 1980.
Downbelow Station (also see below), DAW, 1981
Wave without a Shore, DAW, 1981.
Merchanter's Luck (sequel to *Downbelow Station*), DAW, 1982.
Port Eternity, DAW, 1982.
Forty Thousand in Gehenna, DAW, 1983.
The Dreamstone (also see below), DAW, 1983.
The Tree of Swords and Jewels (sequel to *The Dreamstone*), DAW, 1983.
Voyager in Night, DAW, 1984.
Angel with the Sword, DAW 1985.
Cuckoo's Egg, DAW, 1985.
(With Janet Morris) *The Gates of Hell*, Baen (New York City), 1986.
(With Morris and Lynn Abbey) *Soul of the City*, Ace (New York City), 1986.

(With Morris) *Kings in Hell*, Baen, 1987.
Legions of Hell, Baen, 1987.
The Paladin, Baen, 1988.
Cyteen, Warner (New York City), 1988.
Cyteen: The Betrayal, Warner, 1989.
Cyteen: The Rebirth, Warner, 1989.
Cyteen: The Vindication, Warner, 1989.
Rimrunners, Warner, 1989.
Heavy Time (also see below), Warner, 1991.
The Goblin Mirror, Ballantine, 1992.
Hellburner (sequel to *Heavy Time*), Warner, 1992.
Foreigner (also see below), DAW, 1994.
Tripoint, Warner, 1994.
Invader (sequel to *Foreigner*), DAW, 1995.
Rider at the Gate, Warner, 1995.
Fortress in the Eye of Time, HarperPrism (New York City), 1995.
Inheritor, DAW, 1996.
Cloud's Rider, Warner, 1996.
Lois & Clark: A Superman Novel, Prima, 1996.
Finity's End, Warner, 1997.
Fortress of Eagles (sequel to *Fortress in the Eye of Time*), HarperPrism, 1998.

"MORGAINE" SERIES

Gate of Ivrel, DAW (New York City), 1976.
Well of Shiuan, DAW, 1978.
Fires of Azeroth, DAW, 1979.
The Book of Morgaine (compilation), Doubleday (Garden City, NY), 1979, published as *The Chronicles of Morgaine*, Methuen (London), 1985.
Exile's Gate, DAW, 1988.

"FADED SUN" TRILOGY

The Faded Sun: Kesrith, DAW, 1978.
The Faded Sun: Shon'Jir, DAW, 1979.
The Faded Sun: Kutath, DAW, 1980.
The Faded Sun Trilogy, Methuen, 1987.

"CHANUR" SERIES

The Pride of Chanur, DAW, 1982.
Chanur's Venture, Phantasia Press, 1984.
The Kif Strike Back, Phantasia Press, 1985.
Chanur's Homecoming, DAW, 1986.
Chanur's Legacy, DAW, 1992.

"RUSALKA" TRILOGY

Rusalka, Ballantine (New York City), 1989.
Chernevog, Ballantine, 1990.
Yvgenie, Ballantine, 1991.

SHORT STORY COLLECTIONS

Visible Light, DAW, 1986.
Glass and Amber, NESFA Press (Cambridge, MA), 1987.

Contributor to numerous science fiction anthologies.

OTHER

(Translator) Charles and Nathalie Henneberg, *The Green Gods*, DAW, 1980.
(Translator) Pierre Barbet, *Star Crusader*, DAW, 1980.
(Translator) Daniel Walther, *The Book of Shai*, DAW, 1981.
(Editor) *Sunfall*, DAW, 1981.
(Translator) Daniel Walther, *Shai's Destiny*, DAW, 1985.
(Editor and contributor) *Merovingen Nights: Festival Moon*, DAW, 1987.
(Editor) *Merovingen Nights: Fever Season*, DAW, 1987.
(Editor) *Merovingen Nights: Smuggler's Gold*, DAW, 1988.
(Editor) *Merovingen Nights: Troubled Waters*, DAW, 1988.
(Editor) *Merovingen Nights: Divine Right*, DAW, 1989.
(Editor) *Merovingen Nights: Flood Tide*, DAW, 1990.
(Editor) *Merovingen Nights: Endgame*, DAW, 1991.

■ Sidelights

Since the publication of her first fantasy novel in 1976, C. J. Cherryh has drawn praise from critics and readers alike as both a consummate storyteller and a writer of what Thomas P. Dunn calls "speculative anthropology" in *St. James Guide to Science Fiction Writers*. Dunn characterizes Cherryh's writing in such works as *Forty Thousand in Gehenna*, *Downbelow Station*, *Heavy Time*, and the "Chanur" series, as that which "[seeks] to describe humanity by using the elements of SF [science fiction] to achieve distance and perspective on the human species." "Cherryh's talents for vivid characterization, insightful explorations of human nature and relationships, and absorbing storytelling are shared by many writers in many genres," adds Karen J. Gould in *Twentieth-Century Young Adult Writers*, "but her ability to create and communicate comprehensible cultures stands, if not alone, then certainly in rare company."

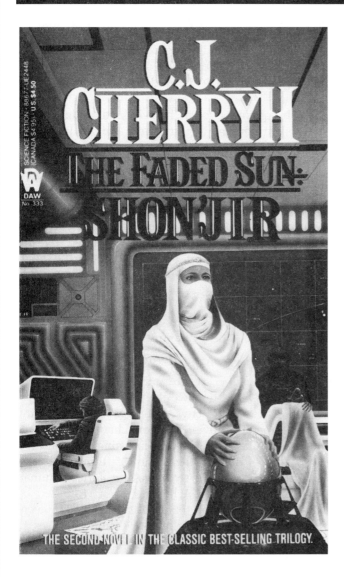

Nium and Melein, the two surviving members of the mri, a warrior-race, have only one possible chance for survival in this installment of Cherryh's acclaimed "Fading Sun" series.

Born in St. Louis, Missouri, in 1942, Cherryh studied Latin at the University of Oklahoma and obtained an advanced degree in the classics from Johns Hopkins University in 1965. After graduation, she taught Latin and ancient history in public schools before embarking on a career as a writer with the successful publication of her first novel, *Gate of Ivrel*, in 1976. Working within both the science fiction and fantasy genres, she has become a prolific writer of both novels and short fiction for teenagers and adults, and has also edited several collections of short stories by other writers.

Cherryh frames each of her novels within a very complicated alien civilization. Setting the stage for her readers involves laying a complex groundwork that includes such things as language, topography, social customs and structures, and psychology. Within each of her fictional worlds, she examines two recurring themes, according to *Dictionary of Literary Biography* contributor Susan Wells: "the theme of absolute power, especially when such power is held by a woman, and the theme of culture as a force shaping the whole of life." Each of these themes are addressed in *Gate of Ivrel*, the first volume in Cherryh's multi-volume "Morgaine" series. In the novel, the lady Morgaine

In this sequel to the Hugo-nominated *Pride of Chanur*, the human Tully establishes a valuable trade agreement with other humans.

helps a group of fellow humans who are working to close "the gates," an interplanetary teleportation network that is slowly destabilizing human worlds. Not one to tread lightly, the intrepid Morgaine and her loyal vassal Vanye cause disruption on the road to the gate of Ivrel, battling the powerful qual, the original gate-builders, on their way through regions where inhabitants "have rightly feared and cursed Morgaine's memory," according to *Magazine of Fantasy and Science Fiction* reviewer Algis Budrys. Morgaine's search for the remaining gates continues through several more novels, including *Well of Shiuan*, *Fires of Azeroth*, and *Exile's Gate*, in which Morgaine

Thorn, a human raised by aliens, must play a crucial role in the future of two worlds in this 1985 work.

confronts Skerrin, a world ruler to whom she may be distantly related. "Brisk pacing, poetic prose, and skilled characterization . . . distinguish this series," according to Roland Green in *Booklist*.

In subsequent novels, Cherryh further developed her talent for creating intricate alien cultures. In *Hunter of Worlds*, for instance, she created three separate alien languages, "each with a distinct grammar and a specific history," as Wells noted. A *Publishers Weekly* reviewer commented of this work: "Cherryh's achievement in creating beings who are convincing yet remain alien is considerable, but most readers will be daunted by the need to master about 50 keywords in the *iduve* language . . . in order to follow the narrative at all comfortably."

The "Chanur" Series

With 1982's *The Pride of Chanur*, Cherryh begins her "Chanur" series, an ambitious future history of an alien race that would unfold through a total of five volumes over the next decade. In the series' opening novel, Pyanfar Chanur, a member of the catlike hani race, is directing her family's ship, the "Pride of the Chanur," through space. She soon discovers a stowaway, a hairless, human creature called Tully, who had been wounded by the violent kif prior to his escape. The kif eventually come seeking Tully, but Pyanfar refuses to hand the frightened human over, thus precipitating a series of battles. *Chanur's Venture* finds Pyanfar developing a trade alliance with her new human allies as she keeps Tully out of the way of the persistent kif. The hapless human finds his way into the clutches of his alien enemies in *The Kif Strike Back;* only with the help of the leonine Pyanfar is Tully released and deadly warfare between rival worlds averted. *Chanur's Legacy* continues the story through the adventures of Hilfy, the niece of Pyanfar and herself captain of a trade ship. In this novel, which *Voice of Youth Advocates* reviewer Katharine L. Kan termed "another winner, an excellent addition to [Cherryh's] previous Chanur novels," Hilfy must contend with a male hani stowaway—the men of her race are not allowed in space due to their violent, unstable character—while on a sensitive diplomatic mission between rival races.

One of Cherryh's most highly acclaimed efforts has been her "Faded Sun" series. Featuring a race

As part of a psychological experiment, young Ari is forced to live out the experiences of a woman from the past in this sequel to the Hugo Award-winning *Cyteen*.

of interplanetary mercenaries called the mri, the "Faded Sun" stories once again place supreme power in the hands of a female, a *she'pan:* commander, priestess, and supreme mother of all mri. Like her later "Rusalka" trilogy, Cherryh's "Faded Sun" books focus on the coming of age of her teen protagonists in the face of the ultimate destruction of their matriarchal culture. Within the novels *Kesrith, Shon'Jir,* and *Kutath,* young Melein and her brother, Niun, must come to terms with the knowledge that they are the last of their species and adapt to a new culture. *Rusalka,* the first volume in a trilogy that falls more into the fan-

tasy classification than "Faded Sun," finds brothers Pyetr and Sasha growing up in a family of wizards in medieval Russia's mystical forests. In *Chernevog,* published in 1990, the forest's magic is abused by an evil force; only with the help of the ghostly Eveshka, wife of Pyetr, can the forces of evil be stopped. Eveshka's fifteen-year-old daughter, the wizard Ilyana, becomes the focus of *Yvgenie,* the final novel in the trilogy, as a handsome young stranger suddenly appears and seduces the young woman despite warnings from both her father and Sasha. Lesa M. Holstine praised the novel in *Voice of Youth Advocates,* calling *Yvgenie* a "powerful" story of "disturbed ado-

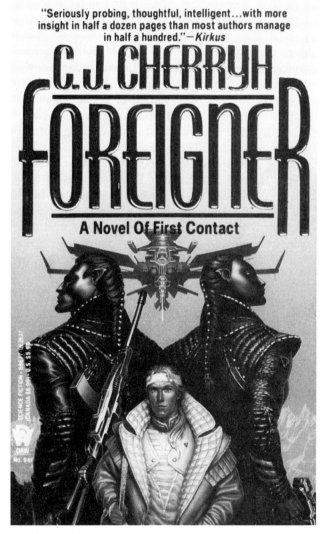

In Cherryh's 1994 novel the humans aboard a lost starship must contend with a culture whose value system is based on betrayal.

lescence, family relations, and the longing for life and love."

Other novels written for a young adult audience include 1980's *Serpent's Reach,* which relates the plight of fifteen-year-old Raen, the only survivor of her race, the Meth-maren, after they are attacked by another species. Given a new home by the insect-like beings that live on her home planet, Raen plots to avenge her family's death. And in *Angel with the Sword,* a 1985 sci-fi adventure, Altair Jones, age seventeen, falls in love with a member of her society's upper class, and finds her emotions embroiling her in Merovingen political intrigue and the vicious Sword of God cult. "Altair is a girl-woman, half worldly-wise, half naive, but full of bravery and honesty, who should appeal to teenage SF fans," noted Betsy Shorb in a *School Library Journal* review.

More fantasy-based, *The Goblin Mirror* finds royal princes Bogdan, Yuri, and Tamas accompanying the wizardly Karoly through the ancient forests of Russia to discover the source of some malevolent magic. After goblins attack the group, Tamas is aided by a troll and a strong-minded, petulant young witch in overcoming the goblins and removing the source of their evil power. And in 1995's *Fortress in the Eye of Time,* the age-old powers of good and evil are again pitted in battle, this time through the older wizards Mauryl and Hasufin, who manipulate demons, souls, and other spirits to fight on their behalf. A naive young man named Tristan is eventually pulled into the fray; handicapped since childhood, he eventually becomes the ally of an earthbound prince who is also battling the forces of evil. Noting that *Fortress in the Eye of Time* contains "much to admire" and that "themes of trust, honor and friendship are beautifully presented," *Voice of Youth Advocates* contributor Diane G. Yates praised the novel as "a major work of high fantasy."

Critical Acclaim

Many reviewers of Cherryh's works continue to praise, in particular, her vivid creation of highly intricate socio-cultural systems. Wide-ranging interests, a broad education, and a great deal of travel have enabled the author to lay claim to this success. "My classical education includes Latin, Greek, anthropology, archaeology, and ancient history, with sidelines in Bronze Age myth and soci-

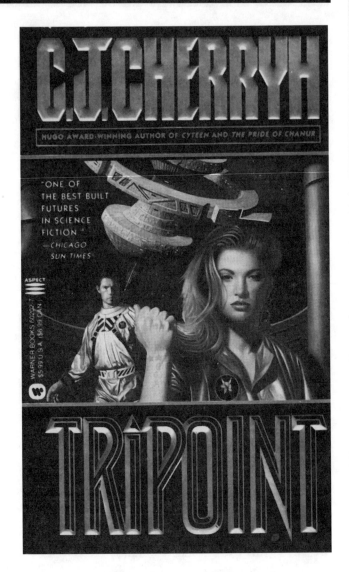

A woman seeks revenge on the man who raped her and fathered her child in this action thriller.

ety; art; geology and climatology," Cherryh once explained. "I have studied literature, religion, music, astronomy; am a passable artist, know French and Italian, with some German and Russian; know fencing and archery and enjoy riding; am active in the pro-space movement and am a constant reader in all sciences and aerospace engineering.

"I have retraced Caesar's campaigns in travels in England, France, Switzerland, and Italy; have hiked about the hills of ancient Thebes and Mycenae in Greece; climbed Mt. Dicte on Crete, where Zeus was born; walked the dead cities of Pompeii, Troy, Ephesus, and Knossos; have visited

If you enjoy the works of C. J. Cherryh, you may also want to check out the following books and films:

Kevin J. Anderson, *Gamearth*, 1989.
Stephen R. Donaldson, *The Illearth War*, 1977.
Joe L. Hensley, *Outcasts*, 1981.
The Planet of the Apes, starring Charlton Heston, 1968.

Rome and Istanbul, Pergamum, Athens and Delphi, lived a week in Sparta; have sailed the Adriatic past Ithaca—all of this while taking photographs and historical notes. I was at [space shuttle] *Columbia*'s maiden launch."

Cherryh's primary motivation for writing in the science fiction and fantasy genres is to broaden her reader's understanding of the future, as space becomes home to the human race and viewpoints are broadened to include concepts that might seem alien today. Cherryh commented in *St. James Guide to Science Fiction Writers*: "Having made a thorough study of the past I am vehemently certain that I do not wish to live in it, nor do I wish to see three quarters of the planet weltering in conditions that should have been left in the past, with the same hunger and disease our ancestors knew. The reach for space and its resources is the make-or-break point for our species, and the appropriate use of technology and the adjustment of human viewpoint to a universe not limited to a blue sky overhead and the curvature of the horizon are absolutely critical to our survival."

■ Works Cited

Budrys, Algis, review of *Gate of Ivrel*, *Magazine of Fantasy and Science Fiction*, June, 1976, p. 39.
Cherryh, C. J., comments in *St. James Guide to Science Fiction Writers*, St. James Press, 1996, pp. 181-82.
Dunn, Thomas P., essay in *St. James Guide to Science Fiction Writers*, St. James Press, 1996, pp. 181-82.
Gould, Karen J., essay in *Twentieth-Century Young Adult Writers*, St. James Press, 1994, pp. 113-15.
Green, Roland, review of *Exile's Gate*, *Booklist*, November 1, 1987, p. 417.
Holstine, Lesa M., review of *Yvgenie*, *Voice of Youth Advocates*, April, 1992, p. 41.
Review of *Hunter of Worlds*, *Publishers Weekly*, July 4, 1977, p. 74.
Kan, Katharine L., review of *Chanur's Legacy*, *Voice of Youth Advocates*, February, 1993, pp. 345-46.
Shorb, Betsy, review of *Angel with the Sword*, *School Library Journal*, November, 1985, p. 105.
Wells, Susan, "C. J. Cherryh," *Dictionary of Literary Biography: Yearbook 1980*, Gale Research, 1981.
Yates, Diane G., review of *Fortress in the Eye of Time*, *Voice of Youth Advocates*, December, 1995.

■ For More Information See

PERIODICALS

Booklist, October 15, 1980, p. 306; April 15, 1981, p. 1138; April 1, 1982, p. 1003; September 1, 1982, p. 27; April 15, 1983, p. 1075; September 1, 1983, p. 29; October 15, 1990, p. 421; October 1, 1992, p. 242; January 15, 1994, p. 904.
Kirkus Reviews, May 15, 1991, p. 640; September 1, 1991, p. 1122; August 1, 1992, p. 953; December 15, 1993, p. 1556; June 15, 1995, pp. 819-20; February 15, 1996, p. 265.
Publishers Weekly, December 4, 1981, p. 49; January 28, 1983, p. 83; April 12, 1985, p. 90; July 19, 1985, p. 49; April 22, 1988, p. 68; April 28, 1989, p. 66; May 3, 1991, p. 66; July 27, 1992, p. 52; January 31, 1994, p. 81; April 10, 1995, p. 57; July 14, 1997, p. 69; December 22, 1997, p. 43.
Voice of Youth Advocates, February, 1981, p. 37; August, 1981, p. 31; February, 1983, p. 43; February, 1984, p. 342; February, 1985, p. 335; August, 1985, pp. 191-92; December, 1986, p. 234; June, 1988, p. 94; June, 1991, p. 106; February, 1992, p. 379; June, 1993, p. 100; August, 1995, p. 168.

Barbara Cohen

■ Personal

Born March 15, 1932, in Asbury Park, NJ; died of cancer, November 29, 1992, in Bridgewater, NJ; daughter of Leo Kauder and Florence (an inn-keeper; maiden name, Marshall) Kauder Nash; married Eugene Cohen (an innkeeper), September 14, 1954; children: Leah, Sara, Rebecca. *Education:* Barnard College, B.A., 1954; Rutgers University, M.A., 1957. *Religion:* Jewish.

■ Career

Educator and author. Public high school teacher of English in Tenafly, NJ, 1955-1957, Somerville, NJ, 1958-60, and Hillsborough, NJ, beginning 1970. *Member:* Authors Guild, Authors League of America, League of Women Voters, Society of Children's Book Writers and Illustrators, Associa-tion of Jewish Libraries, Hadassah, Phi Beta Kappa.

■ Awards, Honors

American Library Association Best Books for Young Adults citations, 1980, for *Unicorns in the Rain,* and 1982, for *Seven Daughters and Seven Sons;* National Jewish Book Awards for *King of the Sev-enth Grade* and *Yussel's Prayer;* Kenneth Smilen Present Tense award for *King of the Seventh Grade;* Association of Jewish Libraries Best Picture Book Award for *Yussel's Prayer;* American Library Asso-ciation Notable Children's Books citations for *Thank You, Jackie Robinson, I Am Joseph,* and *Seven Daughters and Seven Sons;* Sydney Taylor Award for lifetime work.

■ Writings

The Carp in the Bathtub, illustrated by Joan Halpern, Lothrop, 1972.
Thank You, Jackie Robinson, Lothrop, 1974.
Where's Florrie?, illustrated by Joan Halpern, Lothrop, 1976.
Bitter Herbs and Honey, Lothrop, 1976.
The Binding of Isaac, illustrated by Charles Mikolaycak, Lothrop, 1978.
R, My Name Is Rosie, Lothrop, 1978.
The Innkeeper's Daughter, Lothrop, 1979.
I Am Joseph, illustrated by Charles Mikolaycak, Lothrop, 1980.
Unicorns in the Rain, Atheneum, 1980.
Fat Jack, Atheneum, 1980.
Lovely Vassilisa, Atheneum, 1980.
Queen for a Day, Lothrop, 1981.
Yussel's Prayer, Lothrop, 1981.
The Demon Who Would Not Die, illustrated by Antoly Ivanov, Atheneum, 1982.
Seven Daughters and Seven Sons, Atheneum, 1982.

Gooseberries to Oranges, illustrated by Beverly Brodsky, Lothrop, 1982.

King of the Seventh Grade, Lothrop, 1982.

Lovers' Games, Atheneum, 1983.

Molly's Pilgrim, illustrated by Michael Deraney, Lothrop, 1983.

Here Come the Purim Players!, illustrated by Beverly Brodsky, Lothrop, 1984.

Roses, Lothrop, 1984.

The Secret Grove, illustrated by Michael Deraney, Union of American Hebrew Congregations, 1985.

Coasting, Lothrop, 1985.

Four Canterbury Tales, illustrated by Tina Schart Hyman, Lothrop, 1987.

The Christmas Revolution, Lothrop, 1987.

Even Higher, illustrated by Anatoly Ivanov, Lothrop, 1987.

First Fast, Union of American Hebrew Congregations, 1987.

Headless Roommate, Bantam, 1987.

The Donkey's Story, Lothrop, 1988.

The Orphan Game, Lothrop, 1988.

Tell Us Your Secret, Bantam, 1989.

The Long Way Home, Lothrop, 1990.

Two Hundred Thirteen Valentines, Holt, 1991.

The Chocolate Wolf, illustrated by Troy Howell, Philomel, 1993.

David: A Biography, illustrated by Charles Mikolaycak, Clarion, 1993.

Make a Wish, Molly, illustrated by Jan Naimo Jones, Doubleday, 1994.

Robin Hood and Little John, illustrated by David Rey, Philomel, 1995.

■ Adaptations

A 1985 film version of *Molly's Pilgrim,* written and directed by Jeff Brown, won an Academy Award in the Best Live Action Short Subject category.

■ Sidelights

The late Barbara Cohen explained in a 1989 essay for the *Something about the Author Autobiography Series (SAAS)* that "everything I write . . . grow[s] out of my own experience." To a large extent, that is the reason why Cohen, who was of Jewish heritage, initially became known as a writer of children's stories about Jewish themes and characters. Cohen, however, was a master storyteller with eclectic interests and as her literary career progressed, the appeal of her fiction was no longer limited by its ethnicity. Her writings were enjoyed by a wide range of readers, particularly those in the early primary school grades. This was an audience she knew well, having taught for seventeen years before becoming a full-time writer. Although her first book was not published until 1972, when she was already thirty-nine years old, Cohen was prolific, crafting more than thirty-five books in her late-blooming literary career.

Cohen was born in 1932 in Asbury Park, New Jersey, a coastal community about twenty miles south of New York City. The eldest of three children, she fell in love with the world of books as a girl. Her mother, Florence, was a school teacher; her father, Leo Kauder, ran a poultry produce business. During the Great Depression, money was tight, and so the Kauder family, like so many others, made much of their own fun. Young Barbara spent many happy summer nights sitting on the front porch of her grandparents' house reading or listening to her elders as they talked and told stories about those family members who were not present. These sessions kindled the girl's imagination and fired her passion for the world of letters. "I started writing about the same time I started reading, which means I can scarcely remember not being able to do either," she wrote in *SAAS.* "I loved reading right from the beginning, and wanted, also right from the beginning, to make things like those books I loved so much."

The Kauders moved to Somerville, New Jersey, in early 1940, when Barbara was eight years old. Her father had suffered a serious heart attack and his doctor suggested he find a less stressful line of work. The business that he settled on was reopening the Somerville Inn, an establishment that had gone bankrupt the year before. Sadly, the family's move was futile, for Leo died in early 1942, leaving his wife with three young children, a rundown inn, and a stack of bills. Florence Kauder stuck it out, and Barbara, her sister Susan, and her brother Louis grew up at the inn. Complicating the family's life was the covert anti-Semitism they encountered in the town of Somerville. Cohen recalled in *SAAS* that because her family's lifestyle and Jewishness left her feeling isolated from her schoolmates, she spent a lot of time playing with her siblings or writing stories and reading by herself.

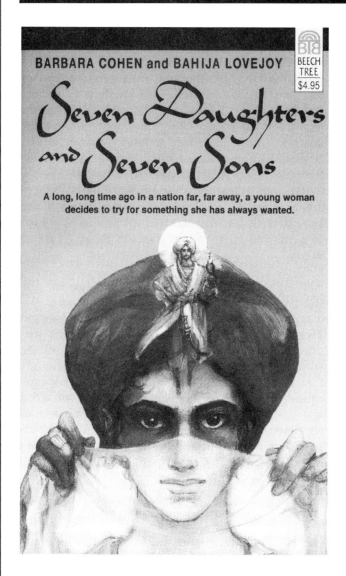

BARBARA COHEN and BAHIJA LOVEJOY

Seven Daughters and Seven Sons

A long, long time ago in a nation far, far away, a young woman decides to try for something she has always wanted.

BEECH TREE
$4.95

A young Arab woman disguises herself as a man in order to seek her fortune in this American Library Association Best Book for Young Adults.

Cohen's literary interests matured during her years at Somerville High School and later at Barnard College, where she studied creative writing. She was in her senior year at Barnard when she began writing seriously. Her stepfather, who owned a chain of three weekly newspapers in New Jersey, asked her to write a column for five dollars a week. These journalistic efforts didn't last long, though, for Cohen got married in September 1954, just a few months after graduating with her bachelor's degree. She spent the next twenty years raising three daughters and earning her living by teaching school. Cohen worked as a newspaper reporter one summer and occasionally wrote sto-

ries or plays for amateur theater groups, but otherwise her dreams of becoming a writer were shelved until one spring day in 1971. Cohen and her husband were visiting friends when they fell into a conversation about the upcoming Jewish holiday of Passover. One of the women present told a story about how as a girl growing up in Brooklyn her mother had kept a live carp in the bathtub so the family would be assured of having fresh fish to make gefilte fish, a Passover culinary delicacy. That anecdote fired Cohen's imagination, and a few days later she sat down at her typewriter and began writing a children's book entitled *The Carp in the Bathtub*. "The story poured out of me. I had the ambience from stories my own mother had told me about growing up in Brooklyn around the time of World War I," Cohen recalled in *SAAS*.

"A Delightfully Warm Book. . . ."

When the carp manuscript was completed, one of Cohen's writer friends suggested she send it to Edna Barth, an editor at the New York children's book publisher Lothrop, Lee and Shepard. Barth, who liked the story, agreed to publish it if Cohen would make a few changes. When she did, *The Carp in the Bathtub*, illustrated by artist Joan Halpern, became Cohen's first book. "[It was] a universal idea cast in a particular ethnic mold," she wrote in explaining the book's appeal, "it is a story to which children (and grown-ups) of every background can relate. At the same time it provides insight into Jewish customs and ceremonies."

The book-buying public obviously agreed with the *Publishers Weekly* reviewer who praised *The Carp in the Bathtub* as "a delightfully warm book," for sales were brisk. Cohen proudly noted in her 1989 essay in *SAAS* that unlike most children's books, *The Carp in the Bathtub* was still in print. Its success encouraged Cohen to continue writing.

Cohen's second book also grew out of her own experiences. Jackie Robinson, the first African American player in Major League Baseball, had died on October 23, 1972, and afterwards Cohen wrote a letter of condolence to her brother, now a lawyer in Washington, D.C. As a boy, Louis Kauder had cheered for the Brooklyn Dodgers (who by 1972 had moved west to Los Angeles) and had idolized the fleet-footed Robinson, one of the Dodgers' star players. A subsequent exchange of letters between Cohen and her brother sparked some long forgotten childhood memories for her. During the summer vacation in 1973, Cohen set out to capture them in prose. In just a couple of weeks, she had completed a first draft of *Thank You, Jackie Robinson*. This young adult novel is about a fatherless white boy named Sam who befriends a black man named Davy, a cook at the inn run by the boy's mother; Sam and Davy become pals because of their mutual adulation of Jackie Robinson. When Davy falls ill and dies, Sam finds solace—just as he did when his own father died—in his memories of Davy and of the good times they had attending ball games together.

New York Times Book Review reviewer Marilyn Sachs praised *Thank You, Jackie Robinson* for doing "for kids what *The Boys of Summer* by Roger Kahn did for adults. It establishes the Brooklyn Dodgers (1947-50) as one of the most endearing teams in baseball history and moved Jackie Robinson up there to the Mt. Olympus of Baseball Gods. . . . The author's style is lively [and] her baseball facts lovingly detailed." In retrospect, Cohen realized that the book's emphasis was less on baseball and more on the human elements of the story. "Both *The Carp* and *Jackie,* in their different ways, were about children coping with loss," she explained in *SAAS*; "what I'd *really* written about [was] not my brother's feelings concerning my father's death, but my own."

Following the same pattern that she had established with her first two books, Cohen's next efforts were a second children's story called *Where's Florrie?*, also illustrated by Joan Halpern, and another young adult novel, *Bitter Herbs and Honey*. Both books were firmly rooted in Cohen's own life experiences. The former grew out of some stories that her mother had told her about growing up in Brooklyn in the early years of the twentieth century; the latter chronicled a year in the life of a young girl named Becky, who struggles to cope with the hardships and restrictions of being Jewish in a small New Jersey town in 1915 and 1916. Although all of the fictional events described took place years before she was born, Cohen realized that her brother was correct when he pointed out to her that "Becky is really you."

Despite the success of her first four books and the fact that she was working on a fifth, Cohen began feeling frustrated. By the fall of 1976, her eldest daughter Leah was in college and her sisters, Sara and Becky, were in high school, yet Cohen still had neither the time nor the energy that she felt she needed, and wanted, to devote to her writing. "I grew uncomfortable if I had to let a book hang untouched for months waiting for the next vacation to roll around," Cohen wrote. "I realized I could no longer live so many lives. I couldn't be a wife, a mother, a housekeeper, a writer, and a teacher. One of those jobs was going to have to go. I wasn't going to leave the kids, divorce the husband, or sell the house. Much as I enjoyed it, teaching was the thing I had to dump."

Although Cohen's family no longer needed the steady pay check she earned from teaching, she was initially uncertain that she had made the right decision; she need not have been. Cohen, who was grimly determined to succeed, forced herself to stick to a rigorous work schedule. She felt strongly that this was the only way to succeed in her new career. "The ones who achieve a body of work are the ones who are disciplined, the ones who sit down every day and simply go to work, inspired or not inspired. I believe inspiration grows out of the work," Cohen explained in *SAAS*.

Becoming A Full-time Writer

Having the time to do so, Cohen now plunged into her writing with renewed vigor and enthusiasm. The result was an astounding literary output; in the period between 1977 and 1991, scarcely a year went by in which Cohen did not produce at least one new book. She plumbed her own experiences as well as those of her own family and her friends for ideas that became the raw material of her fiction. Among her considerable output were two more young adult novels that were clearly based on Cohen's own childhood experiences: *R, My Name is Rosie* in 1978 and *The Innkeeper's Daughter* in 1979. Cohen confided that the latter, which tells the story of the coming-of-age of a teenage girl named Rachel, was the "most directly autobiographical" of all her books. However, it also proved to be one of Cohen's least commercially successful efforts, despite the fact it contained what she felt was some of her best writing and earned some solid reviews. "The hotel atmosphere . . . is deftly and engagingly captured," wrote a reviewer for *Kirkus Reviews*. A

If you enjoy the works of Barbara Cohen, you may also want to check out the following books and films:

Kathryn Lasky, *Beyond the Divide*, 1983.
Madeleine L'Engle, *Many Waters*, 1986.
Albert Murray, *The Spyglass Tree*, 1991.
My Brilliant Career, starring Judy Davis, 1979.

critic in the *Bulletin of the Center for Children's Books* agreed that the characters were convincingly drawn, the dialogue was natural, and the story flowed smoothly. The main problem with the book was that "the story proceeds with little drama until the end."

Cohen also continued to write the kind of children's stories and young adult "coming-of-age" stories that had won her an audience. One of these, a book entitled *Molly's Pilgrim*, was turned into a successful short movie that in 1986 was awarded an Academy Award in the Best Live Action Short Subject category. The resulting publicity was an enormous boost to Cohen's career, an irony that was not lost on her. She noted that while her books had garnered a host of literary awards, it was not until the film version of *Molly's Pilgrim* won an Oscar that many people she knew paid any attention to what she did for a living. "Every neighbor, every long-lost relative, every old college chum now living in West Nerdsville, heard about the Oscar and wrote or called," Cohen quipped in *SAAS*. "Well, it was fun, but it was not important. I don't make movies. I write children's books."

As the years passed, Cohen turned to fresh sources for inspiration. These included an eclectic mix of her own favorite tales from the Bible and classics of English literature. The first of these efforts was the 1980 book *I Am Joseph*, which was a retelling of the Biblical story of Joseph and his brothers. Georgess McHargue, writing in the *New York Times Book Review*, commented that Cohen "has told her story admirably, if perhaps a trifle lengthily." Paul Heins of *Horn Book* agreed, noting that the author had adhered "to the details and theological intent of the account as found in Genesis." Among the others stories which Cohen "retold" were ones derived from the rich tradi-

tion of Jewish mythology, the timeless legend of Robin Hood and Little John, and Geoffrey Chaucer's fourteenth-century epic poem *The Canterbury Tales*. The latter, aimed at teenage readers, was widely praised by reviewers and educators. Cohen selected, translated, and adopted four of Chaucer's stories in prose form: the Nun Priest's tale, the Pardoner's, the Wife of Bath's, and the Franklin's. Cohen's *Four Canterbury Tales* "deserves to be celebrated for it is an incredible achievement," wrote Mary M. Burns of *Horn Book*. Francine Prose of the *New York Times Book Review* was not entirely comfortable with what she felt was at times "a faux folksiness," but she praised Cohen for "the courage and ambition of [her] undertaking."

Despite the death of her husband, Gene, in 1990, Cohen continued writing right up until 1991, when she fell ill with cancer and was unable to work. She was just sixty years old when she died at her home in Bridgewater, New Jersey, on November 29, 1992. Cohen left four books unpublished at the time of her death that have been published posthumously. Cohen recalled in *SAAS* how Gene had once quipped that she was twelve years old when she was born and she would be twelve years old when she died. "I was always there," Barbara Cohen concluded. "That's OK. It's worked out."

■ Works Cited

Burns, Mary M., review of *Four Canterbury Tales*, *Horn Book*, March-April, 1989, p. 214.

Review of *The Carp in the Bathtub*, *Publishers Weekly*, August 7, 1972, p. 49.

Cohen, Barbara, essay in *Something about the Author Autobiography Series*, Volume 7, Gale, 1982.

Heins, Paul, review of *I Am Joseph*, *Horn Book*, August, 1980, p. 425.

Review of *The Innkeeper's Daughter*, *Bulletin of the Center for Children's Books*, January, 1980, pp. 90-91.

Review of *The Innkeeper's Daughter*, *Kirkus Reviews*, January 15, 1980, p. 70.

McHargue, Georgess, review of *I Am Joseph*, *New York Times Book Review*, June 15, 1980, p. 21.

Prose, Francine, review of *Four Canterbury Tales*, *New York Times Book Review*, December 11, 1988, pp. 20-21.

Sachs, Marilyn, "Momentos From The Past," *New York Times Book Review*, May 5, 1974, p. 40.

■ For More Information See

BOOKS

Twentieth-Century Children's Writers, 4th edition, St. James Press, 1995, pp. 229-31.

PERIODICALS

Booklist, November 1, 1972, p. 242; July 15, 1978, p. 1732; December 1, 1979; April 1, 1980, p. 1122; September 1, 1980, p. 39; October 1, 1982, p. 243; September 1, 1983, p. 80; March 1, 1984, p. 963; February 15, 1985, p. 852; November 1, 1985, p. 14; September 15, 1987, p. 132; September 1, 1988, p. 74; May 15, 1989, p. 1638; October 15, 1990, p. 442; March 1, 1994, p. 1269; March 15, 1996, p. 1289.

Bulletin of the Center for Children's Books, December, 1972, p. 242; June, 1978, p. 156; January, 1981, p. 89; May, 1981, p. 167; November, 1981, p. 42; December, 1982, p. 630; October, 1983, p. 24; February, 1984, p. 104; January, 1986, p. 83; September, 1987, p. 5; July, 1988, p. 224; November, 1988, p. 67; July/August, 1989, p. 270; January, 1992, p. 121.

Chicago Tribune Book World, May 3, 1981.

Kirkus Reviews, August 1, 1982, pp. 870-71; September 1, 1985, p. 913.

New York Times Book Review, November 3, 1974, p. 53; February 20, 1983, p. 25; March 27, 1994, p. 21; June 18, 1995, p. 25; August 11, 1996, p. 19.

Publishers Weekly, July 10, 1978, p. 136; February 15, 1980, p. 110; October 3, 1980, p. 66; March 16, 1984, p. 87; July 10, 1987, p. 69; August 14, 1987, p. 105; June 10, 1988, p. 81; October 28, 1988, p. 81; May 19, 1989, p. 86; December, 1993, p. 69; April 17, 1995, p. 62; March 18, 1996, p. 69.

School Library Journal, October, 1976, p. 87; September, 1977, p. 124; September, 1978, p. 105; October, 1980, p. 143; November, 1980, p. 84; January, 1982, p. 61; October, 1982, p. 138; November, 1982, p. 79; November, 1983, p. 175; November, 1985, p. 94; November, 1987, pp. 88, 113; November, 1988, p. 110; May, 1989, p. 124; October, 1990, p. 113; November, 1991, p. 91; April, 1994, p. 101; July, 1995, p. 84; June, 1996, p. 99.

Tribune Books (Chicago), November 13, 1988, p. 6.

Voice of Youth Advocates, April, 1981, p. 32; April, 1986, p. 28; October, 1987, p. 198.

Washington Post Book World, June 8, 1980; August 10, 1980.

■ Obituaries

BOOKS

Contemporary Authors, Volume 40, Gale, 1993.

PERIODICALS

Detroit Free Press, December 2, 1992, p. 7B.

Los Angeles Times, December 5, 1992, p. A26.

New York Times, December 1, 1992, p. B12.

School Library Journal, January, 1993, p. 18.*

—*Sketch by Ken Cuthbertson*

Gillian Cross

member of Parliament, an assistant to a village baker, a childcare worker, and a clerical assistant. *Member:* Society of Authors.

■ Awards, Honors

Carnegie highly commended book, 1982, and Guardian Award runner-up, 1983, both for *The Dark Behind the Curtain;* American Library Association's (ALA) Best Books for Young Adults citation, 1984, Whitbread runner-up, 1984, Notable Books of the Year citation, ALA, 1985, and Edgar Award runner-up, 1986, all for *On the Edge;* Carnegie commended book, 1986, and Best Books for Young Adults citation, ALA, 1987, both for *Chartbreaker;* Notable Books of the Year citation, ALA, 1987, for *Roscoe's Leap; On the Edge, Born of the Sun,* and *Roscoe's Leap* were Junior Literary Guild selections; Carnegie Medal, 1990, for *Wolf;* Whitbread Children's Novel Award, and Smarties Book Prize, both 1992, both for *The Great Elephant Chase* (published in U.S. as *The Great American Elephant Chase).*

■ Personal

Full name, Gillian Clare Cross; born December 24, 1945, in London, England; daughter of (James) Eric (a scientist and musician) and Joan (an English teacher; maiden name, Manton) Arnold; married Martin Cross (an examinations director of the Royal Society of Arts), May 10, 1967; children: Jonathan George, Elizabeth Jane, Colman Anthony, Katherine Clare. *Education:* Somerville College, Oxford, B.A. (with first-class honors), 1969, M.A. 1972; University of Sussex, D.Phil. 1974. *Hobbies and other interests:* Playing the piano, gardening, reading, and orienteering, "which involves running around strange forests, map and compass in hand, looking for control flags."

■ Addresses

c/o Oxford Children's Books, Oxford University Press, Walton Street, Oxford, OX2 6DP, England.

■ Career

Author of juvenile and young adult books. Worked previously as a teacher, an assistant to a

■ Writings

JUVENILE FICTION

The Iron Way, illustrated by Tony Morris, Oxford University Press, 1979.
The Runaway, illustrated by Reginald Gray, Methuen, 1979.
Revolt at Ratcliffe's Rags, illustrated by Tony Morris, Oxford University Press, 1980.

Save Our School, illustrated by Gareth Floyd, Methuen, 1981.

A Whisper of Lace, Oxford University Press, 1981, Merrimack, 1982.

The Dark Behind the Curtain, illustrated by David Parkins, Oxford University Press, 1982, Merrimack, 1984.

The Demon Headmaster (see also below), illustrated by Gary Rees, Oxford University Press, 1982, Merrimack, 1984.

The Mintyglo Kid, illustrated by Gareth Floyd, Methuen, 1983.

Born of the Sun, illustrated by Mark Edwards, Holiday House, 1984.

On the Edge, Oxford University Press, 1984, Holiday House, 1984.

The Prime Minister's Brain (sequel to *The Demon Headmaster*), Oxford University Press, 1985.

Chartbreak, Oxford University Press, 1986, published as *Chartbreaker,* Holiday House, 1987.

Swimathon!, illustrated by Gareth Floyd, Methuen, 1986.

Roscoe's Leap, Holiday House, 1987.

A Map of Nowhere, Oxford University Press, 1988, Holiday House, 1989.

Rescuing Gloria, illustrated by Gareth Floyd, Methuen, 1989.

Twin and Super-Twin, illustrated by Maureen Bradley, Holiday House, 1990.

Monster from Underground, illustrated by Peter Firmin, Heinemann, 1990.

Gobbo the Great, illustrated by Philippe Dupasquier, Methuen, 1991.

Rent-a-Genius, illustrated by Glenys Ambrus, Hamish Hamilton, 1991.

Wolf, Holiday House, 1991.

Beware Olga!, illustrated by Arthur Robins, Walker, 1993.

The Furry Maccaloo, illustrated by Madeleine Baker, Heinemann, 1993.

The Great American Elephant Chase, Holiday House, 1993 (published in England as *The Great Elephant Chase*).

The Tree House, illustrated by Paul Howard, Methuen, 1994.

What Will Emily Do?, illustrated by Paul Howard, Methuen, 1994.

Hunky Parker Is Watching You, illustrated by Maureen Bradley, Oxford University Press, 1994, republished as *The Revenge of the Demon Headmaster,* Puffin, 1995.

The Crazy School Shuffle, Methuen, 1995.

Posh Watson, Walker, 1995.

New World, Holiday House, 1995, Viking, 1996.

Pictures in the Dark, Holiday House, 1996.

The Demon Headmaster Strikes Again, Puffin, 1997.

■ Sidelights

The spectrum of Gillian Cross's writing is wide and varied. Her stories for children and young adults delve into history, suspense, or simply the inherent problems of school life; no matter what the theme, she aims to strike a chord with her readers, particularly reluctant ones. Reviewers frequently point to her well-realized characterizations and her sympathy for the difficulties of growing up. Her willingness to deal bluntly with some of the nastier parts of childhood and adolescence has won her many readers. Writing in the *Times Literary Supplement,* Sarah Hayes observed, "in all her writing Gillian Cross reveals a certain darkness that is sometimes shown as pure evil and sometimes a symptom of human weakness or need." As Cross told *School Librarian,* "I like to write for children and young people because then I feel free to write about important things: love, death, moral decisions. . . ." Even in her lightest vein, Cross has the utmost respect and interest in her audience—her popularity proves she understands her readers well.

Born in London on December 24, 1945, Gillian Clare Arnold grew up surrounded by books. Her mother was an English teacher, and her father, who held a Ph.D. in chemistry, was managing director of a paint company, as well as an organist and choirmaster. The family lived in the London suburbs, first in Wembley and later near Harrow. The household teemed with books, which filled tabletops and shelves and even spilled out of boxes. In the *Sixth Book of Junior Authors and Illustrators,* Cross recalled her parents' natural storytelling abilities: "Before we could read our mother made up stories to tell us and our father read stories onto tape on his big reel-to-reel tape recorder—long before commercial story cassettes were dreamt of."

Cross soon regaled her younger brother and sister and her classmates with her own tales. She attended North London Collegiate School for Girls, an academically prestigious day school. To speed up the long commute, Cross made up stories using her friends as characters, incorporating their requests in an ongoing saga. She liked school and did very well. Cross also wrote stories, but made a separation between her academic work and what she termed her "fast fiction." In the *Sixth Book of Junior Authors and Illustrators,* she described a craving for "every spare blank page I could find," adding that she even "begged for paper as a birthday present."

Between secondary school and university, Cross volunteered as a teacher for teenagers in a depressed area of London. After her comfortable life in the London suburbs, she found herself confronted with new insights. As she once told *Contemporary Authors,* "I began to see that life was

GILLIAN CROSS

point

WOLF

DON'T LOOK NOW.

Scholastic 0-590-45608-3 / $3.25

SCHOLASTIC

Cross received the Carnegie Medal for this psychological tale of a thirteen year old who leaves her grandmother's home to live with her mother.

more varied and more demanding than I had realized." Cross then attended Somerville College at Oxford, concentrating on English. She married John Martin Cross in 1967, while still an undergraduate. She postponed her studies for a year to care for their first child, working as a baker's assistant in Garsington, near Oxford. The brick oven and traditional approach of her employer later became grist for her own detailed description in *The Iron Way.*

Cross returned to Somerville and graduated in 1969 with first-class honors. She went on to the University of Sussex, where she was awarded a Ph.D. in English literature; her thesis was on G. K. Chesterton. She briefly considered teaching but decided against it. It was the combination of finishing her doctorate—a sustained piece of writing that proved to Cross that she could handle something long—and the stories that clamored to be told that made her sit down to write. As she told *CA:* "For the first time in my life I had lots of free time and no 'official' writing to do. And I was up to the knees in stories. I had two children by then, and I was always making up stories for them and making them small, illustrated books."

Her first manuscript found no takers. In the afterword to *The Iron Way,* Cross noted that during the six or seven months it took to complete this manuscript, "I tried very hard and worked it all out carefully. . . . I made sure there were good psychological explanations for everyone's behavior. Into that first book of mine, I put everything that I thought a book should have. It was terrible. . . . I'm incredibly relieved, now, that it has never been published."

Serious Issues and the Seriously Demonic Headmaster

Before she had time to absorb the rejections that came in response to this first effort, she found herself "hooked" on writing—already well into her second manuscript. By 1979, she had completed five novels and found herself in the happy position of publishing two in the same year, *The Iron Way* and *The Runaway.* The idea for *The Iron Way,* which takes place during a period of railway construction in the South Downs of England, came to Cross as an image: a boy watching the railway men change the very composition of his world by bringing trains to rural England. When his family takes in one of the "navvies" (as the Irish workmen are known) as a lodger, the boy must come to terms with the prejudices that dog the foreign workers. Writing in the *New Statesman*, Alan Ryan commended the book for "The solidity of the research behind the historical stories, the quality of the writing. . . ." *Booklist*'s Marilyn Kaye deemed the story "gripping," adding that its "personalities are sharply defined, mainly through dialogue, and the tension is painfully apparent throughout the course of events."

Social, political, and ethnic differences quickly emerged as frequent themes in Cross's work. In *The Runaway*, two contemporary urban children of different economic and ethnic backgrounds hide out together in an abandoned house. In her next book, *Ratcliffe's Rags*, three teenagers from different social backgrounds are assigned a project on local factories. They choose Ratcliffe's Clothing, where one of the children's mother works. An eventual labor dispute pits them against one another. "An excellent English novel on a subject unusual in children's books—labor problems . . .," wrote Ann A. Flowers in *Horn Book*. In the *Times Educational Supplement*, Peter Fanning lauded the "shifting tide of convictions and loyalties" in "a well-worked plot . . . powerfully told despite the predictable characters." Ann Thwaite of the *Times Literary Supplement* deemed Cross "a writer to watch," and praised the book not only for telling a compelling story, but for helping "to fill in the pieces of the jig saw, to make more sense of that extraordinary adult world which touches children whether they like it or not."

Cross revealed more of her humor in *Save Our School*, the first of what became a series of stories that revolve around three friends—Clipper (Caroline Young), Spag (James Barlow), and Barny (Gobbo)—and their efforts to preserve the honor of their school, Bennett Junior High, as well as their own reputations. Of the characters, *Times Literary Supplement* reviewer Anne Carter commented: "Racy, frequently vulgar and abounding in character, Barny, Spag and Clipper . . . are as real and recognizable as the streets among which they live." Reviewing the book for *Growing Point*, Margery Fisher was less enchanted, finding that "in spite of a cheerful style and plenty of incidental humour, there is hardly enough particularity to make this more than a routine piece of fiction."

Cross continued the series with three more installments, *The Mintyglo Kid* (1983), *Swimathon!* (1986), and *Gobbo the Great* (1991). *Books and Bookmen* critic Mary Cadogan admired the "progressive tone" and the "very funny exploits" with which Cross treated issues such as racism, sexism, and, through an elderly, wheelchair-bound character, even ageism. In *Swimathon!*, the friends organize a swim meet to raise funds for their school. Barny and Spag assume—wrongly—that the athletic Clipper can swim. The book details the mayhem that results. In *Books for Keeps*, reviewer Nigel Spencer found "How they succeed in demolishing their opponents, in spite of the handicap of Clipper being a non-swimmer, is rather far-fetched, but all's well that ends well." *Gobbo the Great* finds the three friends involved in a school competition to envision the next 100 years. Cross has written in *School Librarian* that her books are aimed at an imaginary reluctant reader for whom she's "trying not to write something that would break the spell, that would make him remember that he's reading and put the book down."

Another series of novels included *The Demon Headmaster* (1982), *The Prime Minister's Brain* (1985), *The Revenge of the Demon Headmaster* (1995), and *The Demon Headmaster Strikes Again* (1997). The first book began as an essay Cross imagined for Clipper to write as part of a school competition. When Cross told the story to her then-eight-year-old daughter Elizabeth, she was encouraged by her enthusiasm to expand it into a full-length story. For the first time, Cross incorporated a fantastic element: the villainous demon headmaster's ability to hypnotise the entire school. He is ultimately defeated by SPLAT—Society for the Protection of Our Lives Against Them—a group of students led by Dinah Glass who are suspicious of the thrall under which the rest of their classmates have fallen. *Booklist* critic Ilene Cooper found that "The malevolent mood is well described. . . ." For Audrey Laski in the *Times Educational Supplement*, the book made "important points about independence of mind, about certain kinds of cowardice, and about sibling relationship, through its fantastic tale. . . ."

Sheer popularity drove Cross to return to the headmaster again—that and her sudden recognition, as she explained in an afterword to *The Prime Minister's Brain*, that "the Demon Headmaster must like computers." When the headmaster takes the most adept young computer students in Brit-

GILLIAN CROSS

PICTURES IN THE DARK

In this 1996 novel, Charlie's unexplainable photograph leads to his involvement with a troubled boy and his family.

character whom children love to hate" and noted that the tale of SPLAT's efforts to subvert the headmaster's active interest in genetic engineering is "action packed."

Suspense Becomes Key

Cross took up an historical theme again in *A Whisper of Lace* (1981), the first of several suspense novels. A brother and sister are revealed as smugglers of French lace into England by their younger brother. Critiquing the book in the *Junior Bookshelf*, M. Hobbs enjoyed the "modern and satisfying realism of character. . . . The reader experiences both setting and events almost physically through the writer's vivid sensual descriptions." *School Librarian* reviewer Sudbery found the writing "subtle" and concluded that: "The book grips to the end, and is the kind about which one thinks: 'Good, still two more pages. What will happen now?'"

In *The Dark Behind the Curtain* (1982), Cross used elements of the supernatural to add to the suspense of a high school theater production of *Sweeney Todd* that appears to be haunted by ghosts of the real Sweeney Todd's victims. In *Horn Book*, Mary M. Burns praised the book as "a skillfully crafted thriller—richly detailed and plausibly designed." E. Colwell of the *Junior Bookshelf* termed it "a grim story, suffused with malice, hatred and the betrayal of trust. It makes compulsive reading, however, for the build-up of atmosphere is powerfully contrived." The novel was chosen as a Carnegie highly commended book and was a runner-up for the Guardian Award. Critics have picked up on Cross's unapologetic use of violence and betrayal in much of her work. In her essay in *School Librarian*, Cross termed violence "crucial" to children's literature. "Death and danger and injury are hard, definite, dramatic things . . . Love. Hate. The struggle for power. Irrevocable choices. Physical damage . . . It's all there. As absolute, as heroic in its dimensions as anything in Tolkien—or Shakespeare."

In *Born of the Sun* (1984), Cross examined the forces at work on a displaced family when the father, an explorer, decides to track down an ancient lost city in Peru, accompanied by his daughter and wife. Eventually, the teenaged Paula realizes the quite different purpose of the trip: her father is deathly ill, convinced that this will be

ain hostage, it's up to SPLAT to rescue them. Anthony Horowitz, reviewing the book for the *Times Literary Supplement*, praised Cross for inventing that "most compelling of villains; a man motivated not by greed or lust for power but by the simple conviction that his dream of an ordered and efficient world is right." Rodie Sudbery of the *School Librarian* predicted that the book would "go down well with readers who like fast-moving, far-fetched stories." In *Revenge of the Demon Headmaster*, the evil administrator transmits subliminal messages during the Hunky Parker television show. Though SPLAT members manage to foil his scheme, the headmaster escapes only to surface once more in *The Demon Headmaster Strikes Again*. A *Books for Keeps* reviewer welcomed the return of "an evil his last adventure. In *Growing Point*, Margery Fisher lauded "Paula's enforced understanding of her parents and of herself is honestly shown as an inevitable welding of sorrow and the lightening of spirit that comes from maturity in sight."

Cross continued to set herself new challenges with *On the Edge* (1984), an elaborate parallel story of three teenagers, each caught in the vise of arbitrary power. The protagonist, Tug Shakespeare, has been taken hostage by a terrorist group eager to send a message to his mother, an investigative reporter. *Times Literary Supplement* reviewer Dominic Hibberd praised Cross for creating "not just another hostage adventure but a study of why and how far families matter. . . . Despite some unrealistic details, this is an ingenious and stimulating book." Burns, in *Horn Book*, found that Cross had "crafted a tense, compelling adventure-mystery" that led to a "chilling dénouement." Writing in the *Junior Bookshelf*, M. Crouch put a complimentary spin on his criticism that "it does, I feel, fall just short of greatness; and it is a measure of her [Cross's] ability that we expect her to be great." *On the Edge* was among the American Library Association's Best Books for Young Adults and runner-up for the Edgar and the Whitbread awards.

Cross's readers were taken in another direction entirely with her first-person novel *Chartbreaker* (1987), which details the rock business. Janis May Finch, the seventeen-year-old narrator, runs away from home to join a rock group. Many of the tensions she felt at home are at work in the group—and the problems often have to be resolved in the spotlight of public performances. *Chartbreaker* was chosen as one of the American Library Association's Best Books for Young Adults and was also a Carnegie commended book. Jack Forman, writing in *School Library Journal*, found the novel "thoroughly consistent and uncompromising," declaring it "an engrossing pathbreaker, bringing the rhythms and rhymes of rock music in the 80s to the young adult novel." Anne Everall of the *School Librarian* praised the "hard-hitting story" for "successfully avoid[ing] clichés that this type of novel can so easily fall into."

Family ties coupled with suspense are central to *Roscoe's Leap* (1987), which takes place in a house whose wings span a river and are connected by a passageway beneath a waterfall. A mother and her two teenagers live in one wing, their great

If you enjoy the works of Gillian Cross, you may also want to check out the following books and films:

Elisabeth Mace, *Under Siege,* 1990.
Gillian Rubinstein, *Space Demons,* 1988.
Vivian Vande Velde, *User Friendly,* 1991.
WarGames, starring Matthew Broderick, 1983.

uncle and his guardian in the other. The discovery of a life-size model guillotine in one of the rooms leads to questions no one wants to answer and an eventual disruption of the repressed household. Cross met with some criticism for the book, such as the review by Anne Duchene in the *Times Literary Supplement:* "Gillian Cross is demonstrably very able; but here she has set herself too many jumps too close together. . . . The sadly true little story at its heart, about human misunderstanding and pain, needs more space, and time, in which to be developed." Fisher, in *Growing Point*, disagreed, citing Cross as "a past master in establishing through seemingly ordinary words an atmosphere of danger and disturbance" and finding *Roscoe's Leap* "her most powerful essay in Gothicised fiction."

By the time Cross embarked on *A Map of Nowhere* (1988), her two oldest children were teenagers, and she had had two more. She paid a sitter for the twelve hours of writing time she set aside per week. Like *Chartbreaker*, *A Map of Nowhere* was in part a result of her exposure to her children's interests—and her visit to the adventure-game club of her son's former school. In the novel, the protagonist Nick Miller is faced with excruciating moral choices in his attempts to fit in with his older brother and his delinquent friends. Their insistence that he make elements of his adventure games real by spying on a family to case them for an eventual hold-up puts Nick in terrible moral dilemmas. The situation is complicated by the family's own less than pure motives, which are hidden by their seeming goodness. A *Kirkus Reviews* critic called *A Map of Nowhere* "spellbinding" and Burns, writing in *Horn Book*, deemed the work "impeccably constructed" and noted that it involved "the reconciliation of self-gratification with self-esteem." Zena Sutherland, writing in *Children & Books*, found "sharp insight," praising

Cross for being "particularly skilled at combining a dramatic, contemporary structure and an exploration of issues that transcend time." In her review in the *Wilson Library Bulletin*, Cathi MacRae lauded the "complex morality tale. In shifts between fantasy and reality the concepts of right and wrong are explored; life is a game in which ethical choices are made. . . . In the penetrating light that Cross shines on disenchanted youth, teen readers may see beyond black and white."

Animals as a Powerful Metaphor

Wolf (1991) showed the author's more serious side. Cassy, the thirteen-year-old protagonist, leaves the shelter of her grandmother's house for an uncertain existence with her mother and mother's boyfriend in their London squat. In the course of the novel, she must come to terms with the fact that her father, a shadowy, distant figure, is an IRA terrorist; not only does this call to mind the wolf that's been haunting her nightmares, but Cassy becomes fascinated by the animals themselves. The novel was awarded the Carnegie Medal. Fisher, in *Growing Point*, found it "electrifying and absorbing." Brian Slough, reviewing the work in the *Times Educational Supplement*, deemed *Wolf* "an outstanding achievement in its genre, true to conventions while rising beyond them." A *Publishers Weekly* critic noted that "the nature of fear itself [is] among the subjects tackled in this meticulously plotted novel." Ruth S. Vose of *School Library Journal* deemed it "an exciting, multilayered, and thought-provoking thriller," and *Horn Book* reviewer Burns found the use of the wolf metaphor "heavy-handed but powerful, and the psychological depth of the narrative is both rich and subtle."

Reprising an historical theme, Cross set *The Great American Elephant Chase* (1993) in nineteenth-century Nebraska. By running away with the circus, Tad, an orphan, escapes his grim foster home. He befriends Cissie, whose father had been the elephant's trainer until his recent death. Soon Tad is involved in protecting Khush, the resident elephant, from the clutches of a pair of criminals from his former hometown. Though Cross generally sets her stories in England, she effectively captured the feel of the western United States through research. She also spent time at the London zoo, carefully observing and even touching elephants. Her meticulous research nearly bogged her down until, she said in an interview, she re-

alized that this was simply a story of two people and an elephant.

The Great American Elephant Chase won both the Smarties Book Prize and the Whitbread Children's Novel Award. A *Publishers Weekly* reviewer praised the work for offering "more than mere adventure; along with rescuing the great elephant, Tad saves something just as important—his sense of self." Elizabeth S. Watson, in *Horn Book*, especially admired the portrayal of Cissie "as quick-witted a heroine as anyone could wish for . . . an impetuous, stubborn, sometimes high-handed young woman. . . . " For Emily Melton of *Booklist*, the story was "Charmingly told with humor and warmth, it's never gushy or silly, and it keeps the reader's attention from the first page to the last."

In *New World* (1995), Cross explored virtual reality games. Her three teenage protagonists become obsessed, competing with one other via computer in New World, the terrifying game of the title. Eventually, they buck the prohibition of the game's creators and meet each other in person—united in their recognition that they have served as little more than guinea pigs for the adult creators of the game. In *Horn Book* Maeve V. Knoth wrote that "Cross develops strong, individual characters and places them in a tightly woven, taut plot—once again proving herself a master of suspense." A reviewer in *Publishers Weekly* noted that the "ambitious" themes of the story "never really come together in the sort of revelatory collision of metaphor and narrative that characterizes Cross's best works. . . . " In *School Library Journal*, Susan L. Rogers had similar reservations about the novel, but wrote that this "cleverly plotted, suspenseful mystery . . . should grab readers. . . . "

As in *Wolf*, Cross made an animal central to *Pictures in the Dark* (1996). When Charlie, a young photographer, takes a picture of an otter, he suddenly finds himself involved with the odd Luttrell family, whose troubled son Peter has a peculiar connection with the animal. Jo Goodman, a reviewer for *Magpies*, liked the "stunning combination of realistic characters and relationships." Reviewing the work in *Bulletin of the Center for Children's Books*, Deborah Stevenson lauded Cross's "masterful job of uniting the threads here, with the visuality of the photographic theme enhancing both the otherworldly aspect of the book and the intensely depicted human story."

The enormous appeal of Cross's writing stems from her genuine interest in the lives of her readers, in inspiring them to read and identify with her characters. As Jane Inglis summed up in *School Librarian*, "the best tradition of Gillian Cross's novels . . . [is] above all, a tremendously strong emotional range and an acute awareness of the stresses of growing up."

■ Works Cited

Burns, Mary M., review of *Chartbreaker, Horn Book*, September/October, 1984, p. 596.

Burns, Mary M., review of *On the Edge, Horn Book*, July/August, 1985, p. 453.

Burns, Mary M., review of *A Map of Nowhere*, *Horn Book*, May/June, 1989, p. 375.

Cadogan, Mary, "High Flyers and Dragon Slayers," *Books and Bookmen*, July, 1985, p. 25.

Carter, Anne, "Encouraging Stories," *Times Literary Supplement*, March 27, 1981, p. 340.

Colwell, E., review of *The Dark Behind the Curtain, Junior Bookshelf*, October, 1982, p. 197.

Cooper, Ilene, review of *The Demon Headmaster, Booklist*, June 15, 1983, pp. 1336-37.

Cross, Gillian, "Twenty Things I Don't Believe About Children's Books," *School Librarian*, May, 1991, pp. 44-46.

Cross, Gillian, comments in *Contemporary Authors*, Volume 38, Gale, 1993.

Crouch, M., review of *On the Edge, Junior Bookshelf*, April, 1985, pp. 87-88.

Duchene, Anne, "Across the Ravine," *Times Literary Supplement*, November 20-26, 1987, p. 1285.

Everall, Anne, review of *Chartbreak, School Librarian*, August, 1987, p. 252.

Fanning, Peter, "Nasties in the Woodshed," *Times Educational Supplement*, November 21, 1980, p. 32.

Fisher, Margery, review of *Born of the Sun, Growing Point*, January, 1984, p. 4189.

Fisher, Margery, review of *Swimathon!, Growing Point*, November, 1986, p. 4716.

Fisher, Margery, review of *Chartbreak, Growing Point*, March, 1987, p. 4759-60.

Fisher, Margery, review of *Roscoe's Leap, Growing Point*, January, 1988, pp. 4905-6.

Forman, Jack, *School Library Journal*, April, 1987, p. 108.

Goodman, Jo, review of *Pictures in the Dark, Magpies*, May, 1997, pp. 37-38.

Review of *The Great American Elephant Chase, Publishers Weekly*, February 15, 1993, p. 239.

Hibberd, Dominic, "Family Feelings," *Times Literary Supplement*, February 1, 1985, p. 130.

Hobbs, M., review of *A Whisper of Lace, Junior Bookshelf*, October, 1981, p. 207.

Horowitz, Anthony, "Tapping the Junior Brain-Bank," *Times Literary Supplement*, March 14, 1986, p. 286.

Kaye, Marilyn, review of *The Iron Way, Booklist*, January 1, 1980, p. 666.

Knoth, Maeve V., review of *New World, Horn Book*, July/August, 1995, p. 465.

Laski, Audrey, "More Than Readers," *Times Literary Supplement*, July 25, 1986, p. 21.

MacRae, Cathi, "Young Adult Perplex," *Wilson Library Bulletin*, March, 1990, pp. 106-7.

Review of *A Map of Nowhere, Kirkus Reviews*, March 1, 1989, p. 375-76.

Melton, Emily, review of *The Great American Elephant Chase, Booklist*, March 15, 1993, p. 1320.

Review of *New World, Publishers Weekly*, March 13, 1995, p. 70.

Rogers, Susan L., review of *New World, School Library Journal*, March, 1995, p. 222.

Sixth Book of Junior Authors and Illustrators, edited by Sally Holmes Holtze, H. W. Wilson, 1989.

Spencer, Nigel, review of *Swimathon!, Books for Keeps*, March, 1988, p. 19.

Stevenson, Deborah, review of *Pictures in the Dark, Bulletin of the Center for Children's Books*, January, 1997, pp. 161-62.

Sudbery, Rodie, review of *A Whisper of Lace, School Librarian*, December, 1981, p. 340.

Sudbery, Rodie, review of *The Prime Minister's Brain, School Librarian*, March, 1986, pp. 67-68.

Sutherland, Zena, review of *Roscoe's Leap* and *A Map of Nowhere, Children & Books*, Longman, 1997, pp. 339-40.

Vose, Ruth S., review of *Wolf, School Library Journal*, April, 1991, p. 141.

Watson, Elizabeth S., review of *The Great Elephant Chase, Horn Book*, September/October, 1993, p. 596.

Review of *Wolf, Publishers Weekly*, February 22, 1991, p. 219.

■ For More Information See

BOOKS

Children's Books and Their Creators, Houghton, 1995.

Dictionary of Literary Biography, Volume 161: *British Children's Writers Since 1960, First Series*, Gale, 1996.

The Oxford Companion to Children's Literature, Oxford University Press, 1984.
Twentieth-Century Young Adult Writers, 1st edition, St. James Press, 1994.
Written for Children, Scarecrow Press, 1996.

PERIODICALS

Books for Keeps, March, 1997, p. 26.
Bulletin of the Center for Children's Books, June, 1995, pp. 340-41.
Horn Book, January/February, 1997, p. 54.
Publishers Weekly, July 19, 1991, pp. 36-37; September 23, 1996, p. 77.
School Librarian, May, 1995, pp. 76-77.
School Library Journal, June, 1989, p. 122.*

—Sketch by C. M. Ratner

Samuel R. Delany

University, 1987; senior fellow at the Institute for the Humanities, University of Michigan, 1993; visiting Penny and Michael Winton scholar, University of Minnesota, 1995.

■ Awards, Honors

Nebula Award for best novel, Science Fiction Writers of America, 1966, for *Babel-17*, 1967, for *The Einstein Intersection*; Nebula Award for best short story, 1967, for "Aye and Gomorrah"; Nebula Award for best novelette, 1969, for "Time Considered as a Helix of Semi-Precious Stones"; Hugo Award for best short story, Science Fiction Convention, 1970, for "Time Considered as a Helix of Semi-Precious Stones"; American Book Award nomination, 1980, for *Tales of Neveryon*; Pilgrim Award, Science Fiction Research Association, 1985; The Dark Room Award for Lifetime Contribution to Black Literature, 1989; William Whitehead Memorial Award, Lifetime Contribution to Gay and Lesbian Writing, 1993.

■ Personal

Born April 1, 1942, in New York, NY; son of Samuel R. (a funeral director) and Margaret Carey (a library clerk; maiden name, Boyd) Delany; married Marilyn Hacker (a poet), August 24, 1961 (divorced, 1980); children: Iva Alyxander. *Education:* Attended City College (now of the City University of New York), 1960 and 1962-63.

■ Addresses

Agent—Henry Morrison, Inc., Box 235, Bedford Hills, NY 10507.

■ Career

Author, editor, and educator. Butler Professor of English, State University of New York at Buffalo, 1975; professor of comparative literature, University of Massachusetts—Amherst, 1988—. Senior fellow at the Center for Twentieth Century Studies, University of Wisconsin—Milwaukee, 1977; senior fellow at the Society for the Humanities, Cornell

■ Writings

SCIENCE FICTION

The Jewels of Aptor (abridged edition bound with *Second Ending* by James White), Ace Books, 1962, hardcover edition, Gollancz, 1968, complete edition published with an introduction by Don Hausdorff, Gregg Press, 1976.

The Ballad of Beta-2 (also see below; bound with *Alpha Yes, Terra No!* by Emil Petaja), Ace Books, 1965, hardcover edition published with an introduction by David G. Hartwell, Gregg Press, 1977.

Empire Star (also see below; bound with *The Three Lords of Imeten* by Tom Purdom), Ace Books, 1966, hardcover edition published with an introduction by Hartwell, Gregg Press, 1977.

Babel-17, Ace Books, 1966, hardcover edition, Gollancz, 1967, published with an introduction by Robert Scholes, 1976.

The Einstein Intersection, slightly abridged edition, Ace Books, 1967, hardcover edition, Gollancz, 1968, complete edition, Ace Books, 1972.

Nova, Doubleday, 1968.

Driftglass: Ten Tales of Speculative Fiction, Doubleday, 1971.

The Tides of Lust, Lancer Books, 1973.

Dhalgren, Bantam, 1975, hardcover edition published with an introduction by Jean Mark Gawron, Gregg Press, 1978.

The Ballad of Beta-2 [and] *Empire Star*, Ace Books, 1975.

Triton, Bantam, 1976.

Empire: A Visual Novel, illustrations by Howard V. Chaykin, Berkley Books, 1978.

Distant Stars, Bantam, 1981.

Stars in My Pocket Like Grains of Sand, Bantam, 1984.

The Complete Nebula Award-Winning Fiction, Bantam, 1986.

The Star Pits (bound with *Tango Charlie and Foxtrot Romeo* by John Varley), Tor Books, 1989.

They Fly at Ciron, Incunabula, 1992.

"FALL OF THE TOWERS" SERIES; SCIENCE FICTION

Captives of the Flame (bound with *The Psionic Menace* by Keith Woodcott), Ace Books, 1963, revised edition published under author's original title *Out of the Dead City*, Sphere Books, 1968.

The Towers of Toron (bound with *The Lunar Eye* by Robert Moore Williams), Ace Books, 1964.

City of a Thousand Suns, Ace Books, 1965.

The Fall of the Towers (trilogy; contains *Out of the Dead City*, *The Towers of Toron*, and *City of a Thousand Suns*), Ace Books, 1970, hardcover edition published with introduction by Joseph Milicia, Gregg Press, 1977.

"RETURN TO NEVERYON" SERIES; SWORD AND SORCERY NOVELS

Tales of Neveryon, Bantam, 1979.

Neveryona; or, The Tale of Signs and Cities, Bantam, 1983.

Flight from Neveryon, Bantam, 1985.

The Bridge of Lost Desire, Arbor House, 1987.

OTHER

The Jewel-Hinged Jaw: Notes on the Language of Science Fiction (criticism), Dragon Press, 1977, revised edition, Berkley Publishing, 1978.

The American Shore: Meditations on a Tale of Science Fiction by Thomas M. Disch—"Angouleme" (criticism), Dragon Press, 1978.

Heavenly Breakfast: An Essay on the Winter of Love (memoir), Bantam, 1979.

Starboard Wine: More Notes on the Language of Science Fiction (criticism), Dragon Press, 1984.

The Motion of Light in Water: Sex and Science Fiction Writing in the East Village, 1957-1965 (memoir), Arbor House, 1988.

Wagner/Artaud: A Play of Nineteenth and Twentieth Century Critical Fictions (criticism), Ansatz Press, 1988.

Straits of Messina (essays; essays by Delany as well as originally published in magazines under pseudonym K. Leslie Steiner), Serconia Press, 1989.

The Mad Man (fiction), Richard Kasek, 1994.

Silent Interviews: On Language, Race, Sex, Science Fiction, and Some Comics (essays), University Press of New England, 1994.

Atlantis: Three Tales (novella), University Press of New England, 1995.

Hogg (fiction), Illinois State University/Black Ice Books, 1995.

Longer Views: Extended Essays (essays), University Press of New England, 1996.

Also author of scripts, director, and editor of two short films, *Tiresias*, 1970, and *The Orchid*, 1971; author of two scripts for the *Wonder Woman* comic book series, 1972, and of the radio play *The Star Pit*, based on his short story of the same title. Editor, *Nebula Winners 13*, Harper and Row, 1989, and coeditor with Marilyn Hacker of *Quark*, issues 1-4, Paperback Library, 1970-71. In addition, Delany contributed to the *Green Lantern/Green Arrow Anthology*.

■ **Sidelights**

"Samuel R. Delany," comments Jane Branham Weedman in her study of the author, "is one of today's most innovative and imaginative writers of science fiction." *School Library Journal* critic John Adams adds, "Delany's not for everyone. . . . But his writing offers one of the most heady, rewarding experiences in modern fiction today." Considered among the most successful of the New Wave writers of science fiction, a group of English and American authors who emerged in the 1960s and favor stylistic experimentation over traditional narratives, Delany is praised as one of the most gifted authors in the genre as well as one of the few African Americans working in his field to have achieved both critical and popular success. Regarded as a brilliant stylist and compelling storyteller whose complex, often demanding novels and stories have expanded the scope of science fiction, Delany uses elements of mythology, anthropology, psychology, sociology, history, and philosophy to probe the natures of language and art, the role of the artist, sexual identity, and societal issues such as racism and sexism while telling action-filled adventure stories often set in alien worlds. Filling his works with intricate meanings, literary and cultural symbols and allusions, flashbacks, and unusual page designs, the author attempts to provide experiences for his readers that parallel the quests of his protagonists. Delany's audience is invited to question themselves and their societies while participating in the act of reading to its fullest extent.

In his essay on Delany in *Dictionary of Literary Biography*, Peter S. Alterman notes, "His are stories in which the creative experience of the reader is as important as the narrative. They invite, wheedle, and bully the reader into confronting the process of his reading and thereby participating in both the creation and the experience of the story." At the center of the web of personal, cultural, artistic, and intellectual concerns that provides the framework for his books is Delany's examination of how language and myth influence reality by shaping perceptions. In his science fiction, the author "creates new myths, or inversions of old ones, by which his protagonists measure themselves and their societies against the traditional myths that Delany includes," observes Jane Branham Weedman. In this way, as Alterman notes, Delany confronts "the questions of the extent to which myths and archetypes create reality." In addition to his contributions to science fiction, Delany has written adult novels and plays, memoirs, and collections of essays as well as scripts for films, comic books, and a radio play;

This autobiographical 1988 work follows Delany's life in New York's East Village during the 1960s, and details his encounters with such persons as Bob Dylan and W. H. Auden.

a professor of comparative literature, he is also the author of several well-received volumes of literary criticism, much of it assessing science fiction as literature. He has also taught writing, co-edited a magazine, and written and directed two short films.

Although Delany does not characteristically address his books to young adults, several of his novels have been adopted by this audience; for example, a reviewer in *School Library Journal* notes that reissues of some of his early paperbacks in hardcover "are primarily for school libraries supporting s-f programs." Adolescent readers have been attracted to the author's imaginative detailing of alternative societies as well as by his fascination with myth and language. In addition, young adults can identify with his characters as they search for selfhood and may relate to Delany's vision of future worlds, including our own, in which, as the author says, things have changed. "In most of my futures," he has noted, "the racial situation has changed and changed for the better." Many of Delany's protagonists are teenage poets or musicians in the process of self-discovery. In these quests, the characters—who are both male and female, are often black or of mixed race, and suffer from some physical or psychological problem—resolve their personal issues while they seek meaning in their respective worlds. These young people are often involved in criminal activities ranging from petty theft to assassination; critics note that Delany equates the artist and the criminal because both figures operate outside mainstream society. In Delany's view, the presence of both archetypes is crucial, since the actions of the artist/criminals push society's values to their limits and provide the experimentation needed to prepare for eventual change.

Delany was born and raised in Harlem, the son of Samuel R. Delany, Sr., a prominent businessman and funeral director, and Margaret Carey Boyd Delany, a library clerk with the New York Public Library whose friends included some of the Harlem Renaissance figures of the 1920s and 1930s. He received most of his education in predominantly white settings, such as the Dalton Elementary School on Park Avenue and the Bronx High School of Science. Expressing his awareness of the differences in the speech he heard at home and at school, Delany noted that he became attuned to "language as an intriguing and infinitely malleable modeling tool." The dichotomies in his daily life affected Delany's behavior, causing him to run away several times between the ages of five and seventeen and to receive psychological counseling. Accepted by his classmates, he was named Most Popular in his last year at Dalton. However, his teachers failed to recognize his dyslexia. In a letter to bibliographers Michael W. Peplow and Robert S. Brayard, Delany describes his youth as a "virtually ballistic trip through a socio-psychological barrier of astonishingly restrained violence," adding that "it wouldn't be too far afield to say that within the metaphorical, or more accurately, the analogical freedom science fiction provides, I have written nothing about nothing but the trip through such socio-psychological barriers ever since."

While at Dalton, Delany began writing short stories. After graduation, he enrolled at the Bronx High School of Science, concentrating on math and physics as well as pursuing extracurricular interests in music, acting, and ballet; at fourteen, he wrote a complete violin concerto. He also continued his writing, winning first place for a short story and second place for an essay in the National Scholastic Writing Awards contest. While a teenager, Delany became enthralled by science fiction writers such as Robert Heinlein, Ray Bradbury, and Alfred Bester and by European and African American writers such as Jean Genet, Albert Camus, Jean Cocteau, Lawrence Durrell, Alexander Trocchi, James Baldwin, Chester Himes, and John O'Killins—as well as James Joyce and

This work, part of Delaney's "Neveryon" quartet of sword and sorcery novels, is set in an ancient world populated by flying dragons, gods, and barbarians.

William Faulkner. At nineteen, he married former classmate Marilyn Hacker, with whom he had edited their school's literary magazine. Hacker had begun working as an assistant editor at Ace Books, a major publisher of science fiction. When she complained to her husband about the poor quality of some of the manuscripts she was seeing, Delany responded by writing a novel inspired by a series of recent nightmares. That story, *The Jewels of Aptor* (1962), became his first published work.

While working for a few years as a singer and musician in Greenwich Village, Delany wrote four additional novels, including *Captives of the Flame* (1963), the first volume of his popular "Fall of the Towers" trilogy that also includes *The Towers of Toron* (1964) and *City of a Thousand Suns* (1965) Over this time, he published *Babel-17* (1966), *Empire Star* (1966), *The Einstein Intersection* (1967), and *Nova* (1968), the first of his works to be printed originally in hardcover. Douglas Barbour, writing in *Dictionary of Literary Biography*, describes these early novels as "colorful, exciting, entertaining, and intellectually provocative to a degree not found in most genre science fiction." Barbour adds that although they do adhere to science fiction conventions, the books "begin the exploration of those literary obsessions that define [Delany's] oeuvre: problems of communication and community; new kinds of sexual/love/family relationships; the artist as social outsider . . .; cultural interactions and the exploration of human social possibilities these allow; archetypal and mythic structures in the imagination."

Earns Recognition, Major Awards

With the publication of *Babel-17* in 1966, Delany began to gain recognition as a writer of science fiction. The novel, which earned its author his first Nebula Award, is a story of galactic warfare between the forces of the Alliance, which includes the Earth, and the forces of the Invaders. The poet Rydra Wong is enlisted by Alliance intelligence to decipher communications intercepted from its enemy. When she discovers that these dispatches contain not a code but rather an unknown language, her quest becomes one of learning the mysterious tongue labeled Babel-17. While leading an interstellar mission in search of clues, Rydra gains insights into the nature of language and, in the process, discovers the unique charac-

ter of the enigmatic new language of the Invaders. When the poet discovers that Babel-17 is the secret weapon of the Invaders, she and her allies use the language to end the war.

After *Babel-17*, Delany wrote *Empire Star* (1966), a novel that is considered specifically directed to young adults. *Empire Star* relates the history of a galactic civilization by portraying its characters at different ages and performing different functions throughout the narrative. The protagonist, teenager Comet Jo, meets older versions of himself who help him as he grows and travels toward Empire Star, the center of the galaxy, to bring word of the freeing of an enslaved alien race, the L11. On his way to Empire Star, he acquires a sophisticated understanding of the cyclical nature of time and history. At the end of the novel, Comet Jo dies, only to be reborn so that he can begin his journey once again. In her essay in *Dictionary of Literary Biography*, Sandra Y. Govan says that *Empire Star*, "ostensibly for younger readers, is actually an allegory of the cycle of oppression, guilt, and responsibility which the enslavement of any group imposes on the free." Delany's second Nebula winner, *The Einstein Intersection*, introduces his theme of the power and influence of myth. The story describes a strange race of beings that occupies a post-apocalyptic Earth thirty thousand years in the future where humans are extinct. The aliens assume the economic, political, and religious traditions of the humans in an attempt to make sense of the remnant world in which they find themselves. The key figure in the novel is Lobey, a musician. The power of Lobey's music is its ability to create order, to destroy the old myths and usher in the new. Lobey is on a quest to find his lost love Friza and to assassinate Kid Death, who is killing the race of beings struggling to become human. At the end of the novel, Lobey participates in the murder of Kid Death, finds and loses Friza, and prepares to leave Earth for other galaxies.

After the publication of his next science fiction novel, the well-received *Nova* (1968), in which the mulatto hero Lorq Von Ray locates a rare element from an exploding star in order to prevent oppression in his galaxy, Delany went through several major changes in lifestyle; Sandra Y. Govan describes his personal life of this period as "a model of Bohemian flexibility." Coming out as a gay man with his Hugo and Nebula Award-winning story "Time Considered as a Helix of Semi-

Precious Stones" (1968), he also engaged himself in conceiving, writing, and polishing what would become his longest, most complex, and most controversial novel, *Dhalgren* (1975). On its shifting surface, this novel, which is set on Earth in the near future, represents the experience of a nameless amnesiac, an artist/criminal, during the period of time he spends in an isolated city that has been scarred by destruction and decay. The central theme of this massive work, which is nearly nine hundred pages long, is the search for identity undertaken by the protagonist, who comes to be called Kid. Throughout the story, Kid, who is usually regarded as Delany's characterization of himself, has many adventures, including a variety of sexual escapades, and becomes both a poet and the leader of a teenage gang. At the end of the book, Kid is disgorged from the city during a cataclysm, but he leaves with both life experience and a name. Dazzlingly varied in structure, *Dhalgren* is considered both rich and overblown; some critics, in fact, do not consider it science fiction at all. "Nobody, however," writes Peter S. Alterman, "criticized Delany's masterful use of language in *Dhalgren*. Indeed, his prose style is brilliant." In the *New York Times Book Review*, Gerald Jonas notes, "If the book can be said to be about anything, it is about nothing less than the nature of reality," and adds, "One thing is certain; *Dhalgren* is not a conventional novel, whether considered in terms of S.F. or the mainstream."

The "Neveryon" Quartet

In the late 1970s and 1980s, Delany continued to experiment with his fiction while contributing to a variety of other genres; he and Hacker separated in 1975, and he began to teach at the university level. A book from this period with special appeal for young adults is *Empire: A Visual Novel* (1978), a space opera in comic strip form with illustrations by Howard V. Chaykin, an artist who had worked on *Star Wars* and several Marvel comics. Another group of Delany's books that is especially popular with young audiences is his "Neveryon" quartet, a series of heroic fantasies set in an ancient past filled with dragons, treasures, and fabulous cities; the quartet includes *Tales of Neveryon* (1979), which was nominated for an American Book Award, *Neveryona; or, The Tale of Signs and Cities* (1983), *Flight from Neveryon* (1985), and *The Bridge of Lost Desire* (1987). Reviewing the third novel, a *Publishers Weekly* critic

This 1992 fantasy novel describes a peaceful village's fight against an invading army.

notes, "Like Nabokov, Delany has created a grand, mirrored mythology around versions of himself. Both may write about dispossessed artists, but instead of Russian exiles, Delany's protagonists tend to be black, homosexual outcasts." The reviewer notes that Delany's "variegated fantasy world" contains flying dragons, gods, and a child empress and that the author describes "its sexual life and its economic life, its waning slavery and gaining literacy, its architecture, politics, religion and children's games." In an assessment of the fourth novel, a *Publishers Weekly* reviewer states, "Around [the] paradigmatic action . . . Delany constructs a world so distant and romantic that it contains dragons and barbarians, yet so close and recognizable that it suffers an AIDS epidemic. In the best entries, he gives us an enthralling tale and at the same time a challenging critique—of sword and sorcery and of the social systems that fantasy so often ignores or trivializes: politics, economics, language, history, sexuality, slavery, and power."

Throughout the series, Delany tells the story of Gorgik, a boy enslaved at fifteen who becomes known as the Liberator when he defeats the Child Empress and abolishes slavery. In the novel-length "Tale of Plagues and Carnivals," one of the first novels published in the United States to deal with AIDS, the author shifts in time from his primitive world to present-day New York and back to examine the devastating effects of AIDS. In the appendices that accompany each of these books, Delany reflects on the creative process itself. Of the four volumes in the series, *Neveryona* has perhaps received the most critical attention. The novel describes how Pryn, a girl who flees her mountain home on the back of a dragon, meets a storyteller who teaches her to write her name and tells her of a hidden treasure in a sunken town. On her journey, Pryn meets Gorgik and finally discovers the city, Neveryona. *Science Fiction and Fantasy Book Review* contributor Michael R. Collings calls the novel "a stirring fable of adventure and education, of heroic action and even more heroic normality in a world where survival itself is constantly threatened." Faren C. Miller finds the book groundbreaking; she writes in *Locus:* "Combining differing perspectives with extraordinary talent for the details of a world—its smells, its shadows, workaday furnishings, and playful frills—Delany has produced a sourcebook for a new generation of fantasy writers."

With the publication of *The Motion of Light in Water* (1988), Delany turned to writing about himself. This memoir of his early days as a writer in New York's East Village is "an extraordinary account of life experienced by a precocious black artist of the 1960s," as E. Guereschi writes in *Choice.* The book details Delany's sexual adventures and nervous breakdown while reflecting the sense of living on the edge in an exciting social and cultural period. Moreover, *The Motion of Light in Water* describes Delany's realization and eventual acceptance of his homosexuality. Thomas M. Disch, writing in the *American Book Review,* finds that Delany "can't help creating legends and elaborating myths. Indeed, it is his forte, the open secret of his success as an SF writer. [Delany's] SF heroes are variations of an archetype he calls

If you enjoy the works of Samuel R. Delany, you may also want to check out the following books and films:

Poul Anderson, *The Boat of a Million Years,* 1989.
Robert A. Heinlein, *Beyond the Horizon,* 1918.
Gene Wolfe, *Urth of the New Sun,* 1987.
The Abyss, starring Ed Harris, 1989.

The Kid. . . . In his memoir, the author himself [is] finally assuming the role in which his fictive alter-egos have enjoyed their success. That is the book's strength even more than its weakness." Disch concludes that *The Motion of Light in Water* "has the potential of being as popular, as representative of its era, as [Jack Kerouac's] *On the Road.*" In the 1990s, Delany has continued to contribute to the genres of both fiction and nonfiction. Young adults may be most interested in *They Fly at Ciron,* a fantasy novella combined with two related short stories that describes how the peaceful village of Ciron fights against domination by the army of Myetra, who kill and enslave many of the Cironians; a main character in the novel is Rahm, a village boy who joins the Cironian resistance. *Booklist* reviewer Carl Hays calls *They Fly at Ciron* "must reading for Delany's fans and, for newcomers, a good introduction to an enduring talent."

Beginning as a wunderkind of science fiction, Delany is now regarded as one of the genre's grand masters. Despite their sophistication and multilayered levels of meaning, his works have found an appreciative audience among both adults and young adults for their literary quality, dynamic structures, and relevant subtexts. Jane Branham Weedman notes, "Few writers approach the lyricism, the command of language, the powerful combination of style and content that distinguishes Delany's works. More importantly," she concludes, "few writers, whether in science fiction or mundane fiction, so successfully create works which make us question ourselves, our actions, our beliefs, and our society as Delany has helped us do." Writing in the *Washington Post Book World,* John Clute places Delany in a central position in modern science fiction. In his best work, Clute believes, Delany "treated the interstellar venues of space opera as analogues of urban life in the decaying hearts of the great American cities. As a black gay New Yorker much too well educated for his own good, Delany . . . illuminated the world the way a torch might cast light in a cellar.

■ Works Cited

Adams, John, review of *Distant Stars, School Library Journal,* November, 1981, p. 114.

Alterman, Peter S., "Samuel R. Delany," in *Dictionary of Literary Biography, Volume 8: Twentieth-Century American Science Fiction Writers,* Gale, 1981.

Review of *The Ballad of Beta-2, Driftglass, Empire Star,* and *Nova, School Library Journal,* May, 1978, p. 94.

Barbour, Douglas, "Cultural Invention and Metaphor in the Novels of Samuel R. Delany," *Foundation,* March, 1975, pp. 105-21.

Review of *The Bridge of Lost Desire, Publishers Weekly,* October 23, 1987, p. 49.

Clute, John, *Washington Post Book World,* August 25, 1991, p. 11.

Collings, Michael R., review of *Neveryona, Science Fiction and Fantasy Book Review,* July-August, 1983, p. 31.

Delany, Samuel R., letter to Michael W. Peplow and Robert S. Brayard reprinted in their *Samuel R. Delany: A Primary and Secondary Bibliography 1962-1979,* G. K. Hall, 1980.

Disch, Thomas M., review of *The Motion of Light in Water, American Book Review,* January, 1989, p. 1.

Review of *Flight from Neveryon, Publishers Weekly,* April 26, 1985, p. 79.

Govan, Sandra Y., "Samuel R. Delany," in *Dictionary of Literary Biography, Volume 33: Afro-American Fiction Writers after 1955,* Gale, 1984.

Guereschi, E., review of *The Motion of Light in Water, Choice,* February, 1989, p. 938.

Hays, Carl, review of *They Fly at Ciron, Booklist,* December 15, 1994, p. 740.

Jonas, Gerald, review of *Dhalgren, New York Times Book Review,* February 16, 1975, p. 22.

Miller, Faren C., review of *Neveryona, Locus,* summer, 1983.

Weedman, Jane Branham, *Samuel R. Delany,* Starmont House, 1982.

■ For More Information See

BOOKS

Bleiler, E. F., editor, *Science Fiction Writers: Critical Studies of the Major Authors from the Early Nineteenth Century to the Present Day,* Scribner, 1982.

Contemporary Literary Criticism, Gale Research, Volume 8, 1978, Volume 14, 1980, Volume 38, 1986.

Kostelanetz, Richard, editor, *American Writing Today,* Whitston, 1991.

McCaffery, Larry, and Sinda Gregory, editors, *Alive and Writing: Interviews with American Authors of the 1980s,* University of Illinois Press, 1987.

McEvoy, Seth, *Samuel R. Delany,* Ungar, 1984.

Platt, Charles, editor, *Dream Makers: The Uncommon People Who Write Science Fiction,* Berkley Books, 1980.

Slusser, George Edgar, *The Delany Intersection: Samuel R. Delany Considered as a Writer of Semi-Precious Words,* Borgo, 1977.

Smith, Nicholas D., editor, *Philosophers Look at Science Fiction,* Nelson-Hall, 1982.

Weedman, Jane Branham, *Reader's Guide to Samuel R. Delany,* Starmont House, 1979.

PERIODICALS

Analog Science Fiction/Science Fact, April, 1985.
Black American Literature Forum, summer, 1984.
Extrapolation, fall, 1982; winter, 1989; fall, 1989.
Fantasy Review, December, 1984.
Globe and Mail (Toronto), February 9, 1985.
Library Journal, May 1, 1995, p. 134.
Los Angeles Times Book Review, March 13, 1988.
Kirkus Reviews, November 1, 1994, p. 1488.
Magazine of Fantasy and Science Fiction, November, 1975; June, 1980; May, 1989.
New York Review of Books, January 29, 1991.
New York Times Book Review, March 28, 1976; October 28, 1979; February 10, 1985.
Publishers Weekly, January 29, 1988; October 19, 1992; April 3, 1995, p. 47.
Science Fiction Chronicle, November, 1987; February, 1990.
Science-Fiction Studies, November, 1981; July, 1987; November, 1990.
Voice Literary Supplement, February, 1985.
Washington Post Book World, January 27, 1985.

—Sketch by Gerard J. Senick

Farrukh Dhondy

Personal

Born in 1944 in Poona, Bombay, India; immigrated to England, 1964; son of an Indian Army officer. *Education:* Attended Bombay University for a year in the early 1960s; Cambridge University, B.A., 1967; received M.A. from University of Leicester.

Addresses

Office—c/o Jonathan Cape Ltd., 32 Bedford Sq., London WC1B 3SG, England.

Career

Henry Thornton Comprehensive School, Clapham, London, England, English teacher; Archbishop Temple School, Lambeth, London, 1974-1980, English teacher, beginning in 1974, became head of department; commissioning editor for multicultural television programs on Channel 4, London, 1984—. Writer of television scripts, plays, and fiction for adults and children.

Awards, Honors

Children's Rights Workshop Other awards, 1977, for *East End at Your Feet,* and 1979, for *Come to Mecca, and Other Stories;* Collins/Fontana Award for books for multi-ethnic Britain, for *Come to Mecca, and Other Stories;* Dhondy's works were represented in "Children's Fiction in Britain, 1900-1990," an exhibition sponsored by the British Council's Literature Department, 1990.

Writings

JUVENILE

East End at Your Feet (short stories), Macmillan (London), 1976.
Come to Mecca, and Other Stories, Collins, 1978.
The Siege of Babylon (novel), Macmillan, 1978.
Poona Company (short stories), Gollancz, 1980.
Trip Trap (short stories; contains "Herald," "The Bride" [also see below], "Homework," "The Mandarin Exam," "Batty and Winifred," "The Fifth Gospel," "Lost Soul," and "Under Gemini"), Gollancz, 1982.
Romance, Romance [and] *The Bride,* Faber, 1985.
(Compiler) *Ranters, Ravers and Rhymers,* Collins, 1991.
Black Swan, Houghton, 1992.

OTHER

Mama Dragon (play), produced in London, England, for the Black Theatre cooperative, 1980.

Trojans (adaptation of a play by Euripedes), produced in London, for the Black Theatre Cooperative, 1982.

(Coauthor with Barbara Beese and Leila Hassan) *The Black Explosion in British Schools*, Race Today Publications, 1982.

Kipling Sahib (play), produced in London, 1982.

Vigilantes (play; produced in 1985), Hobo Press, 1988.

King of the Ghetto (television series), broadcast by British Broadcasting Company (BBC1), 1986.

Bombay Duck (novel), J. Cape, 1990.

C. L. R. James: A Life, Orion (London), 1996.

Also author of the stage plays *Shapesters; Film, Film, Film;* and, with John McGrath and others, *All the Fun of the Fair.* Author of additional television plays, including *Maids in the Mad Shadow*, 1981, *Good at Art*, 1983; *Dear Manju*, 1983; *Salt on a Snake's Tail*, 1983; *The Empress of the Munshi*, 1984; and *To Turn a Blind Eye*, 1986. Also author of *Janaky and the Giant and Other Stories*, 1993. Author of series of ethnic situation comedies for British television, including *No Problem*, with Mustapha Matura, 1983, and *Tandoori Nights*, 1985.

Contributor to Indian periodicals *Debonair* and *Economic and Political Weekly*, and to London periodicals, including *Race Today* and the *Listener*. Former editor of *Carcanet*.

■ Sidelights

A native of India, Farrukh Dhondy came to Great Britain to be a schoolteacher. He was able to identify with the growing number of non-white teens who were coming of age at that time. Living in poor areas and ghettoes, these teens both had a sense of hope for the future and a knowledge that their differences made them outcasts. Dhondy has become known for showing the confusion and anxieties of these young people while using accurate descriptions, dialect, and slang expressions to add emphasis to his tales.

Dhondy grew up in a middle class family in Bombay, India, where his father was an officer in the army. As a child, he loved to read, but reading just for the pleasure of it was rarely praised. "The pressure of opinion in the family and outside it was to achieve some form of professional status. Qualifications were the key, examination passes, degrees. Apart from a firm conviction held

by my mother, no one in my world told me that reading was its own reward," he related in an article in the *Times Educational Supplement*. His father also tried to censor his reading of an American comic book called *The Fox and the Crow*. "To my dad it was bad language and imported American nihilism. He insisted that if [my sister and I] were to read comics we should go to the big booksellers in Madras and buy some educational ones," Dhondy commented in the article.

"For a very few of us, reading was a semi-secret activity," Dhondy confided to the *Times Educational Supplement*. There was one library in his city, which was in an old ramshackle building off the main street. To check out books, one had to pay a subscription price of a rupee a month, and to Dhondy's knowledge, only elderly people ever went in there. Still, his interest in reading drew him to the place. One day a friend and he wandered into the building. Dhondy wrote, "I went through several bookshelves of the Institute, one after the other, at first out of stubbornness . . . and later because the reading had induced a kind of a trance, an addiction," he related.

Dhondy also found himself reading the popular magazines of the day, including *Readers Digest* and *Time*. The latter was mailed to his family from an uncle who lived nearby. While he enjoyed hearing the news of the world, his friends thought the magazine was propagandistic. He found that he agreed with them after *Time*'s coverage of the Goa incident. Goa was the last place on the Indian subcontinent that was still run by a colonial government. The Indian government decided to send in troops so that this small area would be released from Portuguese rule. *Time* ran a blatantly anti-Indian story on the incident. Dhondy realized then that the magazine was not as objective as he thought it was.

Around the same time, he had another epiphany about his world. In his school, everyone was excited by the visit of English novelist John Wain. Wain met with Professor Damle, one of Dhondy's teachers. After the visit, Wain wrote an article about it in the *Encounter*. Wain focused on the poverty of Damle, including the cockroaches in his bungalow, and wondered how this man could teach his poverty-stricken pupils. Remembering that incident, Dhondy related in the *Times Educational Supplement* that "I felt no outrage; only a glowing sense of pride that Poona had made it

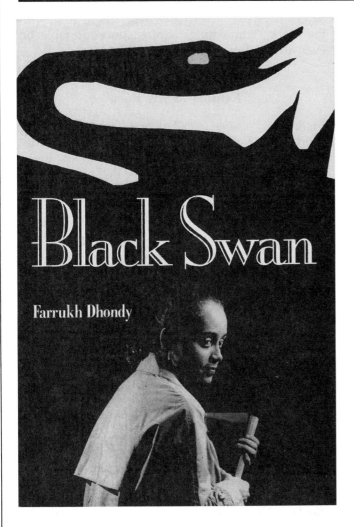

Black Swan

Farrukh Dhondy

What starts for Rose Hassan as a well-paying temporary job transcribing a diary for an elderly, eccentric man turns into a world of secrets and danger in this multilayered mystery.

into the pages of *Encounter*. We were notable at least for our cockroaches. It was an inspiration. I thought to myself, I can be as uncompromising as that with the truth, I can write about India as descriptively, subjectively, harshly. With a little guilt I felt that reading itself had set me apart from those who felt outrage against Wain and *Encounter*. A small lesson: writing was about dishing it out, and reading was about learning to take it."

Career Choices Conflict

Still, it took a while for Dhondy to allow himself the pleasure of this kind of writing. After finish-

ing his secondary education, he moved to Bombay to study chemical technology: "Like all my contemporaries, without exception, I had succumbed to the pressure to 'take up a technical subject'." He moved in with a relative who practiced Ghandian philosophy by dressing simply and practicing vegetarianism. Still, Dhondy's fondness for reading continued, and he read what he could between solving mathematical equations.

Soon, Dhondy's course of study became too much for him. "I was completely bored with the great prospect that yawned before me. An utterly predictable life: you know what kind of house you will have, what sort of person you will marry, where your children will go to school," he told Anwer Bati in the *Times Literary Supplement*. The only solution he knew was to drop out. "I quit chemical engineering and spent the next year truanting from all academe, sitting on a terrace in New Delhi reading anything I could get hold of—Lawrence, Kipling and, for the first time, E M Forster," he told the *Times Educational Supplement*.

Some of Dhondy's friends came to his rescue. They suggested that he try to obtain a scholarship to study abroad. He received the scholarship and was accepted at several prestigious universities, including Stanford University in California, Lumumba University in Moscow, and Pembroke College in Cambridge. He ended up choosing Cambridge because he felt the college matched his bookishness. While there, he joined up with a group of playwrights, wrote for the famous literary magazine *Granta*, and edited a magazine called *Carcanet*.

After graduation, he became a teacher of English at a secondary school in London, England. Liberal to the point of radical in his politics, he was eventually fired from his job, but moved to Archbishop Temple School where he taught for many years, eventually becoming head of the English and Humanities department. It was his tenure at this school that showed him the lives of teenagers, their struggles and hopes, and also gave him a sense of their slang and dialect.

Dhondy's first big literary work was *East End at Your Feet* (1976), a collection of short stories that profiled young adults in the multi-cultural East End of London. In "Dear Manju," Dhondy chronicles the life of a traditional Indian family

If you enjoy the works of Farrukh Dhondy, you may also want to check out the following books and films:

E. M. Forster, *A Passage to India,* 1924.
Victoria Holt, *The India Fan,* 1988.
M. M. Kaye, *The Far Pavilions,* 1978.
My Beautiful Laundrette, starring Daniel Day-Lewis, 1986.

living in London. After his father dies, fourteen-year-old Bhupinder, now the oldest man in the family, finds he must take care of his elder sister. His sister, Manju, however, has other ideas. She aggressively pursues boys, is irreverent, and is happily adjusted to her newer, more liberal country. Bhupinder finds that he can't control her at all. In "K.B.W. (Keep Britain White)," a white teen tries to make sense of the violence and racism that drove his friend's Bangladeshi family out of the neighborhood.

Come to Mecca, and Other Stories (1978), another collection of short stories, established Dhondy as a writer who dealt honestly and openly with the racial problems of Asian and West Indian teenagers in Great Britain. Neil Philip, writing in the *Times Educational Supplement,* praised the work, saying that "Dhondy is subtle, penetrating, witty: one of the few children's authors able adequately to reflect racial differences in the texture of his language. . . . *Come to Mecca* is part of the solution to the problems with which it is concerned."

In 1978, Dhondy published *The Siege of Babylon,* his first novel for young adults. In the work, three black teenagers are persuaded to rob a car rental store by Kwate, an older black man who has been involved in political controversy. During the robbery their plans go astray, and they decide to take hostages. They remain under siege for ten days and are defeated by their lack of nerve. Margery Fisher, writing in *Growing Point,* praises the book for its "subtlety of comment, the intricacy of characterisation, the tight structure and the forceful, idiomatic dialogue which distinguish this book for the intelligent middle 'teens." A. R. Williams, reviewing *The Siege of Babylon* in the *Junior Bookshelf,* enjoyed the author's fine touch with the social commentary in the books and pronounced

the work "stimulating, if often uncomfortable or even disquieting."

Returns to His Roots

In *Poona Company* (1980), Dhondy returns to the short story form, as well as to his native India. He writes about the gossip-filled, spirited atmosphere of the Chowk tea-house, the place where people in his native Poona gathered to catch up and tell tales. The result, according to some reviewers, is illuminating. "We are drawn quietly into this tiny, seething world and we wonder afterwards why we have become so involved in its sordid cruelties and intrigues, its trivial shames and glories," wrote Dervla Murphy in the *Times Literary Supplement.* "The answer can only be that in his unpretentious way Farrukh Dhondy is illuminating not merely a sliver of the Indian scene but a chunk of universal human nature." Gillian Wilce praised the volume in *New Statesman,* writing that "this is the work of a natural story-teller, entertaining and funny and truth-telling in a way that no lesson about other cultures could ever be."

In 1984, Dhondy became head of multi-cultural television programs for a British television station. He was responsible for several situation comedies with Indian characters, including *No Problem* and *Tandoori Nights.* This job, however, left him with less time to write books. In 1992, however, he released *Black Swan,* a new book for young adults. The plot was more convoluted than others he had previously written. When Rose's mother becomes sick, Rose takes over her job. She ends up as personal assistant to the mysterious Mr. B., who gets her started translating a long and complicated document in Elizabethan English. The document becomes a story within a story. It was written by Simon Forman, an Elizabethan doctor who was involved in the theatrical world. It tells about a black man named Lazarus who is involved in much intrigue, including faking his own death, and about Kit Marlowe, who also fakes his death and falls in love with Lazarus. Together, Marlowe and Lazarus write the plays which have been attributed to Shakespeare. Shakespeare himself, a mediocre and drunken actor in this tale, is used merely as a front for the pair's work. Rose ends up being a good companion and translator; later, she finds out that he has tested many people with this job. She ends up being the heir to Mr. B.'s money.

Lucinda Lockwood, writing in the *School Library Journal*, called *Black Swan* "a wobbly mystery with a very muddy solution." A *Junior Bookshelf* reviewer, however, found the book complicated, but interesting: "multi-layered is for once an apt label for a work which should be thoroughly enjoyed by adult readers as well as budding literati." A *Kirkus Reviews* critic thought that the book has "an intriguingly complicated construction . . . [and is] a fast-moving, idea-packed read that will stretch young minds."

"Perhaps what has been lacking until now, at least in England, has been a major contribution to children's literature from coloured writers themselves," claimed David Rees in *Children's Literature in Education*. Dhondy has crossed that gap by producing quality works about non-white teens in Britain. "One of the reasons for his success is that, being coloured himself, he experienced and is able to present vividly some of the complexities of race relations that often escape the notice of white authors of children's books," noted Rees. Rees concluded that Dhondy's work has added significantly to the body of children's literature of Britain, and that Dhondy himself has been a role model to other writers of the genre: "Farrukh Dhondy is one writer who is at least showing the way."

■ Works Cited

Bati, Anwer, "Exposing the Fraud Squad," *Times Literary Supplement*, May 13, 1990, p. H10.

Review of *Black Swan, Junior Bookshelf*, August, 1992, p. 163.

Review of *Black Swan, Kirkus Reviews*, July 15, 1993, p. 932.

Dhondy, Farrukh, "Tale of an Eleventh Hour Child," *Times Educational Supplement*, April 26, 1991, p. 24.

Fisher, Margery, review of *Siege of Babylon, Growing Point*, July, 1978, pp. 3363-64.

Lockwood, Lucinda, review of *Black Swan, School Library Journal*, September, 1993, p. 248.

Murphy, Dervla, "In the Chowk Tea-House," *Times Literary Supplement*, November 21, 1980, p. 1322.

Philip, Neil, "Digging for Gold," *Times Educational Supplement*, January 18, 1980, p. 42.

Rees, David, "Skin Colour in British Children's Books," *Children's Literature in Education*, Summer, 1980, pp. 91-97.

Wilce, Gillian, review of *Poona Company, New Statesman*, November 28, 1980, p. 31.

Williams, A. R., review of *Siege of Babylon, Junior Bookshelf*, August, 1978, p. 200.

■ For More Information See

BOOKS

Children's Literature Review, Volume 41, Gale, 1996, pp. 65-81.

Something about the Author, Volume 65, Gale, 1991, p. 57-58.

Twentieth-Century Young Adult Writers, St. James Press, 1994, p. 176.

PERIODICALS

British Book News, October, 1990.

Bulletin of the Center for Children's Books, September, 1993, p. 8.

Children's Literature in Education, Spring, 1983, pp. 35-43.

School Librarian, March, 1983, pp. 53-54; August, 1991, p. 111.

School Library Journal, December, 1985, pp. 98-99.

Times Educational Supplement, March 18, 1983, p. 35; July 15, 1983, p. 18.

Times Literary Supplement, July 15, 1977, p. 866; April 7, 1978, p. 379; November 26, 1982, p. 1303; June 1, 1990, p. 585.

Voice of Youth Advocates, December, 1993, p. 289.*

—*Sketch by Nancy Rampson*

Philip K. Dick

◾ Awards, Honors

Hugo Award, World Science Fiction Convention, 1962, for *The Man in the High Castle*; Nebula award nomination, 1968, for *Do Androids Dream of Electric Sheep?*; John W. Campbell Memorial Award, 1974, for *Flow My Tears, the Policeman Said*; guest of honor, Science Fiction Festival, Metz, France, 1978; the Philip K. Dick Memorial Award has been created by Norwescon, an annual science fiction convention in Seattle, WA.

◾ Personal

Born December 16, 1928, in Chicago, IL; died of heart failure following a stroke, March 2, 1982, in Santa Ana, CA; son of Joseph Edgar (a government employee) and Dorothy (Kindred) Dick; married wife Jeannette, 1949 (divorced); married wife Kleo, 1951 (divorced); married wife Ann, 1958 (divorced); married wife Nancy, April 18, 1967 (divorced); married Tessa Busby, April 18, 1973 (divorced); children: (third marriage) Laura; (fourth marriage) Isolde; (fifth marriage) Christopher. *Education:* Attended University of California, Berkeley, 1950. *Politics:* "Antiwar, pro-life." *Religion:* Episcopalian.

◾ Career

Writer. Hosted classical music program on KSMO Radio, 1947; worked in a record store, 1948-52; occasional lecturer at California State University, Fullerton; active in drug rehabilitation and antiabortion work. *Member:* Science Fiction Writers of America, Animal Protection Institute.

◾ Writings

SCIENCE FICTION NOVELS

Solar Lottery (bound with *The Big Jump* by Leigh Brackett), Ace Books, 1955, reprinted separately, Gregg, 1976 (published separately in England as *World of Chance*, Rich & Cowan, 1956.

The World Jones Made (bound with *Agent of the Unknown* by Margaret St. Clair), Ace Books, 1956, reprinted, Bart Books, 1988.

The Man Who Japed (bound with *The Space-Born* by E. C. Tubb), Ace Books, 1956.

Eye in the Sky, Ace Books, 1957, reprinted, G. K. Hall, 1979.

The Cosmic Puppets (bound with *Sargasso of Space* by Andrew North), Ace Books, 1957, reprinted separately, Berkley Publishing, 1983.

Time Out of Joint, Lippincott, 1959, reprinted, Bluejay Books, 1984.

Dr. Futurity (also see below; bound with *Slavers of Space* by John Brunner), Ace Books, 1960, reprinted (bound with *The Unteleported Man* by Dick), 1972, reprinted separately, Berkley Publishing, 1984.

Vulcan's Hammer (bound with *The Skynappers* by John Brunner), Ace Books, 1960.

The Man in the High Castle, Putnam, 1962, reprinted, Berkley Publishing, 1984.

The Game-Players of Titan, Ace Books, 1963, reprinted, Random House, 1992.

Martian Time-Slip, Ballantine, 1964, reprinted, 1981.

The Penultimate Truth, Belmont-Tower, 1964, reprinted, Bluejay Books, 1984.

The Simulacra, Ace Books, 1964.

Clans of the Alphane Moon, Ace Books, 1964, reprinted, Bluejay Books, 1984.

Dr. Bloodmoney; or, How We Got Along after the Bomb, Ace Books, 1965, reprinted, Bluejay Books, 1984.

The Three Stigmata of Palmer Eldritch, Doubleday, 1965, reprinted, DAW Books, 1984.

Now Wait for Last Year, Doubleday, 1966, reprinted, DAW Books, 1981.

The Crack in Space (also see below), Ace Books, 1966.

The Unteleported Man (also see below; bound with *The Mind Monsters* by Howard L. Cory), Ace Books, 1966, reprinted (bound with *Dr. Futurity* by Dick), 1972, reprinted separately, Berkley Publishing, 1983.

(With Ray Nelson) *The Ganymede Takeover*, Ace Books, 1967, reprinted, Severn House, 1990.

Counter-Clock World, Berkley Publishing, 1967.

The Zap Gun, Pyramid Publications, 1967, reprinted, Bluejay Books, 1985.

Do Androids Dream of Electric Sheep?, Doubleday, 1968, published as *Blade Runner*, Ballantine, 1982.

Ubik (also see below), Doubleday, 1969.

Galactic Pot-Healer, Doubleday, 1969.

A Philip K. Dick Omnibus (contains *The Crack in Space*, *The Unteleported Man*, and *Dr. Futurity*), Sidgwick & Jackson, 1970.

A Maze of Death, Doubleday, 1970.

Our Friends from Frolix 8, Ace Books, 1970.

We Can Build You, DAW Books, 1972.

Flow My Tears, the Policeman Said, Doubleday, 1974.

(With Roger Zelazny) *Deus Irae*, Doubleday, 1976.

A Scanner Darkly, Doubleday, 1977.

VALIS, Bantam, 1981.

The Divine Invasion, Pocket Books, 1981, reprinted, Random House, 1991.

The Transmigration of Timothy Archer, Pocket Books, 1982.

Puttering about in a Small Land, Academy Chicago, 1985.

Radio Free Albemuth, Arbor House, 1985.

Humpty Dumpty in Oakland, Gollancz, 1986.

Mary and the Giant, Arbor House, 1987.

Nick and the Glimmung, Gollancz, 1988.

The Broken Bubble, Arbor House, 1988.

The Penultimate Truth, Carrol & Graf, 1989.

The Little Black Box, Gollancz, 1990.

Short Happy Life of the Brown Oxford, Carol Publishing, 1990.

Gather Yourselves Together, WCS Books, 1994.

STORY COLLECTIONS

A Handful of Darkness, Rich & Cowan, 1955, reprinted, Gregg, 1978.

The Variable Man and Other Stories, Ace Books, 1957.

The Preserving Machine and Other Stories, Ace Books, 1969.

The Book of Philip K. Dick, DAW Books, 1973 (published in England as *The Turning Wheel and Other Stories*, Coronet, 1977).

The Best of Philip K. Dick, Ballantine, 1977.

The Golden Man, Berkley Publishing, 1980.

Robots, Androids, and Mechanical Oddities: The Science Fiction of Philip K. Dick, edited by Patricia Warrick and Martin H. Greenberg, Southern Illinois University Press, 1984.

Lies, Inc., Gollancz, 1984.

I Hope I Shall Arrive Soon, Doubleday, 1985.

The Collected Stories of Philip K. Dick, 5 volumes, Underwood/Miller, 1987.

The Philip K. Dick Reader, Carol Publishing, 1997.

CONTRIBUTOR

August Derleth, editor, *Time to Come*, Farrar, Straus, 1954.

Frederik Pohl, editor, *Star Science Fiction Stories #3*, Ballantine, 1955.

Anthony Boucher, editor, *A Treasury of Great Science Fiction*, Volume I, Doubleday, 1959.

Harlan Ellison, editor, *Dangerous Visions: 33 Original Stories*, Doubleday, 1967.

Edward L. Ferman and Barry N. Malzberg, editors, *Final Stage*, Charterhouse, 1974.

Willis E. McNelly, editor, *Science Fiction: The Academic Awakening*, College English Association, 1974.

Bruce Gillespie, editor, *Philip K. Dick: Electric Shepherd*, Norstrilia Press (Melbourne), 1975.

Peter Nicholls, editor, *Science Fiction at Large*, Gollancz, 1976, Harper, 1977.

Lawrence Sutin, editor, *The Shifting Realities of Philip K. Dick: Selected Literary and Philosophical Writings*, Pantheon, 1995.

OTHER

Confessions of a Crap Artist, Jack Isidore (of Seville, Calif): A Chronicle of Verified Scientific Fact, 1945-1959 (novel), Entwhistle Books, 1975.

A Letter from Philip K. Dick (pamphlet), Philip K. Dick Society, 1983.

The Man Whose Teeth Were Exactly Alike (novel), Mark Ziesing, 1984.

In Milton Lumky Territory (novel), Ultramarine, 1984.

Ubik: The Screenplay (based on novel of same title), Corroboree, 1985.

The Dark-Haired Girl, Mark Ziesing, 1989.

The Selected Letters, edited by Don Herron, Underwood/Miller, 1991.

Selections from the Exegesis, edited by Larry Sutin, Underwood/Miller, 1991.

Also author of radio scripts for the Mutual Broadcasting System. Contributor of more than 100 stories, some under pseudonym Richard Phillips, to *Magazine of Fantasy and Science Fiction, Galaxy, Amazing Science Fiction Stories,* and other magazines.

■ Adaptations

Do Androids Dream of Electric Sheep? was adapted as *Blade Runner,* Warner Brothers, 1982; "We Can Remember It for You Wholesale," was adapted as *Total Recall,* TriStar, 1990; "The Second Variety" was adapted as *Screamers,* Triumph Films, 1996.

■ Sidelights

The fictional worlds of Philip K. Dick are populated by strange creatures and situations: men with enormous steel teeth, private detectives who own electric animals, self-governing insane asylums. It is from these bizarre places that Dick allows himself to explore the rocky terrain of reality and illusion. His characters are chiefly in charge of this task. "All of his work," Charles Platt wrote in *Dream Makers: The Uncommon People Who Write Science Fiction,* "starts with the basic

assumption that there cannot be one, single, objective reality. Everything is a matter of perception. The ground is liable to shift under your feet. A protagonist may find himself living out another person's dream, or he may enter a drug-induced state that actually makes better sense than the real world, or he may cross into a different universe completely." With inspired plots and exciting worlds to explore, readers have made Dick one of the most popular science fiction novelists of all time.

The beginnings for this popular novelist began in Chicago, Illinois, where he was born to a middle-class family. His twin sister, Jane, weaker than him at birth, died in less than a month. When Dick found out about his twin's death, many years later, he was confused and angry, and often blamed his mother. When Dick was young, the family moved to the San Francisco, California area. When Dick was just five years old, his father was transferred to Reno, Nevada, and his mother refused to move with him. This decision caused some family trauma as Dick's father fought for custody. But Dick's mother was ahead of her time, a staunch feminist when there was hardly a word for that ideal. She held on to her values, and moved Dick to Washington, D.C., where she found a job. Within a few years, she moved Dick back to California, where he lived for the rest of his life.

Dick mastered the skill of typing when he was twelve, and that seemed to unleash his prodigious imagination. Right around this time, Dick read his first science fiction magazine. "And like many troubled boys of the time," commented Alexander Star in the *New Republic,* "he became a voracious reader of the science fiction pulp magazines that were then at their peak." This combination of his feverish reading of science fiction stories and his furious typing propelled him towards his vocation of science fiction writer. His childhood wasn't easy, however. He was prone to strong fears and phobias that followed him into his adult life.

In 1949, Dick became a student at the University of California at Berkeley for one ill-fated term. He took a job at a record store in Berkeley, where he easily memorized volumes and volumes of classical music selections. Working at the store opened up his social life. Star wrote that "after impressing one frequent browser with his musical expertise, Dick married her. Not long after the wedding they quarreled, and the bride's brother threatened to smash his precious record collection. A divorce followed; of his five marriages, it was the shortest."

Continuing to work at the music store, Dick's dream of being a writer soon came to fruition. In 1952, he got married again and the stability seemed to help his work. At the age of twenty-four, Dick published his first science fiction story in the *Magazine of Fantasy and Science Fiction*. His career was just getting moving then—in the years 1953 and 1954, he sold over fifty stories. The market for science fiction short stories seemed to peter out, though, so Dick launched into a fury of novel writing.

Global Game Show

In 1955, Dick published his first novel, *Solar Lottery*. It was bound with another writer's novel. Star wrote that this was "the leading format for science fiction . . . two novels together in one binding with a different lurid cover illustration on each side." The novel sold a respectable 300,000 copies, and received critical praise. The book had hallmark Dick touches—in a feudalistic future society, the elite swear allegiance to corporations while the underclass awaits a chance at greatness through a global game show. Although publication of this book won Dick a powerful literary agent, and his furiously-typed novels continued to find publication, he was unsatisfied with his career. He wanted to get out of the science fiction "ghetto" where his expansive ideas needed to be combined with gadgets and gizmos to attract his readers. He held many of these readers in disdain, complaining of their lack of sophistication. Dick longed for more mainstream acceptance. He tried his hand at mainstream novels, but publishers were put off by the depressing nature of these works.

In 1962, Dick published the novel that would become a classic work of science fiction, *The Man in the High Castle*. This alternate history explored a world where the Allied forces lost during World War II. The United States is divided into three zones, with the Pacific states being ruled by the Japanese, the Rocky Mountain area a neutral zone, and the East coast under the iron hand of the Germans. Americans all over the continent are reading an underground book written by a sup-

In this 1962 novel, the Allies have lost World War II, resulting in a divided United States partly under German and Japanese rule.

posed "man in a high castle," who posits a world where the Allies had won the war. Mr. Tagomi, a Japanese official in the Pacific states, finds himself torn between the racist demands of the Nazis and his own feelings about his native country and the America in which he lives.

This work won Dick a Hugo Award for best science fiction novel of the year, and is considered by many to be his finest work. Patrick G. Hogan, Jr., writing in *Dictionary of Literary Biography*, commented that "perhaps the most chilling effect of the novel . . . is how Dick reveals to the America of 1962, still sure of its international righteousness, how easily this nation would have surrendered its own culture under a Japanese occupation and how compatible American fears, prejudices, and desires were with Nazism. The alternate present again makes significant comments on the real one."

"I did seven years of research for *The Man in the High Castle*," Dick told an interviewer in the *Missouri Review*. "I had the prime-source material at the Berkeley-Cal library right from the gestapo's mouth—stuff that had been seized after World War II. . . . That's . . . why I've never written a sequel to it: it's too horrible, too awful. I started several times to write a sequel, but I [would have] had to go back and read about Nazis again, so I couldn't do it." Dick used the I Ching, an ancient Chinese divining system, to plot *The Man in the High Castle*. At each critical juncture in the narrative, Dick consulted the I Ching to determine the proper course of the plot.

Descent into Drugs

"*The Man in the High Castle* was Dick's most assured and subtle work, and he hoped it would win him a wider audience," Star observed. Upset by his inability to make it in a mainstream literary audience, Dick became heavily involved in his addictions to amphetamines washed down with Scotch whiskey. The drugs, along with his incredible typing speed, spurred him to finish eleven novels in the years from 1964 to 1967. "These are not Dick's most accessible or likeable books, but they are his tours de force," Star commented.

In 1963, Dick reported the first of a continuing series of unexplainable visions that were to have a great impact on his life and works. This vision was of a terrible face in the sky with empty eyes and a face made up of cruel metal. And, most upsetting of all, Dick was convinced it was the face of God. Out of this disturbing vision arose the main character in *The Three Stigmata of Palmer Eldritch*.

The novel is set in the near-future when people from Earth are being evacuated from the planet to Mars because of increasing heat. Life on Mars, however, is far from optimal. Immigrants are forced to live in underground ghettos where the only entertainment is taking the hallucinogenic drug Can-D while playing a game with dolls. When Palmer Eldritch returns from a deep-space exploration, he brings with him a supply of the new and more powerful drug Chew-Z. Eldritch has also acquired three "stigmata"—an artificial

metallic arm, enormous steel teeth, and artificial eyes. His Chew-Z is cheaper and longer-lasting than Can-D, and he soon is selling it to the Martian colonists. But Chew-Z doesn't seem to wear off. The user is moved into a world that seems like his own but with the important difference that Palmer Eldritch has godlike powers. Soon, the colonists who take Chew-Z develop Eldritch's stigmata. "Eldritch seems—. . . like Satan—to function as God's instrument in giving man the capacity to do greater good as well as evil," Hogan commented. Bruce Gillespie, writing in *Philip K. Dick: Electric Shepherd*, called *The Three Stigmata of Palmer Eldritch* "one of the few masterpieces of recent science fiction."

> "There are no heroics in Dick's books, but there are heroes. One is reminded of Dickens: what counts is the honesty, constancy, kindness and patience of ordinary people."
>
> —Ursula K. LeGuin

In *Do Androids Dream of Electric Sheep?* (1968), Dick journeyed into a world of simulacra (his word for electronic beings such as robots and other forms of artificial life) that once again blurred the vision between illusion and reality. The story focuses on Rick Deckard, a bounty hunter who is in charge of searching out and killing renegade androids who have escaped from a work colony. The Earth Deckard inhabits is a post-nuclear wasteland where most animals are extinct and electric animals are a status symbol to own. Deckard himself owns an electric sheep.

The only difference between humans and the rogue androids is that the androids lack the capacity to feel compassion. However, Deckard soon finds himself feeling compassion for the androids he is charged to gun down, and he wonders about the real differences between humans and androids. Writing in *Philip K. Dick*, Patricia S. Warrick called *Do Androids Dream of Electric Sheep?* "one of Dick's finest novels," citing its "complexity of structure and idea." Hogan commented that in this novel "Dick has written a modern version of *Franken-*

stein, for the ambivalence of man toward his own creation tends, . . . to travesty the divine creation." This novel was turned into the popular film *Blade Runner* in 1982, even though many of its central scenes were left out or changed.

In 1972, Dick underwent another event that changed his life. While giving a long, rambling speech to a science fiction convention in Vancouver, Canada, where he railed against the downfall of civilization, he had a nervous breakdown. "Having diagnosed the breakdown of society in his speech," Star related, "Dick suffered a breakdown of his own and checked into a Vancouver clinic." There, he finally put down his drinking and pill-popping addictions, even though he felt the clinic staff were brutal in their methods. Returning to California, he settled down in a nice community, married again, and tried to work on his writing.

Divine Visions

However, peace and quiet were not in store for him. In 1974, he once again experienced visions, but this time it went on for weeks. The visions he received were conflicting and baffling, and they were to influence him and his writing for the rest of his life. "When it was over," Star observed, "[Dick] believed that he had received confirmation that the universe was indeed the 'cardboard fake' that he had long portrayed it to be." Dick postulated that the true god was called a "Vast Active Living Intelligence System" (VALIS)—a title

he used for a later novel. And at that point, Dick began to write a long, sprawling memoir on these visions that he titled the "Exegesis."

Dick published *A Scanner Darkly* in 1977, a semi-autobiographical reflection on himself in his prior drug-induced years. The novel focuses on Bob Arctor, a Los Angeles undercover drug policeman, who is also a junkie. His superiors ask him to spy on himself, and to avoid any suspicions, he agrees. Since the police have perfected a special suit that blurs the person wearing it to surveillance cameras, Arctor is able to carry off his deception for awhile. But as he continues to take the strong drug "Substance D," his personality begins to split so severely that he cannot recognize his alter ego on the surveillance videotapes. Star writes that "With its well-scored drug talk and its terrible portrait of a mind becoming opaque to itself, *A Scanner Darkly* is Dick's funniest novel, and his most affecting."

"Drug misuse is not a disease, it is a decision, like the decision to step out in front of a moving car," Dick commented in the author's note to the novel. In the years to come, Dick took up the fight in the war against drugs. But for himself, it was too late. Drugs had taken a huge toll on Dick's life, causing pancreatic damage and high blood pressure that led to his fatal stroke.

PHILIP K. DICK

THE THREE STIGMATA OF PALMER ELDRITCH

"Dick was one of the genuine visionaries.... His best novels constitute as significant a body of work as that of any writer in this country in the last thirty years." —Steve Erickson, *L.A. Weekly*

Humans living in Martian colonies are seduced by a godlike figure offering a hallucinogenic gum called Chew-Z in this 1965 novel.

In *VALIS* (1981) Dick explores the spiritual themes that had haunted him since the appearance of vi-

Harrison Ford stars as Rick Deckard, a bounty hunter assigned to track down renegade androids, in *Blade Runner*, the 1982 film loosely based on Dick's work, *Do Androids Dream of Electric Sheep?*

sions in his life. In the novel, Dick splits his personality into two characters who carry out a didactic discussion with each other. One character, Horselover Fat, is an insane mystic who has a direct line to god in his head. The other character, Phil Dick, is a writer who tries to grasp the subtleties of Horselover, but he is mostly just patronizing the character. During the novel, it is revealed that Horselover is actually a projection of Dick's imagination. Horselover has been created as a way to allow Dick to deal with the many tragedies and traumas in his life.

Dick left his fifth wife in 1976 and went to live in the peaceful wine country of Sonoma, California. There, he continued work on his "Exegesis," some parts of which were published posthumously, and searched for indications of "VALIS" everywhere. After the death of his friend James Pike, an unorthodox Episcopalian Bishop who

tried to find Jesus in a Jordanian Desert, Dick finished the last novel to be published before his death, *The Transmigration of Timothy Archer*, in honor of Pike.

In the 1980s, Dick finally reached the level of fame and fortune he longed for much earlier in his career. Young writers began to ask him for advice, and *Blade Runner*, the film version of *Do Androids Dream of Electric Sheep?* was filmed (in fact, Dick died after attending a screening of the film). After his death, there was a resurgence in his popularity, resulting in a five-volume reissue of all his short stories, one of which, "I Can Remember It for You Wholesale," was made into the popular film *Total Recall* starring Arnold Schwarzenegger.

Was Philip Dick a mystic or a mental patient, a visionary or a man on an extended drug flash-

If you enjoy the works of Philip K. Dick, you may also want to check out the following books and films:

Orson Scott Card, *Seventh Son*, 1987.

William Gibson, *The Difference Engine*, 1991.

Frederik Pohl and Cyril M. Kornbluth, *The Space Merchants*, 1953.

Kim Stanley Robinson, *Remaking History*, 1991.

William Sanders, *The Wild Blue and the Gray*, 1991.

The works of Robert Silverberg, including *Sailing to Byzantium*, 1985.

Orlando, a film adaptation of a Virginia Woolf novel, 1992.

back? Critics differ on their assessments. Many critics contend that he is one of the greatest science fiction writers of our time. Despite the uneven characteristics of many of his books, several of his works have become science fiction classics. In the *New Republic*, Ursula K. LeGuin commented on the profound moral themes in Dick's writing: "There are no heroics in Dick's books, but there are heroes. One is reminded of Dickens: what counts is the honesty, constancy, kindness and patience of ordinary people." Star concluded that Dick gave the world something rare with his writing. "Visionary literature and realistic fiction, fantasy and conscience, rarely meet. It took a man whose hunger was the match of his instability to bring them together."

■ **Works Cited**

Dick, Philip K., *A Scanner Darkly*, Doubleday, 1977.

Dick, Philip K., interview in *Missouri Review*, Volume 7, number 2, 1984.

Gillespie, Bruce, editor, *Philip K. Dick: Electric Shepherd*, Norstrilia Press (Melbourne), 1975.

Greenberg, Martin Harry, and Joseph D. Olander, editors, *Philip K. Dick*, Taplinger, 1983, pp. 189-214.

Hogan, Patrick G., Jr., "Philip K. Dick," *Dictionary of Literary Biography*, Volume 8: *Twentieth-Century American Science Fiction Writers*, 2 parts, edited by David Cowart and Thomas L. Wymer, Gale, 1981, pp. 134-40.

LeGuin, Ursula K., "Science Fiction as Prophesy," *New Republic*, October 30, 1976, pp. 33-34.

Platt, Charles, *Dream Makers: The Uncommon People Who Write Science Fiction*, Berkley Publishing, 1980.

Star, Alexander, "The God in the Trash," *New Republic*, December 6, 1993, pp. 34-42.

■ **For More Information See**

BOOKS

Aldiss, Brian W., *The Shape of Future Things*, Faber, 1970.

Aldiss, Brian W., *The Billion Year Spree*, Doubleday, 1973.

Contemporary Literary Criticism, Gale, Volume 10, 1979, Volume 30, 1984.

Ketterer, David, *New Worlds for Old: The Apocalyptic Imagination, Science Fiction, and American Literature*, Indiana University Press, 1974.

Knight, Damon, *In Search of Wonder*, Advent Publishers, 2nd edition, 1967.

Major 20th-Century Writers, Gale, 1989.

Nicholls, Peter, editor, *Science Fiction at Large*, Harper, 1976.

Reilly, Robert, editor, *The Transcendent Adventure*, Greenwood Press, 1983.

Rickman, Gregg, *Philip K. Dick: In His Own Words*, Fragments, 1984.

Wolfe, Gary K., editor, *Science Fiction Dialogues*, Academy Chicago, 1982.

PERIODICALS

Chicago Tribune Book Review, July 4, 1982; February 16, 1986.

Detroit Free Press, January 30, 1996, pp. C-2C.

Fantasy Review, October, 1984.

Los Angeles Times Book Review, September 6, 1981.

Magazine of Fantasy and Science Fiction, June, 1963; August, 1968; January, 1975; August, 1978; July, 1980.

New York Times Book Review, July 20, 1975; December 1, 1985; January 12, 1986.

Philip K. Dick Society Newsletter, 1983—.

Science Fiction Review, Volume 5, number 2; Volume 5, number 4; February, 1977; summer, 1983; November, 1983.

Science-Fiction Studies, March, 1975; July, 1980; July, 1983; March, 1984.

Village Voice Literary Supplement, August, 1982.

Washington Post Book World, February 22, 1981; May 23, 1982; June 30, 1985; May 25, 1986; August 2, 1987.*

—Sketch by Nancy Rampson

F. Scott Fitzgerald

the Wind, all 1939. *Military Service:* U.S. Army, 1917-19; became second lieutenant.

■ Writings

NOVELS

This Side of Paradise, Scribner, 1920, reprinted, 1971.

The Beautiful and Damned (first published serially in *Metropolitan Magazine,* September, 1921-March, 1922), revised edition of original text, Scribner, 1922, reprinted, Collier Books, 1982.

The Great Gatsby, Scribner, 1925, reprinted, 1981, Chelsea House, 1986.

Tender Is the Night: A Romance, decorations by Edward Shenton, Scribner, 1934, new edition with Fitzgerald's final revisions, preface by Malcolm Cowley, 1951, reprinted, 1970, revised from original text as *Tender Is the Night,* Scribner, 1960, reprinted, Collier Books, 1986; revised edition published in England as *Tender Is the Night,* with Fitzgerald's final revisions, preface by Cowley, Grey Walls Press, 1953, reprinted, 1970.

The Last Tycoon, first published as *The Last Tycoon: An Unfinished Novel, Together with "The Great Gatsby" and Selected Stories* (includes "Notes for The Last Tycoon"), with additional notes by Fitzgerald, foreword by Edmund Wilson, Scribner, 1941, reprinted, 1977, published as *The Last Tycoon: An Unfinished Novel,* with notes by Fitzgerald, foreword by Wilson, Scribner, 1958, reprinted as *The Last Tycoon,* 1983; published in

■ Personal

Born September 24, 1896, in St. Paul, MN; died of a heart attack, December 21, 1940, in Hollywood, CA; buried in Rockville Union Cemetery, Rockville, MD; reburied near his parents in St. Mary's Cemetery, Rockville, MD, in 1975; son of Edward (in business) and Mary (an heiress; maiden name, McQuillan) Fitzgerald; married Zelda Sayre (an artist, dancer, and writer), April 3, 1920 (died March 10, 1948); children: Frances Scott Fitzgerald Smith (formerly Mrs. Samuel J. Lanahan). *Education:* Attended Princeton University, 1913-17. *Religion:* Catholic.

■ Career

Novelist, poet, playwright, screenwriter, and author of short stories. Worked briefly as a copywriter at Barron Collier Advertising Agency in New York City, 1919; worked sporadically as a screenwriter at motion picture studios in Los Angeles, CA, including Metro-Goldwyn-Mayer and United Artists, 1927-40, contributing to filmscripts such as *Winter Carnival, The Women,* and *Gone With*

England as *The Last Tycoon: An Unfinished Novel*, Grey Walls Press, 1949, as *The Last Tycoon*, Penguin, 1960, 1977, reprinted with notes by Fitzgerald, foreword by Wilson, 1965, 1974.

SHORT STORIES

Flappers and Philosophers (includes "The Offshore Pirate," "The Ice Palace," "Head and Shoulders," and "Bernice Bobs Her Hair"), Scribner, 1920, reprinted, with introduction by Arthur Mizener, 1959, 1972.

Tales of the Jazz Age (contains "The Camel's Back," "May Day," and "The Diamond as Big as the Ritz"), Scribner, 1922, revised as Six Tales of the Jazz Age, and Other Stories, introduction by Frances Fitzgerald Lanahan, Scribner, 1960, reprinted, 1968.

All the Sad Young Men (includes "The Rich Boy," "Winter Dreams," and "Absolution"), Scribner, 1926.

Taps at Reveille (includes "Crazy Sunday" and "Babylon Revisited"), Scribner, 1935, reprinted, 1976.

The Pat Hobby Stories, introduction by Arnold Gingrich, Scribner, 1962, reprinted, 1970, Penguin, 1974.

The Basil and Josephine Stories (includes "The Scandal Detectives"), edited with an introduction by Jackson R. Bryer and John Kuehl, Scribner, 1973, reprinted, 1985.

(With wife, Zelda Fitzgerald) *Bits of Paradise: Twenty-one Uncollected Stories by F. Scott and Zelda Fitzgerald*, selected by Matthew J. Bruccoli, with the assistance of Scottie Fitzgerald Smith, Scribner, 1973.

The Price Was High: The Last Uncollected Stories of F. Scott Fitzgerald (contains "Myra Meets His Family" and "The Pusher-in-the-Face"), edited by Bruccoli, Harcourt, 1979.

The Fantasy and Mystery Stories of F. Scott Fitzgerald, edited by Peter Haining, Robert Hale, 1991.

PLAYS

(And lyricist) *Fie! Fie! Fi-Fi!* (two-act musical comedy; first produced in Princeton, NJ, at Princeton University, December 19, 1914), published in pamphlet form for distribution at performances (extent of Fitzgerald's authorship disputed in some sources [also see below]).

(And lyricist) *The Evil Eye* (two-act musical comedy; first produced at Princeton University, December 18, 1915), published in pamphlet form

for performances (extent of Fitzgerald's authorship disputed in some sources [also see below]).

(And lyricist) *Safety First* (two-act musical comedy; first produced at Princeton University, December 15, 1916), published in pamphlet form for performances (extent of Fitzgerald's authorship disputed in some sources [also see below]).

The Vegetable; or, From President to Postman (first produced at Apollo Theatre, Atlantic City, NJ, November 19, 1923), Scribner, 1923, reprinted, August M. Kelley, 1972, revised and enlarged edition, with previously unpublished scenes and corrections, introduction by Charles Scribner III, Scribner, 1976.

F. Scott Fitzgerald's St. Paul Plays, 1911-1914, edited with an introduction by Alan Margolies, Princeton University Library, 1978.

CORRESPONDENCE

The Letters of F. Scott Fitzgerald, edited by Andrew Turnbull, Scribner, 1963, reprinted, 1981.

Scott Fitzgerald: Letters to His Daughter, edited by Turnbull, introduction by Frances Fitzgerald Lanahan, Scribner, 1965.

Dear Scott, Dear Max: The Fitzgerald-Perkins Correspondence, edited by Kuehl and Bryer, Scribner, 1971, reprinted, 1973.

As Ever, Scott Fitz—: Letters Between F. Scott Fitzgerald and His Literary Agent, Harold Ober, 1919-1940, edited by Bruccoli, with Jennifer McCabe Atkinson, foreword by Scottie Fitzgerald Smith, Lippincott, 1972.

Correspondence of F. Scott Fitzgerald, edited by Bruccoli and Margaret M. Duggan, with Susan Walker, Random House, 1980.

Fitzgerald: A Life in Letters, edited by Matthew J. Bruccoli and Judith S. Baughman, Macmillan, 1994.

COLLECTIONS

The Crack-Up: With Other Uncollected Pieces, Note-Books, and Unpublished Letters (includes "The Crack-Up," "Handle With Care," and "Early Success"), edited by Edmund Wilson, J. Laughlin, 1945, reprinted, 1964; published in England as *The Crack-Up, With Other Pieces and Stories*, Penguin, 1965, reprinted, 1974.

The Portable F. Scott Fitzgerald (includes novels and short stories), selected by Dorothy Parker, introduction by John O'Hara, Viking, 1945, reprinted as *The Indispensable F. Scott Fitzgerald*, Book Society, 1949, 1951.

The Diamond as Big as the Ritz, and Other Stories, first published in limited edition, with an introduction by Louis Untermeyer, for the U.S. Armed Services, 1946, Penguin, 1962, reprinted, 1965.

The Stories of F. Scott Fitzgerald: A Selection of Twenty-eight Stories (includes "Three Hours Between Planes"), introduction by Malcolm Cowley, Scribner, 1951, reprinted, 1984.

Three Novels: The Great Gatsby, With an Introduction by Malcolm Cowley. Tender Is the Night, With the Author's Final Revisions; Edited by Malcolm Cowley. The Last Tycoon, an Unfinished Novel; Edited by Edmund Wilson, Scribner, 1953, reprinted, 1956.

Afternoon of an Author: A Selection of Uncollected Stories and Essays (includes "How to Live on $36,000 a Year"), introduction and notes by Mizener, Princeton University Library, 1957, Scribner, 1958, reprinted, 1981.

The Bodley Head Scott Fitzgerald, six volumes, introduction by J. B. Priestley, Bodley Head, 1958-63.

Babylon Revisited, and Other Stories, Scribner, 1960, reprinted, 1971.

The Stories of F. Scott Fitzgerald, five volumes, Penguin, 1962-68.

The Fitzgerald Reader, edited by Mizener, Scribner, 1963, reprinted, Macmillan, 1978.

The Apprentice Fiction of F. Scott Fitzgerald, edited with an introduction by Kuehl, Rutgers University Press, 1965, reprinted, 1974.

F. Scott Fitzgerald in His Own Time: A Miscellany, edited by Bruccoli and Bryer, Kent State University Press, 1971, reprinted, Popular Library, 1974.

OTHER

Let's Go Out and Play (radio script), first broadcast in New York City on WABC-Radio (CBS), October 3, 1935.

(With Edward E. Paramore, Jr.) *Three Comrades* (screenplay; based on English translation of novel of the same title by Erich Maria Remarque), Metro-Goldwyn-Mayer, 1938 (also see below).

Thoughtbook of Francis Scott Fitzgerald, With an Introduction by John R. Kuehl, Princeton University Library, 1965.

F. Scott Fitzgerald's Ledger: A Facsimile, introduction by Bruccoli, NCR/Microcard Editions, 1972.

The Great Gatsby: A Facsimile, edited with an introduction by Bruccoli, Microcard Editions Books, 1973.

F. Scott Fitzgerald's Screenplay for "Three Comrades," by Erich Maria Remarque (includes original version by Fitzgerald alone), edited with afterword by Bruccoli, Southern Illinois University Press, 1978.

The Notebooks of F. Scott Fitzgerald, edited by Bruccoli, Harcourt/Bruccoli Clark, 1978, reprinted, Harcourt, 1980.

F. Scott Fitzgerald: Triangle Club Songs (cassette recording; songs from three plays produced at Princeton University), performed by After-Dinner Opera Co. of New York, Bruccoli Clark, 1979.

Poems, 1911-1940, edited by Bruccoli, foreword by James Dickey, Bruccoli Clark, 1981.

F. Scott Fitzgerald on Writing, edited by Larry W. Phillips, Scribner, 1985.

Author of "The Count of Darkness," "The Passionate Eskimo," and numerous other fiction works.

Author of unproduced screenplays, such as "Red-Headed Woman" and "Lipstick." Contributor to film scripts, among them *A Yank at Oxford,* 1937; *Infidelity* and *Madame Curie,* both 1938; *Winter Carnival, The Women,* and *Gone With the Wind,* all 1939; and *Cosmopolitan,* 1940.

Author of book reviews, introductions, and forewords. Contributor to periodicals and popular magazines, including *Saturday Evening Post, Esquire, Metropolitan Magazine, Smart Set, American Mercury, Nassau Literary Magazine, New Yorker, Scribner's Magazine, Motor, Bookman, Woman's Home Companion, New Republic, McCall's, Red Book, Collier's,* and *Hearst's International.*

Work represented in hundreds of anthologies, such as *Innocent Merriment: An Anthology of Light Verse,* McGraw, 1942; *Fifty Best American Short Stories, 1915-1965,* Houghton, 1965; *The Age of Anxiety: Modern American Stories,* Allyn & Bacon, 1972; and *The Short Story: An Introductory Anthology,* 2nd edition, Little, Brown, 1975.

■ Adaptations

Writings adapted for film include "Head and Shoulders," adapted as *The Chorus Girl's Romance,* Metro Pictures, 1920; "Myra Meets His Family," adapted as *The Husband Hunter,* Fox Film Corp., 1920; *The Offshore Pirate,* Metro Pictures, 1921; *The*

Beautiful and Damned, Warner Bros., 1922; "The Camel's Back," adapted as *Conductor 1492*, Warner Bros., 1924; *The Great Gatsby*, Players-Lasky-Paramount, 1926, Paramount, 1949 and 1974; "The Pusher-in-the-Face," adapted as a movie short, Paramount, 1929; "Babylon Revisited," adapted as *The Last Time I Saw Paris*, Metro-Goldwyn-Mayer, 1954; *Tender Is the Night*, Twentieth-Century Fox, 1962; and *The Last Tycoon*, Paramount, 1976. The 1924 Film Guild movie *Grit* was based on an original story by Fitzgerald.

Works adapted for stage include *The Great Gatsby*, first produced in New York City at the Ambassador Theatre, February 2, 1926, and produced as a ballet by the Pittsburgh Ballet Theater at State University of New York, State University College at Purchase, NY, March 31, 1989; "Three Hours Between Planes," adapted as a one-act play, 1958; and *This Side of Paradise*, adapted as an Off-Broadway play, 1962. Some of Fitzgerald's writings were also adapted for radio and television.

■ Sidelights

F. Scott Fitzgerald died on the afternoon of December 21, 1940, suffering a fatal heart attack as he was finishing a chocolate bar—one of his placebos for the alcohol that had ravaged both his talent and health. He was with his lover, the British gossip columnist Sheilah Graham, at the time, living in Los Angeles and working as what he termed a Hollywood hack. The author of such classics as *The Great Gatsby* and *Tender Is the Night* had taken any script work he could get in his final years in order to support his wife, Zelda, in a private mental institution, and his daughter, Scottie, at Vassar. Most of America had long forgotten this symbol of the Jazz Age, dead at forty-four—the handsome young writer who had won instant popularity with his first novel, *This Side of Paradise*. Eulogies were left for his few remaining friends to make; the obituary writers were not in a eulogizing mood, and painted Fitzgerald's meteoric rise and fall—it was a scant twenty years from his first success to his death—as visible proof of the hollowness of the excesses of the 1920s.

But what the obituary writers ignored was that Fitzgerald was hard at work on his fifth novel when he died, his first since *Tender Is the Night*. That novel, *The Last Tycoon*, left unfinished, is Fitzgerald's attempt to make sense out of Hollywood. His fictional protagonist, Monroe Stahr, is a self-made man, the head of a major studio, and Fitzgerald's description of Stahr's ambition and his tragic failure, could serve as an epitaph for Fitzgerald himself: "He had flown up very high to see, on strong wings, when he was young. And while he was up there he had looked on all the kingdoms, with the kind of eyes that can stare straight ahead into the sun. Beating his wings tenaciously—finally frantically—and keeping on beating them, he had stayed up there longer than most of us, and then, remembering all he had seen from his great height of how things were, he had settled gradually to earth."

Fitzgerald, following his death, was forgotten for a time, but not lost. By the 1950s, critical evaluation of his accomplishment had turned the corner, and he has been increasingly viewed as one of the most important American writers of the twentieth century, not simply the hagiographer of the flashy 1920s, but an artist who took as his themes fundamentally American motifs: the struggle for success and the costs such a struggle demand; the confusion of image and reality; and yes, also the world of wealth and romance, always tinged with a tragic edge. His novels, *The Great Gatsby* and *Tender Is the Night*—"among the principal achievements of American literature," according to W. R. Anderson in *Dictionary of Literary Biography Yearbook*—have entered the canon of literature survey courses along with the best of his 160 short stories.

From a forgotten writer at his death, Fitzgerald has risen to become one of the best known American authors. A hundred years after his birth, he is still being honored: His works and memorabilia were displayed at a massive exhibition at the University of South Carolina honoring the centenary of his birth in 1996. Speaking at the opening of that exhibit, Fitz-gerald's long-time friend and fellow Hollywood writer Bud Schulberg noted that Fitzgerald's legacy was carried on through the works. As reported in *Library Journal*, Schulberg concluded his speech by saying that "we who read Scott and love his work, we are his immortality." But perhaps the most fitting summation of his life was that given by Alice B. Toklas, the companion of Gertrude Stein, who knew the Fitzgerald's during their Paris years. In her collected letters, *Staying on Alone*, Toklas called Fitzgerald "the most sensitive . . . the most distinguished—the most gifted and intelligent of all his contemporaries. And the most lovable—he is one of those great tragic American figures."

Among the Best and the Brightest

F. Scott Fitzgerald was born on September 24, 1896, in St. Paul, Minnesota, the only son of Edward and Mollie McQuillan Fitzgerald. Irish by ancestry, Fitzgerald was a distant relation of Francis Scott Key, who had penned the "Star-Spangled Banner," and despite financial setbacks the family tried desperately to maintain a patrician or at least upper-middle class lifestyle. Formative events occurred in the family prior to Fitzgerald's birth: Two older sisters died during an epidemic while Mollie was pregnant with her son. Another infant died only hours after its birth in 1900. Fitzgerald thus felt the over-protection that could result from such tragedies. But death was not the only cause for anguish in the Fitzgerald home. As Jeffrey Meyers pointed out in his *Scott Fitzgerald: A Biography*, the future author, "Like many American writers, including Ernest Hemingway, was the son of a weak father and strong mother." For the family, this meant that the father was much better at manners than at business. Edward Fitzgerald regaled his son with stories of his patrician, Confederate past, yet it was the mother's less patrician ancestors who had made successes of themselves in America.

When Scott was two, the family moved to Buffalo and Syracuse, New York, where Edward took a position with Proctor & Gamble. For a decade the father held this position, but in 1908 he lost his job, and the family, including a daughter, Annabel, returned to St. Paul. Thereafter, they lived on Mollie's inheritance, always in rented houses, but in the best part of town. As a youth, Fitzgerald felt like "the outsider, the poor relation," wrote Ruth Prigozy in *Dictionary of Literary Biography*. His father's failure set an early benchmark for Fitzgerald. He was later in life terrified of financial difficulties, and such fear ultimately dictated not only the theme of much of his writing, but also the type of writing he allowed himself to pursue. Lucrative short stories for the *Saturday Evening Post* market would take precedence over his more creative, novel-length efforts.

Fitzgerald was sent to a private school, the St. Paul Academy, from 1908 to 1911, and it was there that he wrote his first short stories, publishing them in the school magazine, *Now and Then.* Always eager to fit in and be admired, he tried out for sports but was too small for football. He found a niche in theater, however, writing plays and performing in school productions. After three years at the St. Paul Academy, poor grades forced him to withdraw. He then enrolled in the Newman School in Hackensack, New Jersey, where he continued his experiments in writing and in the theater. There he met the person "who would become the most influential figure in his early life, both creatively and personally," according to Prigozy. Father Sigourney Fay, a teacher and later director of the school, introduced Fitzgerald to the world of arts and letters, which included the writer, Shane Leslie, and also showed Fitzgerald another side of Catholicism, emphasizing the "beauty and richness of the experience [Fitzgerald] would always try to capture in his writing," as Prigozy noted. In all ways, the Newman experience was more successful for Fitzgerald than had been his years at St. Paul Academy. During the summers he also wrote plays for a St. Paul amateur theatrical society which were performed for charities.

In 1913, Fitzgerald entered Princeton University, and the following years would be central to his development as a writer. At Princeton he won a place for himself not with athletics, but with the pen, composing lyrics for the university's Triangle Club productions and writing for the *Nassau Literary Magazine*. He also made friendships that would continue to be important throughout his life with the future poet, John Peale Bishop, and the future critic and writer, Edmund Wilson, who became his intellectual conscience. He read widely: from Oscar Wilde to Compton Mackenzie, and from Bernard Shaw to H. G. Wells.

Fitzgerald was a handsome if not pretty man, and very much loved the drama and contest of romantic relationships. The Christmas of his sophomore year, he more than met his match in Ginevra King, a young debutante from Chicago whose family wealth put her out of Fitzgerald's league. She became important in another way for him, however—as a fictional prototype of the beautiful but elusive woman he used over and over in his fiction. Despite his social success at Princeton, bad grades once again plagued him, and he had to withdraw from school in 1916. Though he returned the following year, he never graduated. A war and literary fame intervened.

Chronicler of the Jazz Age

Back at Princeton in the fall of 1917, Fitzgerald continued writing stories, but also felt the pull to join the army and get in on the European war. He applied for a commission in the U.S. Army, and in October 1917, he was appointed a second lieutenant, stationed in Montgomery, Alabama. He would spend fifteen months in the service, and never be posted overseas. Yet his military career was far from a total failure. It was in Alabama that Fitzgerald met the eighteen-year-old Zelda Sayre, daughter of a judge on the Alabama Supreme Court, who would become his wife. Zelda was bright, glamorous, and beautiful, fitting Fitzgerald's requirements for a bride, and he courted her with a will. During these early months in the army, Fitzgerald continued writing short stories and also completed the first draft of a novel he entitled "The Romantic Egoist," a loosely autobiographical, coming-of-age story. Submitted to Charles Scribner's Sons, the manuscript fell on the desk of the editor, Max Perkins, who encouraged Fitzgerald to rewrite it.

Discharged from the army in 1919, Fitzgerald worked for a time in New York writing advertising copy. His romance with Zelda had been put on hold—he could not ask for her hand as a penniless wordsmith. Returning to St. Paul, he reworked his novel and submitted it again to Scribner under the title, *This Side of Paradise*. Perkins accepted the manuscript this time, and the book was published in the spring of 1920. While waiting for publication, Fitzgerald also worked on short fiction, and with the help of his new agent, Harold Ober, was able to place several of his stories in national magazines, including the *Smart Set* and *Saturday Evening Post*, the latter buying "Head and Shoulders" for $400, a not inconsiderable sum in 1920. Film rights to the novel were soon sold for another $2,500, and Fitzgerald felt he had arrived. Zelda and he were married in New York on April 3, 1920, a week after publication of his first novel.

This Side of Paradise is Fitzgerald at his most autobiographical, thinly disguising himself as his protagonist, Amory Blaine, whose life parallels Fitzgerald's own. Blaine's fictional Princeton years, in particular, draw on much of the material Fitzgerald had himself experienced: a failed romance, difficulty with grades because of the draw of more seductive pursuits, and the influence of

friends, modeled on the real-life Bishop and Wilson. Writing on Fitzgerald's novels in *Dictionary of Literary Biography*, Scott Donaldson noted that in form "*This Side of Paradise* is less a novel than the collected works, to 1920, of its twenty-three-year-old author." Fitzgerald used poems, short stories, and even fragments of earlier plays in the novel, and though some reviewers found such a form experimental and daring, it was actually a result of Fitzgerald learning his craft on the job. In content, the novel also owed much to Mackenzie's *Sinister Street*, a novel Fitzgerald much admired.

Though reviews were mixed, the novel became quite popular, selling more than 40,000 copies in 1920. Its popularity is somewhat difficult to understand so many years later when mores have so drastically changed. But in its day, the activities of its young protagonists—the casual kiss and drink, the rude treatment of parents—were enough to brand them rebels. It is, in part, this high-spirited refutation of the old order that won the novel readers, but there was also that ineffable quality of spirit and life in the prose. Fitzgerald's college friend, Edmund Wilson, noted this quality in *The Shores of Light: A Literary Chronicle of the Twenties and Thirties*. Though Wilson found the book committed almost every sin of literature, he also concluded that "it does not commit the unpardonable sin: it does not fail to live." Other reviewers at the time were more effusive in praise. H. L. Mencken, in the *Smart Set*, observed that the book was "a truly amazing first novel—original in structure, extremely sophisticated in manner, and adorned with a brilliancy that is as rare in American writing as honesty is in American statecraft." Harry Hansen wrote in the *Chicago Daily News* that the work was "one of the few American novels extant. . . . Fitzgerald has taken a real American type—the male flapper of our best colleges—and written him down with startling verisimilitude."

Fitzgerald's publishers followed up this success with publication of a collection of his short stories, *Flappers and Philosophers*, and thus began a usual cycle at Scribner: publication of a novel followed by a short story collection, establishing the dual career of Fitzgerald as both serious novelist and entertaining short story writer. Fitzgerald often railed at the time he had to spend on his short stories simply to earn enough money for the sort of lifestyle he and Zelda established in the

This Side of Paradise
by F. Scott Fitzgerald

With an Introduction by Tom Dardis

Considered the first American coming-of-age story, Fitzgerald's debut set in the 1920s captured the experiences of a generation.

1920s, yet some of his best work is to be found in the short stories. As Prigozy noted in her critique of Fitzgerald's short fiction in *Dictionary of Literary Biography*, "at least a dozen of [Fitzgerald's] stories rank among the very best short fiction written in the twentieth century." In this first collection, two stories are notable, "The Ice Palace" and "Bernice Bobs Her Hair." In "The Ice Palace," a southern belle cannot tolerate the cold northern climate of her fiance's home, and after being trapped for a time in an ice palace, decides to return to her roots in the South. The daring flapper type was established in "Bernice Bobs Her Hair," when the young female protagonist accepts the dares of her friends to cut her hair short in the new fashion of the day. These two stories,

according to Donaldson in *Dictionary of Literary Biography*, "belong with the best of [Fitzgerald's] tales." Those attracted to Fitzgerald's first novel also purchased his short story collection, and increasingly over the next decade and more, Fitzgerald relied on the magazine market to support him and his family, eventually earning $4,000 per story from the *Saturday Evening Post*. In 1922, he earned $25,000, most of it from short stories.

Fitzgerald needed such sums to finance the whirlwind lifestyle he and Zelda adopted, for the couple never owned a home, rather staying in luxurious hotel accommodations or renting large estates in the United States and Europe. In the first years of their marriage they lived in New York City and Westport, Connecticut, and then traveled to Europe. Returning to the United States, they settled for a time in St. Paul, and then moved on to fashionable Great Neck, Long Island. Already in place in the first two years of their marriage was the heavy drinking and partying the couple would indulge in for the next decade. They were the darling couple, the daring ones, the rule breakers, living out a life Fitzgerald had chronicled in his fiction. Their daughter, Scottie, was born in 1921, but her birth did not slow down their social life.

Yet amid all this frivolous living, Fitzgerald managed to publish his second novel, *The Beautiful and the Damned*, in 1922. This work describes the disintegration of a beautiful young couple, Anthony and Gloria Patch, something of a prescient announcement of what would ultimately happen to Fitzgerald's own marriage. The book was, according to Donaldson, "Fitzgerald's bleakest novel, infected by a tone of cynicism." The reviews were largely negative for this novel, though it sold relatively well. Fitzgerald followed it up with a play, *The Vegetable*, which never made it to Broadway as Fitzgerald had hoped. Important about both these works, however, is the exploration of themes vital to Fitzgerald's later work: the negative effects of too much money, and the tragedy of misplaced love.

In between these two works came publication of a further collection of short stories, *Tales of the Jazz Age*, which contained his popular fantasy tale, "The Diamond as Big as the Ritz," the novella-length "May Day," and "Winter Dreams," which deals with a major Fitzgerald theme—the encounter of wealth by a young man and how it changes him forever. Like so many other Fitzgerald protagonists, Dexter Green of "Winter Dreams" is in love with image over reality, and such a misplaced love costs him dearly. Otherwise, the collection was meager stuff, most of it written before 1920 and more suited to the magazine market, with its happy endings and reliance on plot, than to the book market. But as the humorist and writer Dorothy Parker once noted, Fitzgerald could write a bad story, but he never wrote badly. Steven Goldleaf, reviewing Fitzgerald's short stories in *Reference Guide to Short Fiction*, noted that "Fitzgerald's power derives from his rhythm and imagery, and his weakness was in developing plots and characters. Emphasizing language and de-emphasizing structure is more typical of poetry than prose and Fitzgerald's stories often resemble poems." Fitzgerald's best stories feature one moment of epiphany, of extreme intensity and realization, or, as Fitzgerald himself was fond of describing it, "some sort of epic grandeur."

The Great Gatsby

Fitzgerald's own moment of epic grandeur came with the writing of *The Great Gatsby*, the novel for which he is best remembered, the novel which is widely recognized as an American classic inspiring small libraries of literary criticism. Shortly after Fitzgerald's death in 1940, a critic in the *New Yorker* called *The Great Gatsby* "one of the most scrupulously observed and beautifully written of American novels," and such has remained its repute to this day. The critic Malcolm Cowley noted in his introduction to *Three Novels: The Great Gatsby, Tender Is the Night, The Last Tycoon* that "There is a moment in any real author's career when he suddenly becomes capable of doing his best work. He has found a fable that expresses his central truth and everything else falls into place around it. . . . Something like that happened to Fitzgerald when he invented the story of Jimmy Gatz, otherwise known as Jay Gatsby." Fitzgerald was already mapping out his third novel in 1922 and also devoted part of 1923 to the writing of early portions of the book, but it was not until the family moved to France in 1924—in part to try and live more economically—that he settled down to work in earnest.

Of course, Fitzgerald's attempt at economical living was doomed from the outset. Not for the Fitzgeralds was the bohemian life of the Left Bank, populated by such writers as Ernest Hemingway. Scott and Zelda kept to the fashionable hotels of the Right Bank, eating at the most expensive restaurants. By the end of May, the Fitzgeralds had left Paris for the Riviera, taking a villa near St. Raphael. There they met the wealthy Murphys, Sara and Gerald, with whom they would remain friends for years. Through the Murphys they in turn met many artists of the day, including the painters Pablo Picasso and George Braque, the composer Igor Stravinsky, and a score of others who would help shape literature, art, and music in the twentieth century. Though Fitzgerald was socializing heavily, he managed to finish a first draft of his novel by the end of August. It was that summer, also, that Zelda formed a liaison with a dashing French naval of-

Hope and loss intersect in this 1925 classic about the American dream.

ficer, prompting a crisis in the Fitzgerald home, but also contributing future material for Fitzgerald's *Tender Is the Night*. But despite all these emotional distractions, Fitzgerald was able to promise his editor, Perkins, a revised version of the novel by that fall.

True to his word, Fitzgerald sent off the revised manuscript in late October of 1924. His working titles for the book included a rather macabre list of possibilities: "Gold-Hatted Gatsby," "Trimalchio in West Egg," and "The High-Bouncing Lover." However, at Perkins' insistence, the novel was ultimately published as simply *The Great Gatsby*. Written in France, the book is, however, profoundly American in theme and tone. It is a short novel, only some 50,000 words, but tightly written, and one that blends so many aspects of character with so much incident that it feels much longer. The novel is the story of the mysterious Jay Gatsby, born Gatz, who, during the war as a young officer, met and fell in love with a woman and lost her because of his lack of riches and promise. After the war, Gatsby made his fortune, realizing the American dream—though in a less than legal manner—by bootlegging liquor. Four years later, Gatsby has come to reclaim his lost love, Daisy Buchanan, now married to Tom, whose wealth shields the couple from the real world. Daisy has had a daughter, and Tom has a mistress, Myrtle Wilson, the wife of a garage owner near the Buchanan's Long Island estate where the novel is largely set. Gatsby takes a house across the bay from the Buchanans, and tries in his bumbling and rather uncouth way to win Daisy. The novel thus chronicles the clash of the rich and the poor and the newly rich, the conflict between the old East with its cynical ways, and the raw, brash, but morally upright West.

Gatsby's failed attempt to win the hand of his beloved is narrated by Nick Carraway, himself a young man of the West, who rents a cottage close to Gatsby's estate and witnesses the lavish parties and visits by strange colleagues at the Gatsby residence. Nick is also a cousin of Daisy's and has been to Yale with Tom. Fresh from Minnesota, Nick is in turn aided in this recounting by another witness, Jordan Baker, who helps to supply information to further the story. Critics point out that these narrative devices are reminiscent of both Henry James and Joseph Conrad, and lend the novel a miasma of mystery, for the reader is never really sure of which information is true and

which false. Ultimately, *The Great Gatsby* is a tale of tragic love and murder, for Gatsby is mistakenly killed by Myrtle Wilson's husband, prompting Nick to finally realize that the Buchanans were "careless people . . . who smashed up things and creatures and then retreated back into their money or their vast carelessness, or whatever it was that kept them together, and let other people clean up the mess." It is Gatsby, in the end, who becomes the romantic, tragic hero of the piece, a man who loved well but not wisely, a man who despite his bad taste and illegal money was "worth the whole damn bunch put together," according to Nick.

As Donaldson noted in *Dictionary of Literary Biography*, "*The Great Gatsby* has inspired probably as much critical commentary as any other twentieth-century novel, but it is so intricately patterned and tightly knit . . . that it hardly seems possible that criticism will exhaust the novel." Early reviews were largely positive. Gilbert Seldes, writing in *The Dial*, observed that with *The Great Gatsby*, "Fitzgerald . . . has mastered his talents and gone soaring in a beautiful flight. . . . Scenes of incredible difficulty are rendered with what seems an effortless precision." In a letter to the author, the poet T. S. Eliot concluded that for him, *The Great Gatsby* was "the first step that American fiction has taken since Henry James." Some reviewers of the day, such as H. L. Mencken in his critical study, *F. Scott Fitzgerald: The Man and His Work*, missed the mark, calling the book "no more than a glorified anecdote." John M. Kenny, writing in *Commonweal*, dubbed it "a mediocre novel."

But time has stood on the side of critics like Eliot, and after Fitzgerald's death, the critics looked at *The Great Gatsby* with new eyes, finding it to be a powerful statement about the material culture of the 1920s and of the American dream gone awry. Writing in 1942 in his *On Native Grounds: An Interpretation of Modern American Prose Literature*, the literary critic Alfred Kazin called the novel "one of the most moving of American tragedies," applauding the author's deep understanding of his protagonist, Jay Gatsby. Other critics began comparing it to the greats of the American canon, noting the sophistication of technique, the tight interweaving of various story strands, and the deft hand used to narrate the events of the fable through the voice of Nick Carraway. "One of the happiest decisions was to present *The Great Gatsby* through the mind and eye of a narrator only partially committed to participating in and judging its world," observed Frederick J. Hoffman in his *Modern Novel in America: 1900-1950.* "Gatsby himself, to look at him through Carraway's eyes, is a tragic victim. . . ."

Carraway, as narrator, has himself spawned a cottage industry of criticism, with speculations on both his reliability and sexual orientation. Other critics found the book as a whole to represent the pinnacle of Fitzgerald's art. Douglas Taylor, in the *University of Kansas City Review,* while commenting on the mythic quality of *The Great Gatsby* and the Christ-like character of Gatsby, also declared that "In precision of workmanship, elegance of prose style, and control of dramatic point of view, [*The Great Gatsby*] represents to my mind Fitzgerald's genius at its sustained best." Still other critics have focussed on the themes in the novel, and many have fixed on the contrast of money and power. Writing in his *The American Novel and Its Tradition,* the critic and educator Richard Chase noted that the "special charm of *Gatsby* rests in its odd combination of romance with a realistic picture of raw power—the raw power of the money that has made a plutocracy," and also observed that the novel "gives us an unforgettable . . . sense of the 1920's and what the people were like who lived in them." Barry Gross, writing in *Centennial Review,* summed up Gatsby and his particular power to draw in readers of all generations: "Gatsby represents nothing less than wonder itself, the heightened sensitivity to the promises of life, the extraordinary gift for hope, the romantic readiness that makes life a journey." In the novel, it is left to Nick Carraway, after Gatsby's poorly attended funeral and the glimpse into the real history of the man, to introduce the motif of Gatsby as the romantic searcher. Sitting on the lawn, looking at the green dock light of the Buchanan's which had caught Gatsby's attention, he compares Gatsby's journey and illusion to that of the nation itself: "He had come a long way," Nick observed, "to this blue lawn, and his dream must have seemed so close that he could hardly fail to grasp it. He did not know that it was already behind him, somewhere back in the vast obscurity beyond the city, where the dark fields of the republic rolled on under the night."

Despite favorable reviews, the book did not sell well, going through only two printings of about 24,000 copies in 1925 and earning Fitzgerald about $2,000 after all his advances from Scribner and his agent had been paid back. Though stage and film adaptations of *The Great Gatsby* helped in his continual financial battle, Fitzgerald had to return to the short story.

Tender Is the Night

The Fitzgeralds stayed on in France through 1926. It was during those years that Fitzgerald met Ernest Hemingway, a writer he had earlier championed to his editor, Max Perkins, at Scribner. Fitzgerald was drawn to Hemingway's charm and discipline, and Hemingway in turn found Fitzgerald to be a talented author, though one who never fully achieved his potential. Zelda, during these years, was searching for her own means of expression, first in painting, then in dance, and finally in literature. Another short story collection, *All the Sad Young Men,* was published in 1926, and included the story, "The Rich Boy," a further exploration of some of the themes appearing in *The Great Gatsby,* and a story, according to Donaldson in *Dictionary of Literary Biography,* that was among Fitzgerald's "very best." Sold initially to *Red Book* magazine, this story earned more than the royalties from *The Great Gatsby.*

While still in France, Fitzgerald began taking notes for what would become his fourth novel, *Tender Is the Night.* The book was a long time in the making, not appearing until 1934. Meanwhile, the Fitzgeralds' lifestyle was becoming increasingly destructive, alcohol playing a large part in the mix. Zelda was beginning to show signs of the strain that would ultimately consign her to a mental institution for the rest of her days. In 1926 the Fitzgeralds returned to the United States and Fitzgerald worked in Hollywood for a time, then moved to Delaware to attempt a settled life style. Zelda threw herself into ballet lessons while Fitzgerald turned out short stories for the magazines, primarily the *Saturday Evening Post.*

Returning to France in 1929, the Fitzgeralds were once again living on the edge, and Fitzgerald's novel-in-progress had already gone through several metamorphoses. Summering on the Riviera near their friends, Sara and Gerald Murphy, Fitzgerald made a fresh start on his novel, modeling his protagonists on the Murphys and also incorporating thematic material from his own short story, "The Rough Crossing." Still, writing short stories interfered with the novel—he was earning $4,000 per story now—as well as drinking and an increasingly psychological strain between Fitzgerald and Zelda, who was now also writing short stories. The Stock Market crash of 1929 was a death knell for the excesses of the 1920s; the following spring Zelda suffered a nervous breakdown, and the beautiful young couple was no more. Ultimately Zelda was sent to a Swiss sanatorium where she was diagnosed as a schizophrenic. Though Zelda was released from this sanatorium, it was only to be the first of a series of such experiences. Financing her treatment would henceforth be a major concern for Fitzgerald.

The Fitzgeralds returned to the United States in 1931, and that same year he published the short

Fitzgerald's 1934 work is largely based on the experiences of the author, his wife Zelda, and their friends, and offers observations concerning relationships and society.

story "Babylon Revisited," one of his most-anthologized stories and one which attempted to put some meaning to his own experiences in Europe. For a time, Zelda strengthened and returned to writing, but upon the death of her father in 1932, she suffered another breakdown and thereafter was never free of mental illness. Through it all, however, Fitzgerald continued writing, and finally in 1934, nine years after publication of his previous novel, *Tender Is the Night* was published.

That novel is essentially the story of the disintegration of the psychiatrist, Dick Diver, who marries his patient, Nicole Warren. As usual, Fitzgerald included large dollops of autobiography in his story. When Dick meets Nicole, she is a young patient in a Swiss clinic, daughter of a wealthy Chicago businessman; Diver is a promising young psychiatrist. Ultimately, however, Dick sacrifices his career in order to make Nicole whole again. His attempt fails, and Nicole takes up with another man, while Diver returns to small-town practice in America. On another level, however, the story is also a chronicle of the destructive forces of the 1920s—Dick Diver is not only ruined by his love for Nicole but also by the seductive charm of expatriate life in Paris and on the Riviera. Fitzgerald put many personal experiences into this work, including Zelda's affair with the French aviator and his own shipboard romance with a young American starlet whom he met on one of his many sailings between France and the United States. Fitzgerald told this story not in straight chronological order, but by beginning with the Divers in the prime of their marriage in 1925; then he goes back and forth between 1917 and 1925, and follows their disintegration to 1929 and the Stock Market crash which acts as a symbolic finale. Using this structure, Fitzgerald parallels the destruction of the Divers with the loss of American innocence in the decade following World War I.

Tender Is the Night has often been linked with *The Great Gatsby* as Fitzgerald's crowning achievements. Much of the criticism that appeared upon publication of the novel, however, dealt with its political implications. Reviewers were more interested in reading into it a judgement on the boom-and-bust of the 1920s and the 1930s, rather than examining it as a work of art. Seldes, writing in the *New York Evening Journal*, championed the work, declaring that Fitzgerald had written "the great novel." But most critics of the day voiced disappointment with the work. Henry Seidel Canby observed in *The Saturday Review of Literature* that the novel was "brilliant" in places, but overall complained of Fitzgerald's "laziness" in botched structure, theme, and style. The world had changed since the 1920s. In the midst of the Great Depression, readers and critics were no longer charmed by the excesses of wealthy expatriates. Only 13,000 copies of the novel were sold in the first two years after its publication.

Fitzgerald tried to answer his critics regarding structural problems in the novel with a revised edition, but over the years it is his original version that has been adapted. Time, also, has reversed the earlier negative critical reception. Increasingly, *Tender Is the Night* has been praised for the richness of its style, the intricate interplay of stories, and the depth of its thematic devices. In *Critical Quarterly*, the English poet and critic John Lucas observed that *Tender Is the Night* "is about breakdowns: breakdowns in marriages, friendships, and individuals; breakdowns suggestive of a larger breakdown which, in the last analysis, involves the whole of Western society," and noted that the conclusion, with Dick moving back to the United States, "is a very moving ending and a supremely tactful one."

The thematic depths of the novel have also been acknowledged. Writing in the *Fitzgerald/Hemingway Annual: 1978*, Bruce L. Grenberg concluded that *Tender Is the Night* "presents with the clearest intensity Fitzgerald's profound paradoxical conception that man's nobility lies in his unyielding efforts to be his *best* self—even when faced with certain defeat, that man's tragedy lies in his failure to recognize his own limitations and live with them." As a mirror of his own life and the life of the times he inhabited, *Tender Is the Night* has found a special place in Fitzgerald's collected works. David Littlejohn, writing in *Commonweal*, observed that "Fitzgerald's genius, as *Tender Is the Night* gives witness, was fully to understand the hopelessness, even the appalling viciousness of the romantic ideal he created."

The Last Years and *The Last Tycoon*

The negative reception of *Tender Is the Night* did not stop Fitzgerald from writing short stories. As always, such stories were absolutely essential to

If you enjoy the works of F. Scott Fitzgerald, you may also want to check out the following books and films:

Ernest Hemingway, *The Sun Also Rises*, 1954.
Flannery O'Connor, *Everything That Rises Must Converge*, 1965.
J. D Salinger, *The Catcher in the Rye*, 1951.
The classic film *Of Mice and Men*, 1939.

his finances, even more so now that Zelda required constant treatment. In 1937, Fitzgerald made another foray into the world of screenwriting, accepting a $1,000 per week salary from MGM, despite his decline in popularity and his own self-declared "moral bankruptcy." In Hollywood he worked on the film *Three Comrades*, but other scripts were failures and soon he was left to turning out a series of stories which sold for only $250 each. He continued to drink destructively, though a relationship with the columnist Sheilah Graham did provide some domestic stability. Zelda was lost to him forever, and his daughter was in college. Fitzgerald started one last creative effort in these years, the unfinished novel *The Last Tycoon*.

Monroe Stahr is Fitzgerald's last great romantic hero, a self-fashioned man and head of a powerful studio in Hollywood. Much of the action is recounted by Cecilia Brady, daughter of another studio boss, and a woman who is partly in love with the illusive Stahr. Stahr, meanwhile, is in love with his own creative work as well as with a young actress, Kathleen Moore, whom he ultimately loses. Once again, the quintessential Fitzgerald hero loves unwisely and—as Fitzgerald had sketched in the ending to his novel—comes to ruin. While at work on this fifth novel in 1940, Fitzgerald died, but the unfinished novel was published the following year.

By this time, critics were already beginning the steady reassessment of Fitzgerald's achievement. J. Donald Adams declared in the *New York Times Book Review* that *The Last Tycoon* "would have been Fitzgerald's best novel," and noted that Fitzgerald would be "remembered in his generation." The poet and author Stephen Vincent Benet observed in the *Saturday Review of Literature* that "Wit, observation, sure craftsmanship, the verbal felicity that Fitzgerald could always summon up. . . ." were all included in his final novel, and concluded that Fitzgerald's literary standing "may well be one of the most secure reputations of our time." Other critics speculated that, had Fitzgerald finished the novel, it may have been his best book of all. Edmund Wilson noted in a foreword to a 1951 edition of the novel that *The Last Tycoon,* even in its unfulfilled intention, takes its place among the books that set a standard." The book has also been favorably compared to other Hollywood novels, such as Nathaniel West's *Day of the Locust.*

The Fitzgerald legend has continued to grow since the time of his death, aided in part by biographies by Arthur Mizener, Andrew Turnbull, and the critical work of Matthew J. Bruccoli. Fitzgerald's works have been translated into thirty-five languages and continue to sell about half a million copies a years. Recent critical attention has also placed Fitzgerald among the contemporary masters of the short story. Fitzgerald and his wife were ultimately reunited in death—Zelda died in a fire in a mental hospital in 1948. In 1975 their bodies were interred together in the cemetery at St. Mary's Church in Rockville, Maryland, near where Fitzgerald's parents were buried. The epitaph cut in the couple's gravestone was the last line from *The Great Gatsby:* "So we beat on, boats against the current, borne back ceaselessly into the past."

In the final analysis, perhaps Fitzgerald's biography is, as the biographer Jeffrey Meyers suggested, a cautionary tale. "Fitzgerald's short life was in many ways a tragic one," Meyers wrote in *Scott Fitzgerald: A Biography.* "His greatest work shows what happens to people who pursue illusory American dreams, and how society (which they have rejected) fails to sustain them in their desperate hour. . . . Fitzgerald courageously explored and revealed his own character. He has left us, not a glamorous legend, but a vivid record of self-examination."

■ Works Cited

Adams, J. Donald, "Scott Fitzgerald's Last Novel," *New York Times Book Review,* November 9, 1941, p. 1.

Anderson, W. R., "F. Scott Fitzgerald," *Dictionary of Literary Biography Yearbook, 1981,* Gale, 1982.

Benet, Stephen Vincent, "Fitzgerald's Unfinished Symphony," *The Saturday Review of Literature,* December 6, 1941, p. 10.

Canby, Henry Seidel, "In the Second Era of Democratization," *The Saturday Review of Literature,* April 14, 1934, pp. 630-31.

Chase, Richard, "Three Novels of Manners," *The American Novel and Its Tradition,* Anchor Books, 1957, pp. 157-84.

Cowley, Malcolm, "Introduction: The Romance of Money," *Three Novels: "The Great Gatsby," "Tender Is the Night," "The Last Tycoon,"* Scribner, 1953, pp. ix-xx.

Donaldson, Scott, "F. Scott Fitzgerald," *Dictionary of Literary Biography,* Volume 9: *American Novelists, 1910-1945,* Gale, 1981, pp. 3-18.

Eliot, T. S., letter to F. Scott Fitzgerald on December 31, 1925, *The Crack-Up,* by F. Scott Fitzgerald, New Directions, 1945, p. 310.

Fitzgerald, F. Scott, *The Great Gatsby,* Scribner, 1925.

Fitzgerald, F. Scott, *The Last Tycoon,* Penguin, 1977.

"F. Scott Fitzgerald's Second Act," *Library Journal,* November 1, 1996, p. 16.

Goldleaf, Steven, "Fitzgerald, F(rancis) Scott (Key)," *Reference Guide to Short Fiction,* St. James Press, 1994, pp. 181-83.

Grenberg, Bruce L., "Fitzgerald's 'Figured Curtain': Personality and History in 'Tender Is the Night'," *Fitzgerald/Hemingway Annual, 1978,* 1979, pp. 105-36.

Gross, Barry, "Our Gatsby, Our Nick," *The Centennial Review,* Summer, 1970, pp. 331-40.

Hansen, Harry, review of *This Side of Paradise, Chicago Daily News,* March 31, 1920.

Hoffman, Frederick J., "The American Novel between the Wars," *The Modern Novel in America: 1900-1950,* Henry Regnery and Company, 1951, pp. 89-110.

Kazin, Alfred, "Into the Thirties: All the Lost Generations," *On Native Grounds: An Interpretation of Modern American Prose Literature,* Reynal & Hitchcock, 1942, pp. 312-62.

Kenny, John M., review of *The Great Gatsby, The Commonweal,* June 3, 1925, p. 110.

Littlejohn, David, "Fitzgerald's Grand Illusion," *The Commonweal,* May 11, 1962, pp. 168-69.

Lucas, John, "In Praise of Scott Fitzgerald," *Critical Quarterly,* Summer, 1963, pp. 132-47.

Mencken, H. L., review of *This Side of Paradise, Smart Set,* August, 1920.

Mencken, H. L., "The Great Gatsby," *F. Scott Fitzgerald: The Man and His Work,* edited by Alfred Kazin, Macmillan/Collier, 1962, pp. 89-92.

Meyers, Jeffrey, *Scott Fitzgerald: A Biography*, HarperCollins, 1994, pp. 4, 343.

New Yorker, "The Great Gatsby," January 4, 1941.

Prigozy, Ruth, "F. Scott Fitzgerald," *Dictionary of Literary Biography*, Volume 86: *American Short Story Writers, 1910-1945*, Gale, 1989, pp. 99-123.

Seldes, Gilbert, "Spring Flight," *The Dial*, August, 1925.

Seldes, Gilbert, review of *Tender Is the Night*, *New York Evening Standard*, April 12, 1934.

Taylor, Douglas, "'The Great Gatsby', Style and Myth," *The University of Kansas City Review*, Autumn, 1953, pp. 30-40.

Toklas, Alice B., *Staying on Alone: Letters of Alice B. Toklas*, edited by Edward Burns, Liveright, 1973.

Wilson, Edmund, foreword to *"The Last Tycoon," An Unfinished Novel, Together with "The Great Gatsby,"* Scribner, 1951, pp. ix-xi.

Wilson, Edmund, *The Shores of Light: A Literary Chronicle of the Twenties and Thirties*, Farrar, Straus and Young, 1952, pp. 27-35.

■ For More Information See

BOOKS

Allen, Joan, *Candles and Carnival Lights*, New York University Press, 1978.

Bruccoli, Matthew J., *The Composition of "Tender Is the Night": A Study of the Manuscripts*, University of Pittsburgh Press, 1963.

Bruccoli, Matthew J., editor, *Fitzgerald Newsletter: No. 1-40, Spring, 1958-Winter, 1968*, reprinted, NCR/Microcard Editions, 1969.

Bruccoli, Matthew J., Scottie Fitzgerald Smith, and Joan P. Kerr, editors, *The Romantic Egoists: Scott and Zelda Fitzgerald*, Scribner, 1974.

Bruccoli, Matthew J., *"The Last of the Novelists": F. Scott Fitzgerald and "The Last Tycoon,"* Southern Illinois University Press, 1977.

Bruccoli, Matthew J., *Scott and Ernest: The Authority of Failure and the Authority of Success*, Random House, 1978.

Bruccoli, Matthew J., *Some Sort of Epic Grandeur: The Life of F. Scott Fitzgerald*, Harcourt, 1981.

Bruccoli, Matthew J., *F. Scott Fitzgerald: A Descriptive Bibliography*, revised edition, University of Pittsburgh Press, 1987.

Bruccoli, Matthew J., and Jackson R. Bryer, editors, *F. Scott Fitzgerald in His Own Time: A Miscellany*, Kent State University Press, 1971.

Bruccoli, Matthew J., and Margaret Duggan, editors, *Correspondence of F. Scott Fitzgerald*, Random House, 1980.

Bruccoli, Matthew J., and others, editors, *Fitzgerald/Hemingway Annual*, NCR/Microcard Editions Books/Information Handling Services, 1969-76, Gale, 1977-79.

Bryer, Jackson R., editor, *F. Scott Fitzgerald: The Critical Reception*, Burt Franklin, 1978.

Bryer, Jackson R., *The Short Stories of F. Scott Fitzgerald: New Approaches to Criticism*, University of Wisconsin Press, 1982.

Bryer, Jackson R., *The Critical Reputation of F. Scott Fitzgerald: A Bibliographical Study*, supplement, Archon Books, 1984.

Buttitta, Tony, *After the Good Gay Times*, Viking, 1974.

Concise Dictionary of American Literary Biography: The Twenties, 1917-1929, Gale, 1989.

Cowley, Malcolm and Robert Cowley, editors, *Fitzgerald and the Jazz Age*, Scribner, 1966.

Cross, K. G. W., *F. Scott Fitzgerald*, Oliver & Boyd, 1964.

Dictionary of Literary Biography, Volume 4: *American Writers in Paris, 1920-1939*, Gale, 1980.

Dictionary of Literary Biography Documentary Series, Volume 1, Gale, 1982.

Donaldson, Scott, *Fool for Love: F. Scott Fitzgerald*, Congdon & Weed, 1983.

Donaldson, Scott, editor, *Critical Essays on F. Scott Fitzgerald's "The Great Gatsby,"* G. K. Hall, 1984.

Eble, Kenneth, *F. Scott Fitzgerald*, Twayne, 1963, revised edition, G. K. Hall, 1977.

Eble, Kenneth, editor, *F. Scott Fitzgerald: A Collection of Criticism*, McGraw-Hill, 1973.

Geismar, Maxwell, *The Last of the Provincials*, Houghton Mifflin, 1943.

Goldhurst, William, *F. Scott Fitzgerald and His Contemporaries*, World, 1963.

Graham, Sheilah, *The Rest of the Story*, Coward-McCann, 1964.

Graham, Sheilah, *College of One*, Viking, 1967.

Graham, Sheilah, and Gerold Frank, *Beloved Infidel*, Holt, 1958.

Hemingway, Ernest, *A Moveable Feast*, Scribner, 1964.

Higgins, John A., *F. Scott Fitzgerald: A Study of the Stories*, St. John's University Press, 1971.

Hoffman, Frederick J., editor, *"The Great Gatsby": A Critical Study*, Scribner, 1962.

Kuehl, John, and Jackson R. Bryer, editors, *Dear Scott, Dear Max: The Fitzgerald-Perkins Correspondence*, Scribner, 1971.

LaHood, Marvin J., editor, *"Tender Is the Night": Essays in Criticism*, Indiana University Press, 1969.

Lehan, Richard D., *F. Scott Fitzgerald and the Craft of Fiction*, Southern Illinois University Press, 1966.

Le Vot, Andre, *F. Scott Fitzgerald: A Biography*, translation by William Byron, Doubleday, 1983.

Long, Robert Emmet, *The Achieving of "The Great Gatsby": F. Scott Fitzgerald, 1920-1925*, Bucknell University Press, 1979.

Margolies, Alan, editor and author of introduction, *F. Scott Fitzgerald's St. Paul Plays, 1911-1914*, Princeton University Library, 1978.

Mayfield, Sara, *Exiles from Paradise: Zelda and Scott Fitzgerald*, Delacorte, 1971.

Mellow, James R., *Invented Lives: F. Scott and Zelda Fitzgerald*, Houghton Mifflin, 1984.

Milford, Nancy, *Zelda: A Biography*, Harper, 1970.

Miller, James E., *F. Scott Fitzgerald: His Art and His Technique*, New York University Press, 1964.

Mizener, Arthur, editor, *F. Scott Fitzgerald: A Collection of Critical Essays*, Prentice-Hall, 1963.

Mizener, Arthur, *The Far Side of Paradise*, 2nd edition, Houghton, 1965.

Perosa, Sergio, *The Art of F. Scott Fitzgerald*, University of Michigan Press, 1965.

Piper, Henry Dan, *F. Scott Fitzgerald: A Critical Portrait*, Holt, Rinehart & Winston, 1965.

Piper, Henry Dan, editor, *Fitzgerald's "The Great Gatsby"*, Scribner, 1970.

Ring, Frances Kroll, *Against the Current: As I Remember F. Scott Fitzgerald*, Creative Arts Book Co., 1985.

Shain, Charles E., *F. Scott Fitzgerald*, University of Minnesota Press, 1961.

Short Story Criticism, Gale, Volume 6, 1990.

Sklar, Robert, *F. Scott Fitzgerald: The Last Laocoon*, Oxford University Press, 1967.

Stern, Milton R., *The Golden Moment: The Novels of F. Scott Fitzgerald*, University of Illinois Press, 1970.

Tompkins, Calvin, *Living Well Is the Best Revenge*, Viking, 1971.

Turnbull, Andrew, *Scott Fitzgerald: A Biography*, Scribner, 1962.

Turnbull, Andrew, editor, *The Letters of F. Scott Fitzgerald*, Scribner, 1963.

Twentieth-Century Literary Criticism, Gale, Volume 1, 1978, Volume 6, 1982, Volume 14, 1984, Volume 28, 1988, Volume 55, 1995.

Way, Brian, *F. Scott Fitzgerald and the Art of Social Criticism*, St. Martin's, 1980.

Wilson, Edmund, editor, *"The Last Tycoon": An Unfinished Novel*, Scribner, 1941.

Wilson, Edmund, *Letters on Literature and Politics, 1912-1972*, edited by Elena Wilson, introduction by Daniel Aaron, foreword by Leon Edel, Farrar, Straus, 1977.

PERIODICALS

American Cavalcade, October, 1937.

Bookman, May, 1926.

Chicago Daily Tribune, April 18, 1925.

Chicago Evening Post, September 24, 1920.

Esquire, February, 1936; April, 1936; August, 1936.

Nation, May 9, 1934.

New Yorker, November 15, 1941.

New York Times, April 4, 1989.

New York Times Book Review, March 5, 1922.

New York Tribune, May 7, 1922.

New York World, April 12, 1925.

Princeton University Library Chronicle, Number 5, 1944.

Saturday Evening Post, April 5, 1924.

Saturday Review of Literature, December 6, 1940.

Smart Set, December, 1920; April, 1922.

St. Paul Dispatch, April 12, 1934.

Washington Post, September 25, 1989.*

—Sketch by J. Sydney Jones

Jodie Foster

■ Personal

Born Alicia Christian Foster, November 19, 1962, in Los Angeles, CA; daughter of Lucius III (an air force officer) and Evelyn "Brandy" (a publicist and personal manager; maiden name, Almond) Foster (divorced). *Education:* Yale University, B.A. (literature), 1985.

■ Addresses

Agent—International Creative Management, 8942 Wilshire Blvd., Beverly Hills, CA 90211.

■ Career

Actress, film director, and producer.

■ Awards, Honors

Emmy Award, outstanding actress in a special, 1973, for "Rookie of the Year," *ABC Afterschool Special;* National Film Critics Award, Los Angeles Film Critics Award, David Di Donatello Award, British Academy of Film and Television Arts Award, Academy Award nomination, and New York Film Critics Award nomination, best supporting actress, 1976, all for *Taxi Driver;* British Academy of Film and Television Arts Award, most promising newcomer to leading film roles, and Italian Situation Comedy Award, 1976, both for *Bugsy Malone;* Golden Globe Award, best actress in a motion picture drama, Academy Award, best actress, and David Award, 1989, all for *The Accused;* Academy Award, best actress, 1991, for *The Silence of the Lambs;* Academy Award nomination, best actress, 1995, for *Nell.*

■ Film and Television Work

FILM APPEARANCES

(Film debut) Samantha, *Napoleon and Samantha,* Buena Vista, 1972.
Rita, *Kansas City Bomber,* Metro-Goldwyn-Mayer, 1972.
Martha, *One Little Indian,* Buena Vista, 1973.
Becky Thatcher, *Tom Sawyer,* United Artists, 1973.
Menace on the Mountain, Buena Vista, 1973.
Audrey, *Alice Doesn't Live Here Anymore,* Warner Bros., 1975.
Tallulah, *Bugsy Malone,* Paramount, 1976.
Deirdre Striden, *Echoes of a Summer* (also known as *The Last Castle*), Cine Artists, 1976.

Annabel Andrews, *Freaky Friday*, Buena Vista, 1976.

Iris Steensman, *Taxi Driver*, Columbia, 1976.

Rynn Jacobs, *The Little Girl Who Lives Down the Lane*, American International, 1977.

Fleur Bleue, *Moi, fleur bleue* (also known as *Stop Calling Me Baby!*), Megalo/CIC, 1978.

Casey Brown, *Candleshoe*, Buena Vista, 1978.

Donna, *Carny*, United Artists, 1980.

Jeanie, *Foxes*, United Artists, 1980.

Tersina, *Il cassota* (also known as *The Beach House*), Medusa Distribuzione, 1980.

Barbara O'Hara, *O'Hara's Wife*, Davis-Panzer, 1983.

Helene, *Le Sang des autres* (also known as *The Blood of Others*), Parafrance/Prism, 1984.

Franny Berry, *The Hotel New Hampshire*, Orion, 1984.

Victoria, *Mesmerized*, Thorn-EMI, 1984.

Nancy, *Siesta*, Lonmar, 1987.

Linda, *Five Corners*, Cineplex Odeon, 1987.

Sarah Tobias, *The Accused*, Paramount, 1988.

Katie Chandler, *Stealing Home*, Warner Bros., 1988.

Clarice Starling, *The Silence of the Lambs*, Orion, 1991.

Dede Tate, *Little Man Tate*, Orion, 1991.

Prostitute, *Shadows and Fog*, Orion, 1992.

Anne Benton, *Backtrack*, Vestron Video, 1992.

Laurel, *Sommersby*, Warner Bros., 1993.

Nell, *Nell*, Twentieth Century-Fox, 1994.

Annabelle Bransford, *Maverick*, Warner Bros., 1994.

Ellie Arraway, *Contact*, Warner Bros., 1997.

FILM WORK

Coproducer, *Mesmerized*, Thorn-EMI, 1984.

Director, *Little Man Tate*, Orion, 1991.

Coproducer, *Nell*, Twentieth Century-Fox, 1994.

Director and coproducer, *Home for the Holidays*, Paramount, 1995.

Also directed "Hands of Time," *Americans* (documentary), Time-Life/BBC.

TELEVISION APPEARANCES IN SERIES

(Television debut) *Mayberry, R.F.D.*, CBS, 1969.

Voice of Anne Chan, *The Amazing Chan and the Chan Clan* (animated), CBS, 1972.

Elizabeth Henderson, *Bob and Carol and Ted and Alice*, ABC, 1973.

Voice of Pugsley Addams, *The Addams Family* (animated), NBC, 1973-75.

Addie Pray, *Paper Moon*, ABC, 1974-75.

TELEVISION APPEARANCES IN PILOTS

Henrietta "Hank" Bennett, *My Sister Hank*, CBS, 1972.

Liberty Cole, *Smile Jenny, You're Dead*, ABC, 1974.

TELEVISION APPEARANCES, EPISODIC

Priscilla, *My Three Sons*, CBS, 1965-72.

Joey Kelley, *The Courtship of Eddie's Father*, ABC, 1969-72.

Julie Lawrence, *The Partridge Family*, ABC, 1970-74.

Ghost Story, NBC, 1972.

Love Story, NBC, 1973.

Host, *Saturday Night Live*, NBC, 1976.

Who's Who, CBS, 1977.

Sam, CBS, 1978.

Narrator, "The Fisherman and His Wife," *Storybook Classics*, Showtime, 1989.

Also appeared in *Ironside, Daniel Boone, The Wonderful World of Disney, Adam-12, Julia*, and *Bonanza*, all NBC; *Gunsmoke*, CBS; and *Kung Fu*, ABC.

TELEVISION APPEARANCES, MOVIES

Zoe Alexander, *Svengali*, CBS, 1983.

Helene Bertrand, *The Blood of Others*, HBO, 1984.

TELEVISION APPEARANCES, SPECIALS

Sharon Lee, "Rookie of the Year," *ABC Afterschool Special*, ABC, 1973.

Sue, "Alexander," *ABC Afterschool Special*, ABC, 1973.

Title role, "The Secret Life of T. K. Dearing," *ABC Weekend Special*, ABC, 1975.

The 3rd Annual Hollywood Insider Academy Awards Special, USA, 1989.

The 62nd Annual Academy Awards Presentation, ABC, 1990.

Entertainers '91: The Top 20 of the Year, ABC, 1991.

The 63rd Annual Academy Awards Presentation, ABC, 1991.

Oprah: Behind the Scenes, ABC, 1992.

49th Annual Golden Globe Awards, ABC, 1992.

The 65th Annual Academy Awards Presentation, ABC, 1993.

Behind Closed Doors with Joan Lunden, ABC, 1994.

Voice of Alice Paul, *A Century of Women*, TBS, 1994.

Host, *All About Bette*, TNT, 1994.

■ Writings

"Why Me?", *Esquire*, December, 1982.

Also author of "Hands of Time," *Americans* (documentary), Time-Life/BBC.

■ Work in Progress

Directing and producing *Flora Plum*, Disney/Touchstone; has optioned the film rights for *Alias Grace*, a novel by Margaret Atwood.

■ Sidelights

She is sitting high in Hollywood with a lifetime of work behind her, yet actress, movie director, and producer Jodie Foster still has a whole career ahead of her. She appeared first as a bare-bottomed three-year-old in a Coppertone suntan lotion commercial, and she has been in the public eye ever since. Foster was a child actor who got a typical start in commercials and episodic television, but took an atypical path to movie stardom. Plucky and boyish as a child—she played sidekick Becky Thatcher in *Tom Sawyer* when she might have easily played Tom—she left behind kiddie fare early, getting her first Oscar nomination for her portrayal at age twelve of a child prostitute. She has since become a disciplined, savvy, glamorous-when-she-wants-to-be Hollywood professional, known for the risky, dramatic roles she brings to life—rape victims, troubled adolescents, a struggling single mother, a stalker of serial killers, a "wild" woman of the woods.

"The great anomaly of Foster's career is that she's risen to the top as neither a seductive beauty nor an unbeautiful character actor . . .," Michael Shnayerson wrote in a 1994 interview article for *Vanity Fair*. "What she becomes, by quelling her fears and confronting her enemies, is something no other American actress of our time has embodied with such consistency and aplomb: a hero."

Driven to bring to life cast-aways, the undervalued, women ripe for redemption, Foster's is a chosen heroism that runs along classical lines. "Every acting part that I take is about redeeming somebody. . . . It's like a mission or something," she told Julia Cameron in *American Film.* Cameron writes that in real life, Foster's "bearing more closely resembles the crown prince than some spoiled princess."

Along with an aura of strength and vulnerability, Foster radiates intelligence. She is described by Gerri Hirshey in *Rolling Stone* as "the thinking actor's actor," and is known, according to Melina Gerosa in *Ladies' Home Journal,* for "her penchant for being in control." Linda R. Miller in *American Film* found that "Jodie Foster's allure was a hybrid of child and adult. Even in her earliest performances she displayed a concentration and tension, a worldly self-possession normally associated with much older actors. And this control that she exercised still colors everything in Foster's life. . . . The edge that she held over her generation of actors was won by her years of experience and her braininess."

"Close to Jodie"

"I talk a lot, probably too much. Some of my friends do call me Miss Authoritiva, and I doubtless deserve that," Foster told Hirshey. However, she went on to add, "I'm not a pain in the ass. I'm bossy, but I'm not a pain. And anything I demand is always about the movie. It's not about comfort or vanity."

Foster's acting style is unschooled and technical, developed out of years of practice rather than any studied theory or method. "She can be sitting, joking in French to the makeup man with chewing gum and her glasses on," Jon Amiel, who directed Foster in the 1993 historical romance *Sommersby*, recalled to Shnayerson. "You say, 'Jodie, you're on,' and within 30 seconds she's in front of the camera, delivering a scene that will break your heart. Her experience as a child actor is what enables her to move in and out of character like that," he said, adding, "As grown-ups, we develop overlays, but Jodie combines all the technical facility of a child actor with the maturity of a really seasoned campaigner. If God had designed a perfect acting machine, it would be pretty close to Jodie."

The consummate professional, Foster believes her job is very much her life, and vice versa. "People assume I've been robbed of my childhood," she told Richard Corliss of *Time* in a 1991 interview. "I don't think that's true. I've gotten something

Foster portrayed a twelve-year-old prostitute in Martin Scorcese's searing 1976 film, *Taxi Driver,* starring Robert De Niro as a frustrated, alienated loner who roams the streets of New York City.

extra. Most kids, all they have is school. That's why they get so mad when it's boring and feel so bad if they fail. I have my work; I know how to talk to adults and how to make a decision. Acting has spared me from being a regular everyday kid slob. I used to think of it as just a job, but now it's my whole life, it's all I want to do."

Foster has not been one to talk publicly about her personal life, making her an exception to Hollywood's publicity-at-any cost rule. The little that she does reveal in interviews paints a down-to-earth portrait of someone who drives a station wagon, wants to get a dog, prefers comfortable clothing, loves seeing movies ("I go to cry," she told Gerosa), has learned kick-boxing, and collects photographs. "My time off is regeneration time, and I'm entirely selfish," she explained to Hirshey of *Rolling Stone.* "Somebody calls and says come out and have lunch, and I say no, because be-

tween 12:30 and 2:30, I eat in my car. That's my thing. I eat in my car."

Born Alicia Christian Foster in November 1962, she was the youngest of four children; it was her sisters Lucinda and Constance and brother Buddy, who nicknamed her Jodie. Her parents, Lucius and Evelyn (who goes by the name "Brandy") separated before Foster was born, and so she and her siblings were raised by a single working mother in an eclectic household. Brandy Foster had worked as a Hollywood publicist for a time and later as a dealer in decorative arts, and so the family's modest Los Angeles home near Hollywood Boulevard was often filled with the art objects she sold on consignment. "My mom was just an adventurous soul, a very unconventional soul," Foster said to Ingrid Sischy of *Interview.* Brandy Foster took her children to see foreign movies at odd hours and to browse in shops filled with old, leather-bound books, and they spent quiet weekends at home reading and eating take-out from ethnic restaurants. "We would sit and talk about everything; that was our bond, that was our tie. It was all about staying within four walls and discussing things. I have not lived a 'normal' life. But I think I've lived a very healthy life. I think my upbringing was provocative," Foster told Sischy.

Not the usual movie business mother, Brandy Foster had aims for her children that were academic and cultural, as well as social. She went to the extent of pretending the family lived in an affluent suburb so that Jodie could attend the dancing and manners school there. "Now every time I go to one of those Oscar things, I'm the first one on the dance floor, because it's the only time I get to use my incredible ballroom-dancing skills," Foster said to Gerosa.

Foster was a precocious child who began to speak and then read while still a toddler. She attended Le Lycée Francais, a prestigious French language high school in Los Angeles from which she graduated as valedictorian. By then she had already found her profession, having nabbed the Coppertone commercial by accompanying her actor-brother to the audition and getting hired instead of him. "[Jodie] was never a traditional-looking little girl," Brandy Foster recalled for Miller in *American Film*. "And I think that has a lot to do with her success. It was just at the beginning of women's liberation, and she kind of personified that in a child. She had a strength and uncoquettishness." Under her mother's management, Foster became the family's primary breadwinner, getting parts in commercials (forty-five of them by age thirteen), in television series like *Mayberry, R.F.D., My Three Sons,* and *The Partridge Family,* in *ABC Afterschool Specials,* and eventually in movies. Of her mother's role in her early success, Foster told Gerosa, "When you think about what in your parenting has allowed you to achieve excellence, if winning an Oscar is about excellence, it's not her telling me to wear my raincoat. It was the side of her that encouraged me to fly. And that told me not to hesitate."

She made her film debut in 1972, playing Samantha in *Napoleon and Samantha* and Rita in *Kansas City Bomber.* Other early roles included Martha in *One Little Indian* (1973), Audrey in *Alice Doesn't Live Here Anymore* (1975) and Tallulah in *Bugsy Malone* (1976). Foster remembers in *Interview*

that "there were people on those sets . . . who were like my family—a misfit family of people who did not lead conventional lives. They played with me, but they also reprimanded me when I would get bratty. In terms of real acting, I remember acting in television and stuff, but *Taxi Driver* was the first time I really felt I acted."

Early Oscar Notice

As Iris Steensman in the 1976 movie *Taxi Driver,* the twelve-year-old Foster played a runaway-turned-prostitute alongside Robert De Niro's portrayal of Travis Bickle, an isolated, volatile ex-marine turned New York City taxi driver. The movie, directed by Martin Scorsese, won the Golden Palm at the Cannes Film Festival and earned Academy Award nominations for both De Niro and Foster; she also drew a slew of other awards for the role, including the National Film Critics Award, the Los Angeles Film Critics Award, the British Academy of Film and Television Arts Award, and a New York Film Critics Award nomination, all for best supporting actress.

Roger Ebert of the Chicago *Sun-Times,* writing in 1996 on the occasion of the movie's twentieth anniversary re-release, hailed *Taxi Driver* as "one of the best and most powerful of all films." And Desson Howe of the *Washington Post,* writing at the same time, said that the movie's "theme of bomb-ticking loneliness and, by extension, the notion that we are a nation of angry strangers who vent paranoid resentment toward public figures or the government, couldn't be more resonant today." The insomniac Bickle (known for his lines, "Are you talkin' to me? Well I'm the only one here.") is completely disconnected from and increasingly disgusted by the society that surges and seethes around him. He spends his time driving his cab around a steamy nighttime city and going to pornographic movie theaters. Desperately out of touch, he manages to catch the attention of a presidential candidate's campaign aide, Betsy, played by Cybill Shepherd, but he ruins their one and only date by taking her to a porno flick. He then turns his obsessive attentions toward rescuing Foster's character, and ultimately goes on a killing rampage that he thinks will cleanse what he sees as a debauched world.

Reviewing *Taxi Driver* in the *New Yorker,* Pauline Kael wrote that Foster was "an unusually physical child actress and seems to have felt out her line readings—her words are convincingly hers." It was Foster's first time playing a character that wasn't just a kid like herself, the first time she was required to become someone else. Of De Niro, Foster told Hirshey of *Rolling Stone*, "He didn't tell me anything. . . . He just grabbed me, pulled me into the scene. And we kept doing it, over and over. And over and over again. Until it was only us amid all those people and it was perfect, it was absolutely right."

However, not everyone found it absolutely right to put a child in an R-rated role. The California Labor Board protested and required that Foster undergo a psychological evaluation before allowing her to do the job. "It absolutely infuriated me. I knew morally how strong she was. She had been working years and years," Brandy Foster recalled to Hirshey.

"My mother didn't want me to make hoopla comedies where I would wear cute pigtails and tu-

Foster received her first Oscar for *The Accused*, in which her character is gang-raped in front of a room full of witnesses.

tus. She wanted me to be taken seriously, and to be a moral person, and looked up to as somebody who stood for the right things. And when I did *Taxi Driver*, it's not as if she didn't know who Martin Scorsese was—she dragged me to see *Mean Streets* four times. It's not like she said, 'Oh, a movie about a prostitute; I think I'll put my little girl in that.' She was very aware of Scorsese as a talent," Foster said in the Sischy interview.

After appearing in several more films, including *Carny* and *Foxes*, Foster put her career on hold to attend college, graduating *cum laude* in 1985 with a degree in literature from Yale University—a move that some say helped her to bridge the awkward years of young adulthood that cause many child-actors to self-destruct. But Yale proved to be no escape from celebrity. A bizarre event during her freshman year in March 1981 forever links her name with that of an obsessed fan, John W. Hinckley, Jr., who set out to impress her by trying to assassinate then-President Ronald Reagan, shooting and wounding the President and three other men in the process. Hinckley had supposedly taken his cues from *Taxi Driver*, which he said he had watched repeatedly. (He was eventually found not guilty by reason of insanity and sent away to a Washington, D.C., mental hospital.)

Only days after the shooting, a second *Taxi Driver* fan stalked and threatened Foster, having attended that weekend a campus play in which Foster was performing. The ensuing investigations and publicity, the hate mail and intrusive reactions of strangers and fellow students were overwhelming, yet Foster managed her press conferences herself, and went on to write a December 1982 account for *Esquire* magazine. She has said that the article, titled "Why me?", is her final word on the episode. In it, as recounted by Tom Morganthau in *Newsweek*, she detailed the turmoil after the shootings, examined Hinckley's confusion of love and obsession, and expressed some anger over the public intrusion into her life, concluding that "After a period of death-dodging you learn to believe that you've been picked for survival." She eventually took a leave of absence from her studies to do some movie work and then did a stint at *Esquire* before returning to Yale.

"My career was at a low point when I graduated," Foster said in the *Time* article by Corliss, "but I couldn't let it go without a real push. Then

Fledgling F.B.I. agent Clarice Starling questions serial killer Hannibal "The Cannibal" Lecter in *The Silence of the Lambs*, a 1991 film that earned Foster her second Academy Award for best actress.

it struck me that I wasn't going to do dreck." Corliss notes that she went on to take "roles in some eccentric good films (*Siesta, Five Corners*) and at least one ordinary bad one (*Stealing Home*). Then *The Accused* came along. Or rather, she stormed after it." It won Foster her first best actress Oscar and relaunched her career.

"A daring, acute performance. . . ."

Loosely based on a case in which a group of men gang-raped a woman in a New Bedford, Massachusetts, bar while others watched and cheered, *The Accused* is the story of Sarah Tobias, a tough, wrong-side-of-the-tracks waitress who is similarly gang-raped in the back room of a roadhouse. The prosecuting attorney, played by Kelly McGillis, doubts that Sarah will be a good witness in court, given that Sarah would have to defend herself for drinking and seductive behavior the night of the

attack, so she accepts a plea bargain and the men get only short prison sentences. But an angry Sarah convinces her also to bring charges against the men who watched the rape, and Sarah finally gets a chance to vindicate herself by telling her side of the story in court, through a flashback that, in effect, makes the movie audience a part of the witnessing crowd.

"This is Foster's first full-scale, grown-up performance in the movies, and what she does has range and heart," David Denby wrote in a *New York* magazine review. "*The Accused* is out to prove a thesis—that inducing and watching a violent crime should be treated as a crime in itself. Generically, the move is high-minded melodrama, and what saves it from sententiousness is Jodie Foster's performance—and Jonathan Kaplan's live-wire direction," Denby continued. "The film doesn't show bullets, just basic human cruelty—what happens when people are in a room together. It's not inhuman, which is why it's so scary," Foster said in a *Time* review by Corliss, who called Foster's work in the film "a daring, acute performance."

The performance—with its required courtroom scenes and an alluring dance that Sarah does before the rape scene itself—proved so emotionally taxing for Foster, whose mother was on location with her to lend moral support, that she began making plans to leave Hollywood once and for all and go to graduate school. "I couldn't talk about it for a long time. It was so hard to admit that it was a difficult movie for me," she recalled in an *Entertainment Weekly* article by Mark Harris. "Aside from the publicly happy ending—she was great, she won an Oscar, and the role kicked her into the first rank of young actresses—Foster came out of the experience somewhat more *defined*," Harris wrote, something Foster herself acknowledged. Speaking of her work prior to *The Accused*, Foster told Harris, "It's okay, but it's not the same. I spent a lot of time acting like I thought everyone else on screen was an idiot, and that is the *total* sign of someone not committing to their work."

Her newfound sense of professional self was revealed when Foster, after receiving her Oscar for *The Accused*, "gave one of the most lucid acceptance speeches in recent memory—and then appeared as a presenter [the following year] in a breast-baring jacket that almost upstaged Madonna. Foster has shown that it is possible for a woman in Hollywood to be tough, feminist *and* sexy," wrote Brian D. Johnson in *Maclean's*.

Foster's entire career has been marked by bold moves, ones deemed risky in the beginning and shrewd after the pay-off. "I went to college when, if I wanted to have a career, it was the stupidest thing I could have done," she told Gerosa in *Ladies' Home Journal*. "I directed [*Little Man Tate*] right when I was about to win an Academy Award, when in terms of earning power as an actress you'll never be as high."

Little Man Tate (1991), Foster's directorial debut in which she also starred, began as "a small relationship movie," as Cameron noted in *American Film*, but became to some extent an autobiographical project for Foster. It is a story of triangular conflict between Fred Tate (played by Adam Hann-Byrd), a child genius, who at age seven, is

an accomplished painter, pianist, and mathematician; Dede (Foster), his working-class single mother who is concerned about his emotional needs; and psychologist Jane Grierson (Dianne Wiest), who wants to see Fred's intellect nurtured in the rarefied air of a specialized environment.

"I think of Fred and Dede in terms of my mom having to be on the set with me her whole life. Women give things up for their children. They make sacrifices. My mom made great choices for me. I wasn't about to make large conceptual decisions as a 10-year-old," Foster told Cameron. Foster's siblings had left home by the time she was ten, and so she was familiar with the peculiarities of the relationship her character had with Fred. "There is a sort of romance between a single parent and a child. You do things together that you wouldn't if there were another parent there. Dede dances with Fred, for example. They're partners," Foster added.

Foster had no problem making the transition from actor to director. "So much of acting is letting go of what you think and accommodating other people," Foster explained to Johnson in *Maclean's*. "And that, to me, is much more emotionally exhausting than directing. Being given all the information and having the ultimate voice is so much more relaxing."

Little Man Tate received mixed reviews. Calling Foster "a smart, no-nonsense woman and a superbly honest actress," and noting the autobiographical parallels, David Ansen wrote in *Newsweek* that "While all this makes for good copy, the movie itself is a sweet, disjointed, overly schematic affair that only scratches the surface of its fascinating subject." And John Powers stated in *New York*, "Even as she offers a quietly radical vision of family life . . . she falls into retro cliché. . . . Reducing tricky issues of gender to cheery formulas about the head versus heart, *Little Man Tate* recalls those 'After School Specials' Foster starred in as a kid, back when nobody expected her to know anything about life." Yet Corliss's article in *Time* called *Tate*'s sweet ending "just dessert to a film that offers much chewy food for thought," and included high praise from the late French filmmaker Louis Malle. "Jodie's film is basically about the profound loneliness of childhood, and she's dealt with it head-on. I would be very happy and proud to have made the film she did," he said.

Speaking about *Little Man Tate* in *Interview,* Foster told Sischy, "The film is very American, but there are things about it that I think are European, not because I said, 'Oh, I want this to be European,' but because my favorite movies are films like [Malle's] *Murmur of the Heart, The 400 Blows,* and *Breathless.* This movie deals with the world of the mind, whereas American movies deal more with the world of emotions." (Foster has a strong European following, and has appeared in French films, including the 1978 *Moi, fleur bleue* and the 1984 *Le Sang des autres.*)

Acclaimed *Silence*

Foster won her second Academy Award for Best Actress for her performance in the 1991 film, *The Silence of the Lambs,* directed by Jonathan Demme. (The movie was based on the novel *Silence of the Lambs* by Thomas Harris, who also wrote the popular work *Red Dragon.*) Foster's was another unusually dark and scary role, but this time she ultimately played savior rather than victim. As the fledgling F.B.I. agent Clarice Starling, she descended into the gruesome depths of the psychopathic mind, having to win the help of one serial killer (a jailed Hannibal "The Cannibal" Lecter, played by Anthony Hopkins) in order to catch another—nicknamed Buffalo Bill because he skins his female victims. Calling the movie a "superbly crafted suspense thriller" that "slams you like a sudden blast of bone-chilling, pulse-pounding terror," Peter Travers, writing in *Rolling Stone,* found that "The confrontation scenes between Lecter and Starling are the heart of the picture, and Hopkins and Foster—who is flawless in a performance on a par with her Oscar-winning work in *The Accused*—play off each other with enormous skill." A brilliant psychiatrist as well as psychopath,

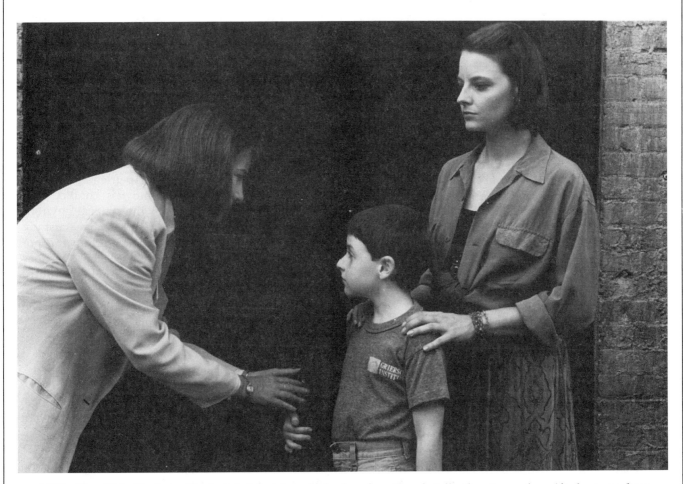

Little Man Tate, Foster's directorial debut in which she also starred, tells the story of a gifted young boy and his relationship with his mother.

Lecter is drawn to try and discover the emotional impetus behind Clarice's career choice, and, in exchange for clues about Buffalo Bill, he gets her to reveal a haunting episode from her childhood, in which she unsuccessfully tried to save a lamb from being slaughtered on the family farm.

The movie's suspense heightens when the killer captures a high-profile victim—a senator's daughter—and there are only three days in which to find and save her. Lecter bargains his way into a jail transfer that leads to his violent escape, but only after Clarice gets what she needs to solve the Buffalo Bill mystery. She then stalks him into his death cocoon—alone. Some reviewers, like Stanley Kauffman in the *New Republic*, who is not a fan of Foster's acting style, found the plot contrived and melodramatic. "The way the danger is resolved, in the dark, is past belief," he wrote, adding that Foster let the role do her work for her. "Her acting choices, from moment to moment, always seem to come from an available stock," he said. Anne Billson, reviewing the movie for *New Statesman and Society*, called it *"The Texas Chainsaw Massacre* for sophisticates; not so much a film, more a case history in how to take a tasteless subject and make it acceptable to a middle-class audience."

For many, however, *Silence* struck the right balance between smart and scary, and it went on to become a commercial success and award winner, taking five of the seven Oscars for which it was nominated, including best picture, actor (to Hopkins), director, and adapted screenplay, along with Foster's award. "For all the unbridled savagery on display, what is shrewd, significant and finally hopeful about *The Silence of the Lambs* is the way it proves that a movie can be mercilessly scary and mercifully humane at the same time," Travers concluded in his review.

"You have to take huge risks to create anything people *want* to see. They'd rather see comedies. They don't want to see a drama unless it's going to take them someplace breathtaking and controversial. Someplace they normally wouldn't have gone. You have to take those risks or all you're ever going to be is mediocre," Foster explained to Hirshey. Yet, good scripts—with good roles for women—are few and far between, and she chooses only those with which she feels a personal connection. More often than not they are characters who are the victims of society or cir-

cumstance, in need of saving or a motivating factor that will enable them to save themselves. "What female actors, and certainly women in history, have to fight against is not so much the obvious things—victimization, etc.—but just being *ignored*. A real hero to me is a woman who has five kids and no money and takes care of them and *survives*. That's a heroic feat," Foster said to Johnson of *Maclean's*.

A Powerful Producer Newly Hatched

Not content to rest on her acting and directing laurels, Foster's next feat was to negotiate a deal with PolyGram to form her own production company, with an initial goal to make six films over a three-year period. Foster named her company Egg Pictures ("because it's feminine and about beginnings and doesn't sound like Greek mythology," she explained to Harris in *Entertainment Weekly*).

Egg's first production was the 1994 film *Nell*, based on the play "Idioglossia" by Mark Handley. Foster was nominated for an Oscar for her portrayal of Nell, a woman raised in isolation in the woods of North Carolina. She speaks an unintelligible language based on the impaired speech of her late mother and the childhood gibberish she shared with her long-dead twin sister. The local doctor, Gerome Lovell (played by Liam Neeson), with the help of psychologist Paula Olsen (Natasha Richardson), observes and befriends her, and the two help play out the movie's conflict over whether Nell is better off in the natural environment that nurtures her or in protective custody where she can be studied and kept from the potential harms of an encroaching society she does not understand. "Foster is hauntingly beautiful . . . a greatly compelling actress," Jack Kroll wrote in *Newsweek*, though he ultimately found the movie too overt in its "sentimental pantheism."

Also noting Foster's "outstanding performance," a review in the *TV Guide* Entertainment Network Motion Picture Database said that although the "film is beautifully made and thought-provoking," it "vacillates too much between the sentimental and the metaphysical," adding that "*Nell*'s approach to the classic argument between Nature and Civilization is rigged from the outset, and no one will be surprised to learn that Nature wins. Nell is the noblest of savages in the best of all

If you enjoy the works of Jodie Foster, you may also want to check out the following books and films:

Jo Jo Dancer, Your Life Is Calling, directed by Debbie Allen, starring Richard Pryor, 1986.
A League of Their Own, directed by Penny Marshall, starring Tom Hanks, 1992.
The Mirror Has Two Faces, directed by Barbara Streisand, 1991.

possible woods; indeed, she's virtually a transcendent being." Along with the sentimental handling of the story's central conflict, other critics cited undeveloped supporting characters (". . . the picture is designed as a Foster vehicle," Kauffman wrote in the *New Republic*) and were disappointed by the implied but unanswered questions about Nell's emerging sexuality. Even though the film may not have been flawless, many agreed that Foster's performance was. "It's as bold as anyone's ever been on film," the movie's director Michael Apted told Melina Gerosa of *Ladies' Home Journal*.

Although Foster has dabbled in comedy (most notably alongside Mel Gibson in the 1994 comic western *Maverick* and in a small role as a prostitute in Woody Allen's 1992 *Shadows and Fog*) and acted on stage during her college days, it is on film that Foster wants to stay, doing the kind of serious dramatic roles that she does so well, bringing to life the kinds of stories that risk-averse Hollywood studios aren't likely to consider. Her part in commercial successes, like the 1997 summer hit *Contact*, directed by Robert Zemeckis, help pave the way. At a time of year when moviegoers face an onslaught of action hero fare and lightweight comedies, *Contact*, based on the novel by the late Carl Sagan, was a visually dazzling surprise based on ideas as much as action, a "solemn two-and-a-half hour reverie on religion, technology and the search for extraterrestrial life" with "the temerity to imagine" heaven as "a gleaming tropical beach with snow-white sand and turquoise surf watched over by a fireworks of wheeling golden stars," as Stephen Holden described it in the *New York Times*.

Foster plays a young astronomer, Ellie Arraway, who has devoted her life to the unyielding pursuit of locating extraterrestrial intelligence. Driven by the tragedies of having had both parents die while she was a child, she has spent her life listening for radio signals from space and fighting for credibility and funds for her work from a skeptical scientific community. When she at last intercepts a signal from the distant star Vega, it turns out to be the coded plans for a space vehicle that eventually is built by a coalition of governments, led by the United States. Ellie's professional rival is chosen for the journey, but when that attempt gets sabotaged by a religious fanatic, Ellie is chosen for a second attempt from a more secure island location. Her life-changing experience on the craft leaves open the question of whether she has made extraterrestrial contact or has had a marvelous hallucination.

"Most of the movie's subsidiary characters are one-dimensional cartoons," wrote Holden, citing in particular the peculiar billionaire S. R. Hadden (John Hurt) who lives on a plane and covertly monitors and finances Ellie's ultimate adventure, and the young minister Palmer Joss (Matthew McConaughey) who "is so underwritten that he remains an enigma." Others echoed the weakness of the Joss character as a spokesman for religious faith, finding that the movie's ultimate science-versus-religion debate doesn't get off the ground because theology is not presented in the same intellectually rigorous light as science. As with *Nell*, some critics found Foster's Ellie to be the character who drives the movie.

"I can't imagine another actress who can bring both the emotion and intellect to the character," Zemeckis said in a *New York Times* article by Bernard Weinraub of his choosing Foster to play Ellie Arraway. Added Foster, "The idea of someone searching for some kind of purity, searching for something out there that she can't find here, was something that was very, very close to myself. I process everything through my head first. I cope through my head. I cope with the disappointments in my life and the pains of my life by using my intellect. That doesn't make me less vulnerable, but I do a good job of hiding it. And that's what this woman is about."

Clearly Foster knows what she is about, and she is not afraid to see it writ large on screen. A seasoned professional with a bankroll of experience, she has wisely invested in her Hollywood future by diversifying and widening her power base, making it possible for more projects that match her high standards to get made. "I realize that I'm in a really exquisite position," she told Harris in *Entertainment Weekly*. "I forget how long I've been doing it, but sometimes it amazes me. Not too many people who have already worked for 25 years have as much energy as I do. Sometimes I can't believe how much I *don't* know, but sometimes I look around . . . and you know what I realize? *I know a lot!*" Taking in stride the royal-like mix of public accessibility and privilege that has been her lot in life, she has gone from being crown prince to "benevolent king" or "queen," as she has more than once described herself to interviewers. With unconquered movie territory ahead of her and a lifetime to make more of it her own, Foster is living into her Hollywood reign.

■ Works Cited

Ansen, David, "No One Is Immune from the Rot," *Newsweek*, October 21, 1991, p. 65.

Billson, Anne, "Dead Silence," *New Statesman and Society*, May 31, 1991, p. 30.

Cameron, Julia, "Burden of the Gift," *American Film*, November, 1991, pp. 47, 48.

Corliss, Richard, "'Bad' Women and Brutal Men," *Time*, November 21, 1988, p. 127.

Corliss, Richard, "A Screen Gem Turns Director," *Time*, October 14, 1991, pp. 68, 70, 72.

Denby, David, "Night Moves," *New York*, October 31, 1988, p. 68.

Ebert, Roger, review of *Taxi Driver* (twentieth anniversary edition), *Sun-Times* (Chicago), March 1, 1996.

Gerosa, Melina, "Jodie Loses Her Cool," *Ladies' Home Journal*, February, 1995, pp. 152, 154-55, 224.

Harris, Mark, "Jodie Foster: Meet the New Boss," *Entertainment Weekly*, April 2, 1993, pp. 16-17, 19.

Hirshey, Gerri, "Jodie Foster," *Rolling Stone*, March 21, 1991.

Holden, Stephen, review of *Contact*, *New York Times*, July 11, 1997.

Howe, Desson, review of *Taxi Driver* (twentieth anniversary edition), *Washington Post*, March 1, 1996.

Johnson, Brian D., "Jodie Foster's 'Best Performance': An Actress Calls Her Own Shots," *Maclean's*, September 16, 1991, pp. 48-49.

Kael, Pauline, "Underground Man," *New Yorker*, February 9, 1976, as reprinted in *For Keeps: 30 Years at the Movies*, Plume/Dutton Signet/Penguin, 1994, p. 683.

Kauffman, Stanley, "Gluttons for Punishment," *New Republic*, February 18, 1991, pp. 48-49.

Kauffman, Stanley, "Early Winter Roundup," *New Republic*, January 23, 1995, p. 31.

Kroll, Jack, "Paradise Found: Jodie Foster in Arcadia," *Newsweek*, December 19, 1994, p. 64.

Miller, Linda R., "Victor of Circumstances," *American Film*, October, 1988, p. 27.

Morganthau, Tom, "Jodie Foster: 'Why Me?',", *Newsweek*, November 8, 1982, p. 34.

Review of *Nell*, in *TV Guide* Entertainment Network Motion Picture Database.

Powers, John, review of *Little Man Tate*, *New York*, October 21, 1991, p. 95.

Shnayerson, Michael, "Pure Jodie," *Vanity Fair*, May, 1994, p. 167.

Sischy, Ingrid, interview with Jodie Foster, *Interview*, October, 1991, pp. 79, 81.

Travers, Peter, "Snapshots from Hell," *Rolling Stone*, March 7, 1991, pp. 87-88.

Weinraub, Bernard, "Using a Big Budget to Ask Big Questions," *New York Times*, July 6, 1997.

■ For More Information See

PERIODICALS

Esquire, December, 1982.

Maclean's, March 12, 1984, p. 66.

New York, March 10, 1980, p. 85.

New Yorker, November 13, 1995, pp. 128-30.

San Francisco Examiner, February 16, 1996, p. D3.

Time, June 16, 1980, p. 50; February 22, 1993, p. 69.

Working Woman, November, 1995, p. 30.*

—Sketch by Tracy J. Sukraw

Russell Freedman

■ Personal

Born October 11, 1929, in San Francisco, CA; son of Louis N. (a publisher's representative) and Irene (an actress; maiden name, Gordon) Freedman. *Education:* Attended San Jose State College (now University), 1947-49; University of California, Berkeley, B.A., 1951. *Hobbies and other interests:* Travel, photography, filmmaking.

■ Career

Associated Press, San Francisco, CA, reporter and editor, 1953-56; J. Walter Thompson Co. (advertising agency), New York City, publicity writer for television, 1956-60; Columbia University Press, New York City, associate staff member of *Columbia Encyclopedia*, 1961-63; freelance writer, 1961—. Editor, Crowell-Collier Educational Corp., 1964-65; writing workshop instructor, New School for Social Research, 1969-86. *Military Service:* U.S. Army, Counter Intelligence Corps, 1951-53; served in Korea. *Member:* Authors Guild, PEN, Society of Children's Book Writers and Illustrators.

■ Awards, Honors

Western Heritage Award, National Cowboy Hall of Fame, and *Boston Globe-Horn Book* Honor Book for Nonfiction, both 1984, Spur Award Honor Book Citation, Western Writers of America, 1985, and Jefferson Cup Award, 1986, all for *Children of the Wild West;* Golden Kite Award Honor Book Citation, Society of Children's Book Writers, 1987, Newbery Medal, American Library Association, and Jefferson Cup Award, both 1988, all for *Lincoln: A Photobiography;* Jefferson Cup Award Honor Book citation, 1988, for *Indian Chiefs;* Golden Kite Award Honor Book citation, 1988, for *Buffalo Hunt;* Golden Kite Award Honor Book citation, 1990, Orbus Pictus Award, National Council of Teachers of English, and Jefferson Cup Award, both 1991, Jefferson Cup Award and Newbery Honor Book citation, both 1992, all for *The Wright Brothers: How They Invented the Airplane; Washington Post*/Children's Book Guild Nonfiction Award, 1992, for distinguished work in the field of nonfiction for children; Golden Kite Award Honor Book citation, 1992, for *An Indian Winter;* Golden Kite Award, 1993, *Boston Globe-Horn Book* Award, 1994, and Newbery Honor Book citation, 1994, all for *Eleanor Roosevelt: A Life of Discovery;* Golden Kite Award, 1994, for *Kids at Work: Lewis Hine and the Crusade against Child Labor;* Laura Ingalls Wilder Medal, American Library Association, 1998, for body of work.

Freedman's books have appeared on numerous "best" or "outstanding" book lists, including lists compiled by such organizations as the American Library Association, the Junior Literary Guild, the Child Study Association of America, and the Children's Book Council, and such periodicals as *School Library Journal*, *Horn Book*, and *Booklist*.

■ Writings

JUVENILE NONFICTION

Teenagers Who Made History, portraits by Arthur Shilstone, Holiday House, 1961.

Two Thousand Years of Space Travel, Holiday House, 1963.

Jules Verne: Portrait of a Prophet, Holiday House, 1965.

Thomas Alva Edison, Study-Master, 1966.

Scouting with Baden-Powell, Holiday House, 1967.

(With James E. Morriss) *How Animals Learn*, Holiday House, 1969.

(With James E. Morriss) *Animal Instincts*, illustrated by John Morris, Holiday House, 1970.

Animal Architects, Holiday House, 1971.

(With James E. Morriss) *The Brains of Animals and Man*, Holiday House, 1972.

The First Days of Life, illustrated by Joseph Cellini, Holiday House, 1974.

Growing Up Wild: How Young Animals Survive, illustrated by Leslie Morrill, Holiday House, 1975.

Animal Fathers, illustrated by Joseph Cellini, Holiday House, 1976.

Animal Games, illustrated by St. Tamara, Holiday House, 1976.

Hanging On: How Animals Carry Their Young, Holiday House, 1977.

How Birds Fly, illustrated by Lorence F. Bjorklund, Holiday House, 1977.

Getting Born, illustrated with photographs and with drawings by Corbett Jones, Holiday House, 1978.

How Animals Defend Their Young, Dutton, 1978.

Immigrant Kids, Dutton, 1980.

Tooth and Claw: A Look at Animal Weapons, Holiday House, 1980.

They Lived with the Dinosaurs, Holiday House, 1980.

Animal Superstars: Biggest, Strongest, Fastest, Smartest, Prentice-Hall, 1981.

Farm Babies, Holiday House, 1981.

When Winter Comes, illustrated by Pamela Johnson, Dutton, 1981.

Can Bears Predict Earthquakes? Unsolved Mysteries of Animal Behavior, Prentice-Hall, 1982.

Killer Fish, Holiday House, 1982.

Killer Snakes, Holiday House, 1982.

Children of the Wild West, Clarion Books, 1983.

Dinosaurs and Their Young, illustrated by Leslie Morrill, Holiday House, 1983.

Rattlesnakes, Holiday House, 1984.

Cowboys of the Wild West, Clarion Books, 1985.

Sharks, Holiday House, 1985.

Indian Chiefs, Holiday House, 1987.

Lincoln: A Photobiography, Clarion Books, 1987.

Buffalo Hunt, Holiday House, 1988.

Franklin Delano Roosevelt, Clarion, 1990.

The Wright Brothers: How They Invented the Airplane, photographs by Orville and Wilbur Wright, Holiday House, 1991.

An Indian Winter, paintings and drawings by Karl Bodmer, Holiday House, 1992.

Eleanor Roosevelt: A Life of Discovery, Clarion, 1993.

Kids at Work: Lewis Hine and the Crusade against Child Labor, Clarion, 1994.

The Life and Death of Crazy Horse, illustrated by Amos Bad Heart Bull, Holiday House, 1996.

Out of Darkness: The Story of Louis Braille, Clarion, 1997.

Martha Graham, A Dancer's Life, Clarion, 1998.

OTHER

Holiday House: The First Fifty Years (adult), Holiday House, 1985.

Contributor to *Columbia Encyclopedia*, 3rd edition, and *New Book of Knowledge Annual*, 1981-89. Also contributor to periodicals, including *Cricket*, *Ranger Rick*, *Horn Book*, and *School Library Journal*.

The manuscripts for *Lincoln: A Photobiography* are housed at the Kerlan Collection in Minneapolis, MN.

■ Adaptations

Lincoln: A Photobiography was adapted as a filmstrip and video, McGraw-Hill Media, 1989.

■ Overview

Russell Freedman has a long career of publishing nonfiction books for children and young adults in a pioneering format, using compelling photographs to illustrate his work. Freedman's technique is to immerse himself in his topic, learning everything he can about the person or subject, and then to complete painstaking research in photographic archives in order to find just the right pictures to illustrate his story. He has written award-winning books about cowboys, animals, and Indians of the American West, as well as biographies of American presidents and inventors. His *Lincoln: A Photobiography* won the 1988 Newbery Medal.

Freedman was born on October 11, 1929, in San Francisco, California, one of two children. He grew up in an atmosphere where literary accomplishments were encouraged. "My father was a great storyteller," Freedman related in his Newbery Medal Acceptance speech, reprinted in *Horn Book*. "The problem was, we never knew for sure whether the stories he told were fiction or nonfiction." Freedman's father, a book salesman, met his mother, a clerk, in the bookstore where she worked. "I had the good fortune to grow up in a house filled with books and book talk," the author stated.

Freedman read voraciously as a youth, diving into any book he could get his hands on. Two of his favorite works were the fiction classic *Treasure Island* and a popular nonfiction book of the day titled *Wild Animals I Have Known*. "In those innocent days I didn't worry about distinctions like fiction and nonfiction. I didn't think I knew the difference. I did know that I was thrilled by both of those books. And I knew that both of them were true. . . . What is important is that I read *Wild Animals I Have Known* with as much pleasure and satisfaction as I have any novel or story. And I've remembered the book ever since," Freedman related in "Pursuing the Pleasure Principle," in *Horn Book*.

Freedman's interest in nonfiction books began to jell when he was a child. Another of his favorite books was *The Story of Mankind* by Hendrik Willem Van Loon. "I think it was the first book that gave me a sense of history as a living thing, and it kept me turning the pages as though I were reading a gripping novel," he related in his Newbery Medal Acceptance speech.

Early biographies for children often fictionalized accounts of a person's life, and Freedman has fond memories of the ways they were written. "I grew up during the cherry-tree era of children's biography," Freedman confessed in his Newbery

speech. "Recently I looked again at a Lincoln biography I read as a boy; it contains my favorite example of invented dialogue. Abe is eleven years old in this scene, and his father is bawling him out: 'Books!' said his father. 'Always books! What is all this studying going to do for you? What do you think you are going to be?' 'Why,' said Abe, 'I'm going to be President.'

The Shadow of Lincoln

Ironically, Lincoln's face was to haunt Freedman during his childhood for a very different reason than the words he read in the biography. Freedman joked in his Newbery speech that he spent a great deal of his time at school in the principal's office, where a portrait of Lincoln hung on one wall. "George Washington may have been the father of our country, but Lincoln was the one who always knew when I was in trouble," he related. Lincoln took on a great importance in young Freedman's life. "His picture reminded me that in America a boy could travel from a log cabin to the White House," he related in his Newbery acceptance speech.

The Freedman household often hosted famous writers because of Louis Freedman's work as

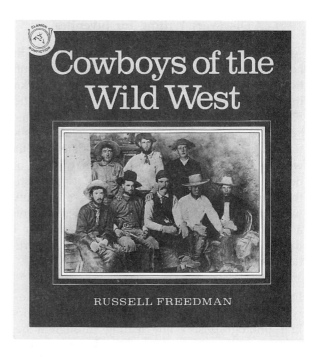

Freedman uncovers the myths about cowboys in this 1985 work.

manager of West Coast sales for Macmillan. Among the dinner guests were John Steinbeck, William Saroyan, and John Masefield. "And they all had leg of lamb, since that was the one thing my mother trusted herself to cook. Whenever she came home from the butcher with a leg of lamb, I knew another author was coming for dinner," Russell Freedman related in an interview with Frank J. Dempsey in *Horn Book.*

From 1947 to 1949, he attended San Jose State College and graduated in 1951 with a B.A. from the University of California at Berkeley. For the next two years he served with the U.S. Counter Intelligence Corps, part of that time in combat duty in Korea with the 2nd Infantry Division. After his stint in the Army, Freedman went to work for the Associated Press in San Francisco as a reporter and editor. "That was where I really learned to write," he told Dempsey. He also wrote publicity pieces for television until he came upon something that would change the direction of his life. Freedman came upon an article about a blind sixteen-year-old boy who had invented a Braille typewriter. Freedman also learned that another blind sixteen-year-old, Louis Braille, had originally developed the Braille system. The article served as the inspiration for *Teenagers Who Made History,* Freedman's first book.

Discovers Writing for Juveniles

After finishing this book, Freedman realized that he had found his true vocation—writing nonfiction works for young adults. He began working in this field full time after the book's publication. His beginning efforts included several technical books on animal life. "They were solid, substantial books, comprehensive and up-to-date, and they were well received. By the time they came out, however, I had become dissatisfied with writing that kind of definitive, comprehensive volume. I wondered, does anyone really sit down and read a book like this from beginning to end? Or do they just dip into it and use it to write reports?" he related in *Horn Book.*

Freedman decided instead that he would like to write a book on animals that included compelling photographs. While leafing through a book about bats, he saw a photo of a baby bat clutching its mother's chest as the pair flew through the air. "The photograph was an enormously af-

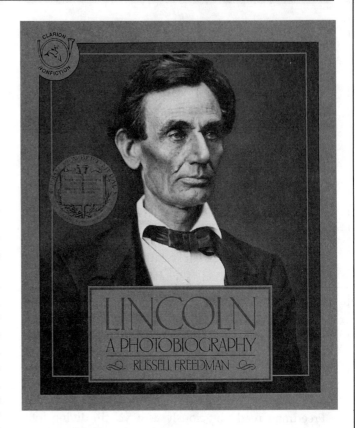

Freedman received the Newbery Award for this work about the sixteenth president.

fecting one and fascinating because the infant's very life depended on its ability to hang on to its mother," he wrote in *Horn Book.* The photograph hatched an idea for a new book, one chronicling all the animal babies who needed to hang on to their mother for survival. After drawing up a list of animals to include in the work, Freedman began his search for photographs. The resulting book featured a variety of animals and the ways their babies hang on to them to survive, from the very rare and exotic to the common house cat. *Hanging On: How Animals Carry Their Young* was published in 1977.

In 1980, Freedman became interested in doing another type of photographic book, this time about people. After attending an exhibit that showed photographs of poor children around the turn of the century, he became inspired to tell their story. "What impressed me most of all was the way that those old photographs seemed to defy the passage of time. They were certainly of their own time, for they depicted, in their vivid details, a particular era from the past. And yet those same photographs were also timeless. They captured scenes from life that are as familiar and recognizable today as they were then, scenes that have been frozen and preserved for future generations to see. . . . I asked my editor, Ann Troy, to visit the exhibit with me, and the outcome was my book *Immigrant Kids* (1980)," Freedman related in *Horn Book.*

Westward Ho!

After completing *Immigrant Kids,* he used the same techniques to write books about children in the Old West. In order to research books on the West, Freedman visited historical societies and libraries throughout the western states, as well as the National Archives and the Smithsonian Institution in Washington, D.C. *Children of the Wild West* (1983) won the Western Heritage Award from the National Cowboy Hall of Fame, and was followed by a sequel, *Cowboys of the Wild West* (1985).

Cowboys of the Wild West uncovered many myths about this often-romanticized group. A *Publishers Weekly* reviewer wrote: "Cowboys, readers discover, were really boys. Many were teenagers, a few 'old hands' were in their early 20s; and they were responsible for driving great herds across the plains in the 1800s." Freedman stays away from romanticizing the cowboys, instead describing the many difficulties of life on the range. George Gleason, writing in the *School Library Journal,* praised the work, declaring that it is "certainly a book to linger over and turn to again and again."

Freedman followed up these two books with a study of Indians entitled *Indian Chiefs* (1987). In it, he features six Indian chiefs from different tribes, including Sitting Bull and Red Cloud. Complete with archival black and white photographs, Freedman gave a balanced picture of the lives and decisions of the great chiefs. Karen P. Zimmerman, writing in *School Library Journal,* stated that the account is factual and concluded that Freedman "does not romanticize the Indian viewpoint, nor is he judgmental against the whites." In *Buffalo Hunt* (1988) Freedman chronicles the importance of the great buffaloes to Native Americans and how their disappearance impacted the Indians' lives.

"One of the great joys of writing nonfiction for youngsters is the opportunity to explore almost

any subject that excites your interest," Freedman wrote in his Newbery acceptance speech. Freedman decided to write a biography about Abraham Lincoln after hearing a remark about the former president's melancholy disposition. What struck Freedman was that Lincoln would have had such a multi-layered and moody personality. "I picked Lincoln as a subject because I felt I could offer a fresh perspective for today's generation of young readers, but mostly I picked him because I wanted to satisfy my own itch to know," he related. The result was *Lincoln: A Photobiography.*

Because so much has been written about Lincoln, Freedman faced the daunting challenge of writing from a fresh perspective. Through the proprietor of a Lincoln-related bookshop, Freedman was able to focus his research and pinpoint the documents he wanted to emphasize. Still, writing the book turned out to be more difficult than Freedman had originally anticipated. The problem was that the more he looked into Lincoln's life, the more complex the man became. "The man himself turned out to be vastly more interesting than the myth," he related in his Newbery speech. "Of course, I was never able to understand him completely. I doubt if it's possible to understand anyone fully, and Lincoln was harder to figure out than most people, 'the most secretive—reticent—shutmouthed man that ever lived,' according to his law partner, William Herndon, who knew him as well as anyone. That's something I wanted to get across to my readers—a sense of the mysteries of personality, the fascinating inconsistencies of character." Many critics praised Freedman for his well-told recounting of Lincoln's life. A *Publishers Weekly* reviewer praised *Lincoln,* calling it "a balanced work, elegantly designed and . . . extremely readable." Elaine Fort Weischedel, writing in the *School Library Journal,* called *Lincoln* "an outstanding example of what (juvenile) biography can be." "I've been asked, 'How long did it take to write your Lincoln biography?'" the author wrote in his Newbery acceptance speech. "Well, *Lincoln* was my thirty-fourth book, and let's say it took thirty-three books to write it. And it took the help and support of a great many people."

■ **Update**

Shifting gears slightly after writing his impressive book on Lincoln, Freedman decided to tackle another president who had become an icon in

American politics. For *Franklin Delano Roosevelt* (1990) Freedman once again did painstaking research to write a volume about a man whose life had already been chronicled extensively. In this book, Freedman tries to bring to life the complicated personal world of the famous president, and the result, according to Alan Brinkley in the *New York Times Book Review*, is "sensitive [and] evocative. . . . It presents Roosevelt as an attractive and admirable public figure."

Freedman looks at the young Roosevelt, who, as a relative of Teddy Roosevelt, desired to enter politics when he was very young. His rise to power seems to have come from the public having familiarity with his famous surname, as well as an optimistic and strong disposition that appealed to voters. As a young man, his ideas about social reform were fairly conventional and in line with his wealthy upbringing. It was difficult for him to understand the plight of the "common" person. However, in the prime of his life,

The president who led the United States through the Great Depression and World War II is the focus of this work.

Roosevelt contracted polio, a devastating disease usually affecting children which often causes paralysis. Thereafter, he was confined to elaborate leg braces, or had to use a wheelchair to get around. "Mr. Freedman's account of Roosevelt's slow, painful adaptation to his handicap is the most riveting part of this book," contended Brinkley. Freedman believes that is this experience that helped Roosevelt overcome some of his prejudiced upper-class assumptions of people and become more compassionate.

Roosevelt's wife, Eleanor, was also a great influence on him. She had led a difficult early life and had for years been a social crusader, determined to help the poor and unfortunate. Roosevelt was obsessed with hiding his handicap, going to great lengths to make certain he wasn't photographed while in his wheelchair, perhaps in an attempt to appear a strong leader at all times. However, going to these extremes to hide his physical flaws had another affect—he had to hide his inner self as well in order to appear strong.

Freedman's portrait of Roosevelt attempts to expose the inner struggles and worries of Roosevelt, in an effort to show him as a human being. Although he was one of the most popular Presidents in history, and is credited with helping many people through the Great Depression with his New Deal politics, he has remained somewhat enigmatic. Brinkley concluded that Freedman's "skillful portrait of the most important American President of this century encourages us to admire Franklin Roosevelt more for who he was than for what he did."

Taking Flight

Freedman's interest in inventors led him to write the book *The Wright Brothers: How They Invented the Airplane* (1991). The author's careful research yielded a "completely engrossing volume," according to Margaret A. Bush in the *Horn Book*, which "draws deeply on letters, diaries, and other well-documented sources." Freedman dips into the characters of the Wright brothers, showing that their complimentary personalities and life experiences helped them become the inventors of modern flight. Critics praised Freedman's selection of photographs and his storytelling ability. Bush claimed that the story is a "fresh, illuminating look at an old story."

Freedman next chronicled the life of Franklin D. Roosevelt's famous wife in his 1993 biography, *Eleanor Roosevelt: A Life of Discovery*. Eleanor's early life was very difficult. Her father was an alcoholic, and both of her parents died when she was young. In her youth, she became involved in what would be her lifetime task—social reform, working tirelessly to improve life for the poor in New York City. After marrying Franklin, she bore five children, and then experienced great sorrow as she learned of her husband's marital infidelities. After Franklin's death, she continued to be a social crusader, became a delegate to the United Nations, and formed close relationships with a small cadre of friends that were as important to her as was her marriage. "If there ever was such a thing as a role model for both girls and boys, I think she is one. She's an example of somebody who took control of her own life," Freedman told Shannon Maughan in a *Publishers Weekly* interview.

Freedman also admits that he tried to be as explicit as possible in exploring Roosevelt's personal life. Although some people may consider this approach controversial, Freedman's interest is in accuracy and telling a good biography. "If you're writing a biography for kids in the 1990s," he told *Publishers Weekly*, "you have to be honest. Kids don't have to be protected in the same way they did a generation or two ago. . . . You can't write an honest book about either Franklin Roosevelt or Eleanor Roosevelt without mentioning Franklin's affair with Lucy Mercer, because that changed his life, and it changed Eleanor's life even more. It helped her liberate herself. It gave her permission to assert herself. It isn't fair to kids to conceal that."

A *Publishers Weekly* reviewer wrote that "this impeccably researched, highly readable study of one of the country's greatest First Ladies is nonfiction at its best." Ellen Chesler, writing in the *New York Times Book Review*, praised the book, stating that it teaches that "immense power can be brought to bear against anyone in our society—especially, perhaps, against women who dare to demand that our politics advance a common good, that it be rooted in morality and not in self-interest."

Picks Strong Subjects

Freedman admitted to Maughan that "I'm attracted to subjects who had a strong sense of in-

justice and felt in a very deep personal sense that there were things that are wrong that have to be fixed. And because of that they're controversial; they're stepping on toes and threatening the status quo." Freedman's next book topic was equally controversial as he profiled Lewis Hine, an early photographer of poor children involved in child labor. *Kids at Work: Lewis Hine and the Crusade against Child Labor* was published in 1994. Hine took photographs of children of immigrants in the early 1900s. During those days, it was not uncommon for young children to work in dangerous conditions in the factory. These jobs often left the children seriously injured, or dead. Hine took the photographs to publicize these atrocities to the general public. Freedman told Maughan that Hine was able to use "a camera as a tool for social change."

Freedman explains in the book that this period in history was a time of incredible growth in the economy, and factories, mines, mills, and other businesses needed more workers than were available in the adult workforce. Therefore, it was legal for children under the age of sixteen to toil in very dangerous jobs. Additionally, for most of them the workday was often twelve hours or more, six days a week, and conditions were abysmal. Children were often given the jobs that no one else wanted, and they had little right of recourse. Their parents were often so poor that they counted on the pay from their children to help make ends meet. These conditions made for very desperate situations for the children. Iris Tillman Hill wrote in the *New York Times Book Review* that "Those who want to share a lived sense of history with young children could not do much better than to look at these photographs and read this book with them."

In 1996, Freedman returned to Native American history to write *The Life and Death of Crazy Horse*, a biography of the great Lakota Sioux chief. Unlike other leaders of the era, Crazy Horse was a quiet, modest man who was also an excellent leader and tactician. He led groups in fights along the Oregon and Bozeman trails, including the Battle of the Little Bighorn, in an attempt to stem the tide of infiltration by pioneers. However, he ended his life as a young man, in a U.S. Army prison, with the fate of Native Americans looking very dim. A *Publishers Weekly* reviewer remarked, "No dry history this, but a story certain to sweep readers along its tragic path."

Writes Braille's Story

Early in his career, Freedman was inspired to write a book about a teenager who had created the Braille typewriter in *Teenagers Who Made History*. The inventor of the Braille alphabet, Louis Braille, was only sixteen when he developed the system. Freedman returned to the inventor of this phenomenal alphabet in *Out of Darkness: The Story of Louis Braille* (1997). Braille was blinded at the age of three after a knife accident. He learned not to turn his injury into a tragedy and worked hard to be accepted into a special school for the blind in Paris at the age of twelve. There he would work by himself for hours, attempting to convert an old military code utilizing dots and dashes into an alphabet that the blind could read by touch. Often, Braille toiled at all hours to complete this project. Braille encountered many difficulties in trying to create his alphabet, both technical and bureaucratic. For a while, the system was suppressed but used in secret by other blind students who knew it was their pathway to reading great books, which would build a bridge to the world of the sighted. Finally, Braille's alphabet gained the acceptance of which he had dreamed. Many years after his death, the Braille alphabet is used all around the world. Martha V. Parravano, writing in *Horn Book*, said that *Out of Darkness* "brings the central figure to life as vividly as only Freedman can." In *Booklist*, Hazel Rochman claimed that Freedman "tells the momentous story in quiet chapters in his best plain style."

While Freedman dwells in the electronic age, his writing habits don't always show that. Freedman's office contains a modern fax machine, but is remarkably without a computer or word processor. The author writes out his books longhand on pads of legal paper, and then types up drafts with an Underwood manual typewriter. For his book *Eleanor Roosevelt*, he typed five manuscripts from beginning to end by himself. "If I start at the first word and have to type the whole thing, I have the rhythm of the prose," he told *Meet the Authors and Illustrators*. "I catch things that are missing. I see things that are in there that shouldn't be." In addition, he takes on the task of doing all the photo research by himself, in order to come up with the perfect photos for his text.

Biographies are the form that Freedman most likes to write. He commented in *Meet the Authors and Illustrators* that "Writing a biography is like get-

If you enjoy the works of Russell Freedman, you may also want to check out the following books:

Jim Murphy, *The Boys' War*, 1990, *The Long Road to Gettysburg*, 1992, and *The Great Fire*, 1995.
The historical fiction of Howard Fast, including *Seven Days in June*, 1994.

ting to know a person. You get to know that person better than you know yourself. You study them with such intensity. You read everything there is to read about them and everything they ever said about themselves. You go to bed thinking about that person. You wake up thinking about that person." Writing biographies for children seems to fit his personal style, also. In order to write an adult biography, he would need to do four or five years of research and writing. His books for children take about a year to research and write.

Having made a career of writing nonfiction for children, Freedman has strong opinions about the genre. In his Newbery acceptance speech Freedman noted: "Of the sixty-seven Newbery winners to date, only six, including my own book, have been nonfiction. . . . While nonfiction has never been completely ignored, for a long time it was brushed off and pushed aside, as though factual books were socially inferior to the upper-crust stuff we call literature. Upstairs, imaginative fiction dwelled grandly in the House of Literature. Downstairs, hard-working, utilitarian nonfiction lived prosaically in the servants' quarters. If a nonfiction book were talented and ambitious enough, it could rise above its station, but for the most part, children's nonfiction was kept in its place."

However, Freedman continues to write nonfiction, with the hope that his work will move the genre towards a greater level of respect. Freedman summed up his writing philosophy in *Horn Book*, "Today when I begin a book, I'm hoping to move a stone or two myself. I'm hoping to change the landscape of the reader's mind, if just a little—to leave the reader with a thought, a perception, an insight, perhaps, that she or he did not have before. . . . I want to write a book that will be read willingly, read from beginning to end with a sense of discovery and yes, with a feeling of genuine pleasure."

■ Works Cited

Brinkley, Alan, review of *Franklin Delano Roosevelt,* *New York Times Book Review,* March 17, 1991, p. 26.

Bush, Margaret A., review of *The Wright Brothers: How They Invented the Airplane,* Horn Book, July/August, 1991, pp. 475-76.

Chesler, Ellen, review of *Eleanor Roosevelt: A Life of Discovery, New York Times Book Review,* November 14, 1993, p. 40.

Review of *Cowboys of the Wild West, Publishers Weekly,* November 15, 1985.

Dempsey, Frank J., "Russell Freedman," *Horn Book,* July/August, 1988, pp. 452-56.

Review of *Eleanor Roosevelt: A Life of Discovery, Publishers Weekly,* June 21, 1993, p. 105.

Freedman, Russell, "Pursuing the Pleasure Principle," *Horn Book,* January/February, 1986.

Freedman, Russell, "Newbery Medal Acceptance," *Horn Book,* July/August, 1988, pp. 444-51.

Gleason, George, review of *Cowboys of the Wild West, School Library Journal,* December, 1985, p. 99.

Hill, Iris Tillman, review of *Kids at Work: Lewis Hine and the Crusade against Child Labor, New York Times Book Review,* November 13, 1994, p. 23.

Kovacs, Deborah, and James Preller, interview with Russell Freedman, *Meet the Authors and Illustrators,* Scholastic, Volume II, 1993, pp. 90-91.

Review of *The Life and Death of Crazy Horse, Publishers Weekly,* June 17, 1996, p. 67.

Review of *Lincoln: A Photobiography, Publishers Weekly,* November 27, 1987, p. 86.

Maughan, Shannon, interview with Russell Freedman, *Publishers Weekly,* July 19, 1993, pp. 228, 234.

Parravano, Martha V., review of *Out of Darkness: The Story of Louis Braille, Horn Book,* May/June, 1997, pp. 339-40.

Rochman, Hazel, review of *Out of Darkness: The Story of Louis Braille, Booklist,* March 1, 1997, pp. 1157-8.

Weischedel, Elaine Fort, review of *Lincoln: A Photobiography, School Library Journal,* December, 1987, pp. 93-94.

Zimmerman, Karen P., review of *Indian Chiefs, School Library Journal,* May, 1987, pp. 110-11.

■ For More Information See

BOOKS

Authors and Artists for Young Adults, Volume 14, Gale, 1990.

Children's Literature Review, Volume 20, Gale, 1990, pp. 71-89.

Contemporary Authors, New Revision Series, Gale, Volume 7, 1982, Volume 23, 1988, Volume 46, 1995, pp. 127-29.

Holtze, Sally Holmes, editor, *Sixth Book of Junior Authors and Illustrators,* H. W. Wilson, 1989, pp. 89-91.

Major Authors and Illustrators for Children and Young Adults, Gale, 1993.

Silvey, Anita, editor, *Children's Books and Their Creators,* Houghton, 1995, p. 1194-6.

Something about the Author, Gale, Volume 16, 1979, pp. 115-17, Volume 71, 1993, pp. 69-73.

Sutherland, Zena, *Children and Books,* 9th edition, Longman, 1997, p. 471.

Twentieth-Century Young Adult Writers, 1st edition, St. James, 1994, pp. 222-24.

Ward, Martha E., *Authors of Books for Young People,* Scarecrow Press, 1990.

PERIODICALS

Horn Book, March/April, 1986, pp. 220-21; January/February, 1987, pp. 104-7; July/August, 1987, p. 483; March/April, 1988, p. 222; July/August, 1988, pp. 453-56; March/April, 1991, pp. 213-14.

Publishers Weekly, May 3, 1991, p. 73; May 4, 1992, p. 58.

U.S. News and World Report, December 5, 1994, p. 96.

Wilson Library Bulletin, September, 1994, p. 121.*

—Sketch by Nancy Rampson

Joseph Heller

■ Personal

Born May 1, 1923, in Brooklyn, NY; son of Isaac (a truck driver) and Lena Heller; married Shirley Held, September 3, 1945 (divorced, 1984); married Valerie Humphries (a nurse), 1987; children: (first marriage) Erica Jill, Theodore Michael. *Education:* Attended University of Southern California, 1945-46; New York University, B.A., 1948; Columbia University, M.A., 1949; Oxford University (Fulbright scholar) 1949-50.

■ Addresses

Home—East Hampton, Long Island, New York. *Agent*—Donadio & Ashworth, 231 West 22nd St., New York, NY 10011. *Other*—c/o International Creative Management, 40 W. 57th St., New York, NY 10019.

■ Career

Writer. *Time* magazine, New York City, advertising writer, 1952-56; *Look* magazine, New York City, advertising writer, 1956-58; *McCall's* magazine, New York City, promotion manager, 1958-61; fulltime writer, 1975—; has also worked in the theater, movies, and television. Pennsylvania State University, University Park, instructor in English, 1950-52; Yale University, New Haven, and University of Pennsylvania, teacher of fiction and dramatic writing; City College of the City University of New York, New York City, Distinguished Professor of English, until 1975. *Military service:* U.S. Army Air Forces, World War II, 1942-45; served as B-25 wing bombardier; flew sixty missions; became first lieutenant. *Member:* National Institute of Arts and Letters, Phi Beta Kappa.

■ Awards, Honors

National Institute of Arts and Letters grant in literature, 1963; American Academy Grant, 1963; Prix Interallie (France) and Prix Medicis Etranger (France), both 1985, both for *God Knows.*

■ Writings

NOVELS

Catch-22 (chapter one originally published in *New World Writing,* 1955; previously unreleased chapters published in *Playboy,* December, 1969, and December, 1987), Simon & Schuster, 1961, critical edition, edited by Robert M. Scotto, Dell, 1973.

Something Happened (excerpt originally published in *Esquire*, September, 1966), Knopf, 1974.

Good as Gold (Literary Guild selection), Simon & Schuster, 1979.

God Knows, Knopf, 1984.

Picture This, Putnam, 1988.

Closing Time: A Sequel to Catch-22, Simon & Schuster, 1994.

The drafts, final manuscript, galley proofs, and reviews of *Catch-22* are held at Brandeis University.

PLAYS

We Bombed in New Haven (two-act; first produced in New Haven, CT, at Yale School of Drama Repertory Theater, December 4, 1967, produced on Broadway at Ambassador Theater, October 16, 1968), Knopf, 1968.

Catch-22: A Dramatization (one-act play based on novel of same title; first produced in East Hampton, NY, at John Drew Theater, July 23, 1971), Samuel French, 1971.

Clevinger's Trial (based on chapter eight of novel *Catch-22*; produced in London, 1974), Samuel French, 1973.

The manuscript for *We Bombed in New Haven* is held at Brandeis University.

SCREENPLAYS

(With David R. Schwartz) *Sex and the Single Girl* (based on book of same title by Helen Gurley Brown), Warner Brothers, 1964.

(Uncredited) *Casino Royale* (based on novel of same title by Ian Fleming), Columbia Pictures, 1967.

(With Tom Waldman and Frank Waldman) *Dirty Dingus Magee* (based on novel *The Ballad of Dingus Magee* by David Markson), Metro-Goldwyn-Mayer, 1970.

(Contributor) *Of Men and Women* (television drama), American Broadcasting Companies, 1972.

Also author of other television screenplays during the 1960s.

UNCOLLECTED SHORT STORIES

"I Don't Love You Anymore," *Story*, September-October, 1945.

"Castle of Snow," *Atlantic*, May, 1947.

"Bookies, Beware!," *Esquire*, March, 1948.

"Girl from Greenwich," *Esquire*, June, 1948.

"A Man Named Flute," *Atlantic*, August, 1948.

"Nothing to Be Done," *Esquire*, August, 1948.

"MacAdam's Log," *Gentlemen's Quarterly*, December, 1959.

"World Full of Great Cities," *Nelson Algren's Own Book of Lonesome Monsters*, edited by Algren, Lancer, 1962.

"Love, Dad," *Playboy*, December, 1969.

"The Day Bush Left," *Nation*, June 4, 1990.

Also contributor of short stories to periodicals, including *Smart* and *Cosmopolitan*; contributor of reviews to periodicals, including *New Republic*.

OTHER

(With Speed Vogel) *No Laughing Matter* (autobiography), Putnam, 1986.

Dear God: Children's Letters, Doubleday, 1987.

Conversations with Joseph Heller, edited by Adam J. Sorkin, University of Mississippi, 1993.

Now and Then: From Coney Island to Here, Knopf, 1997.

■ Adaptations

Audio versions of *Catch-22* and *Closing Time* have been produced, including a sound recording read by Alan Arkin, Listen for Pleasure, 1985. *Catch-22* was produced as a motion picture by Paramount in 1970; the film was directed by Mike Nichols, adapted by Buck Henry, and starred Alan Arkin as Yossarian. *Good as Gold* has been adapted as a screenplay. *Catch-22* (an unsold television pilot for a comedy series), was written by Hal Dresner, directed by Richard Quine, and starred Richard Dreyfuss as Yossarian when produced in 1973.

■ Sidelights

When Joseph Heller learned that the *New York Times Book Review*'s response to his first novel was negative, he and his family were terribly depressed. "Waiting for that review to come out," he later told David Streitfeld of *New York*, "I didn't think any of us would ever smile again." The *New York Times Book Review* critic, Richard G. Stern, acknowledged Heller's talent, but declared that *Catch-22* "gasps for want of craft and sensibility. . . . The book is no novel."

Despite initial negative reviews, Heller and his work soon won fame. "I believe that Joseph Heller is one of the most extraordinary talents now among us," exclaimed Robert Brustein in *The Critic as Artist* some ten years after *Catch-22* was released. Decades after its publication, Heller's *Catch-22* is regarded as a classic which has won a place in American history as well as American literature for its biting social criticism. Rich and complex, the novel continues to attract scholars intent on interpreting it, and it is frequently assigned to high school and college students. *Catch-22* has sold over ten million copies, and the term "Catch-22" has become a familiar catch-phrase.

Catch-22 is a satirical, often surreal novel which tells the story of a World War II bombardier who is crazy enough to want to stop going out on bombing missions, but not crazy enough to be sent home. The novel does more than emphasize the absurdity of war through the perspective of its anti-hero, Yossarian, and the use of "black humor"; it criticizes bureaucracy, commodification, and contemporary American ideals. According to Thomas R. Edwards, writing in the *New York Review of Books*, the novel is "brave and essentially truthful in saying what organizations, military or otherwise, do to the minds and values of their members."

Heller's other works, less enthusiastically received than his first novel, are linked thematically and stylistically with *Catch-22*. As George J. Searles noted in the *Dictionary of Literary Biography*, Heller's first three novels have different targets (the military in *Catch-22*, "the corporate realm" in *Something Happened*, and the government in *Good As Gold*), but in "each context, he focuses on an alienated, antiheroic protagonist struggling to identify his own priorities and reconcile them with the large system by which he is ensnared and controlled. In presenting his characters' misadventures, he alternates between straightforward, realistic narration and grotesque, comic exaggeration, thereby creating an uneasy sense of dislocation that mirrors the protagonists' own confusions."

Heller was born in Coney Island, Brooklyn, New York, as the second child of Russian immigrants. Heller's father, who worked as a bakery truck driver, died during an operation when Heller was just five years old. Heller's mother Lena was left to care for her two sons alone during the Great Depression. Heller attended Public School No. 188

and Abraham Lincoln High School. After graduating in 1941, Heller worked in an insurance office, and then for a blacksmith in the Norfolk Navy Yard. In October 1942, Heller enlisted in the U.S. Army Air Force. With the Twelfth Air Force, he was sent to Corsica, Italy; he flew sixty combat missions as a wing bombardier.

"Sure there's a catch," Doc Daneeka replied. "Catch-22. Anyone who wants to get out of combat duty isn't really crazy."

—from Joseph Heller's novel *Catch-22*

Heller reached the rank of first lieutenant and was discharged in 1945. He married Shirley Held, and, with the help of the G.I. Bill, he began to study at the University of Southern California. Heller later transferred to New York University, where he earned a bachelor's degree in English. During his years in college, Heller began to write seriously. He sold short stories to *Esquire* and the *Atlantic* from 1947 to 1948. Heller went on to Columbia University, where he earned a master's degree. On a prestigious Fulbright Scholarship, he spent one year at Oxford University.

Heller returned to the United States and began teaching at Pennsylvania State University. In 1952, he left academia to work as an advertising manager at *Time* magazine. It was around this time that he began to work on the novel he called "Catch-18," and he published a chapter of it in 1955 in *New World Writing*. Before the novel (with more than four hundred pages) was published by Simon & Schuster in 1961, Heller had to change the title of the novel to *Catch-22*, because Leon Uris had published a novel similarly titled *Mila 18*.

Catch-22

Catch-22 is a complex work. The plot often seems implausible, language is used to emphasize the absurd, and, as Inge Kutt explained in the *Dictionary of Literary Biography*, "The chronological structure of the plot is deliberately obfuscated." To make comprehension of the story more difficult, as Christopher Buckley pointed out in the *New Yorker*, the novel "has sixty characters." *Catch-22* is set on a fictional army base on the island of Pianosa (which is actually located off the Italian coast) in 1944. Much of the action occurs on the base, but scenes in America and Rome are related as well. The third-person narrative focuses primarily on the perspective of Yossarian (the main character), as well as on those of other characters.

As *Catch-22* opens, readers find Yossarian in the hospital, pretending to be suffering from liver trouble, where he is given the task of censoring letters. Yossarian is faking illness because he is afraid of being killed on a bombing mission, and his superiors continually raise the number of flights he must complete before they will discharge him. He cannot stand life in the hospital, however, so he returns to his unit and his duties as a bombardier.

Readers are then introduced to the other men in Yossarian's unit. Orr intends to continue his career as a bomber despite the fact that he has been shot down many times. Nately is helplessly in love with a prostitute from Rome (referred to in the novel as "Nately's whore"). McWatt terrorizes Yossarian by flying in low over his tent. Yossarian's superiors include Major Major, who avoids the men in the unit, and Colonel Cathcart, who insists that the men continue to go on bombing missions to ensure his own promotion. Another officer, Milo Minderbinder, serves as the mess officer but really works to gain profit for himself on the black market, despite the consequences for the men of the unit.

Readers also learn that Yossarian has done more than pretend to be sick to escape his bombardier duties. During the course of the novel, Yossarian poisons his own squadron with soap, changes a map, and sabotages his own plane. He also asks his superiors to be grounded. In one scene, he asks Doc Daneeka why Orr, who seems to be insane, has to fly. Doc replies, "'. . . there's a catch. . . . Catch-22. Anyone who wants to get out of combat duty isn't really crazy.'

"There was only one catch and that was Catch-22, which specified that a concern for one's own safety in the face of dangers that were real and immediate was the process of a rational mind. Orr was crazy and could be grounded. All he had to

do was ask; and as soon as he did, he would no longer be crazy and would have to fly more missions. . . . Yossarian was moved very deeply by the absolute simplicity of this clause of Catch-22 and let out a respectful whistle."

As Yossarian realizes that there is no way out of flying more missions, he also learns that Milo Minderbinder is selling the unit's supplies and cheating people with complicated transactions. He even arranges for the enemy to bomb the unit. Milo feels no guilt when his dishonesty harms the men in the unit, and he bears no loyalty to his country; he only cares about profit. To add to the horror of Milo's actions, his superiors do not punish him when they find out about his deeds; instead, they praise him for his profit-making efforts.

Life in the unit gets worse and worse. One day, while McWatt is flying low in jest, he accidently runs into Kid Sampson and kills him. McWatt then crashes into a mountain, killing himself. Nately, attempting to stay close to the prostitute he loves, takes on more missions and is killed in a plane collision. Yossarian has the sad task of informing the prostitute that Nately has died; she is so upset, she attempts to kill Yossarian. For the rest of the novel, Yossarian has to avoid her. To make matters worse, Orr's plane crashes, and he is presumed dead.

After learning that Nately's whore has disappeared along with her young sister, Yossarian goes absent-without-leave (AWOL) to look for them. On the streets of Rome, he finds a hellish reality, and is disturbed by the squalor in which people are living. Upon his return to his room, he discovers that one of the men in his unit, Yossarian's navigator Aarfy, has raped a woman and thrown her out the window. The police appear, but instead of apprehending Aarfy, they arrest Yossarian because he is AWOL.

Finally, Yossarian is offered a way to go home. His superiors promise him that all he has to do is forget their activities and behavior. After Yossarian agrees to this deal, Nately's whore stabs him and he goes back to the hospital. There, he completes the sporadic recall of a traumatic event which is presented by Heller in some of the most evocative and disturbing scenes in *Catch-22*. High in the air, out on a mission, Yossarian's friend Snowden is wounded. Yossarian tries to help him by bandaging the only wound he sees on Snowden, which is on his leg. But Snowden keeps complaining that he is cold. Finally, when Yossarian removes Snowden's flack jacket and checks for other wounds, Snowden's insides roll out onto the floor. Yossarian realizes that without the spirit, man is nothing. Later, Yossarian is too overwhelmed to attend Snowden's funeral. Naked, he watches it from the branches of a tree.

Eventually, Yossarian informs one of his superiors that he will not take the deal they've offered him after all. At the same time, he learns that Orr is alive and has escaped to Sweden. Yossarian determines to follow Orr after he makes a trip to Rome to look for the younger sister of Nately's

Heller's unique work of social criticism offered a new perspective on war and American ideals.

whore. Just as he leaves the hospital, at the conclusion of the novel, Nately's whore ambushes him again. This time she misses him, and Yossarian runs away.

Some influential reviewers were critical of *Catch-22* when it was first published. Norman Mailer exclaimed in *Esquire* that *Catch-22* "is an original. There's no book like it anyone has read. Yet it's maddening." He went on to argue, "One could take out a hundred pages anywhere from the middle of *Catch-22*, and not even the author could be certain they were gone." In 1963, a critic writing in *Daedalus: Journal of the American Academy of Arts and Sciences,* asserted, "*Catch-22* is worthless." The reviewer continued: "The appalling fact is that author, publisher, and reviewers seem unaware that the book is destructive and immoral. . . . *Catch-22* is immoral because it follows a fashion in spitting indiscriminately at business and the professions, at respectability, at ideals, at all visible tokens of superiority."

Other critics and authors praised the work as one of the best American novels ever written. Reviewers in the *Nation* and the *New Republic* lauded *Catch-22*. In the *Spectator*, Julian Mitchell wrote that *Catch-22* is "an extraordinary book," one "of enormous richness and art, of deep thought and brilliant writing." It was not long before *Catch-22* became an underground classic, promoted by word of mouth. "For many readers," explained David Streitfeld, "*Catch-22* quickly became a touchstone—an anticipation, explanation, and confirmation of the anti-military and anti-government sentiments that blossomed during the Vietnam years." Sales of *Catch-22* were steady during the 1960s. Then, in 1970, Paramount released *Catch-22*, a movie directed by Mike Nichols, and the novel finally made the bestseller list. Heller became a sought-after literary star.

Catching on to *Catch-22*

Over time, as scholars began to seriously assess *Catch-22*, Heller's brilliance and the deep complexity of the novel were revealed. In the words of Jerry H. Bryant in *The Open Decision*, Heller's "satire is directed against the institutions that make up this society, business, psychiatry, medicine, law, the military. . . ." "The emphasis [in *Catch-22*] is never on battle, and even the antiwar theme is soft-pedaled when the question of relative morality involves choosing between life-negating war or life-negating bureaucracy. Heller deals instead with one real terror that haunts the novel of the sixties—the organized institution which in the name of reason, patriotism, and righteousness has seized control over man's life . . . ," explained Raymond M. Olderman in *Beyond the Waste Land*. With the presentation of Milo Minderbinder's character and activities, explained Darren Felty in *Novels for Students*, "Heller condemns the unscrupulous expansion of commercial interests that exploit people for profit or even reduce them to the status of commodities."

Many critics have praised the use of humor in *Catch-22*. Robert Brustein wrote in *The Critic as Artist* that he is "ready to argue that this is one of the most bitterly funny works in the language." Yet humor in *Catch-22*, as Louis Hasley noted in the *Midwest Quarterly*, is not used "as a goal, but as a means to an end. . . . It is not a 'comic war novel' despite the fact that comedy and war are held more or less in solution, for the war is *not* comic but horrible—this we are not allowed to forget." Hasley concluded, "The responsive reader of *Catch-22* is thus made to walk a tight-rope as he leans first to riotous humor and then tips to the side of black tragedy. . . . Where Heller comes through in unalleviated horror is where the message lies. The book's humor does not alleviate the horror; it heightens it by contrast."

Similarly, the absurdity of the work calls attention not just to the irrationality of war, but to how we are trapped into believing it is rational. The work has its own logic, which according to Brustein is "unconventional but utterly convincing" internally. "It is a triumph of Mr. Heller's skill that he is so quickly able to persuade us (1) that the most lunatic are the most logical, and (2) that it is our conventional standards which lack any logical consistency." Hasley quoted the novel, "'So many monstrous events were occurring that he [the chaplain] was no longer positive which events *were* monstrous and which *were* really taking place.' That quoted sentence can stand as characterizing the events of the entire book."

Carol Pearson wrote in the *CEA Critic* that *Catch-22* "is an examination of the destructive power of language when language is used for manipulation rather than communication." According to Pearson, "Catch-22" "is a linguistic construct that requires people to do whatever their superiors wish." Pearson explains that people create what seem to be rational systems with language, but that expressions of these systems in language are myths rather than true reflections of reality. "Catch-22, accordingly, points out the discrepancy between our myths and our realities and suggests that we would do better to stop creating rational systems and to start living in tune with an irrational universe."

"For many readers Catch-22 *quickly became a touchstone—an anticipation, explanation, and confirmation of the anti-military and anti-government sentiments that blossomed during the Vietnam years."*

—David Streitfeld

The work also has "a basic narrative structure," in the words of Clinton S. Burhans in *Twentieth Century Literature*, although this structure is not readily apparent. Heller has created "an ingenious fusion of time planes into the simultaneity of existential time, a fusion entirely consistent with what seems to be the fundamental existential theme of the work." Robert Merrill stated in *Studies in American Fiction* that "the book's more puzzling features—its bewildering chronology, its repetitiveness, its protagonist's belated change of heart—all fit together to advance Heller's radical protest against the modern social order. What appears to be formless chaos is in fact a brilliant strategy to expose not only the worst excesses of the modern bureaucracy but also the complacent acceptance of this system on the part of everyone involved, including Heller's readers. The structural complexity of *Catch-22* thus embodies Heller's meaning more thoroughly than even his admirers have been willing to suggest."

Inge Kutt elaborated on the chronological structure of *Catch-22* in the *Dictionary of Literary Biography*, stating that the structure "is reassimilated through his [Heller's] use of *deja vu*. The characters in *Catch-22* have the impression that what is happening to them has happened before. The reader, like the characters, also experiences *deja vu*. . . . This technique has caused many critics to accuse Heller of needless repetition." Quoting James Mellard, Kutt goes on to say that "'*deja vu* is actually neither simply repetitive nor redundant but is rather complexly incremental and progressive. . . . The characters, both real and symbolic . . . gradually gain in significance, a thematic concept such as Catch-22 also changes in meaning as it recurs.' The use of *deja vu* serves as a guideline through the maze of plot, characters and chronology."

As radically different as *Catch-22* was when it emerged on the American literary scene in the 1960s, some critics noted the work's similarity to other classics of American literature. In the *CEA Critic*, Walter R. McDonald compared Yossarian to other rebels in American literature, including the title character of *Huckleberry Finn* and Hester Prynne in *The Scarlet Letter*. "In Heller's intention, Yossarian is not copping out, is not taking the easy way, but rather 'moved off dead center finally' and in his peculiar world of horror and absurdity, he is ironically a 'traditional' American rebel, like so many other cultural mavericks who have made their separate, principled peace."

Other critics have gone beyond American literature to see the relationship between *Catch-22* and universal classics. As early as 1962, Julian Mitchell recognized the epic quality of *Catch-22* and its similarity to the work of Homer. *Catch-22* "is, in fact, a surrealist Iliad, with a lunatic high Command instead of gods, and a coward for hero." Writing in *Critique* in 1970, Victor J. Milne also argued that the work's plot "offers notable parallels to the Iliad," and that "Heller makes use of some of the generic devices of the epic form." Heller "uses the mock-epic form to reject the pre-Christian (and sub-Christian) values of the military-economic complex, whose competitive ethic is another manifestation of the ancient heroic code." Marcus K. Billson III, in *Arizona Quarterly*, observed a similarity between Yossarian and Adam in the Biblical story of Adam and Eve. "Heller's allusion to Genesis suggests the lineaments of an intertextuality between the Bible and the novel, which exists within and without literary history: within, since the novel derives meaning and irony from its reference to Genesis; without, because the novel undermines the first text's historical status as it promotes a new parable of origins. . . ."

By the early 1980s, critics began to assess the role of *Catch-22* in the meeting of history and litera-

ture. "*Catch-22* (1961) has probably contributed more than any other work to the literary apprehension of war during the last two decades," explained Jeffrey Walsh in *American War Literature 1914 to Vietnam*. Others began to approach *Catch-22* as a cultural artifact, and to view its success as a key to understanding recent American history. Morris Dickstein, for one, remarked in *Gates of Eden: American Culture in the Sixties*, "I think the popular success of the book can be attributed to the widespread spiritual revulsion in the sixties against many of our most sacrosanct institutions, including the army; to which our leaders replied by heightening just those things that had caused the disgust in the first place, especially the quality of fraud, illusion, and manipulation in our public life. Just as the response to war-protest was escalation and the solution to the failures of the bombing was more bombing, so the push for more honesty in public debate was met by more public relations and bigger lies."

Writing in the Wake of a Classic Work

After the success of *Catch-22*, Heller was able to write full time. Although he made surprisingly little on the sales of the novel, he did earn enough to live on the Upper West Side of Manhattan, and in the Hamptons. In addition to teaching at universities, he worked on a number of projects, including movie scripts for *Sex and the Single Girl*, *Casino Royale*, and *Dirty Dingus Magee*. Heller wrote *We Bombed in New Haven*, a play containing themes and settings from *Catch-22*; it was produced at the Yale School of Drama and later, on Broadway. The play met with poor reviews. Heller next adapted *Catch-22* itself for the stage as *Catch-22: A Dramatization*. This play, published in 1971, presents the story in the novel in chronological order, and omits several characters and scenes. Heller also worked on a second novel. Heller's fans got a peek at it when a selection was published in *Esquire* in 1966.

Something Happened, narrated by its protagonist, Bob Slocum, is composed of "ruminations, memories, gags, guilts, self-analysis, fears-at-the-abyss," as Eliot Fremont-Smith observed in *New York*. Slocum, an executive, is unhappy at work and at home in Connecticut, yet he is terribly afraid of losing his job and cannot relate to his family. He finds that he does not know how to want, or what to want; his life is monotonous, superficial, and unfulfilling. At the conclusion of the long novel, Slocum's son is hit by a car. Rushing to his side, Slocum sees the boy's terror and, for comfort, embraces him. The boy dies, not from his wounds, but from asphyxiation at his father's hands.

Critics and fans had very high expectations for Heller's second novel. Some of the critics who had waited eagerly for *Something Happened* worked through its some six hundred pages only to express confusion or disappointment afterward. "*Something Happened* has none of the joyous energy of *Catch-22*, nor much of its comic invention. It is a novel of bleak landscapes and shadowy characters. It begins in anxiety and ends in despair. Nothing happens in *Something Happened*," lamented Joseph Epstein in the *Washington Post Book World*. "The new book is as morose, slow, and thoughtless as the first was morose, fast, and buoyant," argued Walter Clemons in *Newsweek*. "*Something Happened* . . . is a monstrous effort to make literature out of pettiness," wrote Calvin Bedient in the *Nation*.

Other critics found more merit in *Something Happened*. According to Kurt Vonnegut, Jr., writing in the *New York Times Book Review*, the book is "splendidly put together and hypnotic to read." Vonnegut added that if *Something Happened* is "astonishingly pessimistic," it is because the work "is at all points precisely what" Heller "hoped it would be." Heller's message, "baldly" related, is that "many lives, judged by the standards of the people who live them, are simply not worth living." William Kennedy stated in the *New Republic* that the work "is exhaustive and exhausting, a major contemporary novel." He explained, "The book is a baring of what Heller thinks is everybody's soul, at least everybody who shares the values of the corporate state, the company scramble, the family debacle." Noting that the "principal theme" of the book may be "the bankruptcy of the contemporary middle-class American experience," George J. Searles asserted in *Critique* that "in one important respect" *Something Happened* is "a better book" than *Catch-22*. "*Something Happened* is actually far more sophisticated in its method. Heller has turned from hyperbole to implication; in opting for a less strident, less obvious statement, he has produced a more mature work." Eliot Fremont-Smith wrote in *New York* that the novel was "very fine, wrenchingly depressing. . . . It gnaws at one, slowly and almost

nuzzlingly at first, mercilessly toward the end. It hurts. It gives the willies."

In Heller's third novel, *Good As Gold*, the writer again calls upon his own experience. This time, however, his protagonist is Jewish, a man who, like Heller, grew up on Coney Island. As Malcolm Bradbury has explained in the *Observer*, Heller tells "two stories: a tale about one of the most massively anguishing of all fictional Jewish families, and a tale about the absurdist world of contemporary American politics." Bruce Gold is a middle-aged English professor and well-known writer. As Gold begins to question his accomplishments and his personal life, he is offered a position in the White House by an old graduate school friend. As Gold works his way into the fashionable political scene, the book takes up life in Washington. "As a send-up of Capital conventions and clichés, *Good As Gold* is sometimes funny," wrote Benjamin DeMott in *Atlantic Monthly*.

Some critics found much to fault in *Good As Gold*. Pearl K. Bell, writing in *Commentary*, argued that Heller did not take the time to understand what it meant to be Jewish, and had little business writing about it or Washington. Both of these "targets" of Heller's "free-floating cynicism," according to Bell, "demand the kind of complex understanding and moral courage that are beyond his [Heller's] grasp, and they have stubbornly resisted his glib antics and crude literary tricks." Eliot Fremont-Smith was troubled by the presentation of Jews in *Good As Gold*, and wrote that they "are uniformly portrayed as sniveling, deceitful, self-aggrandizing, and ambitious beyond their worth." He concluded, "*Good as Gold* doesn't deal with evil, it merely gets off on it." Other reviewers, like Charles Berryman, writing in *Chicago Review*, found the work redeeming. "*Good as Gold* is a major step forward in Heller's career. The novel combines many of the virtues of his first two books while avoiding most of their faults. . . . *Good as Gold* is unified and coherent . . . [and] reveals a steady wit that is fully integrated with character and situation." He concluded, "After more international fame than any first novel could possibly support, after the great suspense and disappointment with his second book, Heller has at last found his assured place among the great comic writers of modern literature."

Heller's fourth book also dealt with Jewishness. *God Knows* is the story of Kind David, told by

If you enjoy the works of Joseph Heller, you may also want to check out the following books and films:

Alice Munro, *Open Secrets: Stories,* 1994.
Kurt Vonnegut, *Slaughterhouse-Five,* 1969.
Thomas Wolfe, *Electric Kool-Aid Acid Test,* 1968.
One Flew Over the Cuckoo's Nest, starring Jack Nicholson, 1975.

the King himself as he lies on his deathbed. The biblical elements of King David's life, told in flashbacks, are embellished with Heller's imagination, humor, commentary, and anachronisms. The work is replete with jokes. David, according to *Commonweal* reviewer Joel Wells, is seen by Heller as "the first stand-up Jewish comedian, a forerunner of Mel Brooks, Lennie Bruce, and Woody Allen, and God is his straight man." Al J. Sperone noted in *VLS* that the story Heller retells in *God Knows* "parallels parts of Heller's last two novels, and David on his deathbed now joins Heller's ongoing dynasty of bummed-out middle-aged men. . . . The structure of *God Knows* recalls *Something Happened,* which itself was an echo and extension of the dying-Snowden episodes of *Catch-22.* . . . While that plot [in *God Knows*] moves slowly forward, the narrative circles obsessively around a few central episodes from the past."

Noting that Heller "doesn't so much tell a story as peel it like an onion," Mordecai Richler of the *New York Times Book Review* argued that the work, "like all truly grand comic novels . . . is ultimately sad." "Clearly Mr. Heller is dancing at the top of his form again," asserted Richler. Though Richard Cohen of the *Washington Post Book World* found the book to be "entertaining, in places very funny, in still other places touching, even occasionally wise," he added that the *Good as Gold* "does not quite work . . . it's somewhat repetitive, often annoying, sometimes in bad taste, a bit at odds with itself, more of a nightclub schtick than a novel and by no means the classic that *Catch-22* was. . . ."

Heller, who was partially and temporarily paralyzed by Guillain-Barré syndrome in 1981, wrote a book with his friend Speed Vogel about the ex-

perience. The book recounts how Heller suffered, especially as he was in the process of divorcing his first wife, how his friends helped him, and how he fell in love with the nurse who cared for him. In *New York,* Rhoda Koenig remarked that the "point seems to be to show us what a great guy Joe Heller is, and what a fine friend he has in Speed. In this it fails. . . ." Campbell Geeslin, writing in *People,* offered a different view: "*No Laughing Matter,* strangely enough, is a collection of dark guffaws."

A Sequel to *Catch-22*

Heller signed a contract with Putnam Publishing Group for his next novel, *Picture This,* and a sequel to *Catch-22. Picture This,* whose characters include the painter Rembrandt, the Greek philosophers Socrates and Plato, and various U.S. presidents, received negative reviews. As Streitfeld reported in *New York,* the "book fizzled—selling so poorly, Heller says, that for the first time in his career he didn't earn out his advance." The contract with Putnam was dissolved, but Heller wrote the sequel to *Catch-22* anyway. Eventually, the book was published by Simon & Schuster as *Closing Time.*

Barbara Gelb of the *New York Times Book Review* explained that in this book, "fans of 'Catch-22' will find Yossarian once again fearfully trying to sidestep his own imminent death. When the story opens, the twice-divorced Yossarian is living uneasily in Manhattan, knowing that this time there's no possible way out." Yossarian now works as an ethics consultant for M & M Enterprises & Associates, "the giant conglomerate founded during the war by his old comrades Milo Minderbinder and ex-PFC Wintergreen, those dark angels of capitalism," as Thomas R. Edwards noted in the *New York Review of Books.* "But worldly success has made Yossarian no happier than he ever was."

The story in *Closing Time,* like those in Heller's other novels, is told with numerous flashbacks. Several characters are portrayed in addition to Yossarian. The focus this time, however, is on a Jewish character, Sammy Singer, who appears to be the small, unnamed, and fainting tailgunner in *Catch-22.* Other characters in the work include Sammy's friend Lew, and from *Catch-22,* Wintergreen, Milo, and Chaplain Tappman. The action takes place on Coney Island (before and after

World War II), New York (a hellish, baroque wedding scene is set in the Port Authority Bus Terminal), and Washington, D.C. As the characters deal with health problems and with their children, they confront their memories and wrestle with the fear of death. The novel concludes as Yossarian is forced to make a moral decision involving his own demise as the world ends in a nuclear disaster.

"To its imaginative credit if not its formal advantage, *Closing Time* accommodates a directness and depth of feeling that *Catch-22* largely excluded," observed Edwards. Christopher Buckley of the *New Yorker* wrote, "For all its flaws, 'Closing Time' is a summing up by one of the last of the great writers of the Second World War generation." He concluded, "As the critics sharpen their knives and aim for the dotted lines marked 'Cut here,' it seems we can afford to celebrate *Catch-22*'s thirty-third anniversary by welcoming Yossarian, Sammy, Milo, Lew, Wintergreen, and Chaplain Tappman, even as we take leave of them, and give credit to their creator, who has given us such consequential imperfections, and has dared not to leave well enough alone." "What is clear is that Mr. Heller has invested a lot of himself in a few of his characters, enough to give them the third dimension usually absent from his fiction. One has the sense that, like Yossarian, he is determined to live forever in his writing, or at least to die trying," concluded William H. Pritchard in the *New York Times Book Review*.

In 1997, Heller published the autobiographical work, *Now and Then: From Coney Island to Here*. At seventy-four years of age, Heller may indeed write another novel. As he once told Gelb, "I have nothing else to do." Whether or not Heller writes another book full of jarring humor, disturbing scenes, and anti-heroes, he remains a celebrated hero of American literature.

■ Works Cited

Bedient, Calvin, "Demons Ordered from Sears," *Nation*, October 19, 1974, pp. 377-78.

Bell, Pearl K., "Heller & Malamud, Then & Now," *Commentary*, June, 1979, pp. 71-75.

Berryman, Charles, "Heller's Gold," *Chicago Review*, Spring, 1981, pp. 108-18.

Billson, Marcus K. III, "The Un-Minderbinding of Yossarian: Genesis Inverted in 'Catch-22'," *Arizona Quarterly*, Winter, 1980, pp. 315-29.

Bradbury, Malcolm, "Catch-79," *Observer*, April 29, 1979, p. 37.

Brustein, Robert, "Catch-22," *The Critic as Artist: Essays on Books 1920-1970*, edited by Gilbert A. Harrison, 1972, pp. 47-54.

Bryant, Jerry H., *The Open Decision: The Contemporary American Novel and Its Intellectual Background*, The Free Press, 1970, pp. 156-59, 163.

Buckley, Christopher, "Götterdämmerung-22," *New Yorker*, October 10, 1994, pp. 104-9.

Burhans, Clinton S., "Spindrift and the Sea: Structural Patterns and Unifying Elements in *Catch-22*," *Twentieth Century Literature*, October, 1973, pp. 239-49.

Review of *Catch-22, Daedalus: Journal of the American Academy of Arts and Sciences*, Winter, 1963, pp. 155-65.

Clemons, Walter, "Comedy of Fear," *Newsweek*, October 14, 1974, pp. 116, 118.

Cohen, Richard, "Old Testament Time Warp," *Washington Post Book World*, September 30, 1984, pp. 1-2.

DeMott, Benjamin, "Heller's Gold and a Silver Sax," *Atlantic Monthly*, March, 1979, pp. 129-32.

Dickstein, Morris, "Black Humor and History: The Early Sixties," *Gates of Eden: American Culture in the Sixties*, 1977, Penguin Books, 1989, pp. 91-127.

Edwards, Thomas R., "Catch-23," *New York Review of Books*, October 26, 1994, pp. 20, 22-23.

Epstein, Joseph, "Joseph Heller's Milk Train: Nothing More to Express," *Washington Post Book World*, October 6, 1974, pp. 1-2.

Felty, Darren, critical essay in *Novels for Students*, Volume 1, edited by Diane Telgen, Gale, 1997, pp. 106-8.

Fremont-Smith, Eliot, "Heller's Hell," *New York*, September 30, 1974, pp. 78-79.

Fremont-Smith, Eliot, "Kvetch-22," *Village Voice*, March 5, 1979, pp. 74-75.

Geeslin, Campbell, review of *No Laughing Matter*, *People*, March 10, 1986, pp. 22-23.

Gelb, Barbara, "Catch-22 Plus: A Conversation With Joseph Heller," *New York Times Book Review*, August 28, 1994, pp. 3, 18.

Hasley, Louis, "Dramatic Tension in *Catch-22*," *Midwest Quarterly*, January, 1974, pp. 190-97.

Heller, Joseph, *Catch-22*, Simon & Schuster, 1961.

Kennedy, William, "Endlessly Honest Confession," *New Republic*, October 19, 1974, pp. 17-19.

Koenig, Rhoda, review of *No Laughing Matter*, *New York*, March 3, 1986, pp. 122-24.

Kutt, Inge, "Joseph Heller," *Dictionary of Literary Biography*, Volume 2: *American Novelists Since World War II*, edited by Jeffrey Helterman and Richard Layman, Gale, 1978.

Mailer, Norman, "Some Children of the Goddess," *Contemporary American Novelists*, edited by Harry T. Moore, Southern Illinois University Press, 1964, pp. 3-31.

McDonald, Walter R., "He Took Off: Yossarian and the Different Drummer," *CEA Critic*, November, 1973, pp. 14-16.

Merrill, Robert, "The Structure and Meaning of 'Catch-22'," *Studies in American Fiction*, Autumn, 1986, pp. 139-52.

Milne, Victor J., "Heller's 'Bologniad': A Theological Perspective on 'Catch-22'," *Critique: Studies in Modern Fiction*, 1970, pp. 50-69.

Mitchell, Julian, "Under Mad Gods," *Spectator*, June 15, 1962, p. 801.

Olderman, Raymond M., "The Grail Knight Departs," *Beyond the Waste Land: A Study of the American Novel in the Nineteen-Sixties*, Yale University Press, 1972, pp. 94-116.

Pearson, Carol, "'Catch-22,' and the Debasement of Language," *CEA Critic*, November, 1974.

Pritchard, William H., "Yossarian Redux," *New York Times Book Review*, September 25, 1994, pp. 1, 36-37.

Richler, Mordecai, "He Who Laughs Last," *New York Times Book Review*, September 23, 1984.

Searles, George J., "'Something Happened': A New Direction for Joseph Heller," *Critique: Studies in Modern Fiction*, 1977, pp. 74-81.

Searles, George J., "Joseph Heller," *Dictionary of Literary Biography*, Volume 28: *Twentieth-Century American-Jewish Fiction Writers*, edited by Daniel Walden, Gale, 1984, pp. 101-7.

Sperone, Al J., "Maybe He's Just Like His Father," *VLS*, October, 1984, pp. 6-7.

Stern, Richard G., "Bombers Away," *New York Times Book Review*, October 22, 1961, p. 50.

Streitfeld, David, "Catch-23," *New York*, September 12, 1994, pp. 100, 102-5.

Vonnegut, Kurt, Jr., *New York Times Book Review*, October 6, 1974.

Walsh, Jeffrey, "Towards Vietnam: Portraying Modern War," *American War Literature 1914 to Vietnam*, Macmillan Press Limited, 1982, pp. 185-207.

Wells, Joel, "A Psaltery of One Liners," *Commonweal*, October, 1984, pp. 561-62.

■ For More Information See

BOOKS

Aichinger, Peter, *The American Soldier in Fiction, 1880-1963*, Iowa State University Press, 1975.

Bier, Jesse, *The Rise and Fall of American Humor*, Holt, 1968.

Friedman, Bruce Jay, editor, *Black Humor*, Bantam, 1965.

Kazin, Alfred, *The Bright Book of Life: American Novelists and Storytellers from Hemingway to Mailer*, Little, Brown, 1973.

Keegan, Brenda M., *Heller: A Reference Guide*, 1978.

Moore, Harry T., editor, *American Dreams, American Nightmares*, Southern Illinois University Press, 1970.

Nagel, James, editor, *Critical Essays on Joseph Heller*, Hall, 1984.

Pinsker, Sanford, *Understanding Joseph Heller*, University of South Carolina Press, 1991.

Potts, Stephen W., *From Here to Absurdity: The Moral Battlefields of Joseph Heller*, Borgo Press, 1982.

Scotto, Robert M., editor, *A Critical Edition of Catch-22*, Delta, 1973.

Seed, David, *The Fiction of Joseph Heller: Against the Grain*, Macmillan, 1989.

Whitbread, Thomas B., editor, *Seven Contemporary Authors*, University of Texas Press, 1966.

PERIODICALS

America, October 26, 1974.

Detroit Free Press, March 18, 1979.

Life, January 1, 1968.

Harper's Bazaar, September, 1988, pp. 260-63.

Los Angeles Times Book Review, May 7, 1995, p. 1.

New York Times Book Review, February 15, 1998, p. 32.

Playboy, June, 1975.

Publishers Weekly, August 1, 1994, p. 69; December 8, 1997, p. 60.

Time, September 24, 1984, pp. 74-76; October 3, 1994, p. 80.

Times Literary Supplement, October 21, 1994, p. 21.

Writer's Digest, December, 1981, pp. 21-28.

Yale Review, Summer, 1975.*

—*Sketch by R. Garcia-Johnson*

Jon Krakauer

■ Personal

Born in Brookline, MA, in 1954; son of Lewis Krakauer (a physician) and an art teacher; married Linda Moore, 1980. *Education:* Attended Hampshire College, MA, in the early 1970s. *Hobbies and other interests:* Mountain climbing.

■ Addresses

Home—Seattle, WA. *Office*—c/o Villard Publishers, 201 East 50th St., New York, NY 10022.

■ Career

Freelance journalist. Contributing editor to *Outside* magazine. Worked previously as a carpenter and a commercial fisherman.

■ Awards, Honors

National Magazine Award nominee, for an article that formed the basis of *Into the Wild*.

■ Writings

Eiger Dreams: Ventures among Men and Mountains (essay collection), Lyons and Burford, 1990.
(Photographer) David Roberts, *Iceland: Land of the Sagas* (travelogue), Abrams, 1990.
Into the Wild (nonfiction), Villard, 1996.
Into Thin Air: A Personal Account of the Mount Everest Disaster (nonfiction), Villard, 1997.

■ Adaptations

Into Thin Air was adapted for television by TriStar Television and broadcast on ABC-TV, 1997, and into an audiocassette read by Krakauer, BDD, 1997.

■ Sidelights

"Straddling the top of the world, one foot in Tibet and the other in Nepal, I cleared the ice from my oxygen mask, hunched a shoulder against the wind, and stared absently at the vast sweep of earth below. I understood on some dim, detached level that it was a spectacular sight. I'd been fantasizing about this moment, and the release of emotion that would accompany it, for many months. But now that I was finally here, standing on the summit of Mount Everest, I just couldn't summon the energy to care," writes Jon Krakauer in his "Into Thin Air" account for *Outside* magazine, later speculating: "Reaching the top of Everest is supposed to trigger a surge of intense elation; against long odds, after all, I had just attained a goal I'd coveted since childhood. But the summit was really only the halfway point. Any impulse I might have felt toward self-congratulation was immediately extinguished by apprehension about the long, dangerous descent that lay ahead."

Krakauer was right to feel apprehension; as he began his descent down Everest a winter storm invaded the mountain top, stranding several of the climbers who had reached the summit after him. Lucky to make it back to camp in the diminished visibility caused by the storm and the darkness of descending dusk, Krakauer stumbled into his tent, thinking the others would be back soon. It wasn't until several hours later that he learned of the life-and-death struggle taking place further up the mountain, a struggle that ended with the deaths of eight climbers. Haunted by this tragedy and his role in it, Krakauer first wrote the *Outside* article for which he was sent on the commercially-guided Everest expedition. When this format wasn't enough to do the tragic story justice or to bring its author the peace he sought, Krakauer expanded it into the bestselling book *Into Thin Air: A Personal Account of the Mount Everest Disaster*.

"I guess I don't try to justify climbing, or defend it, because I can't," relates Krakauer in a discussion of *Into Thin Air* with Mark Bryant for *Outside*. "There's no way to defend it," he continues, "even to yourself, once you've been involved in something like this disaster. And yet I've continued to climb. I don't know what that says about me or the sport other than the potential power it has. What makes climbing great for me, strangely enough, is this life and death aspect. It sounds trite to say, I know, but climbing isn't just another game. It isn't just another sport. It's life itself."

Climbing and other risk-taking activities became a part of Krakauer's life at a young age. Born in Brookline, Massachusetts, in 1954, Krakauer was only two when he moved with his family to Corvallis, Oregon, experiencing his first climb a few years later at the age of eight. Krakauer's father, who led his son up Oregon's 10,000-foot South Sister, was acquainted with Willi Unsoeld, a member of the first American expedition to Everest in 1963. Thus Krakauer's heroes became Unsoeld and his fellow-climber Tom Hornbein,

and his dream became the Everest Summit. "I'd had this secret desire to climb Everest that never left me from the time I was nine and Tom Hornbein and Willi Unsoeld . . . made it in '63," Krakauer admits to Bryant. "They were my childhood heroes, and Everest was always a big deal to me, though I buried the desire until *Outside* called."

Between his early dreams of Everest and his actual ascent of the mountain Krakauer made several other climbs that eventually led to a writing career. It was while attending Hampshire College in Massachusetts during the early 1970s that Krakauer was introduced to Alaska by climbing writer David Roberts. "I became this climbing

In this 1996 work, Krakauer traces the life of Chris McCandless, a naive young adventurer who starved to death in the Alaskan wilderness.

bum," recalls Krakauer in a *People* interview with William Plummer. "I worked as a carpenter in Boulder, Colo., five months of the year, climbed the rest." Toward the end of the 1970s he met Linda Moore, a student at the University of Colorado at Denver, and married her three years later. Also a climber at one point in her life, Linda believed Krakauer would quit the risky sport, but he found himself unable to do so. As Krakauer explains in an *Outside Online* interview with Jane Bromet, ". . . when we got married I promised I'd quit climbing, and a few years later when I started climbing again I came within a millimeter of wrecking our marriage. So, then we went through a bunch of years where climbing was a big issue. Now it is less of an issue. It is how I make my living, to no small degree. . . . It's a huge part of who I am, and I wouldn't be a writer if it wasn't for climbing and Linda understands that and she accepts it."

Writing and climbing first mixed for Krakauer back in 1974 when he climbed the Alaskan Arrigetch Peaks in the Brooks Range, making three ascents of previously unexplored peaks. These accomplishments prompted the American Alpine Club to request an article for its journal; it was the first article Krakauer ever wrote. Three years later his first income-generating article, on climbing the Devil's Thumb, was published in the British magazine *Mountain.* With the encouragement and advice of Moore and Roberts (his climbing partner and writing mentor), Krakauer learned the craft of writing query letters and began pursuing the career of a freelance writer; in 1983 he quit his carpentry job and wrote full time.

"I have never received any formal training as a writer," Krakauer admits in an *Outside Online* question and answer session. "I have always been a voracious reader, however, and whenever I read something that moves me, I re-read it many times to try and figure out how its author has worked his or her magic. . . . Like any craft, the harder and longer you work at your writing, the more likely you are to get better at it." While trying to hone his new craft, Krakauer wrote several different kinds of articles that drew on his past experiences; since he had been a carpenter he wrote about architecture for *Architectural Digest,* and having been a commercial fisherman he queried *Smithsonian* about penning an article on a commercial fishery in Alaska, which they accepted. "I was setting quotas that I would write ten query

letters a week, and I definitely worked hard, but I got lucky," he observes in an online *Bold Type* interview. "Because I wanted to pay the rent, I didn't have any grandiose ambitions of being an artiste; I wanted to pay the . . . bills, so I worked really hard."

As his new career progressed, however, Krakauer found himself focusing on outdoor subjects more than any others. "The problem is that none of them have captured my interest as much as the outdoor pieces," he observes in his *Bold Type* interview. "The pieces I've written for *Outside* magazine are definitely my best work, and they're virtually all about the outdoors." Krakauer's first book, *Eiger Dreams: Ventures among Men and Mountains,* published in 1990, is a collection of several magazine articles originally published in *Outside* and *Smithsonian.* While describing his experiences climbing Mt. McKinley, the North Face of the Eiger in Switzerland, and many others, Krakauer attempts to answer the question of why anyone would want to risk his life climbing a mountain. "The reader who knows little about climbing will learn much from *Eiger Dreams,* but Mr. Krakauer has taken the literature of mountains onto a higher ledge," maintains Tim Cahill in the *New York Times Book Review.* "His snow-capped peaks set against limitless blue skies present problems that inspire irrefutable human experiences: fear and triumph, damnation and salvation. There is beauty in his mountains beyond that expressed in conventional sermons. His reverence is earned, and it's entirely genuine."

An Alaskan Mystery

The exploration of the impulse that drives risk-taking is the major thread that ties all of Krakauer's books together. In 1992 *Outside* magazine asked him to write about the life and death of twenty-four-year-old Christopher McCandless, an honors graduate whose admiration of Leo Tolstoy, the Russian author and social reformer, prompted him to shed all of his worldly possessions and return to nature in search of transcendental experiences. Giving away his savings, McCandless adopted the name Alex Supertramp and wandered through the American West, eventually making his way to Alaska. There he hiked into the wild Alaskan bush near Denali National Park to live off the land; four months later he was found starved to death.

While researching McCandless's life, Krakauer found similarities in his own youthful adventures, similarities that helped him identify with this young man's life and death. "In 1977, when I was 23—a year younger than McCandless at the time of his death—I hitched a ride to Alaska on a fishing boat and set off alone into the backcountry to attempt an ascent of a malevolent stone digit called the Devils Thumb, a towering prong of vertical rock and avalanching ice, ignoring pleas from friends, family, and utter strangers to come to my senses," writes Krakauer in his *Outside* article "Death of an Innocent." He goes on to point out: "The fact that I survived my Alaskan adventure and McCandless did not survive his was largely a matter of chance; had I died on the Stikine Icecap in 1977 people would have been quick to say of me, as they now say of him, that I had a death wish. . . . I was stirred by the mystery of death; I couldn't resist stealing up to the edge of doom and peering over the brink. The view into that swirling black vortex terrified me, but I caught sight of something elemental in that shadowy glimpse, some forbidden, fascinating riddle."

Krakauer's fascination with McCandless continued long after the publication of this original article. "I was haunted by the particulars of the boy's starvation and by vague, unsettling parallels between events in his life and those in my own," explains Krakauer in his introduction to *Into the Wild*. And so Krakauer spent the next year tracing the complex and twisting path that led to McCandless's death, the result of which became the author's first full-length book: *Into the Wild*, published in 1996. "In trying to understand McCandless," continues Krakauer in his introduction, "I inevitably came to reflect on other, larger subjects as well: the grip wilderness has on the American imagination, the allure high-risk activities hold for young men of a certain mind, the complicated, highly charged bond that exists between fathers and sons."

Reconstructing McCandless's last two years of life, Krakauer drew from journal entries and postcards McCandless had written, as well as interviews with anyone who knew him during this time period. Thomas McNamee, writing in the *New York Times Book Review*, asserts that as Krakauer "picks through the adventures and sorrows of Chris McCandless's brief life, the story becomes painfully moving. Mr. Krakauer's elegantly constructed narrative takes us from the ghoulish moment of the hunters' discovery back through McCandless's childhood, the gregarious effusions and icy withdrawals that characterized his coming of age, and, in meticulous detail, the two years of restless roaming that led him to Alaska. The more we learn about him, the more mysterious McCandless becomes, and the more intriguing."

"I won't claim to be an impartial biographer," Krakauer states in his introduction to *Into the Wild*. "McCandless' strange tale struck a personal note that made a dispassionate rendering of the tragedy impossible. Through most of the book, I have tried—and largely succeeded, I think—to minimize my authorial presence. But let the reader be warned: I interrupt McCandless' story with fragments of a narrative drawn from my own youth. I do so in hope that my experiences will throw some oblique light on the enigma of Chris McCandless." McNamee maintains that Krakauer does just what he set out to do: "Christopher McCandless's life and his death may have been meaningless, absurd, even reprehensible, but by the end of *Into the Wild*, you care for him deeply."

Everest

Like *Into the Wild*, Krakauer's next book began as an article requested by *Outside* magazine—an article on the commercialization of Mt. Everest climbing expeditions. In order to tell the story, Krakauer became a member of a team guided by Rob Hall, a respected and experienced climber who had been on Everest seven times before. And so one of Krakauer's childhood dreams became a reality. "Secretly, I dreamed of climbing Everest myself one day; for more than a decade it remained a burning ambition," Krakauer confesses in his article "Into Thin Air," adding: "It wasn't until my mid-twenties that I abandoned the dream as a preposterous boyhood fantasy. Soon thereafter I began to look down my nose at the world's tallest mountain. . . . Despite the disdain I'd expressed for Everest over the years, when the call came to join Hall's expedition, I said yes without even hesitating to catch my breath. Boyhood dreams die hard, I discovered, and good sense be damned."

As he became acclimated to the altitude (higher than 17,600 feet) and culture of base camp, Krakauer met several of the other teams and

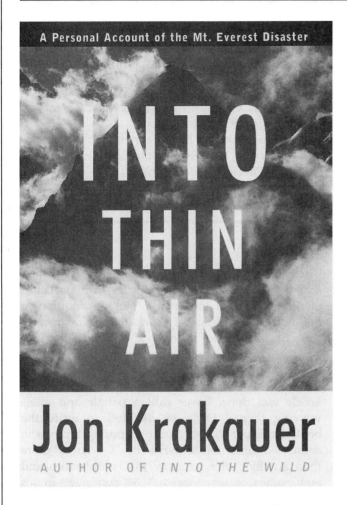

A Personal Account of the Mt. Everest Disaster

INTO THIN AIR

Jon Krakauer

AUTHOR OF INTO THE WILD

In this bestselling work, Krakauer recounts the events of May 1996, when a blinding snowstorm on Mt. Everest led to tragedy for several climbing teams.

climbers, commenting on them in his *Outside Online* interview with Bromet: "It's really appalling. There's a lot of inexperienced people here— and many people would say I'm one of them— and that's sort of scary. There's a lot of people here who shouldn't be here. And maybe I shouldn't be here." Krakauer notes that despite the guides and the Sherpas who would assist the climbers, the ascent would provide a formidable challenge. "I don't care how much you paid or what kind of guides or Sherpas you have, it's not going to be easy, I can tell that already. It demands determination and physical reserves. If you can get to the top of Everest, I say more power to you."

By the time summit day was upon him, Krakauer and his teammates had already made three trips (over the course of six weeks) above base camp, going approximately 2,000 feet higher each time. This was Hall's way of acclimating his team to the altitude, a method which he assured them would enable them to climb safely to the 29,028-foot summit. From the beginning, Hall planned May 10th as his team's summit day, mainly because the most favorable weather of the year was likely to fall on or around this date. This, of course, meant that other teams had their sights set on the same day, which could result in a dangerous gridlock on the summit ridge; so Hall and the other leaders held a meeting and assigned summit dates to the various groups. In the end, it was decided that Krakauer's team would share the May 10th date with Scott Fischer's team and all other groups (except the South African team, whose leader declared they would go to the top whenever they pleased) agreed to steer clear of the top of the mountain on this date.

Climbing with oxygen for the first time, Krakauer reached the South Col, the final camp from which his team would make its summit bid, on May 9th at one in the afternoon, several hours before the last stragglers on Fischer's team. By 11:35 p.m. on the night of May 9th, conditions were excellent and the teams left their tents on the South Col and headed toward the summit. The most important thing Hall had ingrained in his team was the predetermined turnaround time of one o'clock in the afternoon on May 10th: no matter how close you were to the summit at this time, you were to turn around and head back down.

During the ascent various members of both teams suffered from numerous problems, including hypoxia, blindness, and several bottlenecks along the climbing route. Despite these obstacles, on May 10th Krakauer arrived at the summit with two other climbers and began his descent at approximately 1:17 p.m., reaching the South Summit around three. As he continued down from this point, the first clouds began to move in and it began to snow; these weather conditions in combination with the diminishing light made it difficult to determine where the mountain ended and the sky began. The lower Krakauer went, the worse the weather became, but by 5:30 p.m. he was within 200 vertical feet of camp, making it down the final steep bulge of rock-hard ice without a rope and stumbling into his tent about a half hour later. At this point he was unaware that one teammate was already dead and that twenty-three others were in a life-and-death struggle to make it back to camp. The events that unfolded from there made heroes out of some, and are the reason that Krakauer has been unable to overcome his guilt for not having been able to do anything for the other climbers. In the end, a total of eight climbers died, including team leaders Fischer and Hall, and several others were severely injured.

Krakauer writes in "Into Thin Air," "Days later . . . people would ask why, if the weather had begun to deteriorate, had climbers on the upper mountain not heeded the signs? Why did veteran Himalayan guides keep moving upward, leading a gaggle of amateurs . . . into an apparent death trap?

"Nobody can speak for the leaders of the two guided groups involved, for both men are now dead. But I can attest that nothing I saw early on the afternoon of May 10 suggested that a murderous storm was about to bear down on us."

"Climbing mountains will never be a safe, predictable, rule-bound enterprise," muses Kra-kauer in "Into Thin Air." "It is an activity that idealizes risk-taking; its most celebrated figures have always been those who stuck their necks out the farthest and managed to get away with it. Climbers, as a species, are simply not distinguished by any excess of common sense. And that holds especially true for Everest climbers: When presented with a chance to reach the planet's highest summit, people are surprisingly quick to abandon prudence altogether." As proof of this, one need look no further than May 24th, just a couple weeks following the disaster Krakauer experienced; on this date the South African team launched its summit bid. One of the climbers, Bruce Herrod, fell far behind yet continued alone—past the frozen body of Fischer—to reach the summit at 5:00 p.m., where he found himself alone, tired, and out of oxygen. At 7:00 p.m. Herrod radioed camp a final time and was never heard from again; he is presumed to be dead. The desperate radio calls and deaths of the previous weeks had no effect on him during his quest for the summit.

Lasting Effects

Krakauer's Mt. Everest experience has had a deep, long-lasting effect on the writer. Upon his return he wrote his article for *Outdoor*, "Into Thin Air,"

If you enjoy the works of Jon Krakauer, you may also want to check out the following books and films:

Alden R. Carter, *Between a Rock and a Hard Place*, 1995.
Sebastian Junger, *The Perfect Storm : A True Story of Men Against the Sea*, 1997.
Gary Paulsen, *Hatchet*, 1987.
Ivy Ruckman, *No Way Out*, 1988.
Twister, starring Helen Hunt, 1996.

discovering only after it was already published that there were some discrepancies in his account of the events that took place. This, in addition to his incredible feelings of guilt, drove Krakauer to turn his story into a book, also titled *Into Thin Air*. "So writing this book became all I could think about; I was obsessing about it," explains Krakauer in his *Bold Type* interview. "Even after the article was done, I was calling people and interviewing them." Once he decided to write the book, Krakauer did so quickly, ignoring those who counseled him not to write it. "I wanted more than anything else to show the complexities and ambiguities of this tragedy," he continues in his *Bold Type* interview. "That it's not simple and it's not easy to assign blame, and it's rooted not in greed and the crassness of thrill-seeking or trophy hunting, but it's much deeper and more profound. The motives for people who climb Everest are, in some ways, noble, as misguided as they often are. It's wanting to reach beyond yourself. There's also a lot of hubris there and selfishness. . . . I just wanted to tell the story in its full complexity."

The resulting book generated much criticism from friends and families of the victims as well as other climbers who survived the expedition. They accuse Krakauer of being too judgmental of the actions of others, and of earning money off the tragedy of others. "In writing the book I tried very hard to recount the events truthfully, in an even-handed, sympathetic manner that did not sensationalize the tragedy or cause undue pain to friends and families of the victims," contends Krakauer in another *Outside Online* discussion. He also answers some of the other criticisms during his interview with Bryant: "Plenty of people have said to me, 'Who are you to assess someone else's role or lack of experience or skill?' But I'm a working journalist, and I was there, and I was there to do a job—to tell what happened as best I could. I certainly feel bad that some people are hurt by my assessments, but somebody needed to step up and tell what went on up there. Jesus, people died—a lot of people died."

Despite criticisms from those involved in the tragedy, *Into Thin Air* was well-received by both critics and readers, who kept the book on the bestseller list for weeks. "Every once in a while a work of nonfiction comes along that's as good as anything a novelist could make up," maintains James M. Clash in *Forbes*. "Krakauer's new book, *Into Thin Air*, fits the bill." Alastair Scott, writing for the *New York Times Book Review*, points out that with *Into Thin Air* Krakauer "has produced a narrative that is both meticulously researched and deftly constructed. Unlike the expedition, his story rushes irresistibly forward. But perhaps Mr. Krakauer's greatest achievement is his evocation of the deadly storm, his ability to re-create its effects with a lucid and terrifying intimacy." *Sports Illustrated* contributor Ron Fimrite similarly praises Krakauer's account: "In this movingly written book, Krakauer describes an experience of such bone-chilling horror as to persuade even the most fanatical alpinists to seek sanctuary at sea level. Not that they're likely to do so."

In this way, Krakauer gets across the all-consuming need for climbers to climb, a need he himself cannot shake even after this tragedy: he continues to climb mountains. "There's something about it that is important to me—for some of us it's an important antidote to modern life," Krakauer states in his interview with Bryant. "But climbing, for me, does have this transcendental quality, this ability to transport you, to enforce humility, to cause you to lose yourself and simply live in the moment. What other people may get from attending midnight mass, I still get from climbing. These are bad cliches, I know, but they're cliches that nevertheless ring true for me." And so through his climbing and writing Krakauer continues to work toward overcoming the tragedy of Everest. "Writing's a way to hang on to your sanity," he concludes in an *Entertainment Weekly* interview with David Hochman. "It's still very painful to me, but I think I've had an incredibly good life and have been lucky in climbing and writing. Now it's just a matter of getting the rest of my life under control again."

■ Works Cited

Bromet, Jane, "Summit Journal 1996: Jon Krakauer Turns His Eye—and Lungs—toward Everest," *Outside Online*, April 15, 1996.

Bryant, Mark, "Everest a Year Later: False Summit," *Outside*, May, 1997.

Cahill, Tim, "Travel," *New York Times Book Review*, June 10, 1990, p. 48.

Clash, James M., review of *Into Thin Air*, *Forbes*, May 19, 1997, p. 291.

Fimrite, Ron, review of *Into Thin Air*, *Sports Illustrated*, May 12, 1997, p. 18.

Hochman, David, "Cliff Notes," *Entertainment Weekly*, April 25, 1997, pp. 40-43.

Krakauer, Jon, "Death of an Innocent: How Christopher McCandless Lost His Way in the Wilds," *Outside*, January, 1993.

Krakauer, Jon, "Author's Note," *Into the Wild*, Villard, 1996.

Krakauer, Jon, "Into Thin Air," *Outside*, September, 1996.

Krakauer, Jon, responses to reader's questions, *Outside Online: The Lodge*, 1997, at http://outside.starwave.com/disc/guest/krak2/index.html.

Krakauer, Jon, "Summit Journal 1996: Jon Krakauer on Everest," *Outside Online*, May 23, 1997, at http://outside.starwave.com:80/peaks/features/transcript.html.

Krakauer, Jon, *Bold Type* interview at http://www.bookwire.com/boldtype/krakauer/read.article$1258.

McNamee, Thomas, "Adventures of Alexander Supertramp," *New York Times Book Review*, March 3, 1996, p. 29.

Plummer, William, "Everest's Shadow," *People*, June 2, 1997, pp. 53-57.

Scott, Alastair, review of *Into Thin Air*, *New York Times Book Review*, May 18, 1997, Section 7, p. 11.

■ For More Information See

PERIODICALS

Economist, September 6, 1997, pp. 17-18.

Library Journal, November 15, 1995, p. 96.

Newsweek, April 21, 1997, p. 76.

New York Times, May 6, 1997.

New York Times Book Review, December 7, 1997, p. 12.

Outside, February, 1996; May, 1997.

People, February 12, 1996, p. 35.

Publishers Weekly, February 20, 1990, p. 73; November 6, 1995, p. 76; May 5, 1997, p. 20; July 14, 1997, p. 18; September 22, 1997, p. 28.

School Library Journal, August, 1990, p. 178.*

—Sketch by Susan Reicha

Barbara Mertz

■ Personal

Also writes as as Barbara Michaels and Elizabeth Peters; born September 29, 1927, in Canton, IL; daughter of Earl D. (a printer) and Grace (a teacher; maiden name, Tregellas) Gross; married Richard R. Mertz (a professor of history), June 18, 1950 (divorced, 1968); children: Elizabeth Ellen, Peter William. *Education:* University of Chicago, Ph.B., 1947, M.A., 1950, Ph.D., 1952. *Hobbies and other interests:* Reading, needlework, cats, music, football.

■ Addresses

Home—Frederick, MD. *Agent*—Dominick Abel Literary Agency, 146 West 82nd St., Suite 1B, New York, NY 10024.

■ Career

Historian and writer. *Member:* American Crime Writers League, Egypt Exploration Society, American Research Council in Egypt, Society for the Study of Egyptian Antiquities, National Organization for Women.

■ Awards, Honors

Grandmaster award, Bouchercon, 1986; Agatha Award for best mystery novel of 1989, Malice Domestic Convention, for *Naked Once More*; D.H.L., Hood College, 1989.

■ Writings

ROMANTIC SUSPENSE NOVELS; UNDER PSEUDONYM BARBARA MICHAELS

The Master of Blacktower, Appleton, 1966.
Sons of the Wolf, Meredith Press, 1967, published as *Mystery on the Moors*, Paperback Library, 1968.
Ammie, Come Home, Meredith Press, 1968.
Prince of Darkness, Meredith Press, 1969.
The Dark on the Other Side, Dodd, 1970.
The Crying Child, Dodd, 1971.
Greygallows, Dodd, 1972.
Witch, Dodd, 1973.
House of Many Shadows, Dodd, 1974.
The Sea King's Daughter, Dodd, 1975.
Patriot's Dream, Dodd, 1976.
Wings of the Falcon, Dodd, 1977.
Wait for What Will Come, Dodd, 1978.
The Walker in the Shadows, Dodd, 1979.
The Wizard's Daughter, Dodd, 1980.

Someone in the House, Dodd, 1981.
Black Rainbow, Congdon and Weed, 1982.
Here I Stay, Congdon and Weed, 1983.
Dark Duet (includes *Ammie, Come Home* and *Prince of Darkness*), Congdon and Weed, 1983.
The Grey Beginning, Congdon and Weed, 1984.
Be Buried in the Rain, Atheneum, 1985.
Shattered Silk, Atheneum, 1986.
Search the Shadows, Atheneum, 1987.
Smoke and Mirrors, Simon and Schuster, 1989.
Into the Darkness, Simon and Schuster, 1990.
Vanish with the Rose, Simon and Schuster, 1992.
Houses of Stone, Simon and Schuster, 1993.
Stitches in Time, HarperCollins, 1995.
The Dancing Floor, HarperCollins, 1997.
The Game of Troy, HarperCollins, 1997.

MYSTERY NOVELS; UNDER PSEUDONYM ELIZABETH PETERS

The Jackal's Head, Meredith Press, 1968.
The Camelot Caper, Meredith Press, 1969.
The Dead Sea Cipher, Dodd, 1970.
The Night of 400 Rabbits, Dodd, 1971 (published in England as *Shadows in the Moonlight,* Coronet, 1975).
The Seventh Sinner ("Jacqueline Kirby" series), Dodd, 1972.
Borrower of the Night ("Vicky Bliss" series), Dodd, 1973.
The Murders of Richard III ("Jacqueline Kirby" series), Dodd, 1974.
Crocodile on the Sandbank ("Amelia Peabody" series), Dodd, 1975.
Legend in Green Velvet, Dodd, 1976 (published in England as *Ghost in Green Velvet,* Cassell, 1977).
Devil-May-Care, Dodd, 1977.
Street of the Five Moons ("Vicky Bliss" series), Dodd, 1978.
Summer of the Dragon, Dodd, 1979.
The Love Talker, Dodd, 1980.
The Curse of the Pharaohs ("Amelia Peabody" series), Dodd, 1981.
The Copenhagen Connection, Congdon and Lattes, 1982.
Silhouette in Scarlet ("Vicky Bliss" series), Congdon and Weed, 1983.
Die for Love ("Jacqueline Kirby" series), Congdon and Weed, 1984.
The Mummy Case ("Amelia Peabody" series), Congdon and Weed, 1985.
Lion in the Valley ("Amelia Peabody" series), Atheneum, 1986.
Trojan Gold ("Vicky Bliss" series), Atheneum, 1987.

Deeds of the Disturber ("Amelia Peabody" series), Atheneum, 1988.
Naked Once More ("Jacqueline Kirby" series), Warner Books, 1989.
The Last Camel Died at Noon ("Amelia Peabody" series), Warner Books, 1991.
The Snake, The Crocodile, and The Dog ("Amelia Peabody" series), Warner Books, 1992.
Night Train to Memphis ("Vicky Bliss" series), Warner Books, 1996.
The Hippopotamus Pool, Warner, 1996.

UNDER NAME BARBARA MERTZ

Temples, Tombs, and Hieroglyphs: The Story of Egyptology, Coward, 1964, new revised edition, Peter Bedrick, 1990.
Red Land, Black Land: The World of the Ancient Egyptians, Coward, 1966, new revised edition, Peter Bedrick, 1990.
(With Richard R. Mertz) *Two Thousand Years in Rome,* Coward, 1968.
Gertrude Käsebier: The Photographer and her Photographs, Abrams, 1992.

OTHER

Contributor of short stories to *Sisters in Crime,* edited by Marilyn Wallace, Berkeley, 1989.

■ **Adaptations**

Ammie, Come Home was broadcast by ABC-TV in 1969.

■ **Sidelights**

Barbara Mertz began her fiction-writing career in 1966. Since that time she has published dozens of mystery and suspense novels under the pseudonyms of Barbara Michaels and Elizabeth Peters. As Barbara Michaels, she creates romantic tales that involve suspense and the supernatural, and as Elizabeth Peters she is noted for humorous mysteries that often have a historical basis. During her career Mertz has remained one of the most prolific and best-loved writers of popular romance and suspense fiction. Dulcy Brainard commented in *Publishers Weekly* that all of Mertz's books feature "female protagonists who survive danger and solve mysteries with wit, intelligence, good humor and, usually, good fortune in romance." Deirdre Donahue noted in *USA Today* that "Few heroines are more bold—or hilarious—than the ones created by Barbara Mertz." Although Barbara Michaels is the more widely read of the two "authors," Elizabeth Peters has the most ardent following. In an interview in *Contemporary Authors (CA)*, Mertz commented, "I have more readers as Barbara Michaels, but I think Peters fans are more hard-core. They can quote chapter and verse. Sometimes when I speak in public, people will ask when someone in one of the books did something. My face goes totally blank, but someone in the audience generally knows the answer."

Asked about the fact that by writing under two pen names she has essentially three identities, Mertz replied, "We all present different faces to different people. Writing under the pseudonyms lets me do this in an official sort of way. And I'm rather proud of the fact, if I may brag a bit," Mertz continued, "that my three alter egos are so different from one another. I know a lot of other people do different series under different names, but I do think mine are quite different. This is wonderful, because it gives me a chance to be all the different people I really am." The author said that whether she writes a Michaels or a Peters book depends on her contract: ". . . at a certain point, a certain book is due for one publisher or another, and the next one happens to be either a Michaels or a Peters. What I do next depends on which book is due next. . . . I simply turn to the next one. Also, by that time I'm usually a little tired of being the person I've just been; I'm ready to switch to being silly after being serious or to taking up a more serious theme after I've been silly. It's worked out beautifully—so far, anyway."

Mertz was born in a small town in Illinois. In comments for *Something about the Author (SATA)* she recalled "thrilling" visits to her grandmother's farm nearby, where she fed the lambs, played with the other animals, and collected berries. When she was eight her family moved to Oak Park, a suburb of Chicago, Illinois. Mertz discovered her talent in a creative writing class at Oak Park-River Forest High School. In fact, a teacher once called her out of the classroom and asked if she had copied a sonnet titled "To a Book," which she had turned in for an assignment. Eventually the teacher realized Mertz had not plagiarized her work, an event Mertz fondly recalled in *SATA* as "the first time anyone took my writing seriously."

She did not return to writing for several years. Instead she majored in Egyptology in college, then went on to earn a Ph.D. in the field.

After Mertz was married she settled into being a housewife and mother; she and her husband, Richard R. Mertz, had two children. She found few opportunities to pursue a career in her highly specialized profession because her husband's work required the family to travel frequently. While they were living in Europe, however, Mertz became interested in history, architecture, and art. Once her children were in school she used her research materials as the basis for three nonfiction books. The first two, *Temples, Tombs, and Hieroglyphs: The Story of Egyptology* and *Red Land, Black Land: The World of the Ancient Egyptians,* stemmed from her interest in Egypt. The third, which she co-authored with her husband, was *Two Thousand Years in Rome.* She and her husband had also written several spy stories together in the 1950s, but none had ever been published. After completing the book on Rome, Mertz decided to try writing a romantic suspense novel, which was becoming a popular genre. The result was *The Master of Blacktower,* and it immediately found a publisher. In *SATA* she described the book as "very derivative." But it was also "very educational" because she "learned a lot about plotting and character development." Moreover, she discovered, "writing is hard work!"

Mertz and her husband were divorced in 1968, and she began writing full time to support her children. Since then she has published about two novels a year under the Barbara Michaels and Elizabeth Peters pen names. Both "authors" have faithful fans—young readers as well as adults—who look forward to each new Michaels or Peters novel. She gained early success as Barbara Michaels with *Ammie, Come Home.* The story opens with the heroine, Sara, coming to visit her Aunt Ruth, who is living in an old house in the Georgetown section of Washington, D. C. Briefly married years ago, Ruth rediscovers romance when Sara introduces her to Pat MacDougal, an anthropology professor. Sara also awakens ghosts in the house who were involved in tragic events during the 1780s. Sara and her boyfriend, along with Ruth and Pat, manage to lay the ghosts to rest. A reviewer for *Horn Book* praised the book for making "cries in the night, shadowy manifestations in the parlor, and possession by demons seem almost possible."

The Author as Barbara Michaels

A later Michaels novel, *Here I Stay*, also features a ghost in an old house. Andrea Torgeson and her brother Jim, who lost his leg in a car accident, have inherited a mansion in Maryland. They invest nearly all their money in turning the house into an inn. Their first guest is a writer named Martin Greenspan, who likes the place and decides to extend his stay. When Jim and Martin begin researching the history of the house, a ghost pays the level-headed Andrea a visit. Soon Andrea and Martin become romantically involved, and the novel culminates in a shocking tragedy. Priscilla Johnson noted in *School Library Journal* that the "themes explored in this fine story, as well as its fast-paced plot, make it especially suitable for YAs." A *Publishers Weekly* reviewer praised the characterization, calling *Here I Stay* "a very good ghost story" that goes "right to the heart of the dilemma of a woman who cannot help being overly possessive toward those she loves."

Michaels's novels *Shattered Silk* and *Into the Darkness* portray heroines who encounter terror in human form. In *Shattered Silk*, Georgetown is once again the setting as newly divorced Karen Nevitt moves back to her home in the city. After working for awhile in a vintage clothing shop, she makes plans to open her own store. By chance Karen meets a former boyfriend, Congressman Mark Brinckley. Then someone begins stalking her, and the story builds to an action-filled conclusion. Susan Penny predicted in *School Library Journal* that the book would keep young adult readers "engrossed until the final page." Similarly, a *Publishers Weekly* reviewer observed that Michaels "adroitly keeps the suspense mounting."

In the bestseller *Into the Darkness*, which Michaels wrote in 1990, Meg Venturi returns to her New England home. After unexpectedly inheriting a jewelry business from her recently deceased grandfather, she learns she has a co-owner named A. L. Riley. According to town rumors, Riley was responsible for her grandfather's death. As she readjusts to life in her hometown, Meg discovers shocking family secrets involving her father. In the process she comes to realize that her life is in danger, and she struggles to find the answers to mounting questions. Critics registered mixed responses to *Into the Darkness*. A *Publishers Weekly* reviewer, for instance, stated that "Memorable characters and complex mystery make this one of Michaels's best novels of romantic suspense." On the other hand, Denise Perry Donavin noted in *Booklist* that "Michaels has written far better suspense stories (such as *Shattered Silk*). . . ." During the 1990s Michaels continued her prolific output with several other novels, including *The Dancing Floor*, *The Walker in Shadows*, and *The Wizard's Daughter*.

Continued Success as Elizabeth Peters

Mertz has been equally successful and prolific as Elizabeth Peters. (She created the pen name by

A librarian must help solve a murder—and prevent another—in this 1984 mystery novel.

using the first names of her daughter and son.) Early Peters novels include *The Jackal's Head* and *The Camelot Capers,* which were followed by *The Dead Sea Cipher.* A popular work, it features the adventures of Dinah Van der Lyn, a minister's daughter and opera singer. While touring the Middle East, Dinah spends some time in Beirut, Lebanon. Since a woman cannot venture out at night alone, she is confined to her hotel. One evening she overhears an argument in Arabic in the room next door. Thus begins a whirlwind of events caused by the discovery of an ancient scroll and involving spies and counterspies—all pursuing Dinah. A *Publishers Weekly* reviewer commended the book for its "fine, authentic background [and] lots of thrills and romance." Mary Kent Grant wrote in *Library Journal,* "[*The Dead Sea Cipher*] is fun."

Mertz's most popular creation as Elizabeth Peters is Amelia Peabody Emerson. A plucky, fearless sleuth, Amelia is a proper Victorian Egyptologist who encounters adventure at every turn on archeological digs. When asked by *CA* whether Amelia resembles her, Mertz replied, "In fact, I have gotten to be more like Amelia than she has like me, which is a scary phenomenon. Since I started writing about her, I have taken on a lot of her characteristics. In a way she gave me the courage to speak my mind. She does too, and I admire that. I think that's the way people should be. I was Miss Mealymouth for the first forty years of my life. Now people laugh raucously when I say that, which I take as a great compliment."

Mertz conducts extensive research for all of her books, but she told *CA* she finds she does the most work for the Amelia novels: "Oddly enough, I do more research for the Amelia books, probably, than for any of the others, because of the historical background. I made the big mistake early on of tying myself down to a specific chronology," Mertz admitted. "Readers know exactly what year an Amelia story is set in, and I have to make very sure that I don't commit any anachronisms. You can't talk about the tomb of Tutankhamen when it wasn't discovered until twenty years later; that's an obvious one." She said there are other "little pitfalls along the way, and not just in archaeology." She must be concerned about historical accuracy: "There are all the societal activities and the inventions. When can I have Amelia start using a flashlight, for example?

When did they have field glasses? When can I mention a machine gun? It's wonderfully fascinating, but I work myself to death getting the Amelia books right."

In the first Amelia novel, the character is single. By the second she has married Radcliffe Emerson, an archeologist. With their son Ramses and cat Bastet she continues her adventures, which feature, in the words of Brainard, "Murder, intriguing archeological lore and, always, the frisson of ancient superstition." Amelia meets Radcliffe in *Crocodile on the Sandbank,* when she is traveling in Egypt with Evelyn Barton-Forbes. As Amelia and Evelyn journey up the Nile they encounter Radcliffe and his brother, Walter, who are on an

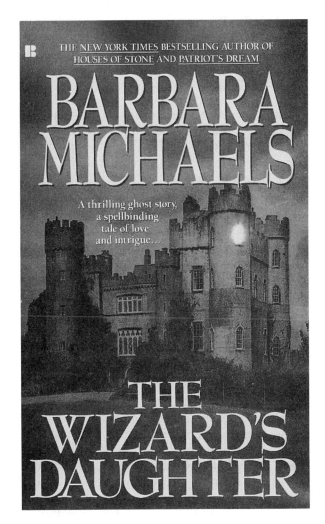

A young orphan with psychic powers discovers the dangers of knowing too much in this Barbara Michaels fantasy novel.

archeological dig. Walter falls in love with Evelyn, a mummy haunts the dig, and strange accidents take place. A *Publishers Weekly* reviewer stated that Peters is "at her best," calling *Crocodile on the Sandbank* a "brilliantly sustained, pulse-quickening narrative." A *Booklist* reviewer also enjoyed the work, commenting that "Well-realized setting and archaeological detail add to a delightful story. . . ." Jon L. Breen recommended the novel in *Wilson Library Bulletin* for its "charm and humor."

When Amelia next appears, in *The Curse of the Pharaohs*, she has married Radcliffe and has had a child—the squalling, bratty Ramses. They join a group of archeologists at a dig in the Valley of the Kings, which is plagued by a series of deaths. Locals are convinced "the curse of the pharaohs" has doomed the project. Amelia is not so sure, and she ignores Radcliffe's objections to investigate the mystery. A *Publishers Weekly* reviewer called the novel "high comedy," and Cathy Clancy observed in *School Library Journal* that Amelia is "credible and entertaining as a liberated late-Victorian lady."

The fifth novel in the Amelia Peabody series is *Deeds of the Disturber*, which continues Amelia's adventures with Radcliffe and the precocious Ramses. Offering exotic settings, colorful characters, a dizzying pace, and a wealth of archeological and Victorian details, the novel earned high marks from reviewers. Kevin Moore observed in the Chicago *Tribune Books* that "no one is better at juggling torches while dancing on a high wire than Elizabeth Peters." Annette DeMeritt predicted in *School Library Journal* that *Deeds of the Disturber* is "sure to delight Peters' fans."

The Last Camel Died at Noon is another work in the Amelia Peabody series. This time Amelia and her family are in the Sudan searching for a lost civilization in an oasis city ruled by descendants of an Egyptian dynasty. Amelia, Radcliffe, and Ramses are stranded in the Nubian Desert when their last camel dies. Unable to reach their archeological dig, they are caught up in a revolution. There is also a flashback to the Peabody-Emerson home in England, which introduces a subplot involving a missing British aristocrat. Naturally, Amelia must get to the bottom of things—*Locus* reviewer Scott Winnett called her "the most incredibly self-righteous serene busybody in fiction"—and she triggers a number of shocking revelations as they travel down the Nile. Although

---

If you enjoy the works of Barbara Mertz, you may also want to check out the following books and films:

Warren Adler, *Immaculate Deception*, 1991.
Joan Aiken, *The Haunting of Lamb House*, 1993.
Jim Lehrer, *Short List*, 1992.
Dead Again, starring Kenneth Branagh and Emma Thompson, 1991.

Winnett found Amelia to be a better sleuth than an adventurer, he considered the style "gloriously ripe, the dialog funny, and the plotting clever." Peter Theroux observed in the *New York Times Book Review* that a "mixture of the beautiful and unsettling . . . sustains *The Last Camel Died at Noon*." Praising the author's "knack for a light, even mock-trashy style," he concluded that her "wonderfully witty voice and her penchant for history lessons of the Nile both ancient and modern keep this high adventure moving for even the highest brows."

Another of Peters's sleuths is Jacqueline Kirby, a Coldwater College (Nebraska) librarian who has appeared in *The Seventh Sinner*, *The Love Talker*, and other novels. In *Die for Love*, Jacqueline attends a meeting of the Historical Romance Writers of the World in New York City. Needing a break from her job and her boyfriend in dreary Nebraska, she wants to learn how to write a romance novel and become rich. After two women are killed at the conference, however, Jacqueline cannot resist getting involved in the murder investigation. Noting that *Die for Love* is a satire of mystery and romance novels, a *Booklist* reviewer complimented Peters's "perfect mastery of each [genre]." A critic in *Publishers Weekly*, however, termed the novel "a mildly funny spoof of romance writers wrapped around a moderately interesting murder mystery," concluding that Jacqueline is "either a brashly quirky heroine or a brash pain in the neck."

Jacqueline Kirby returns in *Naked Once More*. Now an ex-librarian and successful romance novelist, she is chosen to write the sequel to a best-seller after the author, Kathleen Darcy, has been declared legally dead. Jacqueline goes to Kathleen's hometown in the Appalachian hills, where Kathleen disappeared, to write the novel. Soon Jacqueline is experiencing the very same accidents that once plagued Kathleen. Then a murder takes place, and Jacqueline suspects several people, including Kathleen's brother, two of her former lovers, another romance writer, and a literary agent. Jacqueline risks her own life to identify the killer.

A reviewer in *Publishers Weekly* noted that Jacqueline "unmask[s] the culprit with panache and mastery remarkably similar to Peters's own." A *Kirkus Reviews* critic observed that although motive "is egg-shell thin" and "there's much padding," the plot "is rather nifty; the touch mostly light, and the entertainment level moderately high." Florence King touched on the novel's themes in the *New York Times Book Review*: ". . . Ms. Peters makes some valuable points about the importance of being selfish for women in the creative arts, delivers some hilariously cynical reflections on book tours and literary fans and wisely avoids the gratuitous sex scenes that spoil so many mysteries. . . ."

In addition to being a bestselling author, Mertz is also known for her feminist philosophy. She was one of the original members of Sisters in Crime, which was formed to advocate fair critical treatment of women writers. She is also involved in the Malice Domestic Convention, a group that meets annually in Washington, D. C., to discuss mystery novels—the majority of which, Mertz pointed out in the *CA* interview, are written by women. Mertz is especially concerned about women mystery novelists being taken more seriously. "I think the prejudice against the traditional mystery exists in part because the traditional mystery deals largely with women's interests and issues," she asserted. "I don't see why these should be any less critically worthy than men's interests and issues."

■ Works Cited

Review of *Ammie, Come Home, Horn Book,* February, 1969, p. 79.

Brainard, Dulcy, "Barbara Michaels/Elizabeth Peters," *Publishers Weekly,* October 23, 1987, p. 39.

Breen, Jon L., review of *Crocodile on the Sandbank, Wilson Library Bulletin,* September, 1973, p. 35.

Clancy, Cathy, review of *Curse of the Pharaohs, School Library Journal,* August 8, 1981, p. 82.

Review of *Crocodile on the Sandbank, Booklist,* May 1, 1975, p. 908.

Review of *Crocodile on the Sandbank, Publishers Weekly,* February 17, 1975, p. 72.

Review of *Curse of the Pharaohs, Publishers Weekly,* April 3, 1981, p. 71.

Review of *The Dead Sea Cipher, Publishers Weekly,* March 9, 1970, p. 82.

DeMeritt, Annette, review of *The Deeds of the Disturber, School Library Journal,* December, 1988, pp. 131-32.

Review of *Die for Love, Booklist,* March 15, 1984, p. 1009.

Review of *Die for Love, Publishers Weekly,* March 16, 1984, p. 70.

Donahue, Deirdre, *USA Today,* July 27, 1987.

Donavin, Denise Perry, review of *Into the Darkness, Booklist,* April 1, 1990, p. 1506.

Grant, Mary Kent, review of *The Dead Sea Cipher, Library Journal,* May 1, 1970, p. 1763.

Review of *Here I Stay, Publishers Weekly,* July 29, 1983, pp. 64-65.

Review of *Into the Darkness, Publishers Weekly,* April 27, 1990, p. 52.

Johnson, Priscilla, review of *Here I Stay, School Library Journal,* February, 1984, p. 87.

King, Florence, review of *Naked Once More, New York Times Book Review,* October, 15, 1989, p. 46.

Mertz, Barbara, comments in *Something about the Author,* Gale, Volume 49, 1987.

Mertz, Barbara, interview in *Contemporary Authors, New Revision Series,* Gale, Volume 36, 1992.

Moore, Kevin, review of *The Deeds of the Disturber, Tribune Books* (Chicago), April 24, 1988, p. 7.

Review of *Naked Once More, Kirkus Reviews,* July 1, 1989, p. 957.

Review of *Naked Once More, Publishers Weekly,* July 14, 1989, p. 61.

Penny, Susan, review of *Shattered Silk, School Library Journal,* February, 1987, p. 99.

Review of *Shattered Silk, Publishers Weekly,* August 1, 1986, p. 70.

Theroux, Peter, review of *The Last Camel Died at Noon, New York Times Book Review,* October 20, 1991, p. 34.

Winnett, Scott, review of *The Last Camel Died at Noon, Locus,* November, 1991, p. 35.

■ For More Information See

BOOKS

Bestsellers, Number 90, Issue 4, Gale, 1991.

Contemporary Novelists, St. James Press, 1996.

Great Women Mystery Writers, Greenwood Press, 1994.

Legends in Their Own Time, Prentice Hall, 1994.

St. James Guide to Crime and Mystery Writers, 4th edition, St. James Press, 1996.

Twentieth-Century Romance and Historical Writers, St. James Press, 3rd edition, 1994.

PERIODICALS

Booklist, June 1, 1992, p. 1733; October 15, 1993, p. 418; May 1, 1995, p. 1531; January 1, 1997, p. 779.

Chicago Tribune, December 27, 1987; September 7, 1989.

Globe and Mail (Toronto), August 30, 1986.

New Republic, September 14, 1974.

New York Times Book Review, October 4, 1970; June 24, 1984; November 9, 1986; October 15, 1989.

Publishers Weekly, March 7, 1986; September 20, 1993, p. 62; January 13, 1997, p. 53.

School Library Journal, November, 1995, p. 139.

Tribune Books (Chicago), December 25, 1988; July 8, 1990.

Washington Post, April 28, 1984; November 27, 1987; June 11, 1989.

Washington Post Book World, January 6, 1980; March 16, 1980; September 4, 1983; January 5, 1986.

—Sketch by Peggy Saari

Richard Peck

■ Personal

Born April 5, 1934, in Decatur, IL; son of Wayne Morris (a merchant) and Virginia (a dietician; maiden name, Gray) Peck. *Education:* Attended University of Exeter, 1955-56; DePauw University, B.A., 1956; Southern Illinois University, M.A., 1959; further graduate study at Washington University, 1960-61. *Politics:* Republican. *Religion:* Methodist.

■ Addresses

Home—155 East 72nd St., New York, NY 10021. *Office*—c/o Delacorte Press, 1 Dag Hammarskjold Plaza, New York, NY 10017. *Agent*—Sheldon Fogelman, 10 East 40th St., New York, NY 10016.

■ Career

Southern Illinois University at Carbondale, instructor in English, 1958-60; Glenbrook North High School, Northbrook, IL, teacher of English, 1961-63; Scott, Foresman Co., Chicago, IL, textbook editor, 1963-65; Hunter College of the City of New York City, instructor in English and education, 1965-71; writer, 1971—. Assistant director of the Council for Basic Education, Washington, DC, 1969-70; English-Speaking Union fellow, Jesus College, Oxford University, 1973; lecturer. *Military Service:* U.S. Army, 1956-58; served in Stuttgart, Germany. *Member:* Authors Guild, Authors League of America, Delta Chi.

■ Awards, Honors

Child Study Association of America's Children's Book of the Year citations, 1970, for *Sounds and Silences,* 1971, for *Mindscapes,* and 1986, for *Blossom Culp and the Sleep of Death;* Writing Award, National Council for the Advancement of Education, 1971; Edgar Allan Poe Award runner-up, Mystery Writers of America, 1974, for *Dreamland Lake;* Best Books of the Year citations, American Library Association (ALA), 1974, for *Representing Super Doll,* 1976, for *Are You in the House Alone?,* and 1977, for *Ghosts I Have Been;* ALA Notable Book citations, 1975, for *The Ghost Belonged to Me,* and 1985, for *Remembering the Good Times;* Friends of American Writers Award (older category), 1976, for *The Ghost Belonged to Me;* Edgar Allan Poe Award for best juvenile mystery novel, 1976, and Author's Award, New Jersey Institute of Technology, 1978, both for *Are You in the House Alone?;* School Library Journal's Best Books of the Year citations, 1976, for *Are You in the House Alone?,* 1977, for *Ghosts I Have Been,* and 1985, for *Remembering the Good Times; New York Times* Outstanding Book of the Year citation, 1977, for *Ghosts I Have Been;* Illinois Writer of the Year citation, Illinois Association of Teachers of English, 1977; *School Library Journal*'s Best of the Best 1966-1978 citations, for *Dreamland Lake* and *Father Figure;* New York Public Library Books for the Teen Age citation, 1980, for *Pictures That Storm inside My Head,* 1981, for *Ghosts I Have Been,* and 1982, for *Are You in the House Alone?* and *Close Enough to Touch;* ALA Best Books for Young Adults citations, 1981, for *Close Enough to Touch,* 1985, for *Remembering the Good Times,* 1987, for *Princess Ashley,* and 1995, for *The Last Safe Place on Earth; School Library Journal*'s Best Books for Young Adults citations, 1981, for *Close Enough to Touch,* 1983, for *This Family of Women,* and 1985, for *Remembering the Good Times;* ALA's Young Adult Services Division's Best of the Best Books 1970-1983 citations, for *Are You in the House Alone?* and *Ghosts I Have Been;* ALA's Margaret Edwards Young Adult Author Achievement Award, and the National Council of Teachers of English/ALAN Award for outstanding contributions to young adult literature, both 1990; University of Southern Mississippi Medallion, 1991.

■ Writings

YOUNG ADULT NOVELS

Don't Look and It Won't Hurt, Holt, 1972.
Dreamland Lake, Holt, 1973, Dell, 1990.
Through a Brief Darkness, Viking, 1973.
Representing Super Doll, Viking, 1974.
The Ghost Belonged to Me, Viking, 1975.
Are You in the House Alone? (with teacher's guide), Viking, 1976.
Ghosts I Have Been (sequel to *The Ghost Belonged to Me*), Viking, 1977.
Father Figure, Viking, 1978.
Secrets of the Shopping Mall, Delacorte, 1979.
Close Enough to Touch, Delacorte, 1981.
The Dreadful Future of Blossom Culp (sequel to *Ghosts I Have Been*), Delacorte, 1983.
Something for Joey, Delacorte, 1983.
Remembering the Good Times, Delacorte, 1985.
Blossom Culp and the Sleep of Death, Delacorte, 1986.
Princess Ashley, Delacorte, 1987.
Those Summer Girls I Never Met, Delacorte, 1988.
Voices after Midnight, Delacorte, 1989.
Unfinished Portrait of Jessica, Delacorte, 1991.
Bel-Air Bambi and the Mall Rats, Delacorte, 1993.
Love and Death at the Mall, Delacorte, 1994.

The Last Safe Place on Earth, Delacorte, 1995.
Lost in Cyberspace, Dial, 1995.
The Great Interactive Dream Machine, Dell, 1996.

Audio cassette versions of Peck's young adult books include *The Ghost Belonged to Me,* Live Oak Media, 1976, *Don't Look and It Won't Hurt* (filmstrip with cassette), Random House, and *Remembering the Good Times* (cassette), Listening Library, 1987.

FOR CHILDREN

Monster Night at Grandma's House, illustrated by Don Freeman, Viking, 1977.

ADULT NOVELS

Amanda/Miranda (Literary Guild selection; Reader's Digest Condensed Book Club selection), Viking, 1980.
New York Time, Delacorte, 1981.
This Family of Women (Literary Guild alternate selection), Delacorte, 1983.
Desirable Digs, Viking, 1998.

EDITOR

(With Ned E. Hoopes) *Edge of Awareness: Twenty-five Contemporary Essays,* Dell, 1966.
Sounds and Silences: Poetry for Now, Delacorte, 1970.
Mindscapes: Poems for the Real World, Delacorte, 1971.
Leap into Reality: Essays for Now, Dell, 1972.
Urban Studies: A Research Paper Casebook, Random House, 1973.
Transitions: A Literary Paper Casebook, Random House, 1974.
Pictures That Storm inside My Head (poetry anthology), Avon, 1976.

OTHER

(With Norman Strasma) *Old Town, A Complete Guide: Strolling, Shopping, Supping, Sipping,* 2nd edition, [Chicago], 1965.
(With Mortimer Smith and George Weber) *A Consumer's Guide to Educational Innovations,* Council for Basic Education, 1972.
(With Stephen N. Judy) *The Creative Word 2,* Random House, 1974.
(Contributor) Kenneth L. Donelson and Alleen Pace Nilsen, *Literature for Today's Young Adults,* Scott, Foresman, 1980.

(Contributor) Donald R. Gallo, editor, *Sixteen: Short Stories by Outstanding Young Adult Writers*, Delacorte, 1984.

(Contributor) Donald R. Gallo, editor, *Visions: Nineteen Short Stories by Outstanding Writers for Young Adults*, Delacorte, 1987.

Write a Tale of Terror, Book Lures, 1987.

(Contributor) Donald R. Gallo, editor, *Connections: Short Stories by Outstanding Writers for Young Adults*, Delacorte, 1989.

Anonymously Yours (autobiography), Silver Burdett, 1991.

Author of column on the architecture of historic neighborhoods for the *New York Times.* Contributor of poetry to several anthologies. Contributor of poems to *Saturday Review* and *Chicago Tribune Magazine.* Contributor of articles to periodicals, including *American Libraries, PTA Magazine* and *Parent's Magazine.*

■ Adaptations

Television movies based on Peck's books include *Are You in the House Alone?*, CBS, 1977, *Child of Glass* (based on *The Ghost Belonged to Me*), Walt Disney Productions, 1979, and *Father Figure,* Time-Life Productions, 1980. Cineville Production Company bought the film rights for *Don't Look and It Won't Hurt* in 1991.

■ Overview

Richard Peck is one of the most popular creators of young adult literature. He is highly regarded for the honesty, skill, versatility, and consistency displayed in his work. Although Peck didn't write his first novel until he was thirty-seven years old, he has a unique ability to understand contemporary adolescents and to be aware of their changing needs and interests.

Peck was born and raised in Decatur, Illinois, a place that he refers to as "middle Middle America." Peck was close to his father growing up, and he has fond memories of sitting on his father's lap and pretending to steer the family Packard. "Like many midwestern boys, my first romance was with the automobile," he wrote in *Something about the Author Autobiography Series* (*SAAS*). "I learned words by naming the oncoming cars: DeSoto, Terraplane, Lincoln Zephyr,

LaSalle, Oldsmobile, Hydramatic—the streamlined poetry of progress."

Peck's father, the author recalled, was different from other fathers: "In a neighborhood where other people's fathers went off to offices every morning in white collars and Plymouth sedans, my dad was apt to roar away astride a Harley Davidson." Peck spent a lot of time at his father's Phillips 66 gas station, where "elderly men . . . hung out, telling tales." Twelve-year-old boys also spent time at the station rolling newspapers and telling their own tales. "The old timers had honed their stories with years of retelling and flavored them with tobacco juice," Peck said, while the newspaper boys worked hard on their "macho vocabulary" and hoped that those listening would believe them. "I was bombarded from both sides by the language of other generations, and from these rough tale-tellers I began to learn *style.*"

Peck grew up during wartime, which "made the outside world dangerous and glamorous," he wrote in the *Fifth Book of Junior Authors and Illustrators.* Peck's father had been badly wounded in World War I, and he followed World War II passionately, clenching his fist "in rage at war and killing and Roosevelt." Peck's mother was a dietician who "struggled with wartime menus," and his aunt volunteered as a nurse's aide and wrote letters to cheer the servicemen. Listening to their dinnertime conversations, Peck stated, "I learned viewpoint."

In childhood, Peck was surrounded by "elders of all ages," and he listened to stories about the Victorian days from his grandmother, aunts, and uncles. "Little wonder that old folks stalk through my novels about being young," he wrote in *SAAS.* There is Uncle Miles, the great-uncle in *The Ghost Belonged to Me* (whom Peck based on his own Uncle Miles); Madame Malevich, the wise drama teacher in *Are You in The House Alone?*; and Polly Prior, the third oldest woman in the township in *Remembering the Good Times.* He once commented that when writing for young people, it is important to include the wisdom of people who are at the "other end of life."

Another family member who inspired Peck was his younger sister. "My sister Cheryl was born in the darkest days of the war," Peck commented in *SAAS.* [Later] . . . she looked up in astonishment as the technicolor postwar era came roaring in with unrationed chocolate, toy balloons, and new cars toothy with chrome." Cheryl became the "prototypical protagonist" for many of the author's novels. "I was the typical older child, she the typical younger. I conformed, she questioned. I recorded, she rebelled," Peck noted.

Peck attended Decatur High School, which he described as "the least provincial setting I was ever to inhabit, with the possible exception of the army." The school was racially integrated when many weren't, and it was attended by people from all walks of life. The privileged and prominent people in Decatur sent their children to this public high school, because they considered private schools undemocratic. Carol Patterson, the heroine of Peck's first novel, *Don't Look and It Won't Hurt,* was drawn from his experiences with the "invisible poor" at Decatur High School, and the children who came straight from the farms were the source for the characters seen in Peck's novel *Representing Super Doll.*

While in high school, Peck bagged groceries in the A & P on Saturdays for a wage of $7.45. Most of it was spent on wrist corsages for girls who Peck took to dances, which were popular in Decatur. When Peck was sixteen, he went to visit a relative who had married a dignitary assigned to the United Nations. To save for the ticket on the Pennsylvania railroad, he raked yards and shoveled snow. When he got to New York City, he was glad he had made the trip: "It came as quite a relief to me that the outside world was really there and somewhat better than the movies," he wrote in *SAAS.* He explored the streets of New York and took the subway all the way to Coney Island. New York City, he discovered, was "the place I'd been homesick for all along. . . ."

But Peck's happiness was short-lived. "That first trek into the Great World ended on June 25, 1950, the day the Korean War began," he recalled in *SAAS.* "The postwar era we'd waited for all through grade school had turned out to run less than five years, and the 1950s had truly begun." Peck believed he needed straight A's in high school to earn a college scholarship and avoid the army through a deferment. "I grubbed for grades, yearned for the scholarship [to college], dreaded Korea, and feared the formless future," he stated in *School Library Journal.* He did win the scholarship he had been pursuing and was able to attend DePauw University in Indiana instead of

going to Korea. If a student didn't maintain a grade point average in the upper half of the class, however, the draft board was informed. "When I was a freshman, one of the seniors in the fraternity house allowed his grades to slip and was drafted out of school in mid-semester. This had an electrifying effect on the rest of us . . . ," Peck recalled.

Peck's main interests were literature and history, which led him to study for a year in southwest England at Exeter University. He returned to DePauw University for his senior year, completed

Winner of the Edgar Allan Poe Award, this novel exploring the ongoing effects of the rape of a teenage girl was adapted as a prime-time television movie.

his requirements for teaching, and was "marched off, on cue, to the army." "Everybody who was ever in the army remembers the day he went in and the day he got out. I had the idea that I was going to spend two years without anybody to talk to. . . . This overlooked the fact that virtually every able-bodied member of my sex and generation was going where I was going, and it was a place where you made friends because you needed them, and you kept them for life," Peck recalled in *SAAS*. He served for two years in an army field post near Ansbach, Germany. "It was in this unlikely, muddy locale, that I found out the advantage of writing. I learned that if you can type, punctuate, spell, and improvise in mid-sentence, you can work in a clean dry office near a warm stove," he said in *School Library Journal*. He worked as an army clerk and soon became a ghostwriter of sermons for chaplains of all denominations.

When he returned home, Peck attended Southern Illinois University and began working on a master's degree. He also worked as a teaching assistant at the university. It was then that he decided to be a teacher, because he had been told by many people that he couldn't make a living as a writer. "I realize now that those people were not very well informed," he once told *Contemporary Authors* (CA). "So I became a teacher because teachers were the people in my hometown whom I admired and who were interested in all the things I was interested in. Then I fell in love with teaching," Peck said.

Peck first began to see and understand adolescent problems when he began teaching English at Glenbrook North High School in Northbrook, Illinois, an affluent suburb of Chicago. "From that first day in a class room of my own, I heard the voices of the young, and found that I was no longer one of them," he stated in *Fifth Book of Junior Authors and Illustrators*. "As a teacher, I learned things about the private life of the very young that their parents need never know," he added.

Peck learned that there were timely problems that teens were facing that were almost fashionable—like drugs and drinking and divorce. "But I learned of larger, timeless problems from my students. . . . That being young in an old world is never easy. That the more freedom the young are given, the less they have. That to be over-praised

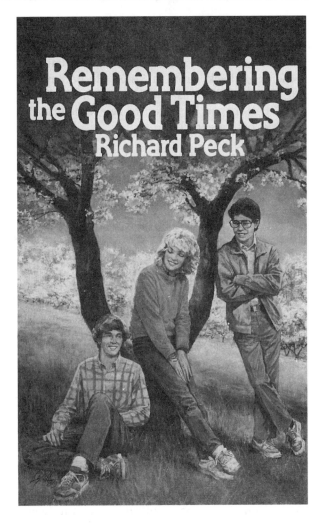

Friendship and suicide are the subjects of this well-received 1985 work, which was based on a true story.

is to be robbed of challenge. That your best friend and your worst enemy tend to be the same person," he said. In the classroom, he also began to identify with his potential readers—the students who liked to read. Peck believed that the most independent and promising students are the quiet ones in the back of the class—the ones who like to read and who are "often overlooked in our crisis-oriented schools," he once told *Something about the Author* (SATA).

In 1965, Peck moved to New York City, where he began teaching English at Hunter College High School, a school for academically gifted girls on Park Avenue in New York City. He found that the world of the young, and the world of teaching, was changing rapidly. "For the first time I was teaching junior-high level students and look-ing high and low for books that reflected their realities, books that were 'relevant,' the battle cry of the age," Peck wrote in *SATA*. He became frus-trated because he was unable to persuade his stu-dents to learn, so he began to re-evaluate and re-examine his career choice.

"I was burning out as a teacher," Peck told *CA*. At that point, Peck felt that it would have been scarier for him to continue to teach than to leave. The Vietnam War was at its peak, teachers were being held legally responsible for students they had never met before, and it was considered "fas-cist" to call roll because a student may be at a protest march in Washington instead of in the classroom. ". . . I quit teaching when I could no longer teach as I had been taught," Peck said. "I moved my typewriter out into the garden of the brick barn in Brooklyn where I live. And I began writing a novel to some of the young people I'd left behind in the classroom," he said.

"The hardest part of being a writer wasn't the uncertainty; it was the solitude," Peck noted in *SAAS*. "I'd been a teacher, and I was so used to being surrounded by students and other teach-ers. . . . Instead, I was sitting alone in a room, staring into a typewriter, trying to make a blank page speak." Four months later, *Don't Look and It Won't Hurt*, a young adult novel about teenage pregnancy, was completed. "It was the junior-high students, the puberty people, who taught me how to be a writer," Peck said. From his students, he had learned that people did not read fiction to be educated. Instead, they read it to be given hope. He decided not to always write happy end-ings to his stories, because the students have "tele-vision for that. But I knew never to leave the reader without hope for the future and a new beginning."

Peck based the book *Don't Look and It Won't Hurt* on the experiences of his friends Jean and Rich-ard Hughes, a couple who took unwed teenage mothers-to-be into their home in suburban Chi-cago. The story is not told from the viewpoint of the mother-to-be, but from her younger sister Carol. Peck identified Carol, a quiet girl who stayed out of trouble, with the students in the back of his classroom.

Peck carried his manuscript to a man named George Nicholson, the Juvenile Editor-in-Chief of

In this 1988 novel, Drew's plans for his sixteenth summer appear to be ruined when he is forced to take a cruise with his little sister and a grandmother he barely knows.

the publishing company Holt, Rinehart and Win-ston. He hardly slept at all that night, but the next day Nicholson called him and said "You can start your second novel." From that point on, Peck devoted himself to writing.

Representing Super Doll was published in 1974. It is the story of a beautiful but not very smart girl named Darlene who goes to New York to partici-pate in the first round of a beauty pageant. Darlene's mother convinces Darlene's friend Verna, who is level-headed and intelligent, to accompany Darlene on her trip. Verna scorns the contest and goes home before the final round, and Darlene does the same, leaving Darlene's mother furious.

The story draws a contrast between Verna, who makes a decision for herself, and Darlene, who has been manipulated and exploited by her mother, who has turned her daughter into a "Super Doll." In *Children & Books*, Zena Sutherland wrote that "The message is firmly feminist, but Peck does not let the message obscure the story. . . ." She went on to say that the plot of *Representing Super Doll* is solid and the treatment of the concerns of adolescents is balanced.

The relationship between a mother and daughter is also a theme in *Princess Ashley*. In this book, the main character, Chelsea, distances herself from her mother until a tragic event allows her to value her mother's work as a guidance counselor. It is also a novel about peer pressure and friendship, and about struggling to develop one's own values.

In 1976, *Are You in the House Alone?*, Peck's novel about a teenage girl who was raped, was published. The book met with critical approval and received the Edgar Allan Poe Award. "I wrote that novel because the victim of rape is not a woman, but a teenage girl—a teenage girl who doesn't have her own lawyer, who doesn't have mobility, who doesn't have a lot of things she will need to be strong in her situation," Peck told *CA*. *Are You in the House Alone?* shows how the victim of the crime continues to be victimized in small ways because of what has happened to her. The book was adapted into a prime-time television movie. "It was a relief when they didn't do what I was terribly worried they would—change the ending to show everything working out all right . . . ," Peck told Jean F. Mercier in *Publishers Weekly*.

Although he has written ghost stories, romances, and thrillers, Peck is still best known for his novels for young adults. He considers *Father Figure* to be one of his best books. It is the story of a seventeen-year-old boy who has been a father to his eight-year-old brother since his parents divorced. When their mother dies, the brothers are reunited with their long-lost father. At first, the father-son relationship is a rocky one. It is only after the teen is able to surrender his little brother to the father that he is also able to rid himself of his anger.

"I have a particular interest in the male relationship in families . . . ," Peck once told *CA*. He feels that it is important to let boys know that it

is okay to express their emotions. "Boys don't know that they can cry. . . . Also, half of them are not living in the same house as their fathers. . . . And some of them who do live in the same house as their fathers do not have that role modeling because there is no real dialogue. That . . . is our number-one problem," Peck said.

To make sure that his topics are relevant, Peck travels widely and meets young people firsthand. "A writer can't afford to sit very long alone. He has to get out among readers, researching their worlds," Peck noted in *SAAS*. This is especially true for the young adult audience, who can change their "protective coloring"—their fads in clothes, speech, and music—every semester. As a

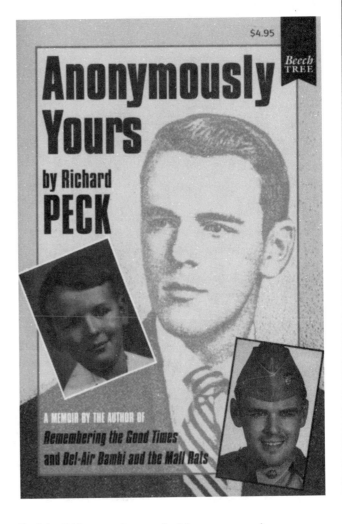

Peck's 1991 memoir reveals his own experiences as a young person, as well as his creative process and unique advice for aspiring writers.

writer, Peck spends about a quarter of his time visiting readers and their teachers and librarians. He sometimes visits schools and speaks at conventions for teachers and librarians, but he also likes to observe young people in different settings around the country.

Secrets of the Shopping Mall, another popular Peck novel, is a satirical look at teen life. "I wrote the novel asking the kids why they felt they had to report to the shopping mall every day, even though home and school were now optional," he told *CA*. "Was it possibly because even in the

Todd discovers that Walden Woods is not as idyllic as it seems when the suburban community becomes divided over censorship of school library books.

cradle they had been conditioned by television commercials to buy happiness with unearned money? Or is it that they're in the suburbs and there is no center for these rootless, blank communities? Or—and here's the real reason—is the shopping mall a place where you can eliminate even the possibility of adult authority?," Peck asked. In *Secrets of the Shopping Mall*, the town mall is being run by a group of runaway teens who have taken up residence in the furniture department of Lord and Taylor, and are ruled with an iron fist by a Hitlerian leader, Barbie, and her friend, Ken. Peck told *CA* that he "experienced Andy Warhol's fifteen minutes of fame when *Time* magazine called this novel 'a Lord & Taylor of the Flies.'"

Remembering the Good Times is based on a real-life story of a boy who told twelve of his classmates that he was going to commit suicide. That night, he did. When people asked the twelve students why they hadn't told anyone, they said that the thought hadn't occurred to them. They didn't know that there were agencies in the community that could have helped the boy, and they weren't accustomed to going to adults for help. Peck wrote *Remembering the Good Times* to make teens aware of the classic signs of suicide.

Knowing that young adults enjoy humor and the supernatural, Peck has written novels in both veins. He blends the two in his four "Blossom Culp" books, which are set in Bluff City, U.S.A., in 1913 and 1914. Blossom Culp is one of several strong female adolescent characters that appear in Peck's novels. He portrays girls who are intelligent and resourceful, and who are able to make their own decisions.

Those Summer Girls I Never Met (1988) is a humorous novel whose main character is sixteen-year-old Drew Wingate. Drew is looking forward to getting a driving license and meeting girls during his sixteenth summer, but instead he is being sent on a Baltic cruise with his fourteen-year-old sister Stephanie and a grandmother he doesn't really know. His grandmother, a tiny, glamorous, and fading singer, is known as the "Sweetheart of Swingtime," and she will perform for the last time on this cruise. During the course of the cruise, Drew and his sister grow to love and respect their grandmother and learn much about their family relationships. In *Horn Book*, a reviewer noted that "Peck writes with a light touch and

If you enjoy the works of Richard Peck, you may also want to check out the following books and films:

Avi, *Nothing but the Truth*, 1991.
Grace Chetwin, *Friends in Time*, 1992.
Peni Griffin, *Switching Well*, 1993.
Back to the Future, starring Michael J. Fox, 1985.

enough underlying psychological truth to make the book entertaining and memorable."

■ Update

Peck has continued to write the young adult novels that are his trademark. *Voices after Midnight* (1989) is a story of a family whose father's business takes them from California to New York. The children are fourteen-year-old Chad, his older sister Heidi, and his little brother Luke. Their new home, a 100-year-old brownstone, is complete with dim voices that can only be heard after midnight. The voices summon the children back to life in the nineteenth century. In *School Library Journal*, Michael Cart called *Voices after Midnight* "a heart-pounding adventure." Cathi Dunn MacRae, writing in *Wilson Library Bulletin*, noted that "With engaging style Peck explores how tuning in to time's fluidity helps us to determine our own destinies. . . ." A critic in the *Horn Book* described *Voices after Midnight* as a "well-paced mystery. . . . This entertaining book deserves and will no doubt have a large audience."

In 1991 *Unfinished Portrait of Jessica* was published. The story concerns a girl named Jessica who becomes resentful toward her mother when her father, a photographer, leaves the family. She misses her father and wants to be with him. At Christmas time, her wishes come true when she is sent to Mexico for a visit with him. Once there, Jessica realizes the truth about both of her parents: her father is charismatic but unreliable and her mother, a well-known romance novelist, is not as drab and boring as she had thought. In a review of *Unfinished Portrait of Jessica* in *Publishers Weekly*, a critic described the book as "the bittersweet journey from a childhood filled with wishful thinking

to a more clearsighted adulthood." Reviewer Lucinda Snyder Whitehurst noted in *School Library Journal* that "While it may not be his [Peck's] most exciting work," *Unfinished Portrait of Jessica* "is well crafted and intellectually satisfying."

In a different vein, *Anonymously Yours* (1991) is an autobiographical work that includes stories about Peck's childhood in the Midwest, his time in college, his stint in the army, his career in teaching, and his work as a writer. In *School Library Journal*, Pat Katka noted that "this memoir is . . . engaging and filled with insight into Peck's creative processes."

Suburban Satires

Bel-Air Bambi and the Mall Rats (1993) is the story of the Babcock family that moves from Los Angeles to the small town of Hickory Fork, where the father grew up. When they reach Hickory Fork, the Babcocks find that it has changed—the cheerleaders and the football team have formed a gang called the "Mall Rats." The adults in the town have allowed the children to take over, and they hide behind closed doors after sunset. The gang trashes the local mall and turns it into a hideout. The Babcock children—Bambi, Buffie, and Brick—band together to try to save the town. In *School Library Journal*, Whitehurst termed the work "a clever, intelligently written, and very funny spoof that pokes fun at one and all in a non-threatening way." In *Wilson Library Bulletin*, MacRae commended the author's ability to use "penetrating insight and humor to make teens aware of issues that endanger them," adding "Thoughtful readers will find plenty to ponder in this deceptively frothy package."

In *The Last Safe Place on Earth*, Peck looks at censorship and democracy and how they affect a family and school in a elitist suburb. Seen through the eyes of the main character Todd Tobin, a high school sophomore, the townspeople of Walden Woods seem unaware of the challenges to their community when censors and hate groups attempt to ban several books. Todd's personal life is disrupted when Laura, a fundamentalist Christian who he befriends, tells stories of witches and devils that traumatize his younger sister. Carol A. Edwards, writing in *School Library Journal*, declared that the author presents "a calm facade" that forms the "backdrop for a truly terrifying novel."

Cyber-Novels

Other Peck novels center around young people's fascination with computers. "Two of my latest attempts to keep pace with the young are a comedy called *Lost in Cyberspace* and its sequel, *The Great Interactive Dream Machine*," Peck noted on, quite fittingly, the Penguin Books Website. ". . . I noticed that twelve year olds are already far more computer-literate than I will ever be. As a writer, I could create a funny story on the subject, but I expect young readers will be more attracted to it because it is also a story about two friends having adventures together."

In *Lost in Cyberspace* (1995), Peck tells the story of two boys, Josh Lewis and his best friend, computer nerd Aaron Zimmer, who travel through time via their computer. Josh already has his own set of problems he is dealing with: his parents have separated, he has an obnoxious older sister, and his mother has hired a succession of wacky English au pairs to take care of him while she is at work. Time traveling just adds to his confusion; he is transported back to 1923 where a housemaid appears to reorganize his life for the better. In *School Librarian*, reviewer Ann G. Hay stated that children who are "accustomed to surfing the Internet" will probably enjoy the book. In *School Library Journal*, reviewer Anne Connor described *Lost in Cyberspace* as "crammed with events and overwhelming . . . computer theory."

In *The Great Interactive Dream Machine* (1996), Josh and Aaron are again facing problems. Josh is worried about the possibility of spending the summer at football camp, and Aaron is concerned about the new computer program he is designing, which is turning his computer into a wish-granting machine. But the program has some problems, and Josh and Aaron find themselves fulfilling the wishes of Josh's boy-crazy sister and the Zimmer family's toy poodle. In the *ALAN Review*, Joyce A. Litton calls *The Great Interactive Dream Machine* a humorous science fiction story that will "appeal to middle school readers of either sex." Connie Tyrrell Burns, in *School Library Journal*, deemed the work a "guaranteed fun, fast-paced adventure," and a contributor in *Publishers Weekly* called the book "an enjoyable light read for science fiction fans."

If Peck's books have one thing in common, it is that they contain a central message of "think and

act independently." Peck declared in a 1986 *Horn Book* article that he writes "counterculture literature of individuality to a conformist readership." As he once told *CA:* "In each of my novels, one of the characters takes a step toward adulthood, and it almost always means taking a step away from the peer group." In his poem "Teenager's Prayer," Peck wrote, "Give me the knowledge that conformity is the enemy of friendship. Give me the understanding that nobody ever grows up in a group so I can find my own way."

In *SAAS*, Peck reflected on his life and career: "There's a saying (or there should be one) that goes 'Be careful what you wish for. You're liable to get it.' When I was a kid, I dreamed privately of being a writer and living in New York and traveling everywhere. I got it all."

■ Works Cited

Burns, Connie Tyrrell, review of *The Great Interactive Dream Machine*, School Library Journal, September, 1996, p. 206.

Cart, Michael, review of *Voices after Midnight*, School Library Journal, September, 1989, p. 276.

Connor, Anne, review of *Lost in Cyberspace*, School Library Journal, September, 1995, p. 202.

Edwards, Carol A., review of *The Last Safe Place on Earth*, School Library Journal, April, 1995, p. 157.

Review of *The Great Interactive Dream Machine*, Publishers Weekly, September 2, 1996, p. 132.

Hay, Ann G., review of *Lost in Cyberspace*, School Librarian, May, 1997, pp. 89-90.

Holtze, Sally Holmes, editor, *Fifth Book of Junior Authors and Illustrators*, H. W. Wilson Co., 1983.

Katka, Pat, review of *Anonymously Yours*, School Library Journal, May, 1992, p. 147.

Litton, Joyce A., review of *The Great Interactive Dream Machine*, ALAN Review, Spring, 1997.

MacRae, Cathi Dunn, review of *Voices after Midnight*, Wilson Library Bulletin, November, 1989, pp. 96-97.

MacRae, Cathi Dunn, review of *Bel-Air Bambi and the Mall Rats*, Wilson Library Bulletin, December, 1993, p. 116.

Mercier, Jean F., "PW Interviews: Richard Peck," Publishers Weekly, March 14, 1980.

Peck, Richard, comments in *Something about the Author*, Volume 18, Gale, 1980.

Peck, Richard, comments in *Contemporary Authors*, Volumes 85-88, Gale, 1980.

Peck, Richard, "Growing Up Suburban: 'We Don't Use Slang, We're Gifted'," *School Library Journal*, October, 1985.

Peck, Richard, essay in *Something about the Author Autobiography Series*, Volume 2, Gale, 1986.

Peck, Richard, "Young Adult Books," *Horn Book*, September/October, 1986, pp. 618-21.

Peck, Richard, comments in *Contemporary Authors, New Revision Series*, Volume 19, Gale, 1987.

Sutherland, Zena, *Children & Books*, 9th edition, Longman, 1997.

Review of *Those Summer Girls I Never Met*, *Horn Book*, January/February, 1989, pp. 79-80.

Review of *Unfinished Portrait of Jessica*, *Publishers Weekly*, October 18, 1991, p. 64.

Review of *Voices after Midnight*, *Horn Book*, November/December, 1989, p. 776.

Whitehurst, Lucinda Snyder, review of *Unfinished Portrait of Jessica*, *School Library Journal*, August, 1991, p. 195.

Whitehurst, Lucinda Snyder, review of *Bel-Air Bambi and the Mall Rats*, *School Library Journal*, September, 1993, p. 234.

Information for this sketch was also taken from a Website located at http://www.penguin.com.

■ For More Information See

BOOKS

Children's Books and Their Creators, edited by Anita Silvey, Houghton Mifflin, 1995, pp. 512-14.

Children's Literature Review, Volume 15, Gale, 1988, pp. 146-66.

Contemporary Literary Criticism, Volume 21, Gale, 1982, pp. 295-301.

Gallo, Donald R., *Presenting Richard Peck*, Twayne, 1989.

Gallo, Donald R., editor, *Speaking for Ourselves: Autobiographical Sketches by Notable Authors of Books for Young Adults*, National Council of Teachers, 1990, pp. 165-66.

Something about the Author, Volume 55, 1989, pp. 126-38.

Twentieth-Century Young Adult Writers, St. James Press, 1994.

PERIODICALS

Booklist, October 1, 1977, p. 300; April 15, 1986, pp. 1226-27; September 5, 1991, p. 137; April 15, 1992, p. 1521; June 1, 1992, p. 1768; September 1, 1993, p. 62; May 1, 1994, p. 1611; January 15, 1995, p. 913; October 15, 1995, p. 402; September 1, 1996, p. 131.

Bulletin of the Center for Children's Books, January, 1974, pp. 83-84; March, 1974, pp. 116-17; November, 1974, p. 51; April, 1986, pp. 155-56; November, 1996, p. 109.

Children's Book Review Service, October, 1972, p. 14; December, 1977, p. 39.

English Journal, October, 1991, p. 96; April, 1992, p. 85; November, 1992, p. 96.

Fantasy Review, August, 1984, p. 50.

Horn Book, September/October, 1997, pp. 529-33.

Junior Bookshelf, October, 1976, p. 283.

Kirkus Reviews, June 15, 1973, p. 648; May 1, 1987, pp. 723-24.

Kliatt, Winter, 1978, p. 4.

New York Times Books Review, November 12, 1972, pp. 8, 10; November 14, 1976, p. 29.

Publishers Weekly, July 17, 1978, p. 168; May 17, 1985, p. 118; August 16, 1993, p. 105; December 19, 1994, p. 55; September 4, 1995, p. 70.

School Library Journal, November, 1973, p. 53; October, 1985, pp. 118-19; May, 1986, pp. 37-39; August, 1987, p. 97; June, 1990, pp. 36-40; October, 1994, p. 49.

Times Literary Supplement, March 25, 1977, p. 348.

Voice of Youth Advocates, October, 1981, pp. 36-37; December, 1983, p. 280.

Wilson Library Bulletin, February, 1989, pp. 84-85; June, 1990, p. 180.*

—Sketch by Irene Durham

Frederik Pohl

■ Personal

Born November 26, 1919, in New York, NY; son of Fred George (a salesman) and Anna Jane (Mason) Pohl; married Doris Baumgardt, 1940 (divorced, 1944); married Dorothy LesTina, August, 1945 (divorced, 1947); married Judith Merril, 1948 (divorced, 1952); married Carol M. Ulf Stanton, September 15, 1952 (divorced, 1983); married Elizabeth Anne Hall (a professor of English), July, 1984; children: Ann (Mrs. Walter Weary), Karen (Mrs. Robert Dixon), Frederik III (deceased), Frederik IV, Kathy. *Education:* Attended public schools in Brooklyn, NY, "dropped out in senior year." *Politics:* Democrat. *Religion:* Unitarian.

■ Addresses

Home and office—855 South Harvard Drive, Palatine, IL 60067.

■ Career

Writer. Popular Publications, New York City, editor, 1939-43; Popular Science Publishing Co., New York City, editor in book department and assis-

tant circulation manager, 1946-49; literary agent, 1946-53; freelance writer 1953-60; *Galaxy* Magazine, New York City, editor, 1961-69; Ace Books, New York City, executive editor, 1971-72; Bantam Books, New York City, science fiction editor, 1973-79. Staff lecturer, American Management Association, 1966-69; cultural exchange lecturer in science fiction for U.S. Department of State in Yugoslavia, Romania, and the Soviet Union, 1974; also lecturer at more than two hundred colleges in the United States, Canada, and abroad; represented United States at international literary conferences in England, Italy, Brazil, Canada, and Japan. Has appeared on more than four hundred radio and television programs in nine countries. County committeeman, Democratic Party, Monmouth City, NJ, 1956-69; trustee, The Harbour School, Red Bank, NJ, 1972-75, and First Unitarian Church of Monmouth City, 1973-75. *Military service:* U.S. Army Air Forces, 1943-45; received seven battle stars. *Member:* Science Fiction Writers of America (president, 1974-76), Authors Guild (Midwest area representative; member of council, 1975—), British Interplanetary Society (fellow), American Astronautical Society, World SF (president, 1980-82), American Association for the Advancement of Science (fellow), World Future Society, American Civil Liberties Union (trustee, Monmouth County, NJ, 1968-71), New York Academy of Sciences.

■ Awards, Honors

Edward E. Smith Award, 1966; Hugo Award, World Science Fiction Convention, 1966, 1967, and

1968, for best editor, 1974, for short story, "The Meeting," 1978, for best novel, *Gateway*, and 1986, for story "Fermi and Frost"; H. G. Wells Award, 1975; Nebula Award, Science Fiction Writers of America, 1977, for best novel, *Man Plus*, and 1978, for best novel, *Gateway*; John W. Campbell Award, Center for the Study of Science Fiction, 1978, for *Gateway*, and 1986, for *The Years of the City*; American Book Award, 1979, for *JEM*; Popular Culture Association annual award, 1982; guest of honor at science fiction convention in Katowice, Poland, 1987.

■ Writings

(Under pseudonym James McCreigh) *Danger Moon*, American Science Fiction (Sydney), 1953.

(With Lester del Rey under joint pseudonym Edson McCann) *Preferred Risk*, Simon & Schuster, 1955.

Alternating Currents (short stories), Ballantine, 1956.

(Under pseudonym Donald Stacy) *The God of Channel 1*, Ballantine, 1956.

(With Walter Lasly) *Turn the Tigers Loose*, Ballantine, 1956.

Edge of the City (novel based on screenplay by Robert Alan Aurthur), Ballantine, 1957.

Slave Ship, Ballantine, 1957.

Tomorrow Times Seven: Science Fiction Stories, Ballantine, 1959.

The Man Who Ate the World, Ballantine, 1960.

Drunkard's Walk, Ballantine, 1960.

(Under pseudonym Ernst Mason) *Tiberius*, Ballantine, 1960.

Turn Left at Thursday: Three Novelettes and Three Stories, Ballantine, 1961.

The Abominable Earthman, Ballantine, 1963.

The Case against Tomorrow: Science Fiction Short Stories, Ballantine, 1965.

A Plague of Pythons, Ballantine, 1965.

The Frederik Pohl Omnibus, Gollancz, 1966.

Digits and Dastards, Ballantine, 1966.

The Age of the Pussyfoot, Ballantine, 1969.

Day Million (short stories), Ballantine, 1970.

Practical Politics, 1972 (nonfiction), Ballantine, 1971.

The Gold at the Starbow's End, Ballantine, 1972.

(With Carol Pohl) *Jupiter*, Ballantine, 1973.

The Best of Frederik Pohl, introduction by Lester del Rey, Doubleday, 1975.

The Early Pohl, Doubleday, 1976.

Man Plus, Random House, 1976.

Gateway, St. Martin's, 1977.

The Way the Future Was: A Memoir, Ballantine, 1978.

JEM, St. Martin's, 1979.

Beyond the Blue Event Horizon, Ballantine, 1980.

Syzygy, Bantam, 1981.

The Cool War, Ballantine, 1981.

Planets Three, Berkley, 1982.

Bipohl, Two Novels: Drunkard's Walk and The Age of the Pussyfoot, Ballantine, 1982.

Starburst, Ballantine, 1982.

Starbow, Ballantine, 1982.

(Author of introduction) *New Visions: A Collection of Modern Science Fiction Art*, Doubleday, 1982.

Midas World, St. Martin's, 1983.

Heechee Rendezvous, Ballantine, 1984.

The Years of the City, Simon & Schuster, 1984.

The Merchant's War, St. Martin's, 1984.

Pohlstars, Ballantine, 1984.

Black Star Rising, Ballantine, 1985.

The Coming of the Quantum Cats, Bantam, 1986.

Chernobyl, Bantam, 1987.

The Annals of the Heechee, Ballantine, 1988.

Narabdela Ltd., Del Rey, 1988.

The Day the Martians Came, St. Martin's, 1988.

Homegoing, Del Rey, 1989.

The Gateway Trip, Del Rey, 1990.

The World at the End of Time, Ballantine, 1990.

Outnumbering the Dead, Century, 1991.

Mining the Oort, Ballantine, 1992.

(With Thomas T. Thomas) *Mars Plus*, Baen, 1994.

The Voices of Heaven, Tor, 1994.

The Other End of Time, Tor, 1996.

The Siege of Eternity, Tor, 1997.

Contributor, sometimes under pseudonyms, to *Galaxy, Worlds of Fantasy, Science Fiction Quarterly, Rogue, Impulse, Astonishing, Imagination, If, Beyond, Playboy, Infinity*, and other magazines. Has written as Elton V. Andrews, Paul Fleur, and Warren F. Howard; and under joint pseudonyms S. D. Gottesman, Lee Gregor, Paul Dennis Lavond, Scott Mariner, Charles Satterfield, and Dirk Wilson.

WITH CYRIL M. KORNBLUTH

(Under joint pseudonym Cyril Judd) *Gunner Cade*, Simon & Schuster, 1952.

(Under joint pseudonym Cyril Judd) *Outpost Mars*, Abelard Press, 1952.

The Space Merchants, Ballantine, 1953, 2nd edition, 1981.

Search the Sky, Ballantine, 1954.

Gladiator-at-Law, Ballantine, 1955.

A Town Is Drowning, Ballantine, 1955.

Presidential Year, Ballantine, 1956.

(Under joint pseudonym Jordan Park) *Sorority House*, Lion Press, 1956.

(Under joint pseudonym Jordan Park) *The Man of Cold Rages*, Pyramid Publications, 1958.

Wolfbane, Ballantine, 1959, reprinted, Garland Publishing, 1975.

The Wonder Effect, Ballantine, 1962.

Our Best: The Best of Frederik Pohl and C. M. Kornbluth, Baen Books, 1987.

WITH JACK WILLIAMSON

Undersea Quest, Gnome Press, 1954.

Undersea Fleet, Gnome Press, 1956.

Undersea City, Gnome Press, 1958.

The Reefs of Space (also see below), Ballantine, 1964.

Starchild (also see below), Ballantine, 1965.

Rogue Star (also see below), Ballantine, 1969.

Farthest Star: The Saga of Cuckoo, Ballantine, 1975.

The Starchild Trilogy: The Reefs of Space, Starchild, and Rogue Star, Paperback Library, 1977.

Wall around a Star, Ballantine, 1983.

Land's End, St. Martin's, 1988.

The Singers of Time, Doubleday, 1991.

The Undersea Trilogy (for children), Baen, 1992.

EDITOR

Beyond the End of Time, Permabooks, 1952.

Star Science Fiction Stories, Ballantine, 1953.

Star Short Novels, Ballantine, 1954.

Assignment in Tomorrow: An Anthology, Hanover House, 1954.

Star of Stars, Doubleday, 1960.

The Expert Dreamer, Doubleday, 1962.

Time Waits for Winthrop, Doubleday, 1962.

The Best Science Fiction from "Worlds of If" Magazine, Galaxy Publishing Corp., 1964.

The Seventh Galaxy Reader, Doubleday, 1964.

Star Fourteen, Whiting & Wheaton, 1966.

The If Reader of Science Fiction, Doubleday, 1966.

The Tenth Galaxy Reader, Doubleday, 1967, published as *Door to Anywhere*, Modern Literary Editions, 1967.

The Eleventh Galaxy Reader, Doubleday, 1969.

Nightmare Age, Ballantine, 1970.

Best Science Fiction for 1972, Ace Books, 1973.

(With Carol Pohl) *Science Fiction: The Great Years*, Ace Books, 1973.

The Science Fiction Roll of Honor, Random House, 1975.

Science Fiction Discoveries, Bantam, 1976.

Science Fiction of the Forties, Avon, 1978.

Galaxy Magazine: Thirty Years of Innovative Science Fiction, Playboy Press, 1980.

Nebula Winners Fourteen, Harper, 1980.

(Co-editor) *The Great Science Fiction Series*, Harper, 1980.

(With son, Frederik Pohl IV) *Science Fiction: Studies in Film*, Ace Books, 1981.

Yesterday's Tomorrows: Favorite Stories from Forty Years as a Science Fiction Editor, Berkley, 1982.

(With wife, Elizabeth Anne Hill) *Tales from the Planet Earth*, St. Martin's, 1986.

(With others) *Worlds of If: A Retrospective Anthology*, Bluejay Books, 1986.

■ Sidelights

Frederick Pohl, an author whom Robert W. Wilcox, in the *St. James Guide to Science Fiction Writers*, has hailed as "a star among stars," is one of the world's most prolific and widely read science fiction writers. Pohl has worn many hats during his sixty-year career, including editor, literary agent, fan, and enthusiastic promoter of science fiction. He was a founding member of the first chapter of the Science Fiction League, and through his involvement he became associated with many of the authors who dominate modern science fiction writing. "Like all the other great men in Science Fiction," wrote Algis Budrys in the *Magazine of Fantasy and Science Fiction*, "Frederick Pohl is idiosyncratic, essentially self-made and brilliant. Unlike many of the others, he has an extremely broad range of interests and education."

Pohl's myriad interests include all kinds of writing, as well as politics, science, and music. Ironically, he is largely self-educated, having dropped out of high school at age seventeen in his senior year—"as soon as it was legal," he noted in a 1984 essay he wrote for *Contemporary Authors Autobiography Series* (*CAAS*). Throughout his life Pohl has worked at many jobs with zeal, but each seemed to lead back to his writing—specifically science fiction. "The act of writing isn't much fun. It's hard work," Pohl once commented in *Something About the Author*. "But once you've finished a book, and are at least reasonably satisfied with it—it's the greatest feeling in the world."

Pohl began writing sci-fi stories in the early 1930s, mostly for "fanzines"—small circulation alternative publications that often were mimeographed rather than printed. In 1939, in his first job as an editor with Popular Publications, he was encouraged to buy what he wrote. And he wrote obsessively, to the detriment of his personal life; his first marriage (of five) fell apart. Pohl speculated in *CAAS* that it may have been the result of the disruptions of the war, or it may simply have been his choice of vocation. "Writers are bad marital risks," he noted. The reason is simple, he added, "a hardworking writer . . . has little time for anything away from his typewriter." Pohl volunteered for the U.S. Army and was serving when his divorce

Pohl received both the Hugo and Nebula Awards for his novel about experimental voyages in ships left behind by an ancient race.

was finalized. After the war, he and his second wife, whom he had married in 1945, both decided to try writing for a living—he as a novelist, she for the theater. Having completed his first novel, set in the advertising industry, Pohl realized that the book, *For Some We Loved*, was unpublishable. To remedy what he decided was his lack of knowledge about advertising, he found a job as a copywriter.

A Sci-Fi Classic

For the next few years, as Pohl noted in *CAAS*, he wrote ads "selling people things they hadn't known they wanted." Pohl's second marriage ended around the same time as his advertising stint; in 1948, a year after his second divorce, he remarried again and changed careers. Pohl became a literary agent; initially he had intended only to help out an old army buddy who had war wounds and could no longer do his job. From 1948 to 1953, Pohl "peddled the writing of others" and continued his own literary efforts, as he recalled in *CAAS*. By 1952, his third marriage was on the rocks, and Pohl had begun collaborating with Cyril Kornbluth, a fellow sci-fi "Futurian." Together, they would write a total of eleven books, one of the best known of which is the 1953 sci-fi novel *The Space Merchants*. Robert Scholes and Eric S. Rabkin in *Science Fiction: History, Science, Vision* have described that book as "a hilarious and pointed satire of contemporary values, achieved through the creation of an ingenious world in which advertising rules everything." Stephen H. Goldman, writing in the *Dictionary of Literary Biography*, commented, "It is on every critic's list of science fiction classics and has never been out of print since its appearance."

The success of *The Space Merchants* boosted Pohl's self-confidence, and he spent the 1950s writing at a feverish pace. Besides his works with Kornbluth, he wrote four science fiction novels of his own, several other books, and countless magazine articles.

Most of Pohl's novels during these years were published by Ballantine Books, whose editor Ian Ballantine became a personal friend. Pohl also wrote for various magazines, mainly *Galaxy*. Again helping a friend who was in poor health, Pohl became the editor of that magazine, as well as its companion publication *If*, and several other

This 1984 collection highlights the author's talent for depicting future scenarios.

In this pioneering work, the authors satirize corporate America, envisioning a future world that revolves around advertising.

helped Pohl finally decide "what his life was really about," as he said in *CAAS*. By 1969, he felt that he was growing stale in his job and that he wanted more time to write, so he quit Ballantine Books. Ironically, as soon as he was free to pursue his own projects, he found that he could not do so. The 1970s began with Pohl suffering from a "mid-life depression." He recalled in *CAAS* how he slowly came out of it when he began "to feel something I had not noticed in a long, long time: enthusiasm." Feeling "reborn," in the winter of 1971 Pohl went to work as executive editor of Ace

magazines that lasted for varying amounts of time. He spent nine years as an editor and loved the work. Pohl explained in *CAAS:* "The pleasure in finding a new writer and giving him an audience, or helping to develop a talent, or finding a way to present a work that no one else has seen a possibility in is almost the same kind of pleasure as writing something of my own that I like."

Another attraction of being an editor was that Pohl had an expense account, which he used to travel widely. As his own fame and popularity as a writer grew, he was in demand as a lecturer at sci-fi conventions and corporate events. All of this

Books, a general interest publishing house. He was unhappy in the job, though, and because of the company's shaky finances, Pohl quit after less than a year. Soon afterward, Bantam Books—then the world's most successful paperback company—offered Pohl a position as their sci-fi specialist. In his new job Pohl was able to take chances on publishing some important "new wave" sci-fi authors—people who were adopting techniques from the literary mainstream, discarding the cliches of the genre, and giving sci-fi new intellectual, creative, and commercial respectability. Among the fresh talents Pohl promoted were Joanna Russ, who wrote the controversial feminist novel *The Female Man*, and Samuel R. Delany, the author of *Dhalgren*, a novel that sold more than a million copies after "wander[ing] homeless as a manuscript until I took my courage in my hand and published it," as Pohl wrote in *CAAS*.

Pohl moved on after six years at Bantam, having finally decided that he did not enjoy working as a member of an editorial team. "Like many writers, I live a large part of my life inside my own head, and there's only room for one person in there," he explained in *CAAS*. "I had finally decided what I wanted to be when I grew up. I wanted to be a writer. Not a writer-editor, or writer agent, or writer copysmith. Just a writer." Pohl's books were by now enjoying considerable popular success. His 1976 novel *Man Plus* won a Nebula Award, one of sci-fi literature's most prestigious awards. The story, set in the not-so-distant future, deals with the creation of a cyborg astronaut. The creature's makers hope that a mission to Mars will divert the Earth's attention away from war and ensure the survival of the human race and the computer age. Reviewer Janet Leonberger in the *School Library Journal* wrote it is "a must for every collection" and "should stimulate lively debate on computer ethics." Gerald Jonas of the *New York Times Book Review* was less impressed, describing the social extrapolation as "simple-minded and the irony heavy-handed."

Pohl Considers *Gateway* Best Novel

Gateway, Pohl's next novel, was published in 1977. In the *New York Times Book Review*, Gerald Jonas stated that *Gateway* is "based on a wonderfully satisfying science fiction premise." The story concerns an ancient interstellar race, the Heechee (a

play on the words "he" and "she"), who left in the solar system an old way station that is equipped with worn-down starships. The ships are programmed to take passengers to predetermined destinations in the cosmos and then return; however, no one knows exactly how the ships work or where they will be transported. Still, desperate people on a resource-depleted Earth jump at the chance to volunteer as crew for missions aboard these ships and have a chance at finding some artifact or scientific discovery that will make them wealthy on their return. The book's protagonist, Robinette Brodhead, wins a lottery and converts his winnings into a one-way ticket to the Heechee

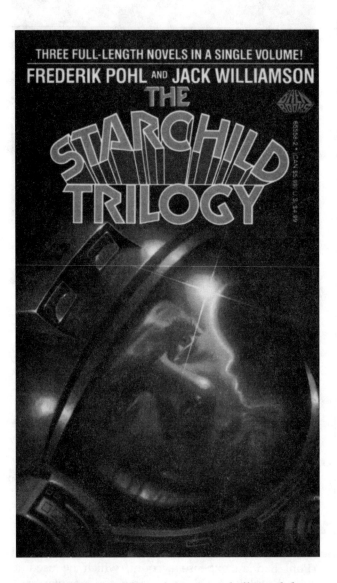

The all-powerful Plan of Man is challenged by a being capable of controlling the stars and the sun in these three inventive novels.

station, known as Gateway. His space experience changes him in unforeseen ways. Mark Rose of the New Republic wrote that *Gateway* "conveys a vivid sense of the pathos and absurdity of human ignorance in attempting to exploit a barely understood universe." *Gateway* won several awards, including the Nebula, the John W. Campbell, and the Hugo Award; in a 1984 interview, Pohl told Jean W. Ross of *Contemporary Authors* that he considers the book to be his "best novel."

Pohl's next book, *The Way the Future Was,* is a memoir that related much of what he had learned in the advertising industry. "Advertising writing should be under constant surveillance by the narcs: it is addictive, and it rots the mind," Pohl stated. "When you spend your days persuading Consumers to Consume articles they would never in their lives dream of wanting, you develop fantasies of power. No, not fantasies. Power. Each sale is a conquest, and it is your silver tongue that had made them roll over and obey. If you do not tend your day with a certain contempt for your fellow human beings, then you are not paying attention to what is that you do." Ray Walters, writing in the *New York Times Book Review,* termed the work "chatty, chummy memoirs. . . ." A *Publishers Weekly* critic praised the author's "youthful energy, which shines through this exuberant memoir."

Pohl's wit and imagination are evident again in the 1979 novel *JEM,* which Gerald Jonas of the *New York Times Book Review* described as "a social satire without humor." The story deals with the first encounters between humans and sentient aliens, as well as the conflicts between humankind's different value systems. Jem is a distant planet offering salvation to humanity, yet its fate is uncertain after a nuclear war devastates Earth. Jonas went on to say, "In Mr. Pohl's dark vision of the future, nothing is what it first appears to be . . . leaving the reader with the impression that nothing can be done." Russell Lord of the *Christian Science Monitor* was more positive in his response; he wrote that it was Pohl's "poetic imagination that elevates this novel to a high position among the author's works." Other critics evidently agreed, for Pohl received the American Book Award for *JEM.*

The 1982 novel *Starburst* was a sequel to Pohl's Hugo Award-nominated novel of a decade earlier,

This story of a newly discovered planet that might bring about either peace or destruction earned the 1979 American Book Award.

The Gold at Starbow's End. Starburst recounts the adventures of four American couples, all geniuses and perfect physical specimens, who are tricked into a space mission to a planet that doesn't exist. The head of the project deceives the explorers because he wants to give them limitless time in space to extend human knowledge. As they send news of their discoveries back to Earth, their coded transmissions overload the planet's computers and bring about catastrophic consequences. "This novel is Pohl at his best, blending science, speculation and satire to fascinate us from first page to last," a *Publishers Weekly* critic opined. A

If you enjoy the works of Frederick Pohl, you may also want to check out the following books and films:

Poul Anderson, *Harvest of Stars*, 1993.
Octavia E. Butler, *Parable of the Sower*, 1993.
William C. Dietz, *Drifter*, 1991.
Millenium, starring Kris Kristofferson, 1989.

---

contributor in *Voice of Youth Advocates* wrote that *Starburst* was a "creatively cryptic blending of narrative, scientific, and mythological description. Speculation at it's best by the master of the genre!"

In 1984, Pohl wrote yet another award-winning novel, *The Years of the City*. The book is a series of five loosely connected novelettes, as well as "a love letter to New York City, cast in the form of a Science Fiction novel whose chapters form individual episodes in the future history of the Big Apple," explained Algis Budrys of the *Magazine of Fantasy and Science Fiction*. Budrys went on to describe *The Years of the City* as "technically stunning, beautifully various, and the best book from Frederick Pohl in years." A *Kirkus Reviews* critic voiced a similar opinion, calling it "the most sure-footed and involving Pohl in some time." A contributor in *Publishers Weekly* stated, "it is written in a clear, clever, rapidly paced and economical style . . . consistently interesting, rich in imagery." But Tom Easton in the *Analog: Science Fiction/Science Fact* felt that the book "reads too often like a tract. The subplots are good but the main plot is all message."

Another of Pohl's more noteworthy works is the *Singers of Time*, one of his collaborations with Jack Williamson (others include *Undersea Quest*, *The Reefs of Space*, *Starchild*, and *Farthest Star*). *Singers of Time* describes what happens when the earth is taken over by a race of giant turtles. Humans have abandoned research, scholarship, and invention in favor of the turtles' more advanced technologies. Eventually, the humans must save the turtles and themselves and they use their new-found power to regain humanity's lost self-respect. Tom Easton in the *Analog: Science Fiction/Science Fact* stated that "the tale felt like little more than a thin excuse to offer you an admittedly nifty

approach to time travel." In contrast, David E. Jones in the *Chicago Tribune* described it as one of sci-fi's "most clever uses of detached seemingly omniscient observers."

An Influential Figure

Although he is approaching his eightieth birthday, the popularity of Frederik Pohl's writing and his influence remain high. "At a time of life when most writers falter or fail, he has somehow emerged as a new master of the genre," Jack Williamson was quoted as saying in the *Dictionary of Literary Biography*. Pohl also remains active in organizations associated with science fiction. He has served as President of the Science Fiction Writers of America, served on the governing council of the Authors Guild and was a founding member of World SF, a world-wide organization established for writers, editors, filmmakers, artists, and academics of science fiction. He remains in demand as a futurologist and his discussions of the future have led to publications in *Playboy*, *Family Circle*, and *Omni*.

Frederik Pohl made his name as one of the most imaginative and original of contemporary sci-fi writers. As he commented in the *St. James Guide to Science Fiction Writers*, "I write what interests me, in the hope that it will interest others. The things that particularly interest me are: the mismatch between what people say and what they do (U.S. presidents being only the most conspicuous example); the turbulence and elegance of science, particularly at its frontiers (science is my favorite spectator sport); the vulnerability and confusion inside the most plastic of human faces; the sound of language, and the amusing tricks that can be played with it, and Morality. How thoroughly I communicate these concerns I can't easily tell, but when I stop trying, I stop writing." That is something he seldom does. "When I was ten years old my wildest ambition was to be a successful science fiction writer," he recalled in *CAAS*. "I thought it would be worthwhile and satisfying and even glamorous way to live . . . and do you know? It is!"

■ Works Cited

Budrys, Algis, review of *Gateway*, *Magazine of Fantasy and Science Fiction*, March, 1978, pp. 63-71.

Budrys, Algis, review of *The Years of the City, Magazine of Fantasy and Science Fiction,* March, 1985, pp. 16-22.

Easton, Tom, review of *The Years of the City, Analog: Science Fiction/Science Fact,* April, 1985, pp. 179-85.

Easton, Tom, review of *The Singers of Time, Analog: Science Fiction/Science Fact,* August, 1991, pp. 162-69.

Goldman, Stephen H., *Dictionary of Literary Biography,* Volume 8: *Twentieth-Century American Science Fiction Writers, Part 2: M-Z,* Gale, 1981.

Jonas, Gerald, review of *Man Plus, New York Times Book Review,* October 17, 1976, p. 43.

Jonas, Gerald, review of *Gateway, New York Times Book Review,* March 27, 1977, p. 43.

Jonas, Gerald, review of *JEM, New York Times Book Review,* May 20, 1979, p. 28.

Jones, David, review of *The Singers of Time, Tribune Books* (Chicago), March 31, 1991, p. 5.

Leonberger, Janet, review of *Man Plus, School Library Journal,* December, 1976, p. 74.

Lord, Russell, review of *JEM, Christian Science Monitor,* June 20, 1979, p. 18.

Pohl, Frederik, comments in *Something about the Author,* Volume 24, Gale, 1981.

Pohl, Frederik, essay in *Contemporary Authors Autobiography Series,* Volume 1, Gale, 1984.

Pohl, Frederik, interview with Jean W. Ross in *Contemporary Authors, New Revision Series,* Volume 11, Gale, 1984, pp. 409-15.

Pohl, Frederik, comments in *St. James Guide to Science Fiction Writers,* 4th edition, St. James Press, 1996.

Rose, Mark, review of *Gateway, New Republic,* November 26, 1977, p. 37.

Scholes, Robert, and Eric Rabkin, *Science Fiction: History, Science, Vision,* Oxford University Press, 1977, pp. 51-69.

Review of *Starburst, Publishers Weekly,* April 23, 1982, p. 89.

Review of *Starburst, Voice of Youth Advocates,* December, 1982, p. 39.

Walters, Ray, review of *The Way the Future Was, New York Times Book Review,* August 26, 1979.

Review of *The Way the Future Was, Publishers Weekly,* July 3, 1978, p. 57.

Wilcox, Robert H., "Frederik Pohl," *St. James Guide to Science Fiction Writers,* 4th edition, St. James Press, 1996.

Review of *The Years of the City, Kirkus Reviews,* June 15, 1984, p. 554.

Review of *The Years of the City, Publishers Weekly,* June 29, 1984, p. 102.

■ For More Information See

BOOKS

Aldiss, Brian, *Billion Year Spree: The History of Science Fiction,* Doubleday, 1973.

Amis, Kingsley, *New Maps of Hell: A Survey of Science Fiction,* Harcourt, 1960.

Carter, Paul A., *The Creation of Tomorrow: Fifty Years of Magazine Science Fiction,* Columbia University Press, 1977.

Contemporary Literary Criticism, Volume 18, Gale, 1981.

Walker, Paul, *Speaking of Science Fiction: The Paul Walker Interviews,* Luna Press, 1978.

PERIODICALS

Analog: Science Fiction/Science Fact, February, 1977; January, 1979; December, 1979; May, 1980.

Books and Bookmen, November, 1979.

Christian Science Monitor, June 20, 1979.

Fantasy Review, September, 1986, p. 29.

Kirkus Reviews, September 1, 1997, p. 1345.

Locus, July, 1994, p. 27.

Los Angeles Times, December 11, 1986.

Magazine of Fantasy and Science Fiction, March, 1978; March 1979, pp. 22-23; September, 1979; July, 1987, p. 26.

New Republic, November 26, 1977.

New Statesman, April 15, 1977; September 26, 1986, p. 33.

New York Times, September 7, 1983.

New York Times Book Review, October 17, 1976, p. 43; March 27, 1977; May 20, 1979; January 18, 1987, p. 33; November 15, 1987; April 24, 1988; July 2, 1989; July 10, 1994, p. 30.

Publishers Weekly, July 31, 1978; September 22, 1997, p. 73.

School Library Journal, September, 1979, p. 168.

Science Fiction and Fantasy Book Reviews, July, 1982, pp. 32-33.

Spectator, January 28, 1978.

Times (London), November 24, 1983; August 8, 1985; January 16, 1988; January 17, 1991.

Times Literary Supplement, January 14, 1977; January 27, 1978; May 14, 1983.

Tribune Books (Chicago), March 15, 1987; August 16, 1987; August 21, 1988; July 15, 1990; December 30, 1990.

Voice of Youth Advocates, April, 1984; December, 1986, p. 240; April, 1987, p. 40; February, 1991, p. 366; April, 1991, pp. 46-47.

Washington Post, October 4, 1987.

Washington Post Book World, March 14, 1980; November 23, 1980; July 25, 1982; July 29, 1984, p. 11; February 28, 1988; April 30, 1989; June 26, 1994, p. 11.*

—Sketch by Kelly Druckenbroad

Carl Sandburg

■ Personal

Also wrote as Charles August Sandburg, Militant, and Jack Philips; born January 6, 1878, in Galesburg, IL; died July 22, 1967, in Flat Rock, NC; buried at Remembrance Rock, Carl Sandburg Birthplace, Galesburg, IL; son of August (a railroad blacksmith; original surname Johnson) and Clara (maiden name, Anderson) Sandburg; married Lilian ("Paula") Steichen (sister of photographer Edward Steichen), June 15, 1908; children: Margaret, Janet, Helga (originally named Mary Ellen; Mrs. George Crile). *Education:* Attended Lombard College, 1898-1902. *Politics:* Formerly Social-Democrat, later Democrat.

■ Career

American poet, biographer, autobiographer, novelist, journalist, songwriter, editor, and author of children's books. Held many odd jobs, including work as milk-delivery boy, barbershop porter, fireman, truck operator, and apprentice house painter; sold films for Underwood and Underwood; helped to organize Wisconsin Socialist Democratic Party;

worked for *Milwaukee Sentinel* and *Milwaukee Daily News*; city hall reporter for *Milwaukee Journal*; secretary to Milwaukee Mayor Emil Seidel, 1910-12; worked for *Milwaukee Leader* and *Chicago World*, 1912; worked for *Day Book* (daily), Chicago, 1912-17; *System: The Magazine of Business*, Chicago, associate editor, February to early fall, 1913 (returned to *Day Book*); worked for *Chicago Evening American* for three weeks in 1917; Newspaper Enterprise Association (390 newspapers), Stock-holm correspondent, 1918, ran Chicago office, 1919; *Chicago Daily News*, 1917-30, served as reporter (covered Chicago race riots), editorial writer, and motion picture editor, later continued as columnist until 1932; wrote weekly column syndicated by *Chicago Daily Times*, beginning in 1941.

Presidential Medal of Freedom lecturer, University of Hawaii, 1934; Walgreen Foundation Lecturer, University of Chicago, 1940. Contributed newspaper columns to Chicago Times Syndicate and radio broadcasts such as "Cavalcade of America" and foreign broadcasts for the Office of War Information during World War II. Lectured and sang folk songs to his own guitar accompaniment.

Military Service: Sixth Illinois Volunteers, 1898; served in Puerto Rico during Spanish-American War. *Member:* American Academy of Arts and Letters, National Institute of Arts and Letters, Phi Beta Kappa (honorary); honorary member of Chicago's Tavern Club and Swedish Club (Chicago).

■ Awards, Honors

Levinson Prize, *Poetry* magazine, 1914; shared Poetry Society of America prize, 1919, 1921; Friend of American Writers award; Phi Beta Kappa poet, Harvard University, 1928, William & Mary College, 1943; Friends of Literature award, 1934, for *Lincoln: The Prairie Years;* Theodore Roosevelt distinguished service medal, 1939; Pulitzer Prize in history, 1939, for *Abraham Lincoln: The War Years;* Pulitzer Prize for poetry, 1951; American Academy of Arts and Letters gold medal for history, 1952, 1953; Poetry Society of America gold medal for poetry, 1953; Taminent Institution award, 1953, for *Always the Young Strangers;* honored by Sweden's Commander Order of the North Star on his seventy-fifth birthday, January 6, 1953; New York Civil War Round Table silver medal, 1954; University of Louisville award of merit, 1955; Albert Einstein award, Yeshiva College, 1956; Roanoke-Chowan Poetry Cup, 1960, for *Harvest Poems, 1910-1960,* and 1961, for *Wind Song;* International Poet's Award, 1963; National Association for the Advancement of Colored People award, 1965, acclaiming Sandburg as "a major prophet of civil rights in our time." Litt.D., Lombard College, 1928, Knox College, 1929, Northwestern University, 1931, Harvard University, 1940, Yale University, 1940, New York University, 1940, Wesleyan University, 1940, Lafayette College, 1940, Syracuse University, 1941, Dartmouth College, 1941, University of North Carolina, 1955; LL.D., Rollins College, 1941, Augustana College, 1948, University of Illinois, 1953; Ph.D., Uppsala University, 1948.

■ Writings

(As Charles A. Sandburg) *In Reckless Ecstasy,* Asgard Press, 1904.
(As Charles A. Sandburg) *The Plaint of a Rose,* Asgard Press, 1905.
(As Charles A. Sandburg) *Incidentals,* Asgard Press, 1905.
(As Charles A. Sandburg) *You and Your Job,* [Chicago], ca. 1906.
(As Charles Sandburg) *Joseffy* (promotional biography; commissioned by a wandering magician), Asgard Press, 1910.
Chicago Poems, Holt, 1916.
Cornhuskers, Holt, 1918.
The Chicago Race Riots, July, 1919, Harcourt, Brace & Howe, 1919, reprinted with new introduction, 1969.

Smoke and Steel (also see below), Harcourt, Brace & Howe, 1920.
Rootabaga Stories (also see below), Harcourt, Brace, 1922.
Slabs of the Sunburnt West (also see below), Harcourt, Brace, 1922.
Rootabaga Pigeons (also see below), Harcourt, Brace, 1923.
Selected Poems of Carl Sandburg, edited by Rebecca West, Harcourt, Brace, 1926.
Songs of America, Harcourt, Brace, 1926.
(Editor) *The American Songbag,* Harcourt, Brace, 1927.
Abraham Lincoln: The Prairie Years (also see below), Harcourt, Brace, 1927.
Abe Lincoln Grows Up, Harcourt, Brace, 1928.
Good Morning, America (also see below), Harcourt, Brace, 1928.
Rootabaga Country: Selections from Rootabaga Stories and Rootabaga Pigeons, Harcourt, Brace, 1929.
Steichen, the Photographer, Harcourt, Brace, 1929.
M'Liss and Louie, J. Zeitlin [Los Angeles, CA], 1929.
Early Moon, Harcourt, Brace, 1930.
Potato Face, Harcourt, Brace, 1930.
(With Paul M. Angle) *Mary Lincoln, Wife and Widow,* Harcourt, Brace, 1932.
The People, Yes, Harcourt, Brace, 1936.
Smoke and Steel [and] *Slabs of the Sunburnt West,* Harcourt, Brace, 1938.
A Lincoln and Whitman Miscellany, Holiday Press, 1938.
Abraham Lincoln: The War Years (also see below), four volumes, Harcourt, Brace, 1939.
Abraham Lincoln: The Sangamon Edition, six volumes, Scribner, 1940.
Bronze Wood, Grabhorn Press, 1941.
Storm Over the Land, Harcourt, Brace, 1942.
Smoke and Steel, Slabs of the Sunburnt West [and] *Good Morning, America* (omnibus volume), Harcourt, Brace, 1942.
Home Front Memo, Harcourt, Brace, 1943.
(With Frederick Hill Meserve) *Photographs of Abraham Lincoln,* Harcourt, Brace, 1944.
Poems of the Midwest, two volumes, World Publishing, 1946.
The Lincoln Reader: An Appreciation, privately printed, 1947.
Remembrance Rock (novel), Harcourt, Brace, 1948.
Lincoln Collector: The Story of Oliver R. Barrett's Great Private Collection, Harcourt, Brace, 1949.
(Editor) *Carl Sandburg's New American Songbag,* Broadcast Music, Inc., 1950.
Complete Poems, Harcourt, Brace, 1950, revised and enlarged edition published as *The Complete Poems of Carl Sandburg,* 1970.

Always the Young Strangers (autobiography), Harcourt, Brace, 1952.

A Lincoln Preface, Harcourt, Brace, 1953.

Abraham Lincoln: The Prairie Years and the War Years, Harcourt, 1954, reprinted, 1974.

Prairie-Town Boy, Harcourt, Brace, 1955.

The Sandburg Range, Harcourt, Brace, 1957.

Chicago Dynamic, Harcourt, Brace, 1957.

The Fiery Trial, Dell, 1959.

Address Before a Joint Session of Congress, February 12, 1959, Harcourt, Brace, 1959 (also published as *Carl Sandburg on Abraham Lincoln,* [Cedar Rapids], 1959, and as *Abraham Lincoln, 1809-1959,* J. St. Onge, 1959).

Abraham Lincoln, three-volume condensation of earlier work, Dell, 1959.

Harvest Poems, 1910-1960, Harcourt, Brace, 1960.

Wind Song, Harcourt, Brace, 1960.

Six New Poems and a Parable, privately printed, 1960.

Address Upon the Occasion of Abraham Lincoln's One Hundredth Inaugural Anniversary, Black Cat Books, 1961.

Honey and Salt, Harcourt, Brace & World, 1963.

The Wedding Procession of the Rag Doll and the Broom Handle and Who Was in It (chapter of Rootabaga stories), Harcourt, Brace & World, 1967.

The Letters of Carl Sandburg, edited by Herbert Mitgang, Harcourt, 1968.

A Sandburg Treasury: Prose & Poetry for Young People, Harcourt, 1970.

Seven Poems, illustrated with seven original etchings by Gregory Masurovsky, Associated American Artists, 1970.

Breathing Tokens, edited by daughter Margaret Sandburg, Harcourt, 1978.

Ever the Winds of Chance, edited by daughter M. Sandburg and George Hendrick, University of Illinois Press, 1983.

Fables, Foibles and Foobles, edited by Hendrick, University of Illinois Press, 1988.

Arithmetic, Harcourt, 1993.

Billy Sunday and Other Poems, Harcourt, 1993.

More Rootabagas, Knopf, 1993.

Poetry for Young People, Sterling, 1995.

Not Everyday an Aurora Borealis for Your Birthday: A Love Poem, illustrated by Anita Lobel, Knopf, 1997.

Also author of commentary for U.S. Government film *Bomber.* Author of captions for "Road to Victory" mural photograph show, 1942. Collaborator on screenplay for the film *King of Kings,* 1960. *The World of Carl Sandburg,* a stage presentation by Norman Corwin, was published by Harcourt in 1961. Contributor to *International Socialist Review, Tomorrow, Poetry, Saturday Evening Post, Masses, Little Review, New Leader, Nation,* and *Playboy.* The Sandburg papers are gathered mainly at the Carl Sandburg Collection of the University of Illinois Library at Urbana-Champaign. Also, more than 10,000 of Sandburg's books and many of his papers are collected at Connemara, the Carl Sandburg Home, in Flat Rock, North Carolina.

■ **Adaptations**

Sandburg recorded excerpts from *Always the Young Strangers,* Caedmon, 1966; he also recorded *The People, Yes, Poems for Children, A Lincoln Album, Carl Sandburg Sings His American Songbag,* and *The Poetry of Carl Sandburg,* for Caedmon.

■ **Sidelights**

"Poetry," wrote Carl Sandburg in his *Good Morning, America,* "is a pack-sack of invisible keepsakes. Poetry is a sky dark with wild-duck migration. Poetry is the opening and closing of a door, leaving those who look through to guess about what is seen during a moment." For millions of Americans and readers around the world, Sandburg opened that magic door to poetry for perhaps the first time. Readers who might have otherwise never approached the carefully metered world of prosody eagerly consumed Sandburg poems, with their free verse incantations of the American quotidian. Sandburg's themes and language are those of the people, of the common man. He had, according to Kenneth Rexroth in his *American Poetry in the Twentieth Century,* "a perfect ear for the beautiful potentials of common speech, something he learned from folk song, but mostly he just learned it from listening." Sandburg indeed listened to the common idiom, for he was not an ivory-tower poet, but a man who participated in the hurly-burly of life, riding the rails with hobos as a youth, working a variety of skilled and unskilled jobs, soldiering and enjoying a good ball game. In his critical study, *Carl Sandburg,* Richard Crowder noted that "Sandburg had been the first poet of modern times actually to use the language of the people as his almost total means of expression. . . . Sandburg had entered into the language of the people; he was not looking at it as a scientific phenomenon or a curiosity. . . . He was at home with it." In collections such as *Chicago Poems, Cornhuskers, Smoke and Steel*, and *The People, Yes*, Sandburg celebrated the life of Everyman in the cities and on the land.

Yet Sandburg's first Pulitzer Prize came not for his poetry, but for the second part of his monumental Lincoln biography, *Abraham Lincoln: The War Years*. Over fifteen years in the writing, Sandburg's six-part biography had no indexes or footnotes, none of the trappings of academic history, but was instead a biography for the people. As the historian Henry Steele Commager noted in a contemporary review in the *Yale Review,* Sandburg "has realized that Lincoln belongs to the people, not to the historians, and he has given us a portrait from which a whole generation may draw understanding of the past and inspiration for the future." Poetry, history, and biography were just three of the professional hats Sandburg wore. Added to those are his fables for children, the *Rootabaga* tales, "some of the first authentic American fairy tales," according to Penelope Niven, writing in *Dictionary of Literary Biography.* Sandburg was also a journalist, and some of his best journalistic writing was involved with race and labor relations, such as those gathered in *The Chicago Race Riots, July, 1919*. In addition to all this were Sandburg's musical contributions. For decades Sandburg toured the country not only reading his poetry, but also gathering and singing folk songs like a modern-day troubadour. A complex man, then, but one who, for all his notoriety and celebrity, maintained a simple mode of life, working right up to the end of his long life.

The Roots of a Populist: A Midwestern Upbringing

Carl August Sandburg was one of seven children born to Swedish immigrant parents, August Sandburg and Clara Anderson Sandburg. The father worked as a blacksmith's helper for the Chicago Burlington and Quincy Railroad in Galesburg, Illinois, where Carl was born on January 6, 1878. Sandburg grew up in this small Midwestern town, which still maintained echoes of Lincoln's time—a local college once held a debate between Lincoln and Stephen Douglas. From an early age then, Carl Sandburg developed an interest in the sixteenth president. He also developed an ear for

colloquial speech, leaving school at thirteen to find work and help supplement the family income. The surrounding prairie and the values of small-town America helped to form the young Sandburg, but as Niven noted in *Dictionary of Literary Biography,* Sandburg was also "restless and impulsive, hungry for experience in the world." He partly assuaged that curiosity by hitting the rails in 1897, traveling for almost four months with hobos and transients, working odd jobs on farms and railroads in Iowa, Missouri, Kansas, Nebraska, and Colorado.

In 1898, Sandburg joined the army to serve in the Spanish-American War, stationed in Puerto Rico for several months. Out of the service, he qualified for free tuition to college, and entered

The poems in this volume celebrate the American experience and the people who built this country.

Lombard College in his hometown, Galesburg. Offered a place at West Point, he took the entrance examination in 1899, but failed in both arithmetic and grammar, and thereafter returned to Lombard College where he remained until 1902. Though Sandburg left college with insufficient credits to graduate, this college experience proved to be a turning point in his life. It was there he first realized a love for poetry, encouraged by a professor, Philip Green Wright, who later published Sandburg's first poems at his independent Asgard Press. These early poems, collected in *In Reckless Ecstasy, Incidentals, The Plaint of a Rose,* and *Joseffy,* were largely "juvenalia," according to Niven, inspired by Walt Whitman and Rudyard Kipling, but they also foreshadowed larger themes which he would explore in his more mature work. These early poems were also published under the name Charles A. Sandburg, for Sandburg had adopted this more American-sounding name in an attempt to leave his Swedish roots behind.

Sandburg as Social Reformer

In the early years of the twentieth century, Sandburg supported himself by a number of jobs, including working as a salesman for stereopticon equipment for Underwood and Underwood. He kept writing poetry and also wrote for various journals. In 1908 he married Lilian Steichen, sister of Edward Steichen, a pioneer in photography. Both Lilian—whom Sandburg called Paula—and Edward Steichen would be powerful influences on Sandburg's life. He and his wife were married for fifty-nine years, and it was she who convinced Sandburg that he should concentrate on his poetry and find his own voice. She also advised him to go back to his christened name of Carl, to reaffirm his immigrant roots.

Another major influence in Sandburg's early development was his involvement in Socialist politics. In 1908, Sandburg campaigned in Wisconsin for the Socialist presidential candidate, Eugene V. Debs, and in 1910 played a key part in the Socialist victory in Milwaukee elections which brought Emil Seidel to the mayor's office. Sandburg and his wife lived in Milwaukee for the next two years, with Sandburg working as private secretary to the mayor. He also wrote for numerous Socialist newspapers and journals, including the *Social Democratic Herald, International Socialist Review,* and the *Chicago Evening Review.* It

was during his years in Milwaukee also that the Sandburgs started a family, eventually comprising three daughters.

In 1914, the Sandburgs moved to Chicago, and the next decade witnessed one of his richest periods of poetic creativity. His first big break came with publication of six of his poems in Harriet Moore's *Poetry* magazine. The publication opened doors to Chicago's literary world for Sandburg, to friendships with Edgar Lee Masters, Vachel Lindsay, and Theodore Dreiser, among others, in what became known as the Chicago Renaissance. Dreiser and Masters encouraged Sandburg to work on a collection of poetry, which was subsequently sent to Alfred Harcourt, a young editor at Henry Holt. Thus was born the first of Sandburg's popular collections, *Chicago Poems,* published in 1916.

The Poet of the People

In *Chicago Poems,* Sandburg made his first statement of poetry for and of the masses. Two types of poetry are represented, as typified in a contemporary review by O. W. Firkins in the *Nation:* "the brawny and the lissome." Of the former, Sandburg dealt with cityscapes and social injustice, and in such poems as "Hog Butcher for the World," painted a portrait of the city as "stormy, husky, brawling." Other poems in the collection are small evocations of everything from fog to deserted brickyards. In "Fog," Sandburg created one of his most anthologized poems whose opening lines have entered the modern idiom: "The fog comes / on little cat feet." Overall, as Niven pointed out in *Dictionary of Literary Biography,* Sandburg's *Chicago Poems* "offered bold, realistic portraits of working men, women, and children," and though his themes "reflect his Socialist idealism and pragmatism," the poems also contain a "wider humanism, a profound affirmation of the common man. . . ."

Reviewers from the outset fell into two camps— those who found Sandburg's free verse and colloquial language refreshing and telling, and those who found such poems to smack of a lack of "discipline," as Firkins commented. Though a contributor in the *New York Times Book Review* of 1916 noted that some of the work in *Chicago Poems* was "good, tremendously good," the reviewer also commented that much of it was prose and not poetry. Yet this same reviewer could not fault

Sandburg's vision: ". . . throughout the book runs a call to a better, finer, and nobler view of human responsibility for what is wrong and sad in our present civilization." Other reviewers, such as Francis Hackett, writing in the *New Republic*, declared that the "free rhythms of Mr. Carl Sandburg are a fine achievement in poetry . . . these imagist verses are as good as any of their kind." Harriet Moore, who had earlier published Sandburg's poems, observed in *Poetry* that Sandburg "has the unassailable and immovable earth-bound strength of a great granite rock which shows a weather-worn surface above the soil," and that his "free-verse rhythms are as personal as his slow speech or his massive gait: always a reverent beating out of his subject."

Sandburg followed this first collection, which painted the city, with a second, *Cornhuskers*, which did the same for rural America. In poems such as "Prairie" and "Wilderness," Sandburg evoked the sounds and feel of mist, dusty earth, running water, and the flow of the seasons. It was, as a critic in the *New York Times Book Review* noted, "a book of the earth, and of the streams which water the earth," and of nature, "indifferently kind and cruel." In this volume Sandburg also demonstrated a penchant for history with his poems about the Civil War. These war poems were, by extension, a statement about war in general, and the devastations of the First World War in particular. Writing in the *Dial*, poet and editor Louis Untermeyer stated emphatically that *Cornhuskers* "brims with an uplifted coarseness, an almost animal exultation that is none the less an exaltation." Untermeyer noted in particular the "confident rhythm" of the opening lines of "Prairie": "I was born on the prairie, and the milk of its / wheat, the red of its clover, the eyes of its / women, gave me a song and a slogan." Untermeyer went on to comment that Sandburg's poems were a "direct answer to Whitman's hope of a democratic poetry that would express itself in a democratic and even a distinctively American speech."

All the while, Sandburg had remained a journalist by trade, writing for the *Chicago Daily News* on the labor beat. He also made his first trip to Sweden, his ancestral home in 1918, just before the close of the First World War. Back in Chicago, he covered the race riots during the summer of 1919, which were later gathered together in *The Chicago Race Riots, July, 1919*. This book was published by his former editor at Holt, Alfred Harcourt, who had since begun his own publishing house, Harcourt, Brace, with whom Sandburg would continue to publish for the rest of his life.

The harshness of post-war life inspired Sandburg's third volume of poems, *Smoke and Steel*, which leaves behind the prairie and Chicago for larger geographical vistas, including New York, the Potomac, and other Midwestern cities and landscapes. Yet Sandburg's message remains unchanged: he sings the song of America, of the struggle of common men and women. Present here is the cataloguing technique that Sandburg would develop further in later volumes, an accretion of images reminiscent of Whitman, as in his description of a Midwestern town: " . . . a spot on the map / And the passenger trains stop there. / And the factory smokestacks smoke / And the grocery stores are open Saturday nights / And the streets are free for citizens who vote / And inhabitants counted on the census. / Saturday night is the big night."

As usual, contemporary critical reaction was mixed. Such plain lyrics—some thought them banal—outraged former champions, such as Arthur Wilson who wrote in the *Dial* that "Sandburg has lost . . . the one and only thing which makes him great—the ability to determine when he has written something good." Others, however, such as Untermeyer, writing in the *New Republic*, praised the book as "an epic of modern industrialism and a mighty paean to modern beauty," and declared that Sandburg and Robert Frost were America's pre-eminent poets. The imagist poet Amy Lowell, at one point critical of Sandburg for being too propagandistic, also joined the ranks of enthusiastic critics. Writing in the *New York Times Book Review*, Lowell noted that "reading these poems gives me more of a patriotic emotion than ever 'The Star Spangled Banner' has been able to do," and concluded that "posterity, with its pruning hand, will mount [Sandburg] high on the ladder of poetic achievement."

A fourth major volume of poetry followed in 1922, *Slabs of the Sunburnt West*, which opened with the famous poem about Chicago, "The Windy City." Rebecca West noted in a preface to the *Selected Poems of Carl Sandburg* that "The Windy City" and the title poem "evoked the essential America which will survive when this phase of commercial expansion is past and the New World is cut

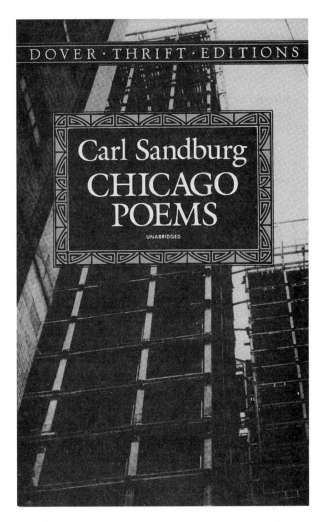

With this book, Sandburg became one of the first American poets to use free verse, authentically capturing the way in which Chicago natives speak.

•

down to the quick as the Old World is to-day: a vast continent which by the majesty of its plains and its waters and its mountains, calls forth a response of power in the men who behold it. . . ." Sandburg used a trip by rail as a connecting device in the title poem, to show past and present in America, in the "wonderful hungry people" who created the nation. He also employed the cataloguing technique to build a resonance of American speech and vistas, a device both applauded and deplored by critics. For Stuart P. Sherman in his *Americans*, such lists painted too broad a stroke. Sandburg, Sherman noted, "seldom individualizes his workingman; almost never does the imaginative work of penetrating the consciousness of any definite individual and telling his story coherently with the concrete emotion belong-

ing to it." Instead, Sherman wrote, Sandburg presented a "rather vague lyrical sense of the surge of but slightly differentiated 'masses'; he gives, as the newspaper does, a collection of accidents to undifferentiated children. . . ." Others, such as Harry Hansen, in his *Midwest Portraits: A Book of Memories and Friendships*, found this fourth volume of poetry to be "a mellowing of Sandburg, contemplating the mass rather than the individual, flinging out his arms and finding room therein for all humankind." Malcolm Cowley, reviewing *Slabs of Sunburnt West* in the *Dial*, noted that the cataloguing technique of Sandburg, with its parallel construction and repetition, created verse that "is highly organized," and built effects as "complex and difficult sometimes as those of Swinburne's most intricate ballads." Yet if reviewers disagreed on style, they did agree on one thing: Sandburg was a thoroughly American poet, and had become, as Niven pointed out in *Dictionary of Literary Biography*, "the Poet of the People."

A Man of Many Talents: Sandburg's Prose

By 1922, Sandburg had carved out a distinguished reputation as a poet: a winner of both prizes and of a large readership. He was a frequent traveler on the lecture circuit, reading his poems and singing folk songs to delighted audiences. The illness of his oldest daughter and subsequent medical bills caused him to increase these lecturing efforts, and he also began writing a series of tales for his children, gathered in the *Rootabaga Stories* of 1922. Sandburg did for fairy tales what he had earlier done for poetry: He gave them a folksy Midwestern setting, in the prairies and small towns he was familiar with, far away from the usual forests and castles such tales inhabit. As noted in *Children's Books and Their Creators*, Sandburg opted for a different cast of characters, as well: "Instead of kings and woodcutters, his characters are whimsical exaggerations of Midwestern rural folks. And instead of fairy princesses and gossamer-winged sprites, corn fairies sew their overalls with corn silk and corn leaves. . . ." This first collection proved so popular that Sandburg wrote a companion volume, *Rootabaga Pigeons*, the following year. These stories led to another turn in the road for Sandburg, a monumental biography of Abraham Lincoln.

For years, Sandburg had been fascinated by the personality and legend of Lincoln. The popularity of his children's stories encouraged him to begin what was intended as a juvenile biography of that famous president. Seventeen years later, this project was brought to a conclusion. Sandburg immersed himself in the times and the history of Lincoln, and what was planned as a children's biography ultimately grew into a six-volume biography. The first two volumes were published in 1926, after extensive revisions. *Abraham Lincoln: The Prairie Years* covered Lincoln's life up to 1861 and created the popular image of the rural, barefoot honest-Abe which has survived to this day. Employing a lyrical approach, Sandburg relied upon anecdote and detailed descriptions of frontier life to create a Lincoln of folkloric dimensions. Writing in the *American Political Science Review,* James A. Woodburn commented that one might never read "a more interesting" Lincoln biography. "There is in it so much of poetry and imagination, so much of tradition mingled with fact, that some may doubt whether it be biography at all. It is clearly not within the canons of historical writing."

Publication of his Lincoln biography brought Sandburg an increased readership as well as financial stability. The opening chapters of that book were also later adapted for a juvenile biography, *Abe Lincoln Grows Up,* and Sandburg thought that he was done with Lincoln; however, he still had a long way to go. Meanwhile, he published a collection of folk songs he had gathered on his travels, *The American Songbag,* and in 1928 turned out a new volume of poetry, *Good Morning, America,* which secured his place as a literary icon of the day. As Percy Hutchison noted in the *New York Times Book Review,* the title poem "is at once a salutation to America, an appreciation, an exhortation, and a prophecy." Though Hutchison felt that Sandburg had shown little growth in his poetry, and that he had "sat too long at the feet of Walt Whitman," most other critics and readers alike agreed that Sandburg once again evoked an America for Americans.

By 1928, Sandburg had decided to write a sequel to his earlier Lincoln biography, this time concentrating on the war years. Another decade of work was dedicated to this project. In 1932, Sandburg finally quit his position at the *Chicago Daily News* to devote himself fulltime to writing and lecturing. His researches on Lincoln continued, and it was not until 1939 that his four-volume *Abraham Lincoln: The War Years* appeared. "Most reviewers

---

If you enjoy the works of Carl Sandburg, you may also want to check out the following books:

Maya Angelou, *And Still I Rise,* 1978.
Robert Frost, *A Witness Tree,* 1942.
Robert Pinsky, *History of My Heart,* 1984.
Diane Siebert, *Heartland,* 1989.
Walt Whitman, *Leaves of Grass,* 1855.

---

were staggered by its sheer bulk," commented Mark E. Neely, Jr., in *Dictionary of Literary Biography.* Less lyrical than the first installment, this second part of Sandburg's Lincoln biography detailed not only the battles of the Civil War, but also the political in-fighting in Washington, D.C., drawing a picture of Lincoln, as Neely pointed out in *Dictionary of Literary Biography,* "as both a stern war leader and a personally forgiving man—an amalgam perhaps most easily seen by a man like Sandburg who had been both a soldier and a kindly Socialist." Allan Nevins, writing in the *Saturday Review of Literature,* credited the success of the book to both its "pictorial vividness, a product of [Sandburg's] graphic style," and "the cumulative force of his detail in building up, step by step, an unforgettable impression of the crowded times. . . ." Nevins concluded that "Mr. Sandburg has written one of the greatest of American biographies." Dubbed "a mountain range of a biography" by the poet Stephen Vincent Benet in the *Atlantic Monthly, Abraham Lincoln: The War Years* was widely popular despite some historical inaccuracies, and won the Pulitzer Prize for history in 1940.

The People, Yes

Sandburg took time out from his Lincoln researches to publish an epic prose-poem in 1936, *The People, Yes,* "the culmination" of his work as a poet, according to Niven in *Dictionary of Literary Biography.* The 107 stanzas of this poem is, according to Niven, Sandburg's "testament to the seekers and the strugglers, the people who were the counterparts of his own immigrant parents." He concluded the piece with typical Sandburg optimism in the power of man: "Man is a long time coming. / Man will yet win. / Brother may yet line up with brother." Once again the critics disagreed over whether Sandburg had created poetry or essay. William Rose Benet wrote in the pages of the *Saturday Review of Literature* that there "is a hypnotic cadence to Sandburg's loose-jointed free verse. . . . He weaves into his verse every old anecdote and adage he has come across." Stephen Vincent Benet, in a review in the *New York Herald Tribune Books,* noted that not all of Sandburg's lusty and humorous verse was poetry, but concluded that "it is the memoranda of the people. And every line of it says 'The People—Yes'." Later critics carried on the same debate. Newton Arvin, in *After the Genteel Tradition: American Writers (1910-1930),* noted that Sandburg's "imagination could not wander far from the democratic center of the American folk tradition," and that *The People, Yes,* "in spite of some air pockets, amply demonstrates . . . how generously the imagination of an American poet can be fed and the art of such a poet be mellowed by that tradition."

The People, Yes was Sandburg's last major work of poetry. During the Second World War, Sandburg committed himself to do all he could as poet, writer, and radio broadcaster to help in the war effort. Working as a syndicated columnist, he published his collected columns, *Home Front Memo,* in 1943. That same year, he decided to try his hand at fiction, signing a contract with Metro-Goldwyn-Mayer for an epic historical novel that could later be filmed. It was not until 1948 that the novel, *Remembrance Rock,* was finally completed and published, but it was poorly received and the film was never made. In 1960, Sandburg, in his eighties, once again worked for Hollywood on the George Stevens film, *The Greatest Story Ever Told.*

In 1945, the Sandburg's left their native Midwest and settled in their final home, a 245-acre estate near Flat Rock, North Carolina, which they called Connemara. There Paula Sandburg gave full rein to her work breeding championship dairy goats. The poet meanwhile continued his touring and writing regimen. In 1950 his *Complete Poems* was published, and the following year he won the Pulitzer Prize for poetry. He also wrote part of an autobiography covering his first twenty-five years of life, *Always the Young Strangers.* Shortly after his eighty-first birthday, Sandburg was honored for his work by being the first private citizen to address a joint session of Congress. That same year he traveled to the Soviet Union with

his brother-in-law, Edward Steichen, to open an exhibition of photos, *The Family Man,* with text which was supplied by Sandburg and which celebrated humanity around the world. Sandburg was still writing at age eighty-five, when he published his last volume of poetry, *Honey and Salt.* Reviews of that final book were mixed, as was the quality of the poems collected. Writing in *Discourse: A Review of the Liberal Arts,* Somner Sorenson felt that "of the seventy-seven poems in the book, about half of them do not merit any serious consideration." However, Richard H. Crowder in *The Vision of this Land,* remarked that over the long course of Sandburg's publishing life—forty-seven years from *Chicago Poems* to

Sandburg's musings about bugs, eggs, dreams, and how the letter X became part of the alphabet in these first truly American fairy tales, first published as *Rootabaga Pigeons.*

Honey and Salt—Sandburg's power had not diminished: "Sandburg is still painting images in varied and brilliant, often dazzling colors." In part summation of his life's work, in part celebration of the Family of Man, *Honey and Salt* affirmed, according to Crowder, Sandburg's "never-discarded esteem for the man of the masses," enabling the poet to create pictures that would be "recognizable to the ordinary reader and also open up the experience of the universe." It was this esteem, as mentioned by Crowder, that made Sandburg loved by young and old readers alike.

Sandburg died on July 22, 1967, at his home in North Carolina. He was eighty-nine, and throughout the course of his long life he had helped change the nature of what was considered poetry; had helped to sing a song of the plains and of the common people. A eulogy presented by his friend and fellow poet, Archibald MacLeish, aptly sums up Sandburg's achievement: "Sandburg had a *subject*—and the subject was belief in man. You find it everywhere." For MacLeish, it was this very readiness to believe, this optimistic nature of Sandburg as displayed in his verse, which was the message. Sandburg's legacy, according to MacLeish, was the act of reminding Americans of their "credulous" heritage, of a daring to believe in beyond what can be proven—an optimism that shapes the future. Sandburg's great achievement, MacLeish concluded, was "that he found a new way in an incredulous, disbelieving, and often cynical time to say what Americans have always known. And beyond that there was another and even greater achievement: that the people listened. They are still listening."

During his lifetime as since his death, Sandburg's critical stock has risen and fallen as literary movements have come and gone. There were critics who prophesied the end of Sandburg's appeal as early as the 1930s with the rise of other modernist poets such as T. S. Eliot, Wallace Stevens, and William Carlos Williams. Williams himself, in a 1951 review of *Complete Poems*, observed that "Carl Sandburg petered out as a poet ten years ago," and that there was a "steady diminution of the poetic charge in his verses from about the time of *Cornhuskers* to *The People, Yes*. He seems to have lost the taste for it." But later critics have challenged that assessment. Phoebe Pettingell, for example, writing in the *New Leader*, while accepting that much of Sandburg's poetry was overstated and overexplained, did remark that "Sandburg's

strength lay in the vernacular," and that his poems never overdo the poet's "deep belief in human dignity." In the final analysis, Pettingell concluded, though "pundits of the literary world . . . had snubbed [Sandburg] for decades," some of Sandburg's best poems "are doubtless closer to the most readers' idea of modern poetry than anything by Eliot, Stevens, Williams, or Lowell. Who knows when a new populist verse may evolve out of Sandburg's generous and hopeful humanity?" Bernard Duffey, writing in the *Centennial Review* more than a decade after Sandburg's death, noted that of the poets of the Chicago literary renaissance, Sandburg was the only one who would endure: "He is in print. His memory has called forth a centenary observance. He has had a special stamp struck off in his honor. He is something, at least, of an institution."

Whether an "institution" or not, Sandburg's popularity has continued. His achievement as a poet of the streets and of rural America, of the hopes and aspirations of the common man, has not been lost or completely drowned out by the voices of other poets. As many critics have pointed out, that enduring popularity is a direct result of Sandburg's humanism, a philosophy that Sandburg carried throughout his work to the very last line of "Timesweep," the final poem in his final book of poetry, *Honey and Salt*: "There is only one man in the world," Sandburg wrote, "and his name is All men."

■ Works Cited

Arvin, Newton, "Carl Sandburg," *After Genteel Tradition: American Writers (1910-1930)*, Southern Illinois University Press, 1964, pp. 67-73.

Benet, Stephen Vincent, "Carl Sandburg—Poet of the Prairie People," *New York Herald Tribune Books*, August 23, 1936, pp. 1-2.

Benet, Stephen Vincent, review of *Abraham Lincoln: The War Years*, *Atlantic Monthly*, December, 1939.

Benet, William Rose, "Memoranda on America," *Saturday Review of Literature*, August 22, 1936, p. 6.

Review of *Chicago Poems*, *New York Times Book Review*, June 11, 1916, p. 242.

Commager, Henry Steele, "Lincoln Belongs to the People," *Yale Review*, December, 1939, pp. 374-77.

Cowley, Malcolm, review of *Slabs of Sunburnt West*, *The Dial*, November, 1922.

Crowder, Richard, *Carl Sandburg*, Twayne, 1964.

Crowder, Richard, "Sandburg's Chromatic Vision in 'Honey and Salt'," *The Vision of this Land: Studies of Vachel Lindsay, Edgar Lee Masters, and Carl Sandburg*, edited by John E. Hallwas and Dennis J. Reader, Western Illinois University Press, 1976, pp. 92-104.

Duffey, Bernard, "Carl Sandburg and the Undetermined Land," *Centennial Review*, Summer, 1979, pp. 295-303.

Firkins, O. W., "American Verse," *Nation*, August 17, 1916, pp. 150-52.

Hackett, Francis, "Impressions," *New Republic*, October 28, 1916, pp. 328-29.

Hansen, Harry, "Carl Sandburg, Poet of the Streets and of the Prairie," *Midwest Portraits: A Book of Memories and Friendships*, Harcourt, Brace, 1923, pp. 15-92.

Hutchinson, Percy, "Carl Sandburg Sings Out: 'Good Morning, America'," *New York Times Book Review*, October 21, 1928, p. 2.

Lowell, Amy, "Poetry and Propaganda," *New York Times Book Review*, October 24, 1920, p. 7.

MacLeish, Archibald, "A Memorial Tribute to Carl Sandburg," *Poetry*, September, 1951.

Moore, Harriet, "Chicago Granite," *Poetry*, May, 1916, pp. 90-93.

"Mr. Sandburg's Poems of War and Nature," *New York Times Book Review*, January 12, 1919, p. 13.

Neely, Mark E., Jr., "Carl Sandburg," *Dictionary of Literary Biography*, Volume 17: *Twentieth-Century American Historians*, Gale, 1983, pp. 378-82.

Nevins, Allan, review of *Abraham Lincoln: The War Years*, *Saturday Review of Literature*, December 2, 1939, pp. 3-4, 20, 22.

Niven, Penelope, "Carl Sandburg," *Dictionary of Literary Biography*, Volume 54: *American Poets, 1880-1945*, Gale, 1987, pp. 388-406.

Pettingell, Phoebe, "The People's Poet," *New Leader*, February 27, 1978, pp. 1920.

Rexroth, Kenneth, *American Poetry in the Twentieth Century*, Seabury Press, 1971, p. 48.

Sandburg, Carl, *Chicago Poems*, Holt, 1916.

Sandburg, Carl, *Cornhuskers*, Holt, 1918.

Sandburg, Carl, *Slabs of Sunburnt West*, Harcourt, Brace, 1922.

Sandburg, Carl, *Good Morning, America*, Harcourt, Brace, 1928.

Sandburg, Carl, *The People, Yes*, Harcourt, Brace, 1936.

Sandburg, Carl, *Honey and Salt*, Harcourt, Brace & World, 1963.

Sherman, Stuart P., "A Note on Carl Sandburg," *Americans*, Charles Scribner's Sons, 1922.

Silvey, Anita, editor, "Sandburg, Carl," *Children's Books and their Creators*, Houghton Mifflin, 1995, pp. 573-73.

Sorenson, Somner, "Poets New and Old: Reviews of Ammons and Sandburg," *Discourse: A Review of the Liberal Arts*, Spring, 1965, pp. 138-52.

Untermeyer, Louis, "Strong Timber," *Dial*, October 5, 1918, pp. 263-64.

Untermeyer, Louis, review of *Smoke and Steel*, *New Republic*, December 15, 1920, pp. 86, 88.

West, Rebecca, preface to *Selected Poems of Carl Sandburg*, Harcourt Brace, 1926, pp. 15-28.

Williams, William Carlos, "Carl Sandburg's Complete Poems," *Poetry*, September, 1951.

Wilson, Arthur, "Sandburg: A Psychiatric Curiosity," *Dial*, January, 1921, pp. 80-81.

Woodburn, James A., review of *Abraham Lincoln: The Prairie Years*, *American Political Science Review*, August, 1926, pp. 674-77.

■ **For More Information See**

BOOKS

Callahan, North, *Carl Sandburg: His Life and Works*, Pennsylvania State University Press, 1987.

Concise Dictionary of American Literary Biography: Realism, Naturalism, and Local Color, 1865-1917, Gale, 1988.

Contemporary Literary Criticism, Gale, Volume 1, 1973, Volume 4, 1975, Volume 10, 1979, Volume 15, 1980, Volume 35, 1985.

Crane, Joan St. C., compiler, *Carl Sandburg, Philip Green Wright, and the Asgard Press, 1900-1910*, University of Virginia Press, 1975.

Detzer, Karl William, *Carl Sandburg*, Harcourt, 1941.

Durnell, Hazel, *America of Carl Sandburg*, University Press of Washington, 1965.

Golden, Harry, *Carl Sandburg*, World Publishing, 1961.

Haas, Joseph, and Gene Lovietz, *Carl Sandburg: A Pictorial Biography*, Putnam, 1967.

Niven, Penelope, *Carl Sandburg: A Biography*, Scribner's, 1991.

Picture Book of American Authors, Sterling, 1962.

Poetry Criticism, Volume 2, Gale, 1991.

Steichen, Edward, editor, *Sandburg: Photographers View Carl Sandburg*, Harcourt, 1966.

Tribute to Carl Sandburg at Seventy-Five, special edition of the Journal of the Illinois State Historical Society, Abraham Lincoln Book Shop, 1953.

World Literature Criticism, Gale, 1992.

Yanella, Philip R. *The Other Carl Sandburg*, University Press of Mississippi, 1996.

Zehnpfennig, Gladys, *Carl Sandburg, Poet and Patriot*, Denison, 1963.

PERIODICALS

Books, August, 1967.

Chicago Tribune Book World, October 23, 1983.

Commentary, May, 1992, p. 47.

Detroit Free Press, November 30, 1965.

Kirkus Reviews, December 15, 1997, p. 1840.

Life, February 23, 1953; December 1, 1961.

Look, July 10, 1956.

Newsweek, January 12, 1953.

New York Herald Tribune Book Review, October 8, 1950.

New York Public Library Bulletin, March, 1962.

New York Times, January 10, 1968; September 25, 1968.

New York Times Book Review, June 1, 1952; January 4, 1953; January 2, 1966; September 29, 1968; January 1, 1984; November 14, 1993.

Publishers Weekly, January 28, 1963; December 1, 1997, p. 52.

Redbook, February, 1966.

Saturday Evening Post, June 6, 1964.

■ Obituaries

PERIODICALS

New York Times, July 23, 1967.

Time, July 28, 1967, July 31, 1967.*

—Sketch by J. Sydney Jones

Robert Silverberg

■ Personal

Born January 15, 1935, in Brooklyn, NY; son of Michael (an accountant) and Helen (Baim) Silverberg; married Barbara H. Brown (an engineer), August 26, 1956 (separated, 1976, divorced, 1986); married Karen L. Haber, 1987. *Education:* Columbia University, B.A., 1956.

■ Addresses

Home—P.O. Box 13160, Station E, Oakland, CA 94661. *Agent*—Ralph Vicinanza, 111 Eighth Ave., No. 1501, New York, NY 10011.

■ Career

Writer, 1956—; president, Agberg Ltd., 1981—. *Member:* Science Fiction Writers of America (president, 1967-68), Hydra Club (chairman, 1958-61).

■ Awards, Honors

Hugo Award, World Science Fiction Convention, 1956, for best new author, 1969, for novella *Nightwings,* 1987, for novella *Gilgamesh in the*

Outback, and 1990, for novelette *Enter a Soldier, Later: Enter Another; Lost Race of Mars* was chosen by the *New York Times* as one of the best hundred children's books of 1960; Spring Book Festival Award, *New York Herald Tribune,* 1962, for *Lost Cities and Vanished Civilizations,* and 1967, for *The Auk, the Dodo, and the Oryx: Vanished and Vanishing Creatures;* National Association of Independent Schools award, 1966, for *The Old Ones: Indians of the American Southwest;* Guest of Honor, World Science Fiction Convention, 1970; Nebula Award, Science Fiction Writers of America, 1970, for story "Passengers," 1972, for story "Good News from the Vatican," 1972, for novel *A Time of Changes,* 1975, for novella *Born with the Dead,* and 1986, for novella *Sailing to Byzantium;* John W. Campbell Memorial Award, 1973, for excellence in writing; Jupiter Award, 1973, for novella *The Feast of St. Dionysus;* Prix Apollo, 1976, for novel *Nightwings;* Milford Award, 1981, for editing; Locus Award, 1982, for fantasy novel *Lord Valentine's Castle;* Woodward Park Award, 1991, for *Letters from Atlantis.*

■ Writings

SCIENCE FICTION

Master of Life and Death (also see below), Ace Books, 1957.
The Thirteenth Immortal (bound with *This Fortress World* by J. E. Gunn), Ace Books, 1957.
Invaders from Earth (also see below; bound with *Across Time* by D. Grinnell), Ace Books, 1958,

published separately, Avon, 1968, published as *We, the Marauders* (bound with *Giants in the Earth* by James Blish) under joint title *A Pair in Space*, Belmont, 1965.

Stepsons of Terra (bound with *A Man Called Destiny* by L. Wright), Ace Books, 1958, published separately, 1977.

The Planet Killers (bound with *We Claim These Stars!* by Poul Anderson), Ace Books, 1959.

Collision Course, Avalon, 1961.

Next Stop the Stars (story collection; bound with *The Seed of Earth* [novel] by Silverberg), Ace Books, 1962, each published separately, 1977.

Recalled to Life, Lancer Books, 1962.

The Silent Invaders (bound with *Battle on Venus* by William F. Temple), Ace Books, 1963, published separately, 1973.

Godling, Go Home! (story collection), Belmont, 1964.

Conquerors from the Darkness, Holt, 1965.

To Worlds Beyond: Stories of Science Fiction, Chilton, 1965.

Needle in a Timestack (story collection), Ballantine, 1966, revised edition, Ace Books, 1985.

Planet of Death, Holt, 1967.

Thorns, Ballantine, 1967.

Those Who Watch, New American Library, 1967.

The Time-Hoppers (also see below), Doubleday, 1967.

To Open the Sky (story collection), Ballantine, 1967.

Hawksbill Station, Doubleday, 1968 (published in England as *The Anvil of Time*, Sidgwick & Jackson, 1968).

The Masks of Time (also see below), Ballantine, 1968 (published in England as *Vornan-19*, Sidgwick & Jackson, 1970).

Dimension Thirteen (story collection), Ballantine, 1969.

The Man in the Maze (also see below), Avon, 1969.

Nightwings (also see below), Avon, 1969.

(Contributor) *Three for Tomorrow: Three Original Novellas of Science Fiction*, Meredith Press, 1969.

Three Survived, Holt, 1969.

To Live Again, Doubleday, 1969.

Up the Line, Ballantine, 1969, revised edition, 1978.

The Cube Root of Uncertainty (story collection), Macmillan, 1970.

Downward to the Earth (also see below), Doubleday, 1970.

Parsecs and Parables: Ten Science Fiction Stories, Doubleday, 1970.

A Robert Silverberg Omnibus (contains *Master of Life and Death*, *Invaders from Earth*, and *The Time-Hoppers*), Sidgwick & Jackson, 1970.

Tower of Glass, Scribner, 1970.

Moonferns and Starsongs (story collection), Ballantine, 1971.

Son of Man, Ballantine, 1971.

A Time of Changes, New American Library, 1971.

The World Inside, Doubleday, 1971.

The Book of Skulls, Scribner, 1972.

Dying Inside (also see below), Scribner, 1972.

The Reality Trip and Other Implausibilities (story collection), Ballantine, 1972.

The Second Trip, Doubleday, 1972.

(Contributor) *The Day the Sun Stood Still*, Thomas Nelson, 1972.

Earth's Other Shadow: Nine Science Fiction Stories, New American Library, 1973.

(Contributor) *An Exaltation of Stars: Transcendental Adventures in Science Fiction*, Simon & Schuster, 1973.

(Contributor) *No Mind of Man: Three Original Novellas of Science Fiction*, Hawthorn, 1973.

Unfamiliar Territory (story collection), Scribner, 1973.

Valley beyond Time (story collection), Dell, 1973.

Born with the Dead: Three Novellas about the Spirit of Man (also see below), Random House, 1974.

Sundance and Other Science Fiction Stories, Thomas Nelson, 1974.

The Feast of St. Dionysus: Five Science Fiction Stories, Scribner, 1975.

The Stochastic Man, Harper, 1975.

The Best of Robert Silverberg, Volume 1, Pocket Books, 1976, Volume 2, Gregg, 1978.

Capricorn Games (story collection), Random House, 1976.

Shadrach in the Furnace, Bobbs-Merrill, 1976.

The Shores of Tomorrow (story collection), Thomas Nelson, 1976.

The Songs of Summer and Other Stories, Gollancz, 1979.

Lord Valentine's Castle, Harper, 1980.

The Desert of Stolen Dreams, Underwood-Miller, 1981.

A Robert Silverberg Omnibus (contains *Downward to the Earth*, *The Man in the Maze*, and *Nightwings*), Harper, 1981.

Majipoor Chronicles, Arbor House, 1982.

World of a Thousand Colors (story collection), Arbor House, 1982.

Valentine Pontifex, Arbor House, 1983.

The Conglomeroid Cocktail Party (story collection), Arbor House, 1984.

Sailing to Byzantium, Underwood-Miller, 1985.

Tom O'Bedlam, Donald I. Fine, 1985.

Beyond the Safe Zone: Collected Short Fiction of Robert Silverberg, Donald I. Fine, 1986.

Star of Gypsies, Donald I. Fine, 1986.

(Editor) *Robert Silverberg's Worlds of Wonder,* Warner, 1987.

At Winter's End, Warner, 1988.

Born with the Dead (bound with *The Saliva Tree* by Brian W. Aldiss), Tor Books, 1988.

The Masks of Time, Born with the Dead, Dying Inside, Bantam, 1988.

To the Land of the Living, Gollancz, 1989.

(With Karen Haber) *The Mutant Season,* Foundation/Doubleday, 1989.

The New Springtime, Warner, 1990.

In Another Country: Vintage Season, Tor Books, 1990.

(With Isaac Asimov) *Nightfall,* Doubleday, 1990.

Time Gate II, Baen Books, 1990.

The Face of the Waters, Bantam, 1991.

The Queen of Springtime, Arrow Books, 1991.

(With Isaac Asimov) *Child of Time,* Gollancz, 1991.

The Collected Stories of Robert Silverberg, Bantam, 1992.

(With Isaac Asimov) *The Ugly Little Boy,* Doubleday, 1992.

(With Isaac Asimov) *The Positronic Man,* Doubleday, 1993.

Kingdoms of the Wall, Bantam, 1993.

Hot Sky at Midnight, Bantam, 1994.

The Mountains of Majipoor, Bantam, 1995.

Starborne, Bantam, 1996.

JUVENILE FICTION

Revolt on Alpha C, Crowell, 1955.

Starman's Quest, Gnome Press, 1959.

Lost Race of Mars, Winston, 1960.

Regan's Planet, Pyramid Books, 1964, revised edition published as *World's Fair, 1992,* Follett, 1970.

Time of the Great Freeze, Holt, 1964.

The Mask of Akhnaten, Macmillan, 1965.

The Gate of Worlds, Holt, 1967.

The Calibrated Alligator and Other Science Fiction Stories, Holt, 1969.

Across a Billion Years, Dial, 1969.

Sunrise on Mercury and Other Science Fiction Stories, Thomas Nelson, 1975.

(Editor with Charles G. Waugh and Martin H. Greenberg) *The Science Fictional Dinosaur,* Avon, 1982.

NONFICTION

First American into Space, Monarch Books, 1961.

Lost Cities and Vanished Civilizations, Chilton, 1962.

Empires in the Dust: Ancient Civilizations Brought to Light, Chilton, 1963.

The Fabulous Rockefellers: A Compelling Personalized Account of One of America's First Families, Monarch Books, 1963.

Akhnaten: The Rebel Pharaoh, Chilton, 1964.

(Editor) *Great Adventures in Archaeology,* Dial, 1964.

Man before Adam: The Story of Man in Search of His Origins, Macrae Smith, 1964.

Scientists and Scoundrels: A Book of Hoaxes, Crowell, 1965.

The Great Wall of China, Chilton, 1965, published as *The Long Rampart: The Story of the Great Wall of China,* 1966.

Bridges, Macrae Smith, 1966.

Frontiers in Archaeology, Chilton, 1966.

The Auk, the Dodo, and the Oryx: Vanished and Vanishing Creatures, Crowell, 1967.

Light for the World: Edison and the Power Industry, Van Nostrand, 1967.

Men Against Time: Salvage Archaeology in the United States, Macmillan, 1967.

Mound Builders of Ancient America: The Archaeology of a Myth, New York Graphic Society, 1968.

The Challenge of Climate: Man and His Environment, Meredith Press, 1969.

The World of Space, Meredith Press, 1969.

If I Forget Thee, O Jerusalem: American Jews and the State of Israel, Morrow, 1970.

The Pueblo Revolt, Weybright & Talley, 1970.

Before the Sphinx: Early Egypt, Thomas Nelson, 1971.

Clocks for the Ages: How Scientists Date the Past, Macmillan, 1971.

To the Western Shore: Growth of the United States, 1776-1853, Doubleday, 1971.

The Longest Voyage: Circumnavigators in the Age of Discovery, Bobbs-Merrill, 1972.

The Realm of Prester John, Doubleday, 1972.

(Contributor) *Those Who Can,* New American Library, 1973.

Drug Themes in Science Fiction, National Institute on Drug Abuse, 1974.

(Contributor) *Hell's Cartographers: Some Personal Histories of Science Fiction Writers,* Harper, 1975.

(Editor with Byron Preiss) *The Ultimate Dinosaur: Past-Present-Future,* Bantam, 1992.

JUVENILE NONFICTION

Treasures beneath the Sea, Whitman Publishing, 1960.

Fifteen Battles That Changed the World, Putnam, 1963.

Home of the Red Man: Indian North America before Columbus, New York Graphic Society, 1963.

Sunken History: The Story of Underwater Archaeology, Chilton, 1963.

The Great Doctors, Putnam, 1964.

The Man Who Found Nineveh: The Story of Austen Henry Layard, Holt, 1964.

Men Who Mastered the Atom, Putnam, 1965.

Niels Bohr: The Man Who Mapped the Atom, Macrae Smith, 1965.

The Old Ones: Indians of the American Southwest, New York Graphic Society, 1965.

Socrates, Putnam, 1965.

The World of Coral, Duell, 1965.

Forgotten by Time: A Book of Living Fossils, Crowell, 1966.

To the Rock of Darius: The Story of Henry Rawlinson, Holt, 1966.

The Adventures of Nat Palmer: Antarctic Explorer and Clipper Ship Pioneer, McGraw, 1967.

The Dawn of Medicine, Putnam, 1967.

The World of the Rain Forest, Meredith Press, 1967.

Four Men Who Changed the Universe, Putnam, 1968.

Ghost Towns of the American West, Crowell, 1968.

Stormy Voyager: The Story of Charles Wilkes, Lippincott, 1968.

The World of the Ocean Depths, Meredith Press, 1968.

Bruce of the Blue Nile, Holt, 1969.

Vanishing Giants: The Story of the Sequoias, Simon & Schuster, 1969.

Wonders of Ancient Chinese Science, Hawthorn, 1969.

Mammoths, Mastodons, and Man, McGraw, 1970.

The Seven Wonders of the Ancient World, Crowell-Collier, 1970.

(With Arthur C. Clarke) *Into Space: A Young Person's Guide to Space*, Harper, revised edition (Silverberg not associated with earlier edition), 1971.

John Muir: Prophet Among the Glaciers, Putnam, 1972.

The World Within the Tide Pool, Weybright & Talley, 1972.

UNDER PSEUDONYM WALKER CHAPMAN

The Loneliest Continent: The Story of Antarctic Discovery, New York Graphic Society, 1964.

(Editor) *Antarctic Conquest: The Great Explorers in Their Own Words*, Bobbs-Merrill, 1966.

Kublai Khan: Lord of Xanadu, Bobbs-Merrill, 1966.

The Golden Dream: Seekers of El Dorado, Bobbs-Merrill, 1967, published as *The Search for El Dorado*, 1967.

Also author of one hundred other novels, 1959-73, under pseudonyms Dan Eliot or Don Elliott.

OTHER

(With Randall Garrett, under joint pseudonym Robert Randall) *The Shrouded Planet*, Gnome Press, 1957, published under names Robert Silverberg and Randall Garrett, Donning, 1980.

(Under pseudonym Calvin M. Knox) *Lest We Forget Thee, Earth*, Ace Books, 1958.

(Under pseudonym David Osborne) *Aliens from Space*, Avalon, 1958.

(Under pseudonym Ivar Jorgenson) *Starhaven*, Avalon, 1958.

(Under pseudonym David Osborne) *Invisible Barriers*, Avalon, 1958.

(With Randall Garrett, under joint pseudonym Robert Randall) *The Dawning Light*, Gnome Press, 1959, published under names Robert Silverberg and Randall Garrett, Donning, 1981.

(Under pseudonym Calvin M. Knox) *The Plot against Earth*, Ace Books, 1959.

(Under pseudonym Walter Drummond) *Philosopher of Evil*, Regency Books, 1963.

(Under pseudonym Franklin Hamilton) *1066*, Dial, 1963.

(Under pseudonym Calvin M. Knox) *One of Our Asteroids Is Missing*, Ace Books, 1964.

(Under pseudonym Paul Hollander) *The Labors of Hercules*, Putnam, 1965.

(Under pseudonym Franklin Hamilton) *The Crusades*, Dial, 1965.

(Under pseudonym Lloyd Robinson) *The Hopefuls: Ten Presidential Candidates*, Doubleday, 1966.

(Under pseudonym Roy Cook) *Leaders of Labor*, Lippincott, 1966.

(Under pseudonym Lee Sebastian) *Rivers*, Holt, 1966.

(Under pseudonym Franklin Hamilton) *Challenge for a Throne: The War of the Roses*, Dial, 1967.

(Under pseudonym Lloyd Robinson) *The Stolen Election: Hayes versus Tilden*, Doubleday, 1968.

(Under pseudonym Paul Hollander) *Sam Houston*, Putnam, 1968.

(Under pseudonym Lee Sebastian) *The South Pole*, Holt, 1968.

Lord of Darkness (fiction), Arbor House, 1983.

Gilgamesh the King (fiction), Arbor House, 1984.

Contributor, sometimes under pseudonyms, to *Omni, Playboy, Amazing Stories Science Fiction, Fantastic Stories Science Fiction, Magazine of Science Fiction and Fantasy*, and other publications. Also editor of more than sixty science fiction anthologies, including *New Dimensions*, Volumes 1-12, 1971-77, and *The Nebula Awards 18*, 1983.

■ Sidelights

Robert Silverberg is one of the best known science fiction writers in the world today. He has won the prestigious Hugo and Nebula awards, and more of his work has been nominated for awards than that of any other science fiction writer. In *Masters of Science Fiction,* Brian M. Stableford described Silverberg as "the most prolific science fiction writer of the past two decades." What is even more impressive is the fact that Silverberg's science fiction writing makes up only a small percentage of his work; nevertheless, he is renowned for his work in the genre.

Born in Brooklyn, New York, in 1935, Silverberg developed an early interest in science fiction. He had an inquisitive mind as a youngster, and often explored the American Museum of Natural History, where he visited the dinosaur exhibits. "From dinosaurs and other such fantastic fossils to science fiction was only a short journey;" he recalled in an essay in the *Contemporary Authors Autobiography Series* (*CAAS*), "to me the romantic, exotic distant past and the romantic, exotic distant future are aspects of the same thing, a time that is not *this* time."

In the eighth grade Silverberg was introduced to such sci-fi magazines as *Thrilling Wonder Stories* and *Astounding Science Fiction,* and he soon moved on to anthologies. One collection in particular had a huge impact on him: *Portable Novels of Science* by Donald A. Wollheim. Soon Silverberg began writing for school newspapers and magazines, and for the sci-fi magazines. "I was still talking then of some sort of career in the sciences—botany, perhaps, paleontology, astronomy," Silverberg remembered in *CAAS.* "But certain flaws in my intelligence were becoming apparent. I had a superb memory and a quick wit, but I lacked depth, originality, and consistency; my mind was like a hummingbird, darting erratically at great speed. . . . I was noticing that some of my classmates were better than I at grasping fundamental principles and drawing new conclusions from them. . . . But I was already writing, and writing with precocious skill."

Silverberg continued writing while he was a student at Columbia University in New York City. His first story sales were to some obscure science fiction magazines during the early 1950s, and his first published book was a juvenile science fiction

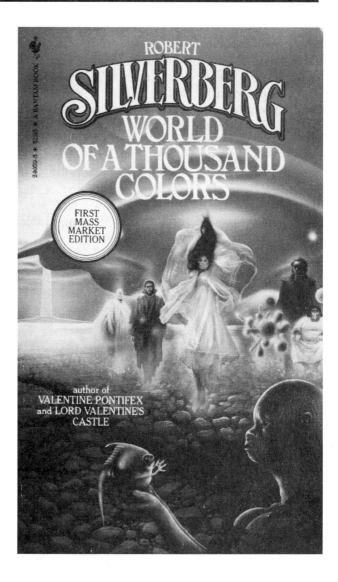

In this 1982 work, Silverberg's early short stories reveal his vivid and diverse vision.

novel, *Revolt on Alpha C,* in 1955. In an interview with Jeffrey Elliot in *Science Fiction Voices* #2 Silverberg explained his decision to become a sci-fi writer. "When I was a boy, I read science fiction and it did wonderful things for me," he said. "I feel a sense of obligation to science fiction to replace what I had taken from it, to add to the shelf, to put something there for someone else that would do for them what other writers had done for me." By the time he was ready to graduate from college, Silverberg was already a successful author. The Science Fiction Convention awarded him the 1956 Hugo Award as best new science fiction writer of the year.

"Two Pieces Every Day"

During the 1950s, Silverberg produced hundreds of stories for science fiction magazines. In fact, he was writing so many that he began to use a number of pseudonyms. Speaking to Charles Platt in *Dream Makers: The Uncommon People Who Write Science Fiction*, Silverberg said: "I was courted by editors considerably back then, because I was so dependable; if they said, 'Give me a story by next Thursday,' I would." However, by the end of the 1950s many science fiction magazines had gone out of business, so Silverberg was no longer able

In this collection from 1984 the author creates a host of new planets and cultures, focusing on the emotional component.

to support himself writing only science fiction. Now, he began writing articles for general interest magazines, churning out about two pieces every day.

He also began publishing novels regularly. *Collision Course* (1961) is one of Silverberg's earliest books. The crew of a spacecraft in the service of a vast Terran empire is investigating a remote planet in the year 2780. They encounter an alien race, the Norglans, who are as committed as the Terrans to extending their supremacy throughout the cosmos. Representative of the two empires fight over who is to have the freer hand in dividing up the universe. They stop fighting when they are captured by the Rosgollans, a powerful and superior race. As George W. Tuma explained in the *Dictionary of Literary Biography*, the Rosgollans are "wise enough to recognize the folly of the two lesser races." And, as stated in the book, they declare that "limits will be drawn for the empire of Earth, and limits for the empire of Norgla. You shall not exceed these bounds in your search for colonies. And in this way your galaxy shall live in peace, forever, and to all eternity, world without end." *Collision Course* takes a harsh look at the arrogance of people who attempt to impose their image on the universe, a theme that is seen in many of Silverberg's works.

In the early 1960s, Silverberg moved from writing magazine articles to writing nonfiction books. His work covered a variety of topics, including Antarctica, ancient Egypt, the American space program, and medical history. "I severed my connections with my sleazy magazine outlets and ascended into this new, astoundingly respectable and rewarding career," he recalled in *CAAS*. Silverberg received awards for many of his nonfiction books, and his *Mound Builders of Ancient America: The Archeology of a Myth* is still considered one of the best works on the subject. He maintained a prolific writing pace, publishing about two million words every year. Barry M. Malzberg, writing in the *Magazine of Fantasy and Science Fiction*, declared that Silverberg "may be, in terms of accumulation of work per working year, the most prolific writer who ever lived."

It was during this time that Silverberg returned to science fiction and started writing what has been described as his first serious work in the genre. He experimented with technique and style and produced the award-winning novels *A Time*

"When I was a boy, I read science fiction and it did wonderful things for me," he said. "I feel a sense of obligation to science fiction to replace what I had taken from it, to add to the shelf, to put something there for someone else that would do for them what other writers had done for me."

—Robert Silverberg

of Changes and *Nightwings,* as well as several acclaimed stories, novellas, and other novels. In the *New York Times Book Review,* Theodore Sturgeon noted that Silverberg had "changed into something quite new and different—his own man, saying things his own way, and doing it with richness and diversity." He had suffered two setbacks in his personal life—he developed an overactive thyroid in 1966 that was attributed to overwork and, curiously, a house fire. The house was a mansion that had once belonged to former New York mayor Fiorello Henry LaGuardia, and Silverberg was devastated by its loss. Silverberg said in *CAAS* that the fire "drained from me, evidently forever, much of the bizarre energy that had allowed me to write a dozen or more significant books in a single year." Silverberg was still a prolific writer, but he began cutting back on his work schedule and would never return to the frantic pace of his early years.

According to Tuma, the primary themes that are developed in Silverberg's major novels are: how alienation can be confronted and overcome; how individuals can discover and develop a new concept of "beingness"; how individuals with special abilities, usually psychic, learn to embrace those abilities and forge new relationships with other individuals; and how individuals adapt to different physical and psychic environments.

Several of these themes are introduced in *Thorns* (1967) and *Hawkbill Station* (1968). In *Thorns,* the protagonist is Minner Burris, a starman whose body has been radically transformed through surgery on the planet Manipol. The surgeons who worked on Burris tried to "improve" him but only change him into their own physical image. When

Burris returns to Earth, he finds himself alienated because of his altered appearance. Lona Kelvin, a young woman in the story, is also feeling alienated because one hundred immature eggs have been taken from her womb, fertilized by a single donor, and then implanted into another woman. In effect, Kelvin is a virgin with one hundred children. Both Burris and Kelvin must learn to accept their own unique natures. A third character, Duncan Chalk, constantly manipulates and exploits people for his own gain. He tries to exploit Kelvin and Burris, but, ironically, his attempts at exploitation result in their liberation and his destruction. In *Thorns,* Silverberg tackles in a most effective manner the themes of alienation, man's ability to exploit others for his own purposes, and the relationship between love and estrangement.

Hawkbill Station is a story about the banishing of political dissidents into the past. It is the early twenty-first century, and the government uses a one-way time machine to send political dissidents back to the Cambrian age, which occurred from 500,000,000 to 600,000,000 B.C. (For "humane reasons," the government does not believe in executing political dissidents.) Silverberg vividly describes the barrenness of the Cambrian age and the isolation that members of the new settlement feel as they are completely separated from their familiar social and physical environment. *Thorns* was nominated for both of science fiction's major awards—the Hugo and the Nebula. The novella version of *Hawkbill Station* was also on both ballots. "But I won no trophies this year," Silverberg wrote in *CAAS.* "Ultimately I was destined to be nominated for more awards than any writer in the history of s-f."

Silverberg was now at the forefront of the science fiction field. But he was dissatisfied with his work. Despite the many awards that he won, Silverberg was disappointed with the public's response to his work. His books were not selling well, and science fiction purists often did not understand the messages in his books. By 1975, all of Silverberg's most serious books were out of print. He published *The Best of Robert Silverberg* and announced that he was retiring from sci-fi. "The reactions were interesting," Silverberg recalled in *CAAS.* "Predictably, the adventure-story fans responded with a 'good riddance.' Others, my loyal audience (and I really had one, I learned) bitterly reproached me for abandoning them, as though I had no right to stop writing."

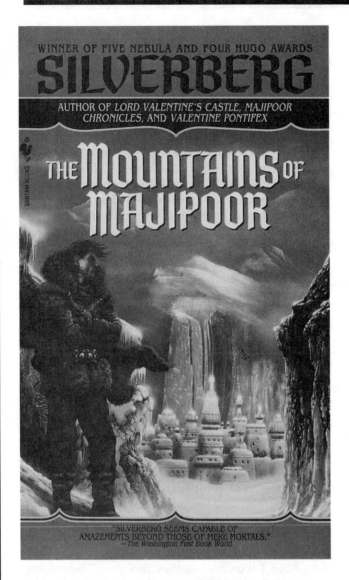

This 1995 novel, part of the author's "Majipoor Cycle," chronicles the adventures of Prince Harpirias as he encounters a barbaric society, the Othinor.

For the next four years, Silverberg wrote no science fiction and worked in the garden outside his home in California. But by 1979, he began writing again, for the most part because he needed money to buy a house for his wife, from whom he had separated. To earn money, he decided to write one last book. The world of science fiction had changed again; a new kind of novel that was more fantasy than science fiction was dominating the book lists. In an interview with *CAAS*, Silverberg remembered how he planned for what he thought would be his last book. "In designing the novel with which I would return, I had no

stomach for concocting pseudo-Tolkien, but I knew I had to avoid anything dark, depressing, or technically demanding." The book that Silverberg planned and wrote was *Lord Valentine's Castle*, a massive novel for which Silverberg received $127,500 from Harper & Row. At the time, this was the largest sum that had ever been paid for a science fiction novel.

Back To Work

Lord Valentine's Castle is the story of a disinherited prince who attempts to regain his throne. It combines elements of science fiction and heroic fantasy. In the *New York Times Book Review*, Jack Sullivan called the novel "an imaginative fusion of action, sorcery and science fiction, with visionary adventure scenes undergirded by scientific explanations." He added that "whatever else it does, *Lord Valentine's Castle* demands that its readers re-examine the relationship between science fiction and fantasy, for in this narrative Silverberg has fused the two together."

The success of *Lord Valentine's Castle* drew Silverberg back into the literary world. He began to write stories for *Omni* magazine, where several of his old friends were working. Times were changing in the science fiction field, due in large part to the success of the *Star Wars* and *Star Trek* movies. In 1982, Silverberg published *Majipoor Chronicles*, a novel compiled from several short stories set on the planet that is introduced in *Lord Valentine's Castle*. Each story is an episode from the history of Majipoor that has been stored on an experience-record. Using a futuristic reading machine, a young boy is able to relive these historical events. With *Valentine Pontifex*, Silverberg did what he said he would not—he wrote a sequel to *Lord Valentine's Castle*. In this book, Lord Valentine has been restored to power as the ruler of Majipoor, but he faces opposition from the Piurivars, an aboriginal race dispossessed years before by Earthling colonists. The Piurivars release plagues and deadly bio-engineered creatures upon the humans. Viewing *Lord Valentine's Castle*, *Majipoor Chronicles,* and *Valentine Pontifex* as a loose trilogy, a critic in the *Voice Literary Supplement* stated that "the trilogy becomes a whole in a way that the form rarely achieves."

Downward to Earth (1979) is considered one of Silverberg's best novels. George W. Tuma noted that the book was partially inspired by Silverberg's travels to Africa and his "growing sense of cosmic consciousness." The novel follows Edmund Gundersen, a sector administrator for the planet Belzagor in the twenty-fourth century. Gundersen comes to realize that he has not allowed the Nildoror, the main species of the planet, any dignity, and has treated them as subhuman because they resemble elephants. *Downward to Earth* tells a story of transformation and redemption.

Silverberg has continued his prolific efforts into the 1990s. He and Isaac Asimov coauthored a

novelization of an Asimov short story, "The Bicentennial Man," which had won a Nebula award in 1976. The novelization, called *The Positronic Man*, was published in 1993, a year after Asimov's death. In *Starborne* (1996), human society has solved all of its problems and is bored with itself. The healthy, wealthy, and bored inhabitants

---

If you enjoy the works of Robert Silverberg, you may also want to check out the following books and films:

Carol Severance, *Reefsong*, 1991.
Dan Simmons, *The Fall of Hyperion*, 1990.
Joan Slonczewski, *A Door into Ocean*, 1986.
Aliens, starring Sigourney Weaver, 1986.

---

of the Earth decide to dispatch a starship, the Wotan, to look for habitable planets elsewhere in the universe. Fifty people are aboard the Wotan, journeying through space and trying to find a new environment that will suit them. In the *New York Times Book Review*, Gerald Jonas noted that "Despite his many awards and honors, he [Silverberg] has never been embraced by the science fiction community. That may have something to do with his predilection for downbeat subjects. . . . The dominant 'mood' of *Starborne* is world-weariness." Tom Easton, writing in *Analog: Science Fiction/Science Fact*, remarked that "Silverberg is immensely skilled, and he has earned a well-deserved following for his many, many contributions to science fiction. But I really don't think this ranks with the best." Christy Tyson, however, writing in *Voice of Youth Advocates*, noted that "Silverberg has never been better than in this stunning combination of space adventure, psychological drama, and metaphysical speculation."

In his many years as a writer, Silverberg has produced an awe-inspiring body of work in several genres; commenting on the author's diversity, George R. R. Martin in the *Washington Post Book World* noted that "few writers, past or present, have had careers quite as varied, dramatic, and contradictory as that of Robert Silverberg." He has been more than a little bit successful as a writer of nonfiction, but it is in the field of science fic-

When twenty-fourth-century ecological disasters poison the air, humans must decide whether to leave earth or to alter themselves so they no longer need to breathe in this work.

tion that he has had his real impact. He is, in the words of Jeffrey Elliot, "a titan in the science fiction field."

In his introduction to *Galactic Dreamers: Science Fiction as Visionary Literature*, Silverberg described what he is trying to achieve in his work: "To show the reader something he has never been able to see with his own eyes, something strange and unique, beautiful and troubling, which draws him for a moment out of himself, places him in contact with the vastness of the universe, gives him for a sizzling moment a communion with the fabric of space and time, and leaves him forever transformed, forever enlarged."

■ Works Cited

Easton, Tom, "The Reference Library," *Analog: Science Fiction/Science Fact*, October, 1996, pp. 145-51.

Elliott, Jeffrey, interview with Robert Silverberg, *Science Fiction Voices #2*, Borgo Press, 1979.

Jonas, Gerald, review of *Starborne*, *New York Times Book Review*, June 30, 1996, p. 28.

Malzberg, Barry M., *Magazine of Fantasy and Science Fiction*, April, 1971.

Martin, George R. R., "The 'True Historie' of Robert Silverberg," *Washington Post Book World*, May 8, 1983, p. 6.

Platt, Charles, *Dream Makers: The Uncommon People Who Write Science Fiction*, Berkley Publishing, 1980.

Silverberg, Robert, *Collision Course*, Avalon, 1961.

Silverberg, Robert, editor, *Galactic Dreamers: Science Fiction as Visionary Literature*, Random House, 1977.

Silverberg, Robert, *Contemporary Authors Autobiography Series*, Volume 3, Gale, 1986, pp. 269-291.

Stableford, Brian M., *Masters of Science Fiction*, Borgo Press, 1981.

Sturgeon, Theodore, "If . . . ?," *New York Times Book Review*, March 5, 1972, p. 37.

Sullivan, Jack, review of *Lord Valentine's Castle*, *New York Times Book Review*, August 3, 1980, p. 12.

Tuma, George W., *Dictionary of Literary Biography*, Volume 8: *Twentieth-Century American Science-Fiction Writers*, Gale, 1981, pp. 106-19.

Tyson, Christy, review of *Starborne*, *Voice of Youth Advocates*, October 31, 1996, p. 221.

Voice Literary Supplement, December, 1983.

■ For More Information See

BOOKS

Aldiss, Brian, and Harry Harrison, editors, *Hell's Cartographers: Some Personal Histories of Science Fiction Writers*, Harper, 1975.

Clareson, Thomas D., *Robert Silverberg: A Primary and Secondary Bibliography*, G. K. Hall, 1983.

Contemporary Literary Criticism, Volume 7, Gale, 1971.

Elkins, Charles L., and Martin Greenberg, editors, *Robert Silverberg's Many Trapdoors: Critical Essays on His Science Fiction*, Greenwood Press, 1992.

MacNee, Marie J., *Science Fiction, Fantasy, and Horror Writers*, Volume 2, Gale, 1995, pp. 334-38.

Major Authors and Illustrators for Children and Young Adults, Gale, 1993.

Rabkin, Eric S., and others, editors, *No Place Else*, Southern Illinois University Press, 1983.

Schweitzer, Darrell, editor, *Exploring Fantasy Worlds: Essays on Fantastic Literature*, Borgo Press, 1985.

Something about the Author, Volume 91, Gale, 1997, pp. 191-98.

PERIODICALS

Booklist, January 1, 1979; September 1, 1984; August 22, 1986; February 1, 1988; April 1, 1990; August, 1991; February 1, 1995, p. 993.

Bulletin of the Center for Children's Books, June, 1969; September, 1969, p. 17; June, 1975, p. 167; November, 1976, p. 48; October, 1987, p. 37.

Extrapolation, December, 1975, pp. 18-28; summer, 1979, pp. 109-17.

Horn Book, June, 1969, pp. 323-25.

Junior Bookshelf, February, 1978, p. 49; August, 1989, p. 194.

Kirkus Reviews, August 1, 1979, p. 896; September 15, 1984, p. 874; February 15, 1992, p. 222.

Library Journal, May 15, 1996, p. 86.

New York Times Book Review, November 11, 1984, p. 13; December 15, 1991, pp. 20-21; May 3, 1992, p. 38; November 14, 1993, p. 74; March 13, 1994, p. 30.

Publishers Weekly, October 20, 1975, p. 74; July 2, 1979, p. 106; January 22, 1982, p. 63; September 30, 1985, p. 112; August 30, 1991, p. 71; November 1, 1993, p. 70; May 27, 1996, pp. 69-70.

School Library Journal, March, 1977, p. 153; April, 1979, p. 72; November, 1979, p. 94; September, 1980, p. 93; May, 1982, pp. 90-91; March, 1987, p. 178; March, 1991, p. 218.

Voice of Youth Advocates, June, 1984, p. 102; April, 1986, p. 42; June, 1988, p. 97; October, 1990, pp. 232-33; December, 1991, p. 322-23; August, 1993, pp. 170-71.*

—Sketch by Irene Durham

Steven Spielberg

■ Personal

Born December 18, 1947, in Cincinnati, OH; son of Arnold (a computer engineer) and Leah (a restaurateur) Spielberg; married Amy Irving (an actress), November 27, 1985, divorced 1990; married Kate Capshaw (an actress), October 12, 1991; children: (first marriage) son Max; (second marriage) daughters Sasha and Mikaela, sons Sawyer and Destry; stepchildren (second marriage) son Theo, daughter Jessica. *Education:* Attended California State College (now University), Long Beach, CA.

■ Addresses

Home—Beverly Hills, CA, and Long Island, NY. *Agent*—Jay Moloney, Creative Artists Agency, 9830 Wilshire Blvd., Beverly Hills, CA, 90212. *Office*—Amblin Entertainment, 100 Universal City Plaza, Bungalow 477, Universal City, CA 91608-1085.

■ Career

Writer and director of motion pictures and television shows. Founder of Amblin Entertainment, Universal City; cofounder of Dream Works SKG,

1994. *Member:* British Academy of Film and Television Arts (fellow).

Began at Universal City Studios, Inc., Universal City, CA, directing television series and movies including *The Name of the Game*, 1968, *Marcus Welby, M.D.*, 1969-70, *Rod Serling's Night Gallery*, 1969-70, *Owen Marshall*, 1971, *The Psychiatrist*, 1971, and *Columbo*, 1971; directed television movies *Duel*, 1971, *Something Evil*, 1972, and *Savage*, 1973. Director of feature films *Sugarland Express*, 1974, and *Jaws*, 1975; writer and director of *Close Encounters of the Third Kind*, 1977; director of *1941*, 1979; director of *Raiders of the Lost Ark*, 1981; director and coproducer of *E.T. The Extra-Terrestrial*, 1982; coproducer of Segment 1 and Prologue, and director of Segment 2 of *Twilight Zone—The Movie*, 1983; director of *Indiana Jones and the Temple of Doom*, 1984; director and coproducer of *The Color Purple*, 1985; director and coproducer of *Empire of the Sun*, 1987; director of *Always*, 1989; director of *Indiana Jones and the Last Crusade*, 1989; director and coproducer of *Hook*, 1991; director and coproducer of *Jurassic Park*, 1993; director and coproducer of *Schindler's List*, 1993; director of *The Lost World: Jurassic Park*, 1997; director of *Amistad*, 1997; director and producer of *Saving Private Ryan*, 1998.

Producer of feature film *An American Tail: Fievel Goes West*, 1991. Executive producer or co-executive producer of feature films, including *I Wanna Hold Your Hand*, 1978; *Used Cars*, 1980; *Continental*

Divide, 1981; *Gremlins,* 1984; *The Goonies, Young Sherlock Holmes,* and *Back to the Future,* 1985; *An American Tail* and *The Money Pit,* 1986; *Innerspace* and *Batteries Not Included,* 1987; *Who Framed Roger Rabbit* and *The Land Before Time,* 1988; *Dad* and *Back to the Future—Part II,* 1989; *Joe Versus the Volcano, Gremlins 2: The New Batch, Back to the Future—Part III,* and *Arachnophobia,* 1990; *An American Tail: Fievel Goes West,* 1991; *We're Back: A Dinosaur's Story, Trail Mix-Up, I'm Mad,* and *The Flintstones,* 1994; *To Wong Foo, Thanks for Everything, Julie Newman, Casper, Balto,* and *The Bridges of Madison Country* (uncredited), 1995; *Twister,* 1996; *Men in Black, The Peacemaker,* and *Mouse Hunt,* 1997; *Mark of Zorro, Cats, Deep Impact,* and *Small Soldiers,* 1998.

Executive producer and segment director of television series *Amazing Stories,* 1985. Executive producer of television series including *Tiny Toons Adventures,* 1990, *Sea Quest,* 1993, *Freakazoid* and *Pinky and the Brain,* 1995, and *High Incident,* 1996. Executive producer of made-for-television films including *Wish for Things That Work,* 1991, *Habitation of Dragons* and *The Water Engine,* 1992, *Class of '61* and *Sea Quest DSV,* 1993, *Tiny Toons Spring Break,* 1994. Executive producer of video production *Tiny Toon Adventures: How I Spent My Vacation,* 1992.

Has also appeared in television shows and films, including *The Blues Brothers,* 1980, *Gremlins,* 1984, as man in electric wheelchair (uncredited), *The Tracy Ullman Show,* 1987, playing himself, and *Animaniacs,* 1993, uncredited voice.

■ Awards, Honors

Won film contest for student film, *Escape to Nowhere;* won prizes at Atlanta Film Festival and Venice Film Festival for student film, *Amblin';* best director award nomination, Academy of Motion Picture Arts and Sciences, 1977, for *Close Encounters of the Third Kind;* recipient of Irving G. Thalberg Award, Academy of Motion Picture Arts and Sciences, 1987, for body of work; named best director, Directors Guild, 1985, for *The Color Purple,* which also received National Association for the Advancement of Colored People Image Awards; named best director, National Board of Review, 1987, for *Empire of the Sun,* which was also named best picture; guest of honor at Moving Picture Ball, American Cinematheque, 1989; Academy

Award for Best Director, Academy of Motion Picture Arts and Sciences, 1993, for *Schindler's List;* American Film Institute Life Achievement Award, 1995.

■ Writings

Close Encounters of the Third Kind (novelization of his film of same title), Dell, 1977.
The Goonies Storybook, Simon & Schuster, 1985.

FILMS

(Author of story) *Ace Eli and Rodger of the Skies,* Twentieth Century-Fox, 1973.
(Author of story, and director) *The Sugarland Express,* Universal, 1974.
(Author of screenplay, and director) *Close Encounters of the Third Kind,* Columbia, 1977.
(Author of screenplay with Michael Grais and Mark Victor, and producer with Frank Marshall) *Poltergeist,* Metro-Goldwyn-Mayer/United Artists, 1982.
(Author of story, and producer) *The Goonies,* Warner Bros., 1985.

Also author and director of amateur films including, *The Last Gun,* 1959; *Escape to Nowhere,* 1961; *Battle Squad,* 1961; *Firelight,* 1965; and *Amblin',* 1969.

■ Overview

"People like [Steven] Spielberg don't come along every day," his friend and colleague George Lucas told a *Time* interviewer, "and when they do, it's an amazing thing. It's like talking about Einstein or Babe Ruth or Tiger Woods. He's not in a group of filmmakers his age; he's far, far away." Spielberg, who is generally regarded as Hollywood's most successful filmmaker, is the director of such megahits as *Jaws, Close Encounters of the Third Kind, Raiders of the Lost Ark, E.T. The Extraterrestrial,* and the two *Jurassic Park* films, as well as such serious features as *The Color Purple* and *Schindler's List.* No matter what subject matter he has chosen, Spielberg's creative sensibilities and unique visual style have found a broad mainstream, middlebrow audience; as Stephen Schiff of the *New Yorker* has pointed out, "For better or worse, Spielberg's graphic vocabulary has engulfed our own." Other critics have pointed out that

Spielberg is the most successful of a generation of "post-literate" Baby Boomer film directors who were weaned on television, fast food, and post-war middle-class, suburban values.

Steven Spielberg was born in Cincinnati, Ohio, as the eldest of four children of Leah and Arnold Spielberg. According to Frank Sanello, the author of *Spielberg: The Man, The Movies, The Mythology* (one of the more than twenty Spielberg biographies), young Steven was "a reluctant Jew" who at bedtime sometimes taped the end of his nose in hopes that it would grow upwards like a gentile's. Spielberg's mother, Leah, a classical pianist, inadvertently fostered her son's insecurities by declining to maintain a kosher diet or to live in a Jewish neighborhood. Instead, she insisted that her family settle in suburbia, the epitome of white, middle-class culture; there her son and his three younger sisters became targets of anti-Semitism.

Spielberg's "workaholic" father was a pioneer in the computer industry in the late 1940s and early 1950s. As a result, Arnold Spielberg moved his family often as he pursued his career. "Just as I'd become accustomed to a school and a teacher and a best friend, the FOR SALE sign would dig into the front lawn and we'd be packing and off to some other state," Spielberg said in a 1985 autobiographical article in *Time*. "I've often considered Arizona, where I was from [age] nine to sixteen, my real home. For a kid, home is where you have your best friends and your car, and your first kiss; it's where you do your worst stuff and get your best grades."

Spielberg's parents and siblings remember him as a relentless practical joker. But he was also a loner, and as a boy he spent many hours alone watching television and movies, despite his parents' prohibitions. When Arnold Spielberg gave his son an old home movie camera to record family camping

Spielberg's first big hit, *Jaws*, about a great white shark that invades a New England tourist area, frightened audiences nationwide during the summer of 1975.

trips and boy scout adventures, Steven Spielberg became obsessed with his new hobby. Leah Spielberg encouraged him by letting him skip school to work on his film projects. On weekends, he sometimes sold tickets to neighborhood children, and in the darkened living room of his parent's home he showed his own films and others that he rented. Spielberg's own efforts at the time were mostly action or horror films inspired by his own childhood fears. "I remember lying there [at night], trying to go to sleep," he told Michiko Kakutani of the *New York Times*, "and I always used to imagine little Hieronymus Bosch-like creatures inside [the walls], peeking out and whispering to me to come into the playground of the crack[s] and be drawn into the unknown. . . ."

Being the only Jew at Arcadia High School in Palo Alto, he recalls being taunted unmercifully. His classmates threw pennies at him and coughed the word "Jew" into their hands whenever he came within hearing range. While Spielberg neither forgot nor forgave them, he figured out how to use his filmmaking talents to win a measure of social acceptance. When the school bully began abusing him, Spielberg found relief by appealing to his tormenter's vanity; he cast the bully in a fifteen-minute film called *Escape to Nowhere*. That 1961 production, which cost $50 to make, won first prize at a local film festival. Another more elaborate effort, a 1965 science fiction film called *Firelight*, starred Spielberg's sisters; it cost $400 to make and proved so successful that it was screened at a local movie theater where it earned its young director $500. Steven Spielberg was already demonstrating a knack for commercial filmmaking. "I felt like a real nerd, the skinny, acne-faced wimp who gets picked on by big football jocks all the way home from school," Spielberg told *Time*. "I hated school. From age twelve or thirteen I knew I wanted to be a movie director, and I didn't think that science or math or foreign languages were going to help me turn out the little 8-mm sagas I was making to avoid homework."

Nothing Holds Him Back

Spielberg's life changed forever the day in 1963 that he took a tour of Universal Studios. He snuck away from his tour group to watch a film being made and chanced to meet Chuck Silver, Universal's film historian. "Instead of calling the guards to throw me off the lot, he talked to me for about an hour," Spielberg told Richard Corliss of *Time* years later. "He said he'd like to see some of my little films, and so he gave me a pass to get on the lot the next day. I showed him about four of my 8-mm films. [Silver] was very impressed. Then he said, 'I don't have the authority to write you any more passes, but good luck to you.'" Spielberg didn't need a pass; he found his own way back onto the Universal lot. "I walked past the guard every day," he told Lynn Hirschberg of *Rolling Stone*, "[I] waved at him and he waved back. I always wore a suit and carried a briefcase, and he assumed I was some kid related to some mogul, and that was that." Spielberg staked claim to an empty office, put his name on the door, and informed the switchboard operator that he was now working at the studio. Incredibly, for the next two years no one asked him what he was doing there. Spielberg claims he spent three days a week at Universal, using the phone and watching how movies are made.

It was around this time that Spielberg's parents divorced. Their 1966 split proved traumatic but seminal for their son. As *Chicago Tribune* writer Dave Kehr has pointed out, "In film after film the same pattern is repeated: A weak, unstable family, burdened with an absent or irresponsible father, is strengthened or saved through the intervention of a supernatural force—a force that can be either sweet or benign (*E.T.*, *Close Encounters [of the Third Kind]*) or evil and destructive (*Jaws*, *Poltergeist*). There is in these films a yearning for authority, a powerful need to feel protected and watched over (or in the dark films, a demand for discipline and strength) that has an obvious nostalgic appeal for young adults freshly booted out of the family nest."

Upon graduating from high school, Spielberg applied to UCLA film school. His marks were not good enough to get in, so he enrolled instead at California State College (now University) in Long Beach. There he majored in English because the school had no film studies program. It did not matter. Spielberg's class attendance was spotty; he preferred to spend his days making films. In 1969, he and a friend shot a twenty-two minute film called *Amblin'*, which told the story of a teenage couple hitchhiking from the Mojave desert to the Pacific Ocean. The friend put up $15,000 to finance the picture, and Spielberg directed. *Amblin'* won awards at film festivals in Venice and At-

Benevolent aliens make contact with humans in *Close Encounters of the Third Kind,* a 1977 feature written and directed by Spielberg.

lanta, and when Chuck Silver screened it for Sid Sheinberg, Universal's head of television production was so impressed that he summoned the film's young director to a job interview. Spielberg biographer Frank Sanello quoted Sheinberg as dismissing the young director as a "nerdlike, scrawny character," but he offered him a job at $275 per week anyway. When Spielberg hesitated, citing his desire to complete his education, Sheinberg demanded, "Do you want to graduate college or do you want to be a film director?" A week later, Spielberg signed the contract and went to work.

Spielberg's directorial debut at Universal was the pilot of a proposed series called *Night Gallery*, which had been written by Rod Serling, the creator of the popular 1950s program *The Twilight Zone.* The segment that Spielberg directed starred legendary screen actress Joan Crawford, who was suffering with alcoholism at the tail end of her career. Crawford initially balked at being directed

by a twenty-year-old unknown, but when Rod Serling spoke up for him, Spielberg was kept on the job. However, that initial directing experience proved so disillusioning that afterward Spielberg took a one-year leave of absence from Universal. He used the time to write several film scripts and to reassess his life. Following his return to work, Spielberg spent the next two years directing segments for various popular weekly television series, including *Marcus Welby, The Name of the Game,* and *Columbo.*

Spielberg's first feature film was *Duel*, a 1971 made-for-television thriller starring Dennis Weaver as a motorist who is pursued through the desert by an unseen driver in a menacing truck. Spielberg finished the $300,000 film in twelve days—three over schedule—but he did so within budget and *Duel* was a hit on U.S. television. It was also shown in theaters in Europe, where it won awards at Italian and French film festivals and caught the eye of the legendary British director David Lean (the maker of epic films such as *Dr. Zhivago* and *Lawrence of Arabia*); according to a 1985 story in *Time,* Lean hailed Spielberg as "a very bright new director" and a kindred spirit. Most important of all from Universal's perspective was the fact that *Duel* made $9 million. That alone landed Spielberg an assignment directing another made-for-television movie. This one was a ghost story called *Something Evil.* Rewarded with more favorable reviews, Spielberg began seeking projects which would allow him even more creative freedom. He directed the pilot episode for a planned weekly television series called *Savage,* starring the real-life husband-and-wife team of Martin Landau and Barbara Bain, of *Mission Impossible* fame. The new show failed to catch on, but it proved to be the final step in Spielberg's apprenticeship; he was now ready to make the leap to directing feature films for the big screen. "Television taught me to how to be a professional in a very chaotic business," Frank Sanello quotes Spielberg as saying.

Spielberg's first theatrical release was *Sugarland Express,* a film based on one of the scripts he had written during his year's sabbatical from Universal. Producers Darryl Zanuck and David Brown hired Spielberg to direct Goldie Hawn and William Atherton in this tale about parents who try to regain custody of their lost children by defying the authorities. *Sugarland Express* "is mostly about cars," wrote Pauline Kael of the *New Yorker.* "Spielberg is a choreographic virtuoso with cars. He patterns them; he makes them dance and crash and bounce back. He handles enormous configurations of vehicles; sometimes they move so sweetly you think he must be wooing them." Kael went on to praise the young director's gift for "very free and easy American" humor, and she predicted that he "could be that rarity among directors, a born entertainer." *New York Times* re-

One of the top-grossing movies of all time, *E.T. The Extra-Terrestrial* warmed the hearts of filmgoers in 1982.

viewer Stephen Farber was decidedly less impressed by *Sugarland Express*. "Everything is underlined," he wrote. "Spielberg sacrifices narrative logic and character consistency for cheap thrills and easy laughs."

Mixed reviews would greet many Spielberg films. While *Sugarland Express* was not the box office hit that producers Zanuck and Brown wanted, they liked Spielberg's work enough to hire him to make another action film. This one was about a great white shark that terrorizes the beaches of a fictional New England summer resort known as Amity Island. *Jaws*, based on a bestselling novel by author Peter Benchley, featured a cast of mostly unknown actors headed by the young Richard Dreyfuss. Dealing with actors was not Spielberg's biggest test in making the movie. The technical and logistical challenges involved in filming in the waters off Martha's Vineyards have become part of Hollywood legend, as have the producers' concerns about the then-daunting $8 million budget. If Zanuck and Brown were worried, they need not have been.

Jaws: First Spielberg Blockbuster

Jaws was a smash hit when it was released in the summer of 1975. That film devoured box office records, taking in more than $450 million and becoming one of the top-grossing films of all time; it also revolutionized American moviemaking—henceforth, summer blockbusters with highly lucrative spin-off merchandising campaigns became part of the business—and it turned Steven Spielberg into a media superstar. "What sets *Jaws* apart from most of the other ceiling busters and makes it a special case," a writer for *Time* observed, "is that it is quite a good movie. For one thing, it is mercifully free of the padding—cosmic, comic, cultural—that so often mars 'big' pictures. If the great white shark that terrorizes the beaches of an island summer colony is one of nature's most efficient killing machines, *Jaws* is an efficient entertainment machine." Most other critics praised *Jaws* for its fast pace and thrilling action.

According to Frank Sanello, Spielberg told a reporter for *Women's Wear Daily* that he earned $4 million "after taxes" from *Jaws*. Media speculation was that he actually made a lot more than that—enough, in fact, to make him independently wealthy. Even more important, in the wake of *Jaws* Spielberg found his directorial skills in demand, even as he was suffering through a critical backlash. "The same people who had raved about [the movie] began to doubt its artistic value as soon as it began to bring in so much money," he complained to Jack Kroll of *Newsweek*. One impact of this was that Spielberg did not receive a hoped for Oscar nomination in the Best Director category. "It hurt me because I felt [*Jaws*] was a director's movie," he admitted.

Undaunted, Spielberg set to work on his next film intent on disproving the skeptics who said his success had been a fluke. *Close Encounters of the Third Kind* was released in the summer of 1977. The title, initially a meaningless phrase to most people, instantly became synonymous with making physical contact with unidentified flying objects (UFOs) and alien life forms. Scores of previous Hollywood movies over the years had depicted visitors from space as bloodthirsty invaders, but *Close Encounters* suggested that these creatures might actually come in peace. Spielberg tells the story of how some UFO sightings in Indiana lead an everyman utility worker, played by Richard Dreyfuss, to discover the craft's eventual landing site in the Wyoming wilderness. When the aliens' huge mothership arrives, it does so bearing a message of hope and goodwill.

After the critical jabs thrown his way over *Jaws*, Spielberg was pleased that so many critics praised the strong storyline of *Close Encounters*. He explained to Chris Hodenfield of *Rolling Stone* that he had gone through six drafts of the script because "you need good storytelling to offset the amount of technique the audience demands, the amount of spectacle audiences demand before they'll leave their television sets. And I think people will leave their television sets for a good story before anything else." The extra attention to plot paid off. *Close Encounters* went on to become one of the top grossing movies ever, earning more than a quarter billion dollars. Audiences were dazzled by the film's special effects; many critics praised the film as being Spielberg's most personal, while others debated its religious overtones. However, a few journalists also chided the director for "manipulating" his audience. Pauline Kael of the *New Yorker* lauded *Close Encounters* as "the most innocent of all technological marvel movies, and one of the most satisfying," but at the same time she noted that it showed "an excess of kind-

In *Schindler's List*, the Oscar-winning 1993 film, Spielberg examined the horrors of the Holocaust through the real-life story of German industrialist Oskar Schindler, who saved the lives of more than a thousand Jews.

ness—an inability (or, perhaps, unwillingness) to perceive the streak of cowardice and ignorance and confusion in the action of the authorities who balk at the efforts of the visionaries to reach their goal."

Close Encounters' popularity solidified Spielberg's reputation as one of Hollywood's most successful directors. It also made him temporarily lose sight of his own strengths as a filmmaker. Spielberg's next directorial effort was an uncharacteristically lavish big-budget slapstick comedy called *1941*. Based on actual historical events that occurred in the wake of Pearl Harbor, the film looks at the "lighter side" of the hysteria that gripped Southern California in late 1941, when a Japanese attack seemed imminent. Spielberg later conceded that he had experienced misgivings about the film even as he was making it. "I kept saying to myself from the first day, 'This is not a Spielberg movie. What am I doing here?'," Sanello quoted him as saying. Those doubts proved well founded;

for once, the public sided with the critics, who lambasted *1941* as tasteless and dull. The movie was a box office flop; incredibly, although *1941* eventually took in more than $90 million, it still lost money.

Spielberg's next film, *Raiders of the Lost Ark*, marked a return to the kind of strong storyline and thrilling special effects that had made *Jaws* and *Close Encounters* so popular. *Raiders of the Lost Ark*, released in 1981, was actually a collaboration between Spielberg and George Lucas (the creator behind the phenomenally popular *Star Wars* series); Lucas was one of the film's producers, while Spielberg directed. This first installment of what would become an adventure trilogy stars Harrison Ford as the intrepid archeologist Indiana Jones. The film, a "cliffhanger classic," as a critic in *Newsweek* termed it, is a fast-paced action film in the style of the old 1930s adventure serials. Roger Ebert of the Chicago *Sun-Times* commented that *Raiders of the Lost Ark* "defined a new energy level for adventure movies." Richard Schickel of *Time* praised it as "an object lesson in how to blend the art of storytelling with the highest levels of technical know-how, planning, cost control, and commercial acumen."

The Little Alien That Could

Any doubts that Spielberg had hit his creative and commercial stride were permanently erased by *E.T. The Extra-Terrestrial*, released in 1982. The film is based on a story that had come to Spielberg when he was in the Tunisian desert filming *Raiders of the Lost Ark*. "I was kind of lonely at the time," Spielberg told Jim Calio of *People*. "My girlfriend was back in Los Angeles. I remember saying to myself, 'What I really need is a friend I can talk to—somebody who can give me *all* the answers.'" The friend that Spielberg dreamed of eventually came to life in the character of E.T., a child-size alien who is inadvertently left behind when the spaceship he arrives on departs without him. After finding his way into a typical suburban American neighborhood, E.T. is taken in and befriended by a boy named Elliott.

When news of the existence of Elliott's secret friend inevitably leaks out, government scientists quarantine the family's home and capture E.T., who has fallen deathly ill. After helping his alien friend beam a radio signal to his distant planet—giving rise to the film's most famous line: "E.T. phone home"—Elliott, his siblings, and their friends rescue the little alien in a magical scene that involves a wild car chase and some flying bicycles. Spielberg has explained that when he first envisioned *E.T.*, it was to have been a modest, low-budget film. As the project grew, so did its cost, leading executives at the Columbia studio to pass on making the film. Some observers were also skeptical because the movie was one of the few that Spielberg has made without first meticulously sketching every scene on storyboards; this time he opted to improvise with his young cast. He told an interviewer from *People*, "while I was doing *Raiders* I felt I was losing touch with the reason I became a moviemaker—to make stories about people and relationships. [E.T.] is the first movie I ever made for myself."

Audiences and critics alike loved the result. *E.T.* became the most successful film ever made to that time, with a total box office of more than $700

million and another $1 billion from sales of spin-off merchandise. At one point in mid-1982, *People* reported that Spielberg was earning a staggering $1 million *a day* from the film. The money was as extravagant as the praise for *E.T.* In the *New York Times* critic Vincent Canby opined that it "may become a children's classic of the space age." *New York* magazine film critic David Denby pronounced it "one of the most beautiful fantasy-adventure movies ever made."

Ironically, the same year that *E.T.* was released, another much darker Spielberg film appeared in movie theaters. *Poltergeist* is a horror story about evil spirits that terrorize an ordinary, middle-class family. Spielberg did not direct this movie, although it is very much a Steven Spielberg creation; he both wrote and produced it. (In fact, at one point director Tobe Hooper charged that in hopes of cashing in on *E.T.*'s success, studio publicists were spreading rumors that Spielberg had secretly directed *Poltergeist*.) Producing films is an aspect of the business in which Spielberg became involved in the late 1970s, when he founded his own production company, Amblin Entertainment, on a corner of the Universal Studios lot. *Poltergeist*, one of the hit films of 1982, was Spielberg's first big success as a producer. He has subsequently produced dozens more movies, among them such hits as *Goonies*, *Back to the Future* (I and III), *Who Framed Roger Rabbit?*, *An American Tail*, *Arachnophobia*, *The Flintstones*, *Casper*, *Twister*, and *Men in Black*; in addition, the television arm of Amblin Entertainment has created a variety of popular programs.

Spielberg has had far more hits than misses in his career as a producer, but it was in this capacity that he experienced one of the most traumatic episodes of his life. Just a few months after the release of *E.T.*, actor Vic Morrow and two young Vietnamese children died in a helicopter accident on the set of the Spielberg-produced *Twilight Zone: The Movie*. Spielberg's colleague and friend John Landis, who like Spielberg directed one of the movie's four segments, faced manslaughter charges. Questions also arose about the use and possible "exploitation" of child actors on the set. Although a court eventually found Landis not guilty, the incident was deeply unsettling for Spielberg and everyone else involved.

It almost seemed as if Spielberg was subconsciously unable to shake his bad memories when he and George Lucas teamed up again in 1984 for a "prequel" to *Raiders of the Lost Ark. Indiana Jones and the Temple of Doom* was a hit, but the film was attacked by critics who pointed out that while *Raiders of the Lost Ark* had been full of non-stop action and fun, *Indiana Jones and the Temple of Doom* was dark, violent, and rife with images of children being brutalized; in one especially disturbing scene, a still-beating heart is ripped from a sacrifice victim's body. Ralph Novak of *People* denounced the middle portion of the film as "a relentless, tedious stream of graphic brutality."

Spielberg continued in a serious vein with his next project: a 1985 movie based on black writer Alice Walker's controversial Pulitzer Prize-winning novel *The Color Purple,* which deals with racism, lesbianism, alcoholism, male violence against women, incest, and other explosive themes. Initially Spielberg was reluctant to direct a film about black women in rural Georgia during the years 1906 to 1940. He changed his mind only after a conversation with black record mogul Quincy Jones, who reminded him, "You didn't have to come from Mars to do *E.T.,* did you?" Accepting what he saw as the biggest challenge of his career, Spielberg directed for a minimum salary of $40,000. He took another chance by casting a couple of then-unknown black actresses in the lead roles. One was a Chicago television talk show host named Oprah Winfrey, the other a young comedian named Whoopi Goldberg. The pair turned in career-making performances, and both became major stars as a result.

Some critics praised *The Color Purple* as Steven Spielberg's most mature and polished film. "It is a great, warm, hard, unforgiving, triumphant movie," wrote Roger Ebert of the Chicago *Sun-Times.* However, some viewers and gay rights advocates chided Spielberg for downplaying lesbian themes in Walker's novel; David Denby of *New York* described it as "inauthentic and unconvincing." Alice Walker herself came to Spielberg's defense, pointing out that the film had focused more attention on her writing than she had ever enjoyed. Nonetheless, the controversy continued, even when *The Color Purple* received eleven Oscar nominations; notably missing once again was a nomination for Spielberg as Best Director. Members of the Academy of Motion Picture Arts and Sciences were less impressed with the film than reviewers were, and when the awards were handed out, *The Color Purple* was virtually ignored.

Some of Spielberg's disappointment was eased when his colleagues in the Directors' Guild honored him with their Best Director of the year award.

Spielberg's next film also had literary roots. *Empire of the Sun* was a 1987 big-budget epic based on British writer J. G. Ballard's semi-autobiographical novel of the same name. That book chronicles the adventures of a nine-year-old British boy who is living with his upper-class family in Shanghai, China, on the eve of the Second World War. The boy is separated from his parents in the rush to evacuate the city when war breaks out, and he ends up in a Japanese civilian internment camp. Conditions are grim, and it is a struggle to survive. *Empire of the Sun* garnered some good reviews, but its dark subject was too intense for audiences. Spielberg professed to be neither surprised nor concerned. "At this point in my career I think I've earned the right to fail commercially," Frank Sanello quoted him as saying. "I knew going in that *Empire of the Sun* wasn't a very commercial project." Ironically, the same year Spielberg flopped at the box office, the Academy of Motion Picture Arts and Sciences finally recognized Spielberg's directorial prowess, bestowing upon him the Irving J. Thalberg Award for lifetime achievement (at the still young age of forty).

Whatever box office appeal Spielberg's *Empire of the Sun* lacked, one of the two new films that he released in 1989 more than made up for. Spielberg had planned to do the movie *Rainman,* starring Dustin Hoffman and Tom Cruise; however, at the last moment Spielberg turned over the project to director Barry Levinson because he had promised George Lucas that he would direct another installment of the adventures of Indiana Jones. That 1989 film, *Indiana Jones and the Last Crusade,* featured Harrison Ford in a reprise of the title role, with Sean Connery as his father. This casting combination proved popular, and Spielberg struck it rich yet again. *Indiana Jones and the Last Crusade* became the biggest hit of the three films in the series, rocketing into what was then fourth spot on the all-time list of top-grossing movies. A critic from the *New York Times* praised the film as "an endearing original [that] attests to the filmmaker's expanding talent." But other reviews were less enthusiastic. "It's enjoyable, but familiar, and the action lacks the exhilarating, leaping precision that . . . Spielberg is famous for," wrote Pauline Kael of the *New Yorker.* Calling *The Last Crusade* a "defi-

The 1997 film *Amistad* details a rebellion aboard a slave ship in 1839.

nite improvement over" *Temple of Doom*, syndicated critic Leonard Maltin noted that "it still bears the mark of one too many trips to the well."

The second Spielberg film released in 1989 was not nearly as successful as the third installment of Indiana Jones' adventures. *Always* was a remake of the 1944 romance movie *A Guy Named Joe*, which Spielberg had seen and enjoyed as a boy. Neither audiences nor critics liked this version; most agreed with Pauline Kael when she wrote, "All [Spielberg] seems to want to do in each scene is get an audience reaction; almost everything is grandiloquent, rushed, [and] confusing."

Spielberg has conceded that he was adrift creatively in the early 1990s. This lack of direction was apparent in his next project: a modern-day version of British writer J. M. Barrie's timeless children's classic *Peter Pan*. The film, released in 1990, was one that Spielberg had long dreamed of making. In fact, in 1985, he explained to a *Time* interviewer, "I have always felt like Peter Pan. I still feel like him. It has been very hard for me to grow up." *Hook* cost $60 million to make and featured a dream cast that included Spielberg's friend Robin Williams, Julia Roberts, and Dustin Hoffman. "I was finally able to break through my 20-year fear of working with movie stars," told *People*. As a result, *Hook* was one of the most eagerly anticipated films of 1990, and it earned $288 million at the box office. While any other director would have considered this to be a major success (especially when he or she received a percentage of the film's gross receipts, as Spielberg did), Spielberg was disappointed by the reviews for the film, which were mostly negative.

■ Update

Undeterred, he demonstrated his unequalled talent for commercial filmmaking once more when he directed the 1993 screen version of author Michael Crichton's bestselling novel *Jurassic Park*. The book is a cautionary science fiction tale about what happens when unscrupulous businessmen clone dinosaurs using DNA extracted from fossils. Things go awry, of course, and the beasts run amuck in the theme park that has been built for them. Spielberg used a state-of-the-art special effects technique called Computer Generated Imagery (CGI) to create amazingly life-like dinosaurs which terrorized the real-life human actors on the

screen. Movie critic Leonard Maltin pronounced *Jurassic Park* to be a "slam bang thriller [that] delivers the goods with action, suspense, and hair-raising chills. . . ." Audiences agreed and the movie became one of the biggest hits in the Hollywood's history, grossing more than $1 billion, with another $1 billion in revenue from sales of *Jurassic Park* merchandise; as a result, Spielberg reportedly earned more than $350 million.

Schindler's List A Watershed For Spielberg

The buzz over *Jurassic Park* still had not subsided when Spielberg released his second film of 1993. *Schindler's List*, a drama based on the book of the same name by Australian writer Thomas Keneally, could not have been more different from *Jurassic Park*. *Schindler's List* tells the real-life story of Oskar Schindler, a German industrialist who was a Nazi, yet who saved more than a thousand Jews from certain death in the extermination camps by employing them in a factory. "Until *Schindler's List*, Spielberg's Judaism never touched his work," David Ansen of *Newsweek* pointed out. In other ways, too, the film was a watershed for Steven Spielberg, one that he has said has forever changed his artistic sensibilities, his moviemaking, and his life. To create *Schindler's List*, he focused every ounce of his consummate talents; the movie was shot on location in Europe—some scenes were actually filmed at Auschwitz—in black-and-white and used *cinéma vérité* techniques to give a documentary feel. It took just seventy-one days to shoot, cost a relatively modest $23 million, and involved more than 125 actors and 30,000 extras. The end product was a stunning, profoundly original drama about the horrors of the Holocaust. A coda (shot in color) showed the actors and their real-life counterparts, who survived because of Schindler, visiting his grave. Spielberg used this technique in an effort to reiterate to his audience the reality and immediacy of the story. It worked; the effects were stunning, even emotionally overwhelming for many people.

Schindler's List became one of the most talked about films in Hollywood history, and it was also a commercial success. Spielberg reportedly took no salary for his work. Instead, he committed his share of the proceeds—about $16 million—to establish a non-profit organization called the Survivors of the Shoah Visual History Foundation. Its purpose is to use the latest computer digital tech-

If you enjoy the works of Steven Spielberg, you may also want to check out the following films:

Backdraft, directed by Ron Howard, starring Kurt Russell, 1991.
Platoon, directed by Oliver Stone, 1986.
Star Wars, directed by George Lucas, starring Mark Hamill, 1977.

nology to record video interviews with as many Holocaust survivors as possible and to make this material available to a mass audience. "What really prompted Spielberg to spend millions on the project was the debt he felt he owed posterity," wrote Frank Sanello.

Even more satisfying for Spielberg than the commercial success of *Schindler's List* was the fact the film was hailed by many observers as an instant classic. Stephen Schiff of the *New Yorker* called it "the finest fiction film ever made about the century's greatest evil," and John Gross of the *New York Review* wrote, "It offers as truthful a picture as we are ever likely to get of the regions where no documentary compilation could ever hope to penetrate." As a result, *Schindler's List* finally won Spielberg the kind of artistic recognition he had always craved. The film garnered seven Oscars, including Best Picture and Best Director for Spielberg; in addition, *Schindler's List* was voted Best Picture by the Los Angeles and New York critics' groups, the Board of Review, and the National Society of Film Critics.

Perhaps reflecting his growing power in Hollywood as much as his own passion for making films that he is personally committed to, in the fall of 1994 Spielberg and two friends—former Walt Disney Corporation executive Jeffrey Katzenberg and record mogul David Geffen—announced they were launching their own studio. DreamWorks SKG was capitalized with $250 million from each of the three partners as well as their creative energies. Hollywood trade publications were full of news stories and gossip about the implications of the move, which upped the ante for executives at rival Hollywood studios. "They're going to rewrite all the rules," producer Steve Tisch predicted to *Entertainment Weekly*.

In the meantime, Spielberg's next film (for Universal) was a much anticipated sequel to *Jurassic Park*, a movie that showed yet again that its creator is what Jack Kroll of *Newsweek* has termed "the great double personality of modern movies." On the one hand, Spielberg can make vastly entertaining thrillers like *Jaws, Raiders of the Lost Ark,* and *Jurassic Park,* and on the other, he can also do a serious film like *The Color Purple* or *Schindler's List. The Lost World: Jurassic Park,* released in the summer of 1997, picked up where *Jurassic Park* had left off. Spielberg used the same CGI technology he had used to such good advantage the first time around, giving his audience even more and better dinosaurs. Although some critics such as David Denby of *New York* magazine felt that "the awe, the giddy sense of curiosity and fear" that had made *Jurassic Park* so thrilling was lacking in the sequel, *The Lost World* was another monster box office hit.

Only a few months after the debut of *The Lost World,* the first film created by the DreamWorks studio arrived in theaters. *Mouse Hunt,* a children's film that did well in the Christmas 1997 season, and *The Peacemaker,* a mediocre action thriller, opened strongly but soon faded. Nonetheless, Cable News Network (CNN) movie analyst Martin Grove was moved to observe, "I think DreamWorks is up and running." That reality was confirmed when Spielberg's next film, his first for DreamWorks, opened just before Christmas 1997. *Amistad,* a historical drama about an 1839 slave revolt, inevitably reminded viewers of *Schindler's List.* "Both films are about the ways good men try to work realistically within an evil system to spare a few of its victims," wrote Roger Ebert of the Chicago *Sun-Times.* "*Amistad* is about the search for truth that, if found, will be small consolation to the millions of existing slaves. As a result, the movie doesn't have the emotional charge of [*Schindler's List*] or of *The Color Purple.*" Critic Peter Howell of the *Toronto Star* agreed. "With *Amistad,* Spielberg positively sweats with desire for more . . . serious filmmaking laurels," he wrote, "but in the end, [*Amistad*] comes up short both as history and entertainment."

Neither harsh words from film critics nor the financial constraints that rule the lives of lesser talents any longer apply to Steven Spielberg, who in 1998 stands atop the mountain in Hollywood. With a personal fortune estimated at more than $1 billion, he is one of the entertainment industry's most powerful figures. He is also one of its busiest, although he insists he is still "only a film director," as he told a *Time* reporter in 1997. Spielberg's deal with DreamWorks calls for him to direct one film for the company for every two that he makes for another studio. In addition, he has reportedly begun moving in new directions, teaming up with Microsoft head Bill Gates to develop a new line of interactive video games.

Meanwhile, Spielberg's personal life seems as successful and secure as his professional life. Divorced in 1989 from actress Amy Irving, he married actress Kate Capshaw (the female star of *Indiana Jones and the Temple of Doom*) in 1991. After making *Jurassic Park* and *Schindler's List,* he took three years off (1994 to 1997) to spend more time with his family, which now includes son Max (whose custody he shares with Irving), a grown step-daughter, an African-American son by adoption, and four children—three boys and a girl—he has fathered with Capshaw. The Spielberg-Capshaw house is a busy place that bustles with noise and activity. "I found true love with Kate, and I don't say that with a Harlequin romance feeling," Spielberg told the *Time* interviewer. "I say it from the most honest part of me."

■ Works Cited

Ansen, David, "Cliffhanger Classic," *Newsweek,* June 15, 1981, pp. 58-61, 63-64.

Ansen, David, "Spielberg's Obsession," *Newsweek,* December 20, 1993, pp. 113-18, 120.

Calio, Jim, "Director Steven Spielberg Takes the Wraps off E.T., Revealing His Secrets at Last," *People,* August 23, 1982, pp. 81-88.

Canby, Vincent, "Enchanted Fantasy," *New York Times,* June 11, 1982, p. B-29.

Corliss, Richard, "I Dream for a Living," *Time,* July 15, 1985, pp. 54-61.

Corliss, Richard, and Jeffrey Ressner, "Peter Pan Grows Up," *Time,* May 19, 1997, pp. 74-82.

Denby, David, "The Visionary Gleam," *New York,* June 14, 1982, pp. 73-75.

Denby, David, "Purple People Eater," *New York,* January 13, 1986, pp. 56-57.

Ebert, Roger, "The Color Purple," *Microsoft Cinemania'94* (CD-ROM).

Ebert, Roger, "Raiders of the Lost Ark," *Microsoft Cinemania'94* (CD-ROM).

Ebert, Roger, "Amistad," *Sun-Times* (Chicago), December 12, 1997.

Farber, Stephen, "Something Sour," *New York Times,* April 28, 1974, p. B-11.

Gross, John, "Hollywood and the Holocaust," *New York Review of Books,* February 3, 1994, pp. 14-16.

Hirschberg, Lynn, "Will Hollywood's Mr. Perfect Ever Grow Up?" *Rolling Stone,* July 19/August 2, 1984, pp. 32-38.

Hodenfield, Chris, "The Sky Is Full of Questions!!," *Rolling Stone,* January 26, 1978.

Howell, Peter, "Slave Ship Tale is Uneven Voyage," *Toronto Star,* December 12, 1997, p. C-3.

Kael, Pauline, "Sugarland and Badlands," *New Yorker,* March 18, 1974.

Kael, Pauline, "The Greening of the Solar System," *New Yorker,* Nov. 28, 1977.

Kael, Pauline, "Always," *Microsoft Cinemania'94* (CD-ROM).

Kael, Pauline, "Indiana Jones and the Last Crusade," *Microsoft Cinemania'94* (CD-ROM).

Kakutani, Michiko, "Steven Spielberg—Horror vs. Hope," *New York Times Biographical Service,* May, 1982, pp. 654-57.

Kehr, Dave, "Uneven Steven: Spielberg is Finding He's a Tough Act to Follow," *Chicago Tribune,* January 10, 1988, p. 6.

Kilday, Gregg, and Benjamin Svetkey, "Three's Company: Katzenberg, Geffen, and Spielberg Start a Studio," *Entertainment Weekly,* October 28, 1994, p. 10.

Kroll, Jack, "T. Rex Redux," *Newsweek,* May 26, 1997, pp. 74-75.

Maltin, Leonard, *Movie and Video Guide 1994,* Signet, 1994.

Novak, Ralph, "Indiana Jones and the Temple of Doom," *People,* June 4, 1984, p. 12.

Park, Jeannie, "Ahoy! Neverland!," *People,* December 23, pp. 92-96, 99-100, 102.

Sanello, Frank, *Spielberg: The Man, The Movies, The Mythology,* Taylor Publishing, 1996.

Schickel, Richard, "Slam! Bang! A Movie Movie," *Time,* June 15, 1981, pp. 42-50.

Schiff, Stephen, "Seriously Spielberg," *New Yorker,* March 21, 1994, pp. 96, 98-104, 106-9.

Spielberg, Steven, "The Autobiography of Peter Pan," *Time,* July 15, 1985, pp. 62-63.

Time, June 23, 1975.

■ For More Information See

BOOKS

Brode, Douglas, *The Films of Steven Spielberg,* Citadel Press, 1995.

Collins, T., *Steven Spielberg, Creator of E.T.*, Dillon, 1983.

Contemporary Literary Criticism, Volume 20, Gale, 1982.

Contemporary Theatre, Film, and Television, Volume 10, Gale, 1993.

Farber, S., *Outrageous Conduct*, Arbor House, 1988.

Halliwell, Leslie, *Halliwell's Film Guide*, 7th edition, Harper & Row, 1989.

Kael, Pauline, *Reeling*, Little, Brown, 1974.

Kael, Pauline, *When the Lights Go Down*, Holt, 1980.

Leather, M., *The Picture Life of Steven Spielberg*, Watts, 1984.

Mabery, D. L., *Steven Spielberg*, Lerner, 1986.

Monaco, James, *American Film Now: The People, the Power, the Money, the Movies*, Oxford University Press, 1979.

Mott, D. R., *Steven Spielberg*, Twayne, 1982.

Sarris, Andrew, editor, *The St. James Film Directors Encyclopedia*, Visible Ink, 1998.

PERIODICALS

Business Week, June 23, 1997, p. 66.

Chicago Tribune, December 23, 1979; June 4, 1982; June 11, 1982; December 11, 1987.

Commonweal, June 20, 1975; January 15, 1988, p. 20.

Detroit Free Press, September 9, 1997; September 25, 1997, p. 12F.

Entertainment Weekly, January 21, 1994, pp. 14-20; December 13, 1996, p. 16.

Film Comment, June, 1978; May, 1982; April, 1986.

Films and Filming, January, 1976.

Globe and Mail (Toronto), November 29, 1997, p. C4.

Interview, December 1991, pp. 68-69.

Journal of Popular Film, Volume 6, number 4, 1978.

Los Angeles Times, June 4, 1982; May 21, 1984; May 23, 1984; December 16, 1986.

Maclean's, June 4, 1984; June 14, 1993, pp. 42-43.

Magazine of Fantasy & Science Fiction, December, 1983, pp. 75-77; March, 1985, pp. 83-91, 121.

Monthly Film Bulletin, July, 1974.

Movietime, October, 1997, p. 64.

Nation, July 10-17, 1982, pp. 59-60, 60-61; February 1, 1986, pp. 124-25; June 19, 1989, p. 862; January 3-10, 1994, p. 30.

New Republic, December 10, 1977; September 6-13, 1980, p. 24; July 4-11, 1981, pp. 26-27; August 5, 1985, p. 24; June 19, 1989, pp. 28-29; December 13, 1993, p. 30.

New Statesman and Society, February 18, 1994, pp. 33-34.

Newsweek, April 8, 1974; June 23, 1975; November 21, 1977; June 27, 1983, p. 80; June 4, 1984; June 27, 1988, pp. 54-59; December 16, 1991, pp. 75, 77; May 24, 1993; June 14, 1993, pp. 64-65; December 20, 1993, pp. 60-61, 116-18, 120.

New York, November 7, 1977; January 7, 1980; June 15, 1981, June 4, 1982; July 15, 1985, pp. 64-66; March 24, 1986; June 21, 1993, pp. 60, 62.

New York Daily News, December 18, 1997.

New Yorker, March 18, 1974; November 28, 1977; September 1, 1980, pp. 80-81; June 15, 1981, pp. 132-35; June 14, 1982, pp. 122-25; June 14, 1984, pp. 100, 103-6.

New York Times, November 13, 1977; December 23, 1979; June 7, 1981; January 10, 1988; May 27, 1997, pp. C11, C15; June 1, 1997, p. B26.

North American Review, fall, 1978.

People, September 15, 1980, p. 34; July 29, 1981; November 1, 1982, pp. 62-64, 67, 69; May 16, 1983, p. 12; May 5, 1986; January 11, 1988, p. 10; June 21, 1993, p. 13; December 13, 1993, p. 17.

Premiere, January, 1994, pp. 67-72, 92-93.

Publishers Weekly, June 16, 1997, p. 20.

Rolling Stone, July 22, 1982; October 24, 1985.

Saturday Review, June, 1981.

Sight and Sound, winter, 1972; summer, 1978.

Take One, January, 1978.

Time, April 16, 1979; May 31, 1982; June 4, 1984; June 27, 1988, p. 72; Dec. 16, 1991, p. 74; April 26, 1993, pp. 49-50; June 9, 1997.

Washington Post, May 31, 1975; February 9, 1987.*

—Sketch by Ken Cuthbertson

Robert Louis Stevenson

■ Personal

Full name Robert Louis Balfour Stevenson; also wrote as Captain George North; born November 13, 1850, in Edinburgh, Scotland; died following a cerebral hemorrhage December 3, 1894, in Apia, Samoa; buried on Mount Vaea, Samoa; son of Thomas (an engineer and designer of lighthouses) and Margaret Isabella (Balfour) Stevenson; married Fanny Vandegrift Osbourne, May 19, 1880; stepchildren: Isobel Strong, Lloyd Osbourne, Hervey Osbourne (deceased). *Education:* Attended Edinburgh Academy and Edinburgh University, 1867-82; studied law in the office of Skene Edwards and Gordon, Edinburgh. *Politics:* Anti-imperialist. *Religion:* Church of Scotland (Presbyterian).

■ Career

Novelist, poet, essayist, and writer of travel books. Called to the Scottish bar, 1875, but never practiced. Traveled widely in Europe, America, and the Pacific Islands, finally settling in Samoa in 1890.

■ Awards, Honors

Silver medal, Royal Scottish Society of Arts, 1871, for a scientific essay on lighthouses.

■ Writings

NOVELS

Treasure Island (first published serially under pseudonym Captain George North in *Young Folks*, 1881-82), Cassell, 1883.
Prince Otto: A Romance, Chatto & Windus, 1885, Roberts Brothers, 1886.
The Strange Case of Dr. Jekyll and Mr. Hyde, Scribner, 1886.
Kidnapped, Scribner, 1886.
The Black Arrow: A Tale of the Two Roses, Scribner, 1888.
The Master of Ballantrae: A Winter's Tale, Scribner, 1889.
(With stepson, Lloyd Osbourne) *The Wrong Box*, Scribner, 1889.
(With Osbourne) *The Wrecker*, illustrated by William Hole and W. L. Metcalf, Scribner, 1892.
David Balfour, Scribner, 1893, published in England as *Catriona: A Sequel to Kidnapped*, Cassell, 1893.
(With Osbourne) *The Ebb-Tide: A Trio and a Quartette*, Stone & Kimball, 1894.
Weir of Hermiston: An Unfinished Romance, Scribner, 1896.

St. Ives: Being the Adventures of a French Prisoner in England (completed by Arthur T. Quiller-Couch), Scribner, 1897.

SHORT STORIES

New Arabian Nights, Holt, 1882.
The Story of a Lie, Hayley & Jackson, 1882, published in America as *The Story of a Lie and Other Tales,* Turner, 1904.
(With wife, Fanny Vandegrift Stevenson) *More New Arabian Nights: The Dynamiter,* Holt, 1885.
The Merry Men and Other Tales and Fables, Scribner, 1887.
The Misadventures of John Nicholson: A Christmas Story, Lovell, 1887.
Island Nights' Entertainments: Consisting of The Beach of Falesa, The Bottle Imp, The Isle of Voices, illustrated by Gordon Browne, Scribner, 1893.
The Body-Snatcher, Merriam, 1895.
Fables, Scribner, 1896.
Tales and Fantasies, Chatto & Windus, 1905.
The Waif Woman, Chatto & Windus, 1916.
When the Devil Was Well, edited by W. P. Trent, Bibliophile Society, 1921.
Two Mediaeval Tales, illustrated by C. B. Falls, Limited Editions Club, 1929.
Tales and Essays, edited by G. B. Stern, Falcon, 1950.
The Complete Short Stories of Robert Louis Stevenson, edited by Charles Neider, Doubleday, 1969.
Tales from the Prince of Storytellers, edited by Barry Menikoff, Northwestern University Press, 1993.

POETRY

Not I and Other Poems, illustrated by the author, S. L. Osbourne, 1881.
Moral Emblems, illustrated by the author, S. L. Osbourne, 1882.
A Child's Garden of Verses, Scribner, 1885.
Underwoods, Scribner, 1887.
Ballads, Scribner, 1890.
Songs of Travel and Other Verses, edited by Sidney Colvin, Chatto & Windus, 1896.
The Poems and Ballads of Robert Louis Stevenson, Scribner, 1896.
R. L. S. Teuila (fugitive lines and verses), privately printed, 1899.
Poetical Fragments, privately printed, 1915.
A Ode of Horace, privately printed, 1916.
Poems Hitherto Unpublished, edited by G. S. Hellman, two volumes, Bibliophile Society, 1916.

New Poems and Varient Readings, Chatto & Windus, 1918.
Poems Hitherto Unpublished, edited by Hellman and W. P. Trent, Bibliophile Society, 1921.
The Poems of Robert Louis Stevenson (complete poems), Gordon Press, 1974.

PLAYS

(With William E. Henley) *Deacon Brodie; or, The Double Life* (first produced at Pullan's Theater of Varieties, Bradford, December 28, 1882), privately printed, 1880.
(With Henley) *Beau Austin* (first produced at Theatre Royal, Haymarket, London, November 17, 1890), privately printed, 1884.
(With Henley) *Admiral Guinea* (first produced at Avenue Theatre, London, November 29, 1897), privately printed, 1884.
(With Henley) *Macaire* (first produced at Strand Theatre, London, November 4, 1900), privately printed, 1885.
(With Henley) *Three Plays: Deacon Brodie, Beau Austin, Admiral Guinea,* Scribner, 1892.
(With Fanny Stevenson) *The Hanging Judge,* edited by Edmund Gosse, privately printed, 1914.
Monmouth: A Tragedy, edited by C. Vale, Rudge, 1928.

TRAVEL BOOKS

An Inland Voyage, Kegan Paul, 1878, Roberts Brothers, 1883.
Edinburgh: Picturesque Notes, with Etchings, Seeley, Jackson & Halliday, 1879, Macmillan, 1889.
Travels with a Donkey in the Cevennes, Roberts Brothers, 1879.
The Silverado Squatters: Sketches from a California Mountain, Chatto & Windus, 1883, Munro, 1884.
Across the Plains, with Other Memories and Essays, Scribner, 1892.
The Amateur Emigrant from the Clyde to Sandy Hook, Stone & Kimball, 1895.
In the South Seas, Scribner, 1896.
A Mountain Town in France: A Fragment, illustrated by the author, J. Lane, 1896.
Essays of Travel, Chatto & Windus, 1905.
Silverado Journal, edited by John E. Jordan, Book Club of California, 1954.
From Scotland to Silverado, edited by James D. Hart, Harvard University Press, 1966.
The Amateur Emigrant with Some First Impressions of America, edited by Roger G. Swearingen, two volumes, Osborne, 1976-77.

ESSAYS

The Pentland Rising, privately printed, 1866.

An Appeal to the Clergy of the Church of Scotland, with a Note for the Laity, Blackwood, 1875.

Virginibus Puerisque and Other Papers, Collier, 1881.

Familiar Studies of Men and Books, Chatto & Windus, 1882, Dodd, Mead, 1887.

Some College Memories, University Union Committee (Edinburgh), 1886, Mansfield & Wessels, 1889.

Memories and Portraits, Scribner, 1887.

Memoir of Fleeming Jenkin, Longmans, Green, 1887.

Father Damien: An Open Letter to the Reverend Dr. Hyde of Honolulu, Chatto & Windus, 1890, Mosher, 1897.

A Footnote to History: Eight Years of Trouble in Samoa, Scribner, 1892.

War in Samoa, privately printed, 1893.

The Morality of the Profession of Letters, Brothers of the Book, 1899.

Essays and Criticisms, Turner, 1903.

Prayers Written at Vailima, with an Introduction by Mrs. Stevenson, Scribner, 1904.

Essays in the Art of Writing, Chatto & Windus, 1905.

Essays, edited by W. L. Phelps, Scribner, 1906.

Lay Morals and Other Papers, Scribner, 1911.

Records of a Family of Engineers, Chatto & Windus, 1912.

Memoirs of Himself, privately printed, 1912.

On the Choice of a Profession, Chatto & Windus, 1916.

Confessions of a Unionist: An Unpublished Talk on Things Current, Written in 1888, edited by F. V. Livingstone, privately printed, 1921.

The Best Thing in Edinburgh: An Address to the Speculative Society of Edinburgh in March 1873, edited by K. D. Osbourne, Howell, 1923.

Selected Essays, edited by H. G. Rawlinson, Oxford University Press, 1923.

The Manuscripts of Robert Louis Stevenson's "Records of a Family of Engineers": The Unfinished Chapters, edited by J. Christian Bay, Hill, 1929.

The Essays of Robert Louis Stevenson, edited by M. Elwin, Macdonald, 1950.

LETTERS AND DIARIES

Vailima Letters: Robert Louis Stevenson to Sidney Colvin, 1890-1894, Stone & Kimball, 1895.

The Letters of Robert Louis Stevenson to His Family and Friends, edited by S. Colvin, Scribner, 1899.

Autograph Letters, Original Mss., Books, Portraits and Curios from the Library of the Late Robert Louis Stevenson (catalog of the Anderson Galleries sale of Stevenson's literary property), three volumes, Brown, 1914-16.

(With Fanny Stevenson) *Our Samoan Adventure*, edited by Charles Neider, Harper, 1955.

R. L. S.: Stevenson's Letters to Charles Baxter, edited by De Lancey Ferguson and Marshall Waingrow, Yale University Press, 1956.

COLLECTIONS

The Works of Robert Louis Stevenson, Edinburgh edition, eighteen volumes, edited by S. Colvin, Chatto & Windus, 1894-98.

The Works of Robert Louis Stevenson, Thistle edition, twenty-six volumes, Scribner, 1902.

The Works of Robert Louis Stevenson, Biographical edition, thirty-one volumes, Scribner, 1905-39.

The Works of Robert Louis Stevenson, Pentland edition, twenty volumes, edited by Edmund Gosse, Cassell, 1906-07.

The Works of Robert Louis Stevenson, Swanston edition, twenty-five volumes, Chatto & Windus, 1911-12.

The Works of Robert Louis Stevenson, Vailima edition, edited by Lloyd Osbourne and Fanny Vandegrift Stevenson, Scribner, 1922-23.

The Works of Robert Louis Stevenson, Tusitala edition, thirty-five volumes, Heinemann, 1923-24.

The Works of Robert Louis Stevenson, South Seas edition, thirty-two volumes, Scribner, 1925.

Robert Louis Stevenson: The Complete Shorter Fiction, edited by Peter Stoneley, Carroll & Graf, 1991.

Robert Louis Stevenson: The Complete Short Stories, Centenary edition, two volumes, edited by Ian Bell, Holt, 1993.

OTHER

The Strange Case of Dr. Jekyll and Mr. Hyde, with Other Fables, Longmans, 1896.

A Stevenson Medley, edited by S. Colvin, Chatto & Windus, 1899.

Diogenes in London, Edwin and Robert Grabhorn for John Howell, 1920.

Diogenes at the Savile Club, Frank M. Morris, 1921.

Robert Louis Stevenson: Hitherto Unpublished Prose Writings, edited by H. H. Harper, Bibliophile Society, 1921.

Castaways of Soledad: A Manuscript by Stevenson Hitherto Unpublished, edited by G. S. Hellman, privately printed, 1928.

The Charity Bazaar: An Allegorical Dialogue, Georgian Press, 1929.

Salute to RLS, edited by F. Holland, Cousland, 1950.

A Newly Discovered Long Story "An Old Song" and a Previously Unpublished Short Story "Edifying Letters of the Rutherford Family," edited by Roger G. Swearingen, Archon, 1982.

Robert Louis Stevenson and "The Beach of Falesa": A Study in Victorian Publishing with the Original Text, edited by Barry Menikoff, Stanford University Press, 1984.

Robert Louis Stevenson: The Scottish Stories and Essays, edited by Kenneth Gelder, University of Edinburgh Press, 1989.

Contributor to the *Illustrated London News,* the *Times,* and numerous magazines, including *Academy, Anthenaeum, Black and White, Contemporary Review, Cornhill Magazine, Edinburgh University Magazine, Fortnightly Review, Fraser's Magazine, London, Longman's Magazine, Macmillan's Magazine, Magazine of Art, New Quarterly Magazine, Pall Mall Gazette, Portfolio, Scribner's Magazine, Temple Bar,* and *Young Folks.* Collections of Stevenson's papers are housed at the Beinecke Rare Book and Manuscript Library, Yale University; the Pierpont Morgan Library, New York City; the Henry E. Huntington Library, San Marino, California; the Widener Library, Harvard University; the Edinburgh Public Library; the Silverado Museum, Saint Helena, California; and the Monterey State Historical Monument Stevenson House, Monterey, California.

■ Adaptations

PLAYS

Robert Brome, *Robert Louis Stevenson's "Markheim"* (one-act), Eldridge Publishing, 1963.

Robert Brome, *Robert Louis Stevenson's "The Suicide Club"* (one-act), Eldridge Publishing, 1964.

FILMS

The Bottle Imp, Jesse L. Laskey Feature Play Co., starring Sessue Hayakawa, 1917.

Treasure Island, Fox Film Corp., 1917; Famous Players-Laskey Corp., starring Lon Chaney, 1920; Metro-Goldwyn-Mayer, starring Jackie Cooper, Wallace Beery, and Lionel Barrymore, 1934; Teaching Films Custodians, 1945; Walt Disney Productions, starring Bobby Driscoll and Robert

Newton, 1950; Turner Network Television and Agamemnon Films, starring Charlton Heston, Christian Bale, and Oliver Reed, 1990.

Kidnapped, Thomas A. Edison, Inc., 1917; Twentieth Century-Fox, starring Freddie Bartholomew and Warner Baxter, 1938; Teaching Film Custodians, 1947; Monogram Pictures, starring Roddy McDowall and Dan O'Herlihy, 1948; Walt Disney Productions, starring James MacArthur and Peter Finch, 1950.

Dr. Jekyll and Mr. Hyde, Pioneer Film Corp., 1920; Famous Players-Laskey Corp., starring John Barrymore and Nita Naldi, 1920; Paramount, starring Frederic March and Miriam Hopkins, 1932; Metro-Goldwyn-Mayer, starring Spencer Tracy and Ingrid Bergman, 1941; Sterling Educational Films, 1959.

The White Circle (adaptation of "The Pavilion on the Links"), Famous Players-Laskey Corp., starring John Gilbert, 1920.

Ebb Tide, Famous Players-Laskey Corp., starring Milton Sills, 1922; Paramount, starring Ray Milland and Barry Fitzgerald, 1937.

Trouble for Two (adaptation of *The Suicide Club*), Metro-Goldwyn-Mayer, starring Robert Montgomery and Rosalind Russell, 1936.

The Body Snatcher, RKO Radio Pictures, starring Boris Karloff and Bela Lugosi, 1945.

Adventure Island (adaptation of *Ebb Tide*), Paramount, starring Rory Calhoun and Rhonda Fleming, 1947.

Adventures in Silverado (adaptation of *The Silverado Squatters*), Columbia Pictures, starring William Bishop and Forrest Tucker, 1948.

The Black Arrow, Columbia Pictures, starring Louis Hayward and Janet Blair, 1948; Walt Disney Productions, starring Oliver Reed and Stephan Chase, 1984.

Lodging for the Night, Realm Television Productions, 1949.

Lord Maletroit's Door, Realm Television Productions, 1949.

The Secret of St. Ives, Columbia Pictures, starring Richard Ney and Vanessa Brown, 1949.

The Treasure of Franchard, Realm Television Productions, 1949.

The Imp in the Bottle, General Television Enterprises, 1950.

The Strange Door (adaptation of "The Sire de Maletroit's Door"), Universal International Pictures, starring Charles Laughton and Boris Karloff, 1951.

The Treasure of Lost Cannon (adaptation of "The Treasure of Franchard"), Universal International

Pictures, starring William Powell, 1951.

The Master of Ballantrae, Warner Bros., starring Errol Flynn, 1953; Time-Life Television/BBC Enterprises (six half-hour episodes), starring Julian Glover and Brian Cox.

Long John Silver (based on characters from *Treasure Island*), Distributors Corp. off America, starring Robert Newton, 1955.

The Wrong Box, Columbia Pictures, staring John Mills, Peter Sellers, Ralph Richardson, and Michael Caine, 1966.

A Child's Garden of Verses, Sterling Educational Films, 1967; McGraw-Hill, 1968; University of California Extension Media Center, 1974.

Muppet Treasure Island, Walt Disney/Jim Henson Productions, 1996.

Treasure Island was also the inspiration for the films *Treasure Island Revisited* and *Treasure Island with Mr. Magoo*, both by Macmillan Films; *Treasure Island with Mr. Magoo* also ran as a thirty minute television series with Robert Newton.

FILMSTRIPS

Kidnapped, Eye Gate House, 1958; Encyclopaedia Britannica Films, 1961; Carman Educational Associates, 1966.

Treasure Island, Encyclopaedia Britannica Films, 1960; Carman Educationsl Associates, 1966; Jam Handy School Service, 1968; Dufour Editions, 1969; Walt Disney Educational Materials, 1970; Universal Education and Visual Arts, 1971; Educational Record Sales, 1971; McGraw-Hill, 1972, Teaching Resources Films, 1974.

The Owl and the Pussy-Cat [and] *My Shadow* (the first by Edward Lear and the second by Stevenson), Cooper Films and Records, 1969.

Garden of Verses (transparencies), Creative Visuals, 1970.

Highlights from Treasure Island, Encyclopaedia Britannica Educational Corp., 1973.

RECORDINGS

Treasure Island (record or cassette), read by Ian Richardson, Caedmon; Spoken Arts, 1971.

Treasury of Great Educational Records (includes *Treasure Island*; twelve records), Miller-Brody Productions; with *Robin Hood*, Columbia Special Products, 1977.

Also *Adventure Library* (includes *Treasure Island* and *Kidnapped*; ten records or sixteen cassettes), Miller-Brody Productions; *Adventure Poets* (five cassettes), United Learning; *A Child's Garden of Verses* (two records), read by Nancy Wickwire and Basil Langton, Miller-Brody Productions; read by Dame Judith Anderson, Caedmon; *Dr. Jekyll and Mr. Hyde* (three records or cassettes), read by Patrick Horgan, Miller-Brody Productions; *Kidnapped* (parts 1 and 2, cassettes only), read by John Franklyn, Alan MacDonald, Pamela Mant, David Thorndike, and Derek Young, Spoken Arts; *Markheim by Robert Louis Stevenson*, CMS Records; *Poetry in Song*, Crofut Productions; *The Strange Case of Dr. Jekyll and Mr. Hyde*, Caedmon, (parts 1 and 2, cassettes only), Spoken Arts.

■ Sidelights

As the author of three of the most-loved adventure novels of all time—*Treasure Island, Kidnapped,* and *The Strange Case of Dr. Jekyll and Mr. Hyde*—Robert Louis Stevenson has won a reputation as a great writer of books for children. Until recently, these three novels were regarded as Stevenson's only major contribution to literature in English. "It is one of the many paradoxes in the life of Robert Louis Stevenson," explains *Concise Dictionary of British Literary Biography* contributor Robert Kiely, "that, though he was a worker and craftsman of extraordinary skill, his literary image is that of a whimsical amateur, an aesthetic drifter."

In the century since his death, however, Stevenson has also earned a reputation among critics as an important writer and novelist, ranking with other Victorian and Edwardian writers such as Henry James, Thomas Hardy, and Joseph Conrad. "We can admit that there have been better writers than Stevenson," states Ian Bell in *Dreams of Exile: Robert Louis Stevenson, a Biography*, "writers more subtle and ambitious, more tenacious, certainly more profound. Then it is necessary to remind ourselves that many of the names offered have long since faded from the public's memory. Whatever Stevenson had they lacked." "R.L.S.," Bell concludes, "commands a place among the few who have created literature of universal appeal, with characters who have achieved an existence outside the pages of the fictions in which they were born. He was a popular artist; the conjunction has become rare."

Robert Lewis (he changed the spelling later) Balfour Stevenson was born in Edinburgh, the son of Thomas and Margaret Stevenson. Thomas was an engineer from a long line of engineers. His father Robert was first engineer of the Board of Northern Lighthouses, and "planned or built twenty-three lighthouses in Scotland, using the catoptric system of illumination and his own invention of 'intermittent' and 'flashing' lights," writes Frank McLynn in *Robert Louis Stevenson: A Biography*, "as well as acting as a consulting engineer for the construction of roads, bridges, harbours, canals and railways." Thomas expanded his father's reputation, making Edinburgh a world center for lighthouse construction and winning the title of "the Nestor of lighthouse illumination." He was also a devoted member of the Church of Scotland, with a strong interest in theology. His wife, Margaret Isabella Balfour, came from a family of Scottish church leaders. Unlike her husband, who tended to be moody, Robert's mother "was cultivated, companionable, affectionate and a born optimist," McLynn explains, "with a noticeable talent for shutting her eyes to trouble or ignoring it rather than finding solutions."

Stevenson's parents provided two of the major influences on their only child's literary works. Another major influence was his home and environment: at first Scotland and, late in life, the South Pacific. Still another was his health. Stevenson was considered very unhealthy throughout his life. Medical historians still disagree as to what caused his poor health. Some of it may have been hereditary; his mother's family, the Balfours, had a history of weak lungs. "The consequence was," writes McLynn, "that the child never enjoyed good health: from the age of two to eleven, apart from the usual childhood ailments, he suffered from digestive upsets, feverish colds, gastric fever, bronchitis and pneumonia. It is also likely that an illness he suffered at twenty-nine months was diphtheria."

However, Stevenson may have had even more deeply rooted health-related problems. McLynn states that "some physicians have speculated from the oddity of his bone structure that there was an endocrinal problem." A poor thyroid gland could explain Stevenson's problems with his nerves and his bad reactions to medication later in life. Other theories suggest that Stevenson suffered from tuberculosis, a lung tumor, or even from a disease known as fibroid bronchitis, which causes damage to the supportive tissue of the lungs. "Stevenson was caught in a dilemma," says McLynn. "He was unable to breathe naturally, therefore the blood could not get enough oxygen, and therefore he had poor health. But he could not exercise his way out of ill-health, for the same symptoms impeded him, and oxygen starvation prevented his putting on weight." His friend, the poet W. E. Henley, described Stevenson in verse in his twenties as "Thin-legged! thin-chested! slight unspeakably, / Neat-footed and weak-fingered."

As a result of his many illnesses, Stevenson spent much of his youth confined to a sickroom. "In some ways," Kiely writes, "the early signs of frail health were a good omen for his career, for they enabled his parents to 'make allowances' for him, go abroad for his health, to rest and to write rather than to pursue the rigors of a 'manly' profession." "His education at Mr. Henderson's school on India Street, near his Edinburgh home, was frequently interrupted by illness between 1855 and 1861," says Kiely. "His later attendance at the Edinburgh Academy, beginning at age eleven, was similarly disrupted by poor health and trips to the Continent in search of better climates." Stevenson's education was haphazard, but he was still able to attend Edinburgh University to study first engineering and later law. However, he soon persuaded his parents to support his writing career. "Partly as a concession to their attitude, partly out of necessity and for the amusement of it," Kiely continues, "Stevenson approached the life of a writer as a long holiday."

"The Angel of My Infant Life"

The inspiration for Stevenson's works came from several major sources, especially his own childhood, and his nurse Alison Cunningham (known as "Cummy"). "She looked after him," writes Bell, ". . . from the age of eighteen months until he was grown, and outlived him by nineteen years." "In Stevenson's childhood she was the sure center of a turbulent, enclosed world," the critic continues. "Cummy sang him ballads and songs, read to him from the Bible and Bunyan (particularly during the long, still Edinburgh Sabbath), and told him 'blood-curdling tales of the Covenanters and their struggles.'" It was to Cummy that Stevenson dedicated his most popular book of poetry, *A Child's Garden of Verses*, first published in 1885, calling her "My second mother, my first wife, / The angel of my infant life." However, "less sentimentally," Bell explains,

Long John Silver's buccaneers are on the attack in this illustration from a 1980
edition of Stevenson's adventure classic, *Treasure Island.*

"Cummy might also be accused of having fed the vulnerable, hyperactive imagination of a child prone to nightmares and often deprived, because of illness, of the company of his peers." "Her idea of a constitutional was to take the child for a stroll through Warriston Cemetery, a habit harmless enough in itself had she not also filled his head with tales of body-snatchers," he states. "His famous personification of storm-swept Edinburgh nights, and their impression on him as a child, have her mark."

Cummy's influence can be seen not only in Stevenson's horror stories, such as "Thrawn Janet" and *The Strange Case of Dr. Jekyll and Mr. Hyde,* but even in *A Child's Garden of Verses.* Critics recognized very soon after the collection's publication that the poems were autobiographical in nature. Some also saw that the poems accurately represented childhood as it is experienced by children, although others felt that the voice of the adult poet intruded. "He seems to us to fall into some confusion between two very different things indeed," states a reviewer in the *Spectator* in March of 1885, "—the verse which children might be supposed to write, and the verse which they would delight to read." Stevenson himself recognized this tendency in the poems, declaring in a letter to a friend, the critic Edmund Gosse, "They look ghastly in the cold light of print; but there is something nice in the little ragged regiment for all—the blackguards seem to me to smile, to have a kind of childish treble not that sounds in my ears freshly; not song, if you will, but a child's voice."

Another early reviewer, William Archer, writes in the *Pall Mall Gazette* that Stevenson's work in *A Child's Garden of Verses* has a "charming simplicity, yet in the selection of his subjects we trace the irony of self-conscious manhood, and here and there we find a touch in which the artist does not quite conceal his art." Archer also suggests that the verses in the collection were unrealistic and unrepresentative of childhood because they showed Stevenson as "a humourist and an artist in words, a man of alert, open-eyed sanity, unconcerned as to the mystery of childhood, but keenly alive to its human grace and pathos, its fantastic gravity, its logical inconsequence, its exquisite egoism." "Mr. Stevenson," Archer concludes, "knows nothing of the fierce rebellions, the agonized doubts as to the existence of justice, human or divine, which mar the music of child-

hood for so many; or if he realizes their existence, he relegates them to that other life, the life of pain, terror, and weariness, into which it is part of his philosophy to look as seldom as possible."

Archer's analysis of *A Child's Garden of Verses* presents most of the problems that later critics have seen in the collection. However, other reviewers have seen a darker side to the poems, reflecting the night-fears of Stevenson's own childhood. "Because there is no sign of effort" in its composition, writes Alfred Noyes in his study *Some Aspects of Modern Poetry,* the collection " . . . is supposed by the unintelligent to be achieved without pains, and because it is so crystal-clear that it takes the infinite to its heart, it is supposed by turbid and shallow minds to be without any depth at all." Many of the poems, Noyes points out, evoke images of darkness and fear. "The book is full of good-nights and good-byes," he states. The poem "North-West Passage," for instance, draws a picture of darkness as a living thing: "All round the house is the jet-black night, / It stares through the window-pane; / It crawls in the corners, hiding from the light, / And it moves with the moving flame." "Now my little heart goes a-beating like a drum / With the breath of the Bogie in my hair;" Stevenson continues, "And all round the candle the crooked shadows come / And go marching along up the stair." "The Land of Nod" and "The Land of Counterpane," among other poems, reflect some of the distress and unhappiness of Stevenson's own sickly childhood. "He was an ailing child; and from an ailing childhood he passed to an ailing boyhood, youth, and manhood," declares H. W. Garrod in *The Profession of Poetry and Other Lectures.* "For children, boys, young men, pirates, soldiers, and sailors, for all naturally healthy life, Stevenson had an affection the more real because, in each successive stage of his own development, the body plucked him back from the desire of the mind."

Enter the Osbournes

Cummy's horror stories and the fervent Calvinism she and Stevenson's parents—especially his father Thomas—practiced left its mark on Robert. While studying for the bar exams in 1872 he nearly alienated his parents by declaring himself an agnostic. In part he turned to writing as a form of rebellion against their influence. Yet, explains William F. Naufftus in the *Dictionary of Lit-*

This 1950 Disney adaptation of *Treasure Island* starred Bobby Driscoll as Jim Hawkins and Robert Newton as Long John Silver.

erary Biography, "despite the most painful and bitter disagreements with their son on theological and moral questions, the parents gave him the financial support that freed him for . . . literary work. This parental support allowed Stevenson to write what he pleased when he pleased and as little as he pleased until he finally developed a voice and form that would both suit him and provide a satisfactory income."

Stevenson's initial success in publishing also came through connections with family and friends. His parents sent him to London to live with relatives after he rejected their Calvinistic Christianity. There he met several figures who became important in his later career: the writer and critic Stanley Colvin, Slade Professor of Fine Arts at Cambridge, who was "Stevenson's first contact with the liter-

ary world of London," says Naufftus. "Through Colvin's good offices he met and befriended other literary figures," the *Dictionary of Literary Biography* contributor continues, "including Edmund Gosse, Leslie Stephen, William Ernest Henley, and George Meredith." Stephen published several of Stevenson's early essays and criticism in his *Cornhill Magazine*. Beginning in 1873, Stevenson also began to spend much of his time in France, in Paris, and at artist's colonies. In 1876, at the artist's colony of Grez, he met another of the great influences on his life: an American woman at least ten years older than himself named Fanny Vandegrift Osbourne.

Fanny Osbourne was born in Indiana in 1840 and married Samuel Osbourne, the secretary to the governor of Indiana, in 1857. Her husband served in the Civil War and, says McLynn, the war probably destroyed his character and his marriage. "Something happened to Sam Osbourne during the four years of fighting (1861-65)," McLynn explains, "for ever afterwards he was a restless, troubled man, as unable to live a settled life in a fixed location as to stay long with any one woman." By the mid-1870s, their marriage was in very bad shape. Fanny took her teenaged daughter Belle and her young sons Lloyd and Hervey and sought refuge in Europe, where she hoped to be accepted as an artist. The trip nearly ruined her; her husband did not support her adequately, and she and her children often suffered from cold and hunger. Malnutrition probably played a role in the death of Hervey, her youngest child, in April of 1876. Shortly before Hervey died Fanny met the Stevensons: first Robert's cousin Bob, then Stevenson himself. "Her American candour, her intrinsic strength, her unusual looks, and perhaps most of all, her experience of the world drew R.L.S. to her almost immediately," writes Bell. "Despite all the apparent obstacles, the two became friends and gradually over a two-year period developed an unusual bond," states Kiely. "When Fanny returned to America, Stevenson's parents assumed the 'danger' was over, but his close friends knew better and were not surprised when Stevenson responded to a telegram by dropping everything and setting off for the New World."

Stevenson left for America in great haste, says Naufftus, "without telling his parents or bothering to collect adequate funds for the voyage." "To make matters worse," the *Dictionary of Literary Biography* contributor adds, "his health was precarious on the Atlantic crossing, during his brief stay in New York, on his railroad trip across the continent, and during the four months he spent in Monterrey . . . and the five months he spent in San Francisco and Oakland before he and Fanny were finally able to marry on 19 May 1880." Stevenson's travel books *The Amateur Emigrant from the Clyde to Sandy Hook* (1895) and *Across the Plains, with Other Memories and Essays* (1892) tell the stories of his Atlantic crossing and his cross-country excursion by rail. *The Silverado Squatters: Sketches from a California Mountain* (1883) is the tale of their honeymoon, spent "in the cabin of an abandoned mine at Silverado, more than two thousand feet up the slope of Mount Saint Helena," explains Kiely. Later that year the couple "left the United States for a reunion with friends

in Liverpool and London, a visit to Stevenson's family in Edinburgh, and a prolonged expedition to Switzerland," Kiely continues. "In the summer of 1881 Stevenson returned to Scotland, rented a cottage in Braemar, and there, surrounded by his American family and the rough and rainy beauty of his own land, began to write *Treasure Island.*"

A Tale of Treasure

The genesis of *Treasure Island,* more than any other of Stevenson's books, is surrounded by stories and legends. In part this was because of the influence of the Osbournes. All of them had a professional as well as a personal interest in promoting Stevenson's own image. Fanny had coauthored a volume of short stories with her husband, while Lloyd was credited as coauthor on three of his stepfather's books and Belle served as his secretary, writing down his final work for him when Stevenson was too sick to use a pen. Upon his death Fanny, Lloyd, and Belle banded together to protect their own vision of Robert. "After 1894," says Naufftus, "all three of the Osbournes became, in various ways, keepers of the Stevenson legend, influencing posthumous publications, collected editions, and authorized biographies and producing memoirs and reminiscences of their own. Among them they did a great deal to create the misleadingly saintly image of Stevenson that emerged in the years before World War I and contributed to the anti-Stevenson reaction that began around 1914 and has not quite yet ended."

Both Fanny and Lloyd Osbourne claimed to have influenced the composition of *Treasure Island.* The most commonly repeated story is that given by Lloyd, who said that "it was his drawing and colouring of an imaginary island that gave Louis the idea," declares McLynn, "and that his original map was used—all of which was later denied by RLS." "There is something distastefully vainglorious about the following," McLynn continues: "'Had it not been for me, and my childish box of paints, there would have been no such book as *Treasure Island.*'" "Fanny did not like the story," says Bell, "finding it 'tedious' (though she changed her mind, and rewrote history, later)." Stevenson's own account, as first published in the magazine *Idler* in August of 1894 and then reprinted in his collection *Essays in the Art of Writing* (1905), supports McLynn's account: "There was a schoolboy in the Late Miss McGregor's Cottage, home from the holidays, and much in want of 'something craggy to break his mind upon.' He had no thought of literature; it was the art of Raphael that received his fleeting suffrages; and with the aid of pen and ink and a shilling box of water colours, he had soon turned one of the rooms into a picture gallery." "My more immediate duty toward the gallery was to be showman; but I would sometimes unbend a little, join the artist (so to speak) at the easel, and pass the afternoon with him in a generous emulation," Stevenson continues, "making coloured drawings. On one of these occasions, I made the map of an island; it was elaborately and (I thought) beautifully coloured; the shape of it took my fancy beyond expression; it contained harbours that pleased me like sonnets; and with the unconsciousness of the predestined, I ticketed my performance 'Treasure Island.'"

McLynn suggests that the original concept of *Treasure Island* had less to do with Stevenson's relationship to his stepson and more to do with his relationship to his father. "All available evidence backs the hypothesis that it was the sixty-three-year old Thomas, not the thirteen-year old Lloyd who was the true inspirer," the critic writes. "My father caught fire at once with all the romance and childishness of his original nature," Stevenson reports in an essay on the work's composition. "His own stories, that every night of his life he put himself to sleep with, dealt perpetually with ships, roadside inns, robbers, old sailors, and commercial travellers before the era of steam. He never finished one of these romances; the lucky man did not require to! But in *Treasure Island* he recognized something kindred to his own imagination; it was *his* kind of picturesque; and he not only heard with delight the daily chapter, but set himself actively to collaborate."

Thomas Stevenson was also instrumental in finding a publisher for the book: Dr. Alexander Japp, a "scholar and journalist, biographer of De Quincey and friend of Mrs. Henry Wood, a man with a legion with contacts in London literary circles," explains McLynn. Japp, who was visiting the Stevensons, "took the manuscript away with him and soon reported that he had placed the serialisation with *Young Folks* and that the expected receipts were £100," although Stevenson actually only received around £30 for the work's first publication. Despite the fact that the editor Robert Leighton, who changed the title of the

work from *The Sea Cook* to *Treasure Island*, considered it "really too 'arty' for juvenile taste," says McLynn, Stevenson was convinced that he had composed a great story. "If this don't fetch the kids," he wrote in a letter to Henley, "why, they have gone rotten since my day." "The story, appearing in the first of seventeen instalments under the pseudonym 'Captain George North' in October 1881, did not do particularly well as a serial," states Bell; "Stevenson's smart friends deplored its publication in such a periodical ('let them write their damn masterpieces for themselves,' he retorted)."

The story of *Treasure Island* is well-known. The book "describes the dangerous adventures of Jim Hawkins and his passage from adolescence to manhood," explains Kiely. Stevenson tells how Jim discovers a map belonging to a former pirate who lived in his parents's inn. The map leads to buried treasure on a small island somewhere in the Caribbean Sea. With Dr. Livesy and Squire Trelawney, Jim sets sail on the *Hispaniola* in pursuit of the treasure. However, the one-legged Long John Silver, the "sea cook" of Stevenson's original title, conspires with the crew to mutiny and, when the ship arrives at Treasure Island, leads them off the boat. "Smuggling himself on land, Jim meets Ben Gunn, once a pirate with Captain Flint," Kiely states, "who buried the treasure. Suddenly, the mutiny breaks out, and Jim, with Dr. Livesy, the squire, and others, takes refuge in an abandoned stockade on the island." Jim manages to sneak back on board the *Hispaniola* and cut the ship adrift, although the pirates catch him as he returns to the island. "Long John Silver, however, protects him, and the pirates turn against them both," says Kiely. "The pirates suspend their harmful actions while they search for the treasure, discovering only an empty chest. Returning to kill Silver and Jim, they are stopped by Ben Gunn and company, who free the two heroes." The protagonists, along with Gunn and Silver, abandon the remaining pirates on Treasure Island and return home. Silver himself jumps ship in the West Indies along with a share of the treasure. Jim returns safely home to write the story of his adventures.

Even though it is Jim that relates the story of *Treasure Island*, the main character—or at least the character that attracts the most attention from readers—is not Jim Hawkins, the narrator and protagonist, but Long John Silver. "Sometimes kind, sometimes cruel, he is an untrustworthy surrogate father who places more faith in Jim than Jim gives to him," declares Bell. "In a novel with an otherwise simple moral plan, Silver is ambiguous. Sometimes it is as though R.L.S. were tempting us to admire this figure whose personality swings like a pendulum, whose character metamorphoses almost in an instant." Silver is the first character among many in Stevenson's works who show this duality of nature. "But *who* Long John actually is seems less important than what, by contrast, he shows the others to be," Bell concludes. "A strong man, he brings out innate strength or weakness in others; a dishonest man, he tests their capacity for truth. And, of course, at the novel's end he escapes; such mercury cannot be caught, as though to show that our moral judgements are not adequate to human variety. John Silver remains a triumph."

With the publication of *Treasure Island* in book form, Stevenson attracted widespread critical attention. "Any one who has read 'The New Arabian Nights,'" one of Stevenson's first collections of short stories, Arthur John Butler writes in *Atheneum*, "will recognize at once Mr. Stevenson's qualifications for telling a good buccaneer story. The blending of the ludicrous with the ghastly, the commonplace with the romantic, of which that book offered examples in plenty, is just what a tale of the search for a pirate's treasure demands." The author of an unsigned review appearing in the magazine *Academy* in December of 1883 states, "[We] shall be surprised if 'Treasure Island' does not satisfy the most exacting lover of perilous adventures and thrilling situation." According to Stevenson's friend Henley, who reviewed the volume for the *Saturday Review, Treasure Island* "is a book for boys which will be delightful to all grown men who have the sentiment of treasure-hunting and are touched with the true spirit of the Spanish Main."

The Black Arrow

Stevenson tried to follow the success of *Treasure Island* with more adventure stories. His next effort, *Prince Otto*, met with less enthusiasm. He completed a third adventure novel, about a conspiracy set in fifteenth-century England, at about the same time, but he set it aside and did not find a book publisher for it until 1888. The story, entitled *The Black Arrow*, tells of how Dick Shelton, the heir to an English estate, discovers that his father was murdered and he himself was defrauded of his inheritance by a knight named Sir Daniel Brackley. Brackley is able to conceal his crime because of the political turmoil surrounding the Wars of the Roses, a dynastic conflict that absorbed all of England from about 1450 to 1485. The novel shows how Shelton attempts to win back his birthright and win the love of Sir Daniel's ward, Joanna Sedley. In the process he encounters many powerful and historical figures, chief among them Richard of Gloucester, future king of England, before winning both his estate and his bride.

"The saga of the Black Arrow, while it reflects the innocent robustness and impulsive romance of Stevenson's mind," states B. Allen Bentley in his introduction to *The Black Arrow,* " . . . also contains hints that his soul was constantly preoccupied with the internal moral struggle of mankind—the conflict of good and evil." "*The Black Arrow* shares with *Treasure Island* the theme of a descent into a chaos world," McLynn explains. "The inadequacies of the Hamlet-like hero are never more fully exposed. It is impossible to find a point of moral leverage, for the adherents of the House of York are just as brutal and villainous as those of the House of Lancaster; such a world, in which he who hesitates is lost indeed, calls for a commitment to action without any certainty that one is on the right side, or even that there is a right side." Dick is forced to make his own decisions about right and wrong, good and evil, and finds his way in the end to his own home with the woman of his choice beside him.

The Black Arrow also reveals Stevenson's fascination with the concept of duality. Unlike Long John Silver, who contains within himself the dual aspects of his nature, Dick Shelton's evil side is separated from him and plays a role in the novel as the character Richard of Gloucester. The work "is the first Stevenson novel to make explicit use of the 'double'—the device for which RLS would achieve everlasting fame in *Dr. Jekyll and Mr. Hyde*," writes McLynn. "Richard of Gloucester is Dick Shelton's *alter ego* and represents the side of himself he dare not acknowledge consciously." Gloucester acknowledges their relationship openly throughout the novel, referring to Dick as his "namesake," McLynn says, "and finally makes his meaning unambiguous: 'two Richards are one.'" At the same time, the critic continues, for Stevenson Richard of Gloucester represents one

Frederic March portrayed the tormented physician in this classic 1931 film version of *Dr. Jekyll and Mr. Hyde.*

form of pure evil: he is "the fictional extension of the devil seen by the infant RLS in his nightmares."

"A Fine Bogey Tale"

Stevenson's devil appeared in a more concrete form in the novel *The Strange Case of Dr. Jekyll and Mr. Hyde,* first published in book form in 1886. "Published in January 1886, *Jekyll and Hyde* was a superseller," states McLynn, "which sold 40,000 copies in six months in Britain and another 250,000 in pirated editions in the U.S.A." Fanny Osbourne's account of the genesis of the work is that she disapproved of Stevenson's first draft and said so. Her husband was at first greatly perturbed by her criticism, but later agreed to rewrite the story and discarded the first draft in the fire. "In reality, she seems to have been genuinely horrified when he burned his manuscript," says Bell. "He may have been teaching her a sharp lesson. Nevertheless, since R.L.S. did, in the end, agree, and did undertake the supreme effort of rewriting his piece from scratch, she is entitled to her version. He often took her advice but just as often ignored it. In this case, wrote Lloyd, 'The culmination was the *Jekyll and Hyde* that everyone knows.'"

The "*Jekyll and Hyde* that everyone knows" is sometimes quite different from the book that Stevenson wrote. The story has been a favorite with motion picture producers since the early days of the industry and has been adapted and changed many times since its original publication over a hundred years ago. "Dr. Jekyll is a fat, benevolent physician, not without human frailties, who at times by means of a potion projects himself into, or concentrates or precipitates, an evil person of brutal and animal nature taking the name of Hyde, in which character he leads a patchy criminal life of sorts," explains novelist Vladimir Nabokov in his *Lectures on Literature.* "For a time he is able to revert to his Jekyll personality—there is a down-to-Hyde drug and a back-to-Jekyll drug—but gradually his better nature weakens and finally the back-to-Jekyll drug fails, and he poisons himself when on the verse of exposure." The story, Nabokov continues, is not a detective story in which investigators try to discover Hyde's identity. Instead, it is the story of a complex personality, Dr. Jekyll, who contains within himself the seeds of Mr. Hyde. "In this

mixture of good and bad in Dr. Jekyll," Nabokov says, "the bad can be separated as Hyde, who is a precipitate of pure evil, a precipitation in the chemical sense since something of the composite Jekyll remains behind to wonder in horror at Hyde when Hyde is in action."

"In *Dr. Jekyll and Mr. Hyde,*" says McLynn, "Stevenson delved deeper into the unconscious than in any other work." Partly this may have been because it was born from his own unconscious mind: the original germ, according to Fanny, came about during a nightmare. Stevenson reproached his wife when she woke him up because, he said, he was enjoying "a fine bogey tale." Some of the thoughts may have been drug-

This 1886 adventure novel, set in the Scottish highlands after the Jacobite rebellion, is considered by some to be Stevenson's best work.

induced, suggests Bell: because of his ill health, Stevenson often took drugs, including laudanum (a derivative of opium that usually also contained alcohol and some morphine), that today would be either illegal or available only under strictly supervised conditions. Stevenson's "experiences of mood-altering substances," Bell writes, "helped to furnish the transformation symbolism of the story." The effects of the drugs, which Stevenson described in a letter to his friend Stanley Colvin as including "partial madness and total imbecility," may have suggested one of the book's chief plot elements: the mixture that changes Dr. Jekyll into Mr. Hyde.

The book also follows the pattern of duality explored in *Treasure Island* and *The Black Arrow*. "Its London (much of it actually a disguised Edinburgh) is a place of good and evil, light and dark," says Bell. "Hyde, as the mark of the devil, arises from the subterranean depths of the psyche, prowls the darkness; Jekyll is a man of science, virtue, and light." "Jekyll, as 'himself,' is the Victorian denial of human appetites and human realities," the critic continues. "Hyde is a monster not because he is an alien creature but because he *is* Jekyll, with his repressions dissolved utterly, out of control." "To many readers that was the Victorian nightmare," Bell concludes, "a parable of those 'not themselves' because of vice, drugs, or alcohol. . . . Louis made the nightmare hairy flesh in Edward Hyde."

Highlands Adventure

The same year that he completed *The Strange Case of Dr. Jekyll and Mr. Hyde*, Stevenson also finished the work most critics regard as his finest: *Kidnapped*, the story of two young men and their journey across the Scottish highlands in an attempt to restore one to his just inheritance and to enable the other to escape a homeland that had become too dangerous for him. "In *Kidnapped*," says Kiely, "Stevenson explores in greater depth and with some subtlety a friendship between a loyal Protestant Whig Lowlander and a rebellious Catholic Jacobite Highlander." "*Kidnapped* says as much about Stevenson as any autobiography," Bell states. "In David Balfour and Alan Breck he gave substance to two sides of his own character, adventurer and rationalist, man of duty and man of passion." "Coming hard on the heels of the *Jekyll and Hyde* sensation, which had been the subject

of Sunday sermons in London churches," writes McLynn, "*Kidnapped* drew the attention of heavyweight members of the Victorian intellectual elite and firmly established RLS as a major British literary figure."

More than most Stevenson novels, *Kidnapped* requires a knowledge of Scottish history in order to understand the underlying tensions and pressures that drive the narrative. James IV of Scotland became James I of England upon the death of Elizabeth I in 1603. He founded the Stuart dynasty, which continued to rule England until 1713. However, his grandson James II was uncrowned and expelled from England in 1685 for openly professing Catholicism in a Protestant country. James II's son James Stuart ("the Old Pretender") tried to reclaim the English throne from the Protestants in 1715 but was defeated and forced to flee. In 1745 his son Charles—"Bonnie Prince Charlie"—tried again. He raised a large army of supporters in northern and western "Highland" Scotland, but his army was decisively defeated at the battle of Culloden in 1746. About six years after the battle one of the Scottish leaders that supported the English king against Bonnie Prince Charlie, Colin Campbell of Glenure, was murdered. "Although James Stuart [a distant relative of the exiled former kings of Scotland] was eventually executed for the murder, there is doubt that he actually committed it," it states in the introduction to the Airmont Books edition of *Kidnapped*, "but he was a Jacobite leader and spent his time trying to right the wrongs committed by the conquering English. It is also known that Alan Breck Stuart, Balfour's companion in the novel, was in Scotland at the time. . . . It is entirely possible that he was in the area when Campbell Glenure was murdered. It is on this murder and these historical figures that Stevenson based his book."

Kidnapped does not introduce new themes for Stevenson to explore. Instead, it revisits the themes of duality and good vs. evil that his other books had investigated. *Kidnapped*'s superiority lies in the way Stevenson weaves the serious themes of his later books with the inspired storytelling of *Treasure Island*. "*Kidnapped* can be read as an adventure story; the historical detail is never so rich nor so deeply woven into the narrative as it is in Stendhal or Count Lev Nikolayevich Tolstoy or the best of Sir Walter Scott," says Kiely. "Still, the daydream is no longer so free and pure as it had

If you enjoy the works of Robert Louis Stevenson, you may also want to check out the following books and films:

Daniel DeFoe, *Robinson Crusoe*, 1909.
Charles Dickens, *David Copperfield*, 1850.
Mark Twain, *The Adventures of Tom Sawyer*, 1875.
The Last of the Mohicans, starring Randolph Scott, 1936.

been in *Treasure Island*. The adult world encroaches both on the unsettled emotions of the young David and on the political ambitions of Alan Breck." "Although it does not probe as deeply into the nature of duality as *Jekyll and Hyde*," McLynn declares, "and yields fewer clues to the author's life, *Kidnapped* is far more satisfying as a novel, and is let down only by the 'framing action' with the wicked uncle at the beginning and end."

"If in *Jekyll and Hyde* Stevenson finally wove together all the philosophical threads of his mental life," states McLynn, "in *Kidnapped* for the first time he managed wholly successfully to dovetail high adventure with deep psychology." "It unites the historical background which so fascinated Stevenson with characters alive *in* their period while never allowing mere facts to detail the narrative," says Bell. "This is not to say that R.L.S. does not try to be faithful to history, only that he never allows himself to be overwhelmed by it in this novel begun 'partly as a lark, partly as a potboiler.'"

The two major characters, David Balfour and Alan Breck Stuart, are not simply types but fully realized individuals. "David Balfour is a naturalistic hero, unlike Jim Hawkins who is a creature of fantasy; where young Jim could shoot and handle a schooner, David has never learned to use a sword," McLynn continues. "Alan Breck is more complex: martial and courageous yet boastful and undependable, both a warrior and a fop. . . . The brilliance of the quarrel scene, . . . is that David and Alan, as opposites, interpenetrate and show that in certain spheres—relating to life in the Highlands and Lowlands—each is helpless without the other. Using his favourite device of ambivalence within an existing ambiguity, Stevenson

shows both the strength of the bonds that mesh the pair *and* the crevasse that divides them."

"Serialized in May [of 1886] in *Young Folks* and published in book form in July," states McLynn, "*Kidnapped* was later hailed by Henry James . . . as the greatest of Louis's books." The book, James continues in his work *Partial Portraits*, "breathes in every line the feeling of moor and loch." The book also won plaudits from the audience that had so recently taken to *The Strange Case of Dr. Jekyll and Mr. Hyde*. "It was another instant success," explains Bell, "and Stevenson was enjoying an extraordinary bout of creativity that would end only with his death."

Last Years

Another event that marked a change in Stevenson's life and personal circumstances happened in 1886: his father Thomas died. Stevenson and his father had been on uneasy terms throughout their lives. It was Thomas's money that supported Stevenson on his expeditions to the Continent, through his illnesses, through his marriage to Fanny, and through the lean years before his writing earned enough to support himself comfortably. Within a year of Thomas's death Robert had become master of a substantial income and was set up comfortably for life, ironically at the same time that his writing was beginning to earn him both fame and fortune. In 1887 the family—including Thomas's widow Margaret—left Scotland for New York, where Robert had obtained a home deep in the Adirondack Mountains. While there he worked on *The Master of Ballantrae*, another Scottish novel in the pattern of *Kidnapped*. In 1888, however, he shook the dust of America from his heels much as he had the dust of Europe the year before. "A new world of wide skies and blue oceans was opening up to the traveller," relates Bell. "The Pacific beckoned and he did not even think to resist."

Stevenson chartered a boat and set off into the South Pacific. During the remainder of 1888 and all of 1889, the family cruised islands and archipelagos. They arrived in Samoa late in the year and early in 1890 Stevenson purchased the estate of Vailima, on the slopes of Mount Vaea above the town of Apia on the island of Upolu. In the remaining four years of his life Stevenson regained much of his health, dedicated much of his attention to stopping "the political and economic exploitation of the natives by European and American colonists," says Kiely, and began several more long books. "Beneath the excitement of seeing new places and adjusting to a new life was the growing realization that he had cut himself off from the cultures and lands that had frustrated but also nourished him," Kiely explains. In the South Seas his thoughts turned more and more to his Scottish homeland. "It was in Samoa that he wrote *Catriona*, the sequel to *Kidnapped*; and his last work—and one that promised to be his greatest if he had lived to finish it—was *Weir of Hermiston* (1896), a book that is Scottish to the core."

Robert Louis Stevenson died suddenly at his home of Vailima on December 3, 1894. "Death came to RLS from an unexpected direction: not from tuberculosis but from a stroke, brought on by stress and overwork," explains McLynn, "which in turn was caused by the demands of his extravagant family." He was buried near the summit of Mount Vaea at the end of a road cut by his Samoan friends and retainers. "Few now would disagree," says Kiely, ". . . that his fiction belongs with that of Scott, Edgar Allan Poe, Herman Melville, and Conrad in that compelling tradition where mystery and psychology, adventure and moral choice converge."

■ Works Cited

Archer, William, review of *A Child's Garden of Verses, Pall Mall Gazette*, March 24, 1885, reprinted in *Robert Louis Stevenson: The Critical Heritage*, edited by Paul Maixner, Routledge, 1981, pp. 154-57.

Bell, Ian, *Dreams of Exile: Robert Louis Stevenson, a Biography*, Holt, 1992.

Bentley, B. Allen, "Introduction" to *The Black Arrow* by Robert Louis Stevenson, Airmont Books, 1963, pp. 3-7.

Butler, Arthur John, review of *Treasure Island, Atheneum*, December 1, 1883, reprinted in *Robert Louis Stevenson: The Critical Heritage*, edited by Paul Maixner, Routledge, 1981, pp. 130-31.

Garrod, H. W., "The Poetry of R. L. Stevenson," *The Profession of Poetry and Other Lectures*, Clarendon Press, 1929, pp. 179-93.

Henley, W. E., review of *Treasure Island, Saturday Review*, December 8, 1883, reprinted in *Robert Louis Stevenson: The Critical Heritage*, edited by Paul Maixner, Routledge, 1981, pp. 131-36.

"Introduction" to *Kidnapped* by Robert Louis Stevenson, Airmont Book, 1963.

James, Henry, "Robert Louis Stevenson," *Partial Portraits*, Macmillan & Co., 1888, pp. 137-74.

Kiely, Robert, "Robert Louis Stevenson," *Concise Dictionary of British Literary Biography, 1890-1914*, Gale, 1991, pp. 293-309.

McLynn, Frank, *Robert Louis Stevenson: A Biography*, Random House, 1993.

"Mr. R. L. Stevenson's Verse for Children," *Spectator*, March 21, 1885, pp. 382-83.

Nabokov, Vladimir, "Robert Louis Stevenson: 'The Strange Case of Dr. Jekyll and Mr. Hyde,'" *Lectures on Literature*, edited by Fredson Bowers, Harcourt, 1980, pp. 179-204.

Naufftus, William F., "Robert Louis Stevenson," *Dictionary of Literary Biography*, Volume 156: *British Short-Fiction Writers, 1880-1914: The Romantic Tradition*, 1996, pp. 330-55.

Noyes, Alfred, "Stevenson," *Some Aspects of Modern Poetry*, Frederick A. Stokes Co., 1924, pp. 96-117.

Stevenson, Robert Louis, letter to Edmund Gosse dated March 12, 1885, published in *Robert Louis Stevenson: The Critical Heritage*, edited by Paul Maixner, Routledge, 1981, p. 147.

Stevenson, Robert Louis, *Essays in the Art of Writing*, Chatto & Windus, 1905, pp. 111-31.

Stevenson, Robert Louis, *A Child's Garden of Verses*, illustrated by Charles Robinson, Shambala Publications, 1979.

Review of *Treasure Island, Academy*, December 1, 1883, published in *Robert Louis Stevenson: The Critical Heritage*, edited by Paul Maixner, Routledge, 1981, pp. 128-29.

■ For More Information See

BOOKS

Bingham, Jane M., editor, *Writers for Children*, Scribner, 1988.

Calder, Jenni, *Robert Louis Stevenson: A Life Study*, Oxford University Press, 1980.

Daiches, David, *Robert Louis Stevenson and His World*, Thames & Hudson, 1973.

Dictionary of Literary Biography, Gale, Volume 18: *Victorian Novelists after 1885*, 1983, Volume 57: *Victorian Prose Writers after 1867*, 1987, Volume 141: *British Children's Writers, 1880-1914*, 1994.

Hennessy, James Pope, *Robert Louis Stevenson*, Simon & Schuster, 1974.

Short Story Criticism, Volume 11, Gale, 1992.

Silvey, Anita, editor, *Children's Books and Their Creators,* Houghton, 1995.

Swearingen, Roger G., *The Prose Writings of Robert Louis Stevenson: A Guide,* Archon Books, 1980.

World Literature Criticism, Gale, 1992.

PERIODICALS

American Heritage, December, 1988, pp. 81-90.

American West, July-August, 1981, pp. 28-35.

Atlantic Monthly, November 1994, pp. 140-47.

Horn Book, April, 1983, pp. 197-201.

New York Review of Books, June 8, 1995, pp. 14-19.

Reader's Digest (Canadian), August, 1991, pp. 104-9.

Saturday Night, May, 1994, pp. 39-42.

Smithsonian, August, 1995, pp. 50-60.

Sunset, May, 1980, p. 10; September, 1982, pp. 42-45.

Vintage, August-September, 1980, pp. 20-26.*

—*Sketch by Kenneth R. Shepherd*

Robert Townsend

vision variety, 1988, for "Robert Townsend and His Partners in Crime," *HBO Comedy Hour.*

■ Personal

Born February 6, 1957, in Chicago, IL; son of Robert (a construction worker) and Shirley (Jenkins) Townsend; married Cherri Jones in 1990; two children. *Education:* Attended Illinois State University, William Paterson College, NJ, and Hunter College of the City of New York.

■ Addresses

Office—Tinsel Townsend Productions, 8033 Sunset Blvd., #890, Los Angeles, CA 90046.

■ Career

Actor, director, producer, and writer. Former member of experimental Black Actors Guild and Second City comedy group; television commercial appearances and stand-up comedy in New York.

■ Awards, Honors

Image Award, National Association for the Advancement of Colored People (NAACP), best tele-

■ Credits

FILM APPEARANCES

Cooley High, American International, 1975.
Streets of Fire, Universal, 1984.
Soldier's Story, Columbia, 1984.
American Flyers, Warner Bros., 1985.
Odd Jobs, TriStar, 1986.
Ratboy, Warner Bros., 1986.
Hollywood Shuffle, Samuel Goldwyn, 1987.
The Mighty Quinn, Metro-Goldwyn-Mayer (MGM)/ United Artists, 1989.
The Five Heartbeats, Twentieth Century-Fox, 1991.
The Meteor Man (also known as *The Meteor Man: An Urban Fairy Tale*), MGM, 1993.

Also appeared in *Willie and Phil,* 1980, and *That's Adequate,* 1989.

TELEVISION APPEARANCES

The Bounty Man, ABC, 1972.
Women at West Point, CBS, 1979.
Senior Trip!, CBS, 1982.
(Rotating host) *The Late Show,* Fox, 1986.
"Rodney Dangerfield: It's Not Easy Bein' Me," *On Location,* HBO, 1986.
"Robert Townsend and His Partners in Crime," *HBO Comedy Hour,* HBO, 1987.
"Uptown Comedy Express," *On Location,* HBO, 1987.

That's What Friends Are For: AIDS Concert '88, Showtime, 1988.

(Also executive producer) "Take No Prisoners: Robert Townsend and His Partners in Crime II," *HBO Comedy Hour,* HBO, 1988.

(Host) *Freedomfest: Nelson Mandela's 70th Birthday Celebration,* Fox, 1988.

The 2nd Annual American Comedy Awards, ABC, 1988.

The 20th Annual NAACP Image Awards, NBC, 1988.

"The Mutiny Has Just Begun: Robert Townsend and His Partners in Crime III," *HBO Comedy Hour,* HBO, 1989.

"Playing the Nutroll: Robert Townsend and His Partners in Crime IV," *HBO Comedy Hour,* HBO, 1989.

MTV's 1989 Video Music Awards, MTV, 1989.

All-Star Tribute to Kareem Abdul-Jabbar, NBC, 1989.

16th Annual Black Filmmakers Hall of Fame, syndicated, 1989.

Motown 30: What's Goin' On, CBS, 1990.

Cutting Edge with Maria Shriver, NBC, 1990.

The 22nd Annual NAACP Image Awards, NBC, 1990.

A Party for Richard Pryor, CBS, 1991.

Go Party!, The Disney Channel, 1991.

A Comedy Salute to Michael Jordan (also known as *Los Angeles and Chicago Salute to Michael Jordan*), NBC, 1991.

Celebrate the Soul of American Music, syndicated, 1991.

(Host) *Ray Charles: 50 Years in Music, Uh-Huh!,* Fox, 1991.

(Host) *The Movie Awards,* CBS, 1991.

Magic Johnson's All-Star Slam 'N Jam, syndicated, 1992.

The Issue Is Race, PBS, 1992.

Comic Relief V, HBO, 1992.

Back to School '92 (also known as *Education First!*), CBS, 1992.

The 24th Annual NAACP Image Awards, NBC, 1992.

Laughing Matters (also known as *Funny Business*), Showtime, 1993.

Count on Me, PBS, 1993.

(Host) *Met Life Presents the Apollo Theatre Hall of Fame,* NBC, 1994.

The Parent 'Hood, WB, 1995—.

Also appeared in *The Great American Dream Machine,* 1971.

STAGE APPEARANCES

(New York debut) *Take It from the Top,* Henry Street Settlement, 1979.

Bones, Riverside Church, New York City, 1980.

FILM DIRECTOR

(And producer) *Hollywood Shuffle,* Samuel Goldwyn, 1987.

(And executive producer) *The Five Heartbeats,* Twentieth Century-Fox, 1991.

The Meteor Man (also known as *Meteor Man: An Urban Fairy Tale*), MGM, 1993.

B.A.P.S, New Line, 1997.

Also director of *Eddie Murphy Raw,* 1987.

TELEVISION DIRECTOR AND EXECUTIVE PRODUCER

"Robert Townsend and His Partners in Crime," *HBO Comedy Hour* (special), HBO, 1987.

"The Mutiny Has Just Begun: Robert Townsend and His Partners in Crime III," *HBO Comedy Hour* (special), HBO, 1989.

"Playing the Nutroll: Robert Townsend and His Partners in Crime IV," *HBO Comedy Hour* (special), HBO, 1989.

Townsend Television (also know as *The Robert Townsend Variety Show,* series), Fox, 1993.

■ Writings

SCREENPLAYS

(With Keenen Ivory Wayans) *Hollywood Shuffle,* Samuel Goldwyn, 1987.

(With Keenen Ivory Wayans) *The Five Heartbeats,* Twentieth Century-Fox, 1991.

The Meteor Man (also known as *Meteor Man: An Urban Fairy Tale*), MGM, 1993.

TELEVISION SERIES

Townsend Television (also known as *The Robert Townsend Variety Show*), Fox, 1993.

TELEVISION SPECIALS

"Take No Prisoners: Robert Townsend and His Partners in Crime II," *HBO Comedy Hour,* HBO, 1988.

"The Mutiny Has Just Begun: Robert Townsend and His Partners in Crime III," *HBO Comedy Hour,* HBO, 1989.

"Playing the Nutroll: Robert Townsend and His Partners in Crime IV," *HBO Comedy Hour,* HBO, 1989.

■ Sidelights

Drug dealers, pimps, muggers, slaves, and servants—these were the roles actor and filmmaker Robert Townsend feared he would play for his entire career. Rather than give in to a system that tended to stereotype non-white actors in a narrow range of possibilities, Townsend took matters into his own hands: he wrote, directed, and starred in *Hollywood Shuffle*, an independent film that poked fun at the very experiences he and his friends were having. Embraced by the studios and the public, *Hollywood Shuffle* put him on the map and gave him the freedom to take on many subsequent film and television projects. As a director, actor, writer, and producer, Townsend has sought to expand the panorama of options for black characters, using his work to show that skin color is the least descriptive aspect of character, that only by eroding the standard categories will all actors have the same choices, regardless of ethnic background.

One of four children, Townsend was born in Chicago on February 6, 1957. Not long after, Townsend's father, a construction worker, divorced his mother. With the help of her own mother, she raised the children on her own, working at the post office to support the family. Eager to protect her children from the violence that surrounded them, she kept Townsend and his siblings in their apartment as much as possible. In an interview with the *Washington Post*'s Richard Harrington, Townsend recalled: "She had four small kids growing up in a tough neighborhood and she didn't want the gangs to mess with us. And so I used to watch a lot of TV. But I was a weird kid—I watched PBS, classic performances like the Royal Shakespeare Company doing *King Lear* and *Othello*." Townsend often mimicked what he heard on these programs; he also performed accomplished imitations of popular actors, to his friends' amusement. At the time, his only goal was to play basketball—he's a little over six feet tall. But his skills seemed to lie elsewhere, and he remembers spending a lot of time on the bench, cheered by the fact that even if he wasn't on the court, his friends found him very funny.

Townsend's mother offered great support, reassuring her children that they were capable of anything. His grandmother was less encouraging, particularly as his interest in theater began to get more serious. By sixteen, Townsend started to perform with the Experimental Black Actors Guild, now known as the Chicago Theater Company, an experience he credited with teaching him about acting and directing. He also attended the John Robert Powers Modeling School in addition to honing his acting skills further with the improvisational Second City troupe. Townsend began to appear at Punchinello's, a Chicago comedy club; his act was composed of a wide range of celebrity impressions, including Edward G. Robinson and Bill Cosby. He began to establish himself in the entertainment business, appearing in commercials and, in 1975, his first film, *Cooley High*.

The actor intended to join Second City professionally as soon as he was graduated from high school. His mother had other ideas; in an interview with Christopher Vaughn for *Entertainment Weekly*, Townsend acknowledged that she had been a hero to him: "She told us we could do anything we wanted, we just had to work at it." For her sake, he went to Illinois State University in Normal, majoring in communications. After he transferred to Paterson College of New Jersey, he spent much of his time shuttling to New York City. His training included a course with well-respected acting teacher Stella Adler, as well as performances in Negro Ensemble Company productions.

His final transfer was to Hunter College of the City of New York, but he soon quit school to focus on his stand-up and improvisational work. In the late 1970s and early 1980s, Townsend had parts in several made-for-television films, including *Women at West Point, Senior Trip,* and *In Love with an Older Woman*. He also had a small part in Paul Mazursky's feature film *Willie and Phil*. Townsend became friendly with comedian Eddie Murphy around this time, and both of them auditioned for an opening on *Saturday Night Live;* Murphy was hired for the weekly comedy show and Townsend was not, but they remained friendly, working together a few years later.

From Run Around to *Shuffle*

Townsend soon settled on the West Coast, where he landed a small part in Walter Hill's *Streets of Fire* in 1984. Later that year he made a more significant appearance in *A Soldier's Story*, Norman Jewison's tale of a murder investigation at an all-black army base in Louisiana during World War II. During the time he wasn't on camera, Townsend

Townsend wrote, directed, and starred in *The Five Heartbeats*, a 1991 film inspired by the great Motown groups of the 1960s.

assisted cinematographer Russell Voight, an opportunity he later described as extremely instructive for his own filmmaking.

Unfortunately, most of the parts he was offered at this point were those of two-bit hoods. Initially, this seemed fine, but it quickly wore thin. As Townsend explained to Stephen Bourne of *Films and Filming*, ". . . when I played a pimp for the thirty-ninth time, I thought, 'Hey, is this it?'" He feared that he would never break out of those roles if he continued to accept them. Speaking with *People* reporter Darlene Donoloe, Townsend remarked: "People aren't going to say, 'Hey, caught you stealing that TV set on *Cagney & Lacey*.' If you whore around, people will say you are a whore." Teaming up with his friend Keenen Ivory Wayans (later the executive producer and star of the popular comedy series *In Living Color*), he made several short films. The first of these, *Sam Ace*, was shot in 1984. This black-and-white

send-up of film noir detectives such as Sam Spade and Mike Hammer showcased the writing talents of Townsend and Wayans, as well as the acting talents of their friends, many of whom had found the same lack of variety in the film roles they were offered. Playing a version of Siskel and Ebert, the television movie critics, Wayans and Townsend discussed their likes and dislikes in *Sneakin' in the Movies*, followed by a mock-documentary on the Black Acting School, where highly trained black actors practice the black dialect they'll need to land the pimp and hood roles awaiting them in films. Over the next two and a half years, Townsend completed several other short parodies which he ultimately combined along with new material, into his first feature, *Hollywood Shuffle*, released in 1987.

During this time, Townsend paid his bills with minor roles in *Odd Jobs*, directed by Mark Story, John Badham's *American Flyers*, and *Ratboy*, directed by Sondra Locke. He sunk $60,000 he had managed to save into his own project, shooting a few days at a time whenever he could. With no film permits, Townsend and his cast had to rely on one take for each scene—just enough time before the police showed up. The actors rehearsed exhaustively, not only to keep shooting time down but to save on film. In a canny move, Townsend convinced the directors with whom he worked at this time to give him any leftover film stock from their better-financed projects.

Even with these frugalities, Townsend came up about $40,000 short. Taking a gamble, he decided to go into serious credit card debt. As he explained to Harrington, he was on the verge of "tearing up" an application for Visa and Mastercard, ". . . then I opened it, and it said, 'Mr. Townsend, you have a credit line of $8,000 on one card and $9,000 on the other.' And I realized, 'Wait a minute, I could *charge* the film.'" As he noted to Harrington, "The most important question when I was finishing the movie was 'Do you take Visa or Mastercard?'" When it bought the rights to the movie, the Samuel Goldwyn Company covered the credit card expenses and gave Townsend some money to reshoot a few scenes.

Bobby Taylor, the hero of *Hollywood Shuffle* played by Townsend, is a young actor looking for a break. Supporting himself with work at the Winky Dinky Dog, he auditions for a series of stereotypical black roles. In his fantasies—the earlier shorts that Townsend made with Wayans—Taylor imagines better roles for himself, simultaneously pointing up the lack of variety in choices for black actors. Writing in *Time,* Richard Corliss remarked on the overall amateurish production, but concluded that "Townsend knows Bobby fully lives where we all live, in dreams of glory, agony, love—of life's infinite possibilities." *New Republic* critic Stanley Kauffmann found the movie "lively, [and] knowledgeable," and saw a more serious message amidst the parodies: ". . . the film finally says: a black's dream isn't worth holding on to if the only way to realize it is by bowing to white strictures. It's a film about black self-deceptions as well as the black self, deceptions at the price of pride." Bourne declared *Hollywood Shuffle* to be "one of the most original and sharpest comedies to come out of Hollywood in the eighties."

Townsend took a little heat for satire that some critics perceived as homophobic, especially in the character of a prissy hairdresser who can't stop blowing kisses. In an interview with Margy Rochlin in *American Film* he apologized for any offense, stating that "I wasn't trying to poke fun at anybody, I really wasn't." The film was a hit with audiences, easily recouping Townsend's initial $100,000 investment—it grossed more than $10 million. Basking in his success, Townsend had no illusions that his film had removed barriers for black actors, but it was a step. As he said to Donoloe, "I got fed up with seeing other people do the work I wanted to do. Why can't I play the roles that Sean Penn is playing?"

After he saw *Hollywood Shuffle,* Eddie Murphy chose Townsend to direct his concert film *Eddie Murphy Raw.* Describing his work on the film, Townsend told the *Wall Street Journal's* Julie Salamon that he had to get around " . . . profanity and lawsuits and down to an 'R' rating." Janet Maslin of the *New York Times* commended his efforts, writing, "*Eddie Murphy Raw* has been filmed simply and invitingly by Robert Townsend . . . who is very much on the actor-comedian's wavelength and does a subtle job of drawing the audience into the show."

Five Heartbeats, a Superhero, and Two Super Shoppers

In 1987, Townsend made the first of several comedy specials for HBO, "Robert Townsend and His Partners in Crime." Reuniting many of the actors from *Hollywood Shuffle,* Townsend presented a series of parodies and sketches. Three other "Partners in Crime" specials followed, including "Take No Prisoners: Robert Townsend and His Partners in Crime II." Writing in the *New York Times,* John O'Connor commented, "*Take No Prisoners* generally adds up to another first-rate credit for Mr. Townsend's résumé. There's a sometimes quirky, decidedly new sensibility at work here. The results are nearly always fascinating." The following year, Townsend returned to films, appearing in *That's Adequate,* an effort that met with disappointing reviews. He met with more success as the supporting actor to Denzel Washington's star role in *The Mighty Quinn.* Playing the prime suspect in a murder investigation headed by Washington, Townsend caught *New York* critic David Denby's attention: "Playing a local legend—a great lover and free spirit—Townsend exudes a physical pleasure in his rascally role."

The Parent 'Hood, a television series starring Townsend as a communications professor with a rambunctious family, looks at contemporary African American life.

If you enjoy the works of Robert Townsend, you may also want to check out the following films:

A Low Down Dirty Shame, directed by Keenen Ivory Wayans, 1994.
Harlem Nights, directed by Eddie Murphy, 1989.
I Like It Like That, directed by Lauren Valez, 1994.

Teaming up once again with Wayans, Townsend co-scripted *The Five Heartbeats,* the first project of his own production company, Tinsel Townsend. Inspired by the R&B groups of the 1960s such as the Temptations and the Four Tops, the film is a biography of a fictional band whose success is leavened with personal problems and setbacks. The film met with mixed reviews. Typical was Brian D. Johnson's assessment in *Maclean's:* "Sadly, it tries to be too many movies at once. . . . The components do not harmonize. . . . *The Five Heartbeats*—a Motown morality play dressed up as Hollywood entertainment—never finds its own rhythm." *Rolling Stone* contributor Peter Travers found that the films shortcomings were redeemed by its "propulsive score, spirited choreography . . . and evocative sets and costumes. . . . Even clichés can't muffle that joyful noise." Although Desson Howe faulted *The Five Heartbeats* for its "sentimental ambition" in his *Washington Post* review, he noted that "there are flashes everywhere of the comic talent that lit up Townsend and Wayans's *Hollywood Shuffle.*"

One of the sequences of *Hollywood Shuffle* featured a black superhero, an idea Townsend returned to in his 1993 release, *The Meteor Man.* Starring in the film, he played a teacher and struggling musician who lives in a drug-ridden Washington neighborhood. When a meteor transforms this average man into a superhero, he can suddenly confront the dealers and criminals who have taken his neighborhood hostage. Although they acknowledged Townsend's good intentions, several critics expressed their disappointment with the film. *New York Times* contributor Stephen Holden was quite unsparing: "With virtually no plot to speak of, the film is a series of disconnected comic-book adventures with little visceral charge, played mostly for laughs but lacking wit." Ralph Novak, writing in

People, remarked that it is to Townsend's credit that the good-natured writer-director-star of "this unfocused, capricious film, that he makes it not only tolerable but often enjoyable."

Capitalizing on the success of his several *Partners in Crime* comedy specials, Townsend hosted *Townsend Television,* beginning in fall of 1993. The show found little favor with the critics. Tom Shales of the *Washington Post* wrote that, "It's as a director that Townsend comes up shortest; his timing seems off so that the commercial parodies and movie spoofs tend to creak and wobble." *New York Newsday*'s Diane Werts faulted the skits for "wander[ing] on too long." She felt that, "the upside here is, Townsend's so amiable that many folks will happily indulge him." Her opinion was not shared by the network, which cancelled the show before the 1993-1994 season had ended.

Townsend tried another television project in 1995, this time a series titled *The Parent 'Hood.* Co-creator and co-producer Townsend stars as a communications professor whose law-student wife and four children keep him on the alert. The critics were not especially impressed, though several commended its efforts to show a middle-class black family. The result is "super dull, even if the effort to uplift is admirable," as Ken Tucker observed in *Entertainment Weekly. People* reviewer David Hiltbrand found the "structure, the timing and the humor all strictly standard, even a little clichéd." In a cover story on Townsend, *Jet* magazine praised the actor for proving that "a positive family image isn't just a thing of the past," making special mention of Townsend's effort to "bring forth not only laughs but also thought-provoking messages." In his interview with Rochlin, Townsend noted, "You look at two great comedians like Eddie [Murphy] and Richard Pryor, whom I both respect, then you look at Bill Cosby. Cosby, I think, is the new wave because his show is clean and intelligent. . . . People are all shocked out by profanity. Cosby's humor is human: it's not black comedy, it's people and life, universal experiences. That's what I'm into." *The Parent 'Hood* has been compared to *Cosby,* but by the second season, Townsend told *Jet* that the show had established itself as an "original."

In 1997, Townsend returned to film directing with *B.A.P.S.,* a fairy tale of two black American princesses who leave their native Decatur, Georgia, to audition for a rap video in Los Angeles. They are spotted as easy marks by a con man and soon find themselves unknowingly aiding him in a scheme to cheat his elderly uncle of his millions. But the girls and the senior citizen become great friends. A critic in *People* termed *B.A.P.S.* an "amiable but botched comedy," noting that Townsend appeared to direct it "sparingly."

What he began in *Hollywood Shuffle* remains Townsend's emphasis: to dislodge the casting habits and prejudices that keep black actors in stock roles. In 1989, Townsend and filmmaker Spike Lee were honorees of the Black Filmmaker's Foundation at a gala to commemorate the group's tenth anniversary. Townsend appeared with Attorney General Janet Reno in August 1993 to celebrate the tenth anniversary of the National Night Out program that helps promote community outreach programs to fight drug and crime problems. Throughout his career, Townsend has never forgotten the power of movies and television to influence people, to send messages about what matters. Speaking with Veronica Webb in *Interview,* Townsend stated, "I don't think it's just enough to entertain people. I mean, there's a side of me that's a comedian, there's a side of me that's very serious in terms of black people. . . . People need inspiration, especially black people."

■ Works Cited

Review of *B.A.P.S.*, *People,* April 14, 1997, p. 20.

Bourne, William, *Films and Filming,* April, 1988.

Corliss, Richard, "Cinema: Art, War, Death and Sex," *Time,* April 27, 1987, p. 79.

Denby, David, review of *The Mighty Quinn, New York,* March 6, 1989.

Donoloe, Darlene, "In *Hollywood Shuffle,* Comic Actor Robert Townsend Wields His Wit Against Movie Industry Racism," *People,* May 18, 1987, pp. 61-62.

Harrington, David, *Washington Post,* March 24, 1987.

Hiltbrand, David, review of *The Parent 'Hood, People,* January 30, 1995, p. 11.

Holden, Stephen, *New York Times,* August 7, 1993.

Howe, Desson, review of *The Five Heartbeats, Washington Post,* March 29, 1991.

Johnson, Brian D., review of *The Five Heartbeats, Maclean's,* April 22, 1991, p. 62.

Kauffmann, Stanley, "Stanley Kauffmann on Films: Comedy, Sharp and Otherwise," *New Republic,* May 4, 1987, p. 26.

Maslin, Janet, review of *Eddie Murphy Raw, New York Times,* December 19, 1987.

Novak, Ralph, review of *The Meteor Man, People,* August 23, 1993, p. 16.

O'Connor, John J., *New York Times,* September 23, 1988.

"Robert Townsend Gives Positive View of Family Life on *The Parent 'Hood, Jet,* January 29, 1996, pp. 24-27.

Rochlin, Margy, "Close-up: Robert Townsend," *American Film,* April, 1987, p. 62.

Salamon, Julie, *Wall Street Journal,* March 19, 1987.

Shales, Tom, *Washington Post,* September 11, 1993.

Travers, Peter, "The Five Heartbeats," *Rolling Stone,* April 18, 1991, p. 101.

Tucker, Ken, review of *The Parent 'Hood, Entertainment Weekly,* February 3, 1995, p. 42.

Vaughn, Christopher, "Homemade Heroes," *Entertainment Weekly,* January 28, 1994, p. 72.

Webb, Veronica, "Interviews by Veronica Webb," *Interview,* February, 1991, pp. 74-76.

Werts, Diane, *New York Newsday,* September 10, 1993.

■ For More Information See

BOOKS

Current Biography Yearbook, Gale, 1994.

PERIODICALS

American Film, July/August, 1989, p. 22; April, 1991, p. 49.

Black Enterprise, July, 1989, p. 36.

Essence, July, 1995, p. 54.

Newsweek, April 6, 1987, pp. 64-66.

Premiere, April, 1993, p. 40.

Vogue, March, 1991, p. 248.*

—Sketch by C. M. Ratner

Paul Yee

Exhibitions: Saltwater City exhibition, Chinese Cultural Centre (CCC), Vancouver Centennial, 1986.

■ Personal

Born October 1, 1956, in Spalding, Saskatchewan, Canada; son of Gordon and Gim May (Wong) Yee. *Education:* University of British Columbia, B.A., 1978, M.A. 1983. *Hobbies and other interests:* Cycling and swimming.

■ Addresses

Home—922 Carlaw Avenue, Toronto, Ontario, Canada M4K 3L3.

■ Career

Writer. City of Vancouver Archives, Vancouver, British Columbia, Assistant City Archivist, 1980-1988; Archives of Ontario, Toronto, Ontario, Portfolio Manager, 1988-91; Ontario Ministry of Citizenship, policy analyst, 1991-97. Teacher in British Columbia schools, and at Simon Fraser University, University of Victoria, University of British Columbia, Vancouver Museum, and Chinese Community Library Services Society of Vancouver.

■ Awards, Honors

Honorable Mention, Canada Council Literature Prizes, 1986, for *The Curses of Third Uncle;* Vancouver Book Prize, 1989, for *Saltwater City: An Illustrated History of the Chinese in Vancouver;* British Columbia Book Prize for Children's Literature, National I.O.D.E. Book Award, and Parents' Choice Honor, all 1990, all for *Tales from Gold Mountain: Stories of the Chinese in the New World;* Ruth Schwartz Award, Canadian Booksellers Association, 1992, for *Roses Sing on New Snow: A Delicious Tale;* Governor-General's Award, Canada Council, 1996, for *Ghost Train.*

■ Writings

Teach Me to Fly, Skyfighter! (stories), illustrations by Sky Lee, Lorimer (Toronto), 1983.
The Curses of Third Uncle (novel), Lorimer, 1986.
Saltwater City: An Illustrated History of the Chinese in Vancouver, Douglas and McIntyre (Vancouver), 1988, University of Washington, 1989.
Tales from Gold Mountain: Stories of the Chinese in the New World, illustrations by Simon Ng, Groundwood Books (Toronto), 1989, Macmillan, 1990.
Roses Sing on New Snow: A Delicious Tale, illustrations by Harvey Chan, Macmillan, 1992.

Breakaway (novel), Groundwood, 1994.

Moonlight's Luck, illustrations by Terry Yee, Macmillan, 1995.

Ghost Train, illustrations by Harvey Chan, Groundwood, 1996.

Struggle and Hope: The Story of Chinese Canadians, Umbrella Press (Toronto), 1996.

■ Sidelights

Born in Spalding, Saskatchewan, in 1956, Paul Yee is a third generation Chinese-Canadian. Perhaps best known for his award-winning children's work *Tales from Gold Mountain: Stories of the Chinese in the New World,* Yee has also written well-received books for both young adults and adults, including *Saltwater City: An Illustrated History of the Chinese in Vancouver* and *Breakaway.* His works address such themes as racism, alienation, and the New World versus the Old World.

Yee grew up in the Chinatown area of Vancouver, British Columbia. His parents died when he was very young, and he was sent to live with a foster family. Later, his aunt and uncle, who had been raising Yee's older brother, took him in as well. As Yee explained to Dave Jenkinson in *Emergency Librarian,* "I think there was a sense of a family responsibility as well as a personal need on my aunt's part. . . . None of her own children that she gave birth to survived. She had adopted an earlier child, and, when we came along, I think she had another opportunity to become a mother."

On the dust jacket of his book, *Saltwater City,* Yee wrote that he had a "typical Chinese-Canadian childhood, caught between two worlds, and yearning to move away from the neighborhood." His aunt ran a strict home—she would not allow English to be spoken and there was no television. Because their aunt wanted the two boys to retain some ties to their culture, Yee and his brother attended Chinese school for several years. After Yee graduated from high school, his aunt encouraged him to further his education. "Going to university was a ticket out of Chinatown and out of poverty," he told Jenkinson. "It was the classic way of escaping one's economic background."

While he attended the University of British Columbia, Yee began volunteering his time back in Chinatown, which had experienced a period of economic decay. Yee explained to Jenkinson that he and others volunteered as a way of rediscovering their roots: "There was a lot of analysis of why we had been dispossessed of our own heritage and of our own connections to the community. . . . Our own families had decided not to tell us a great deal about the past because it had been so dark and gloomy. . . . The flip side to not knowing our history was that, if you knew your history, you controlled the destiny of your community, of how it would move ahead."

Yee decided to major in history and landed a part-time job at the City Archives in Vancouver. "By the end of that year," he related, "I realized I was more intrigued with working with an archives because it was closer to history." An archivist takes care of historical documents that are usually stored in special areas of libraries and cultural or state institutions. These documents or papers are important for historians and other writers to research past events. Spurred by his interest, Yee later took a full-time position at the Archives.

Yee received a Master of Arts degree in history from the University of British Columbia in 1983 after completing his undergraduate work there. Although Yee has taught informally at several institutions in British Columbia, the focus of his career has been on his work as an archivist and policy analyst, in which he researches and analyzes options for government decision-making. He said in an interview for *Junior DISCovering Authors:* "I really don't view myself as a teacher, even though I do classroom visits."

In 1988, Yee moved to Toronto, where he became Multicultural Coordinator for the Archives of Ontario. In his interview, Yee was asked how, as an archivist, he became a writer of children's literature. "It was a fluke," he replied. "Back in 1983, I was involved in doing work for Chinatown, such as organizing festivals, exhibits, and educational programs. Even though I had written some short stories, I had not done anything in children's literature. A Canadian publishing company, Lorimer, knowing about my work in the Chinese community, asked me to write a children's book that would employ my knowledge of Chinese-Canadian life as a background. *Teach Me to Fly, Skyfighter!* was my first children's book that came out of the request by the publishing company." With his series of four related stories about

"...powerful..."
—*Montreal Gazette*

"...a well-written novel with staying power."
—*Quill & Quire*

Paul Yee

Yee's 1994 young adult novel follows the life of Kwok-ken Wong, a teenage soccer player in Depression-era Vancouver who lives and works on his family's struggling farm.

children living in the immigrant neighborhoods of Vancouver, Yee "has succeeded in portraying the personalities, interests, and dreams of four 11-year-old friends whose voices ring true throughout," according to Frieda Wishinsky in *Quill and Quire*.

Yee very much enjoyed writing his first children's book. "It dovetailed with the work I was doing in building awareness of Chinese-Canadian history and community. I saw my target audience as Canadian children of Chinese ancestry who needed to know more about themselves and their heritage," he said in his interview. Three years later,

Lorimer worked with Yee on another book. In 1986, he won honorable mention for his second juvenile novel, *The Curses of Third Uncle*, from the Canada Council Literature Prizes.

Reveals Past Through Writings

The Curses of Third Uncle is a historical novel that deals with the period of the early twentieth century in which Sun Yat-Sen's revolutionary movement fought against the Chinese Empire. Dr. Sun Yat-Sen, called the "Father of Modern China," had led nine uprisings against the Empire by the time he visited Vancouver in 1910 and 1911, Yee recounts in *Saltwater City*. In *The Curses of Third Uncle*, fourteen-year-old Lillian, living in Vancouver's Chinatown, misses her father, who often travels back to China and throughout the British Columbia frontier—presumably to take care of his clothing business. He is actually a secret agent for Dr. Sun's revolutionary movement.

At one point in his travels, Lillian's father fails to return. His absence is hard economically on the family, but Lillian will not believe that her father has deserted them. Her third uncle, however, threatens to send Lillian's family back to China. In her attempts to locate her father by travelling through British Columbia, Lillian discovers that he has been betrayed by his brother, who has been paid to turn him over to his enemies. Comparing the book in the *Emergency Librarian* to historical epics such as *Shogun* or *Roots*, Christine Dewar stated that Yee "has produced a story that is exciting but contrived, with an attractive and reasonably motivated heroine." *Quill and Quire* reviewer Annette Goldsmith similarly commented that *The Curses of Third Uncle* is "an exciting, fast-paced, well-written tale," and praised Yee for his use of legendary Chinese female warriors to reinforce Lillian's story.

Yee's next book, *Saltwater City*, was published in 1988. This book grew out of Yee's work from 1985 to 1986 as chair of the Saltwater City Exhibition Committee of the Chinese Cultural Centre. In the preface to the book, Yee wrote: "The book pays tribute to those who went through the hard times, to those who swallowed their pride, to those who were powerless and humiliated, but who still carried on. They all had faith that things would be better for future generations. They have been proven correct."

Saltwater City is a history of Vancouver's Chinatown from its beginnings in 1858 to the present. Containing more than 200 photographs and documents, the book deals with a number of political, economic, and social issues, and profiles the lives of many individuals. Yee remarked in his interview that there were no special problems in assembling all this material: "I had done a lot of research from the Saltwater City Exhibition Committee and then there was all my previous work with Chinatown. I had worked with many people, and they were happy to tell me their stories and show me their photograph albums. Had I been an outsider, it would have been much more difficult."

Yee pointed out that "while *Saltwater City* is not a children's book, it is an extremely accessible book. It can serve as a child's book not in the sense that it is read from cover to cover, but rather as a reference book the child can open at any page and study a photograph or read a profile or sidebar." He also added that *Saltwater City* "is very much localized to the Vancouver scene. It is therefore most important to Chinese in the Vancouver area and to the grandchildren of the people who appear throughout the book," although he noted that "it would be possible to compare some of the history to Chinese experiences in cities of the United States."

Other than commemorating the Saltwater City Exhibition, Yee said in his interview, the book serves another purpose: "The key thing in the Vancouver Chinese community is that a tremendous change is occurring. Since 1967, the arrival of many new Chinese from Hong Kong and other Asian immigrants has overwhelmed the older, established community. I felt it was necessary to recognize the earlier chapters of our history before the new waves of immigrations changed everything. I did chapters on the newer immigrants, and their stories are different from the problems encountered earlier."

Although Yee started his career as a historian, compiling information such as that in *Saltwater City,* he had no particular difficulty in making the switch to fiction. Nevertheless, he remarked, he found that writing fiction was much more "arduous because instead of merely reporting what has happened in non-fiction, fiction requires the creation of a story" that will be believable and enjoyable. "The difference between nonfiction and

fiction is the difference between reliable reporting and imaginative creating," he concluded.

Examines Cultural Myths

Yee has said that his knowledge of folk literature comes partly from his childhood reading of western fairy tales. From those stories he remembered things such as actions happening in groups of three, a principle he makes use of in some of his stories. Yee used his familiarity with traditional stories to write *Tales from Gold Mountain,* which was published in 1989. This collection of short stories has won Yee high praise from the critics. Lee Galda and Susan Cox, writing in *Reading Teacher,* believed the book "gives voice to the previously unheard generations of Chinese immigrants whose labor supported the settlement of the west coast of Canada and the United States." The book includes stories about the conflict between the manager of a fish cannery and his greedy boss; a young man who arranges the burial of Chinese railroad workers when he meets his father's ghost; a young woman's gift of ginger root to save her fiance's life; a wealthy merchant who exchanges his twin daughters for sons; and clashes between old traditions and new influences.

Betsy Hearne of the *Bulletin of the Center for Children's Books* noted that "Yee never indulges in stylistic pretensions," yet is able to dramatically blend realism and legend. She explained that Yee moves between lighter tales of love and wit to conflicts between the present and past. The result is that the stories "carry mythical overtones that lend the characters unforgettable dimension—humans achieving supernatural power in defying their fate of physical and cultural oppression." In the afterword, Yee said that he hopes to "carve a place in the North American imagination for the many generations of Chinese who have settled here as Canadians and Americans, and help them stake their claim to be known as pioneers, too."

Yee remarked in his interview that most of *Tales from Gold Mountain* was original material, with only "about five to ten percent of the tales [coming] from the stories I heard when I was growing up." He continued: "The rest comes from my imagination. It's really hard to slice up a book to say which is history and which is imagination. The Chinese stories operate within the particular context of new world history. It's not just a blend of the new with the old but the creation of a new world mythology. Every group that comes to North America leaves an imprint of itself that can be shaped into fiction."

Denise Wilms, writing in *Booklist*, believed that Yee's stories "strikingly reflect traditional Chinese beliefs and customs in new world circumstances," and compared the work to Laurence Yep's *Rainbow People*. *School Library Journal* contributor Margaret A. Chang also compared *Tales* to *Rainbow People* and added that Yee's stories "will further expand and enhance understanding of the Chinese immigrant experience." The book is "told in richly evocative language," according to *Horn Book* reviewer Hanna B. Zeiger, and "the stories skillfully blend the hardships and dangers of frontier life in a new country with the ancient attitudes and traditions brought over from China." The critic concluded that the images of *Tales from Gold Mountain* "will stay with the reader for a long time."

As in *The Curses of Third Uncle*, Yee created another strong female character for his 1992 work, *Roses Sing On New Snow: A Delicious Tale*. In the work, Maylin, a cook in her father's restaurant, teaches the secrets of her recipes to the governor of South China, who is visiting her town. In the *Bulletin of the Center for Children's Books*, Betsy Hearne noted that "vivid art and clean writing are graced by a neatly feminist ending." Asked if there had been a feminist twist in *Roses Sing on New Snow*, Yee replied, "Insofar as the novel shows Maylin asserting herself, I would say yes." He explained: "Children need to see representations of reality in their literature: Chinese immigration to North America has had the unique feature of being predominately male since at first the men were coming by themselves to America. That's a fact about our history. Some of the early communities were almost all male." By portraying positive female characters such as Maylin and Lillian in *The Curses of Third Uncle*, Yee counters the male-dominated history with fictional female role models.

In 1994, Yee published *Breakaway*, a novel for young adults. Set in the Chinese community in Vancouver during the Great Depression of the 1930s, the story follows high school student Kwok-ken Wong, who lives with his impoverished family on their small farm. A soccer star, Kwok yearns to attend a university. But he meets with preju-

---

If you enjoy the works of Paul Yee, you may also want to check out the following books and films:

Virginia Hamilton, *The People Could Fly: American Black Folk Tales*, 1985.
Ruthanne Lum McCunn, *Pie-Biter*, 1983.
Laurence Yep, *The Rainbow People*, 1989.
The Joy Luck Club, starring Tsai Chin, 1993.

---

dice: Kwok's scholarship application is rejected and he is forced off his soccer team for being "a Chinaman." His family members have their own struggles—his father and mother are pressured to accept a small offer for their land, and his sister agrees to an arranged marriage to help the family economically. "Yee gives a sensitive yet hard-edged portrayal of the life facing a talented young Chinese man in the 1930s," according to Ronald Jobe in the *Journal of Adolescent and Adult Literacy*. "Readers glimpse the stern reality of the depression—lack of jobs, shortage of money, and constant worry about food." Margaret Mackey, writing in *CM: A Reviewing Journal of Canadian Materials for Young People*, declared that the author is adept at "conveying the complexity and ambivalence of Kwok-ken's life. . . . Kwok's increasing bitterness over his inability to fit in anywhere is well handled."

As a historian and observer of Chinese and other immigrant communities in Canada, Yee has noted significant changes in Canadian attitudes and practices toward its racial minority communities. "The change has been for the better in many ways. There are new state initiatives to improve race relations, and even the private sector is learning about managing diversity and employment equity. I am optimistic about the future." In his writing, he concluded, he strives to articulate this philosophy: "From the past, for the future."

■ Works Cited

Chang, Margaret A., review of *Tales from Gold Mountain: Stories of the Chinese in the New World*, *School Library Journal*, May, 1990, p. 121.
Dewar, Christine, review of *The Curses of Third Uncle*, *Emergency Librarian*, May, 1987, p. 51.

Galda, Lee, and Susan Cox, review of *Tales from Gold Mountain: Stories of the Chinese in the New World, Reading Teacher,* April, 1991, p. 585.

Goldsmith, Annette, "Illuminating Adventures with Young People from Long Ago," *Quill and Quire,* December, 1986, p. 14.

Hearne, Betsy, review of *Tales from Gold Mountain: Stories of the Chinese in the New World, Bulletin of the Center for Children's Books,* March, 1990, p. 178.

Hearne, Betsy, review of *Roses Sing on New Snow: A Delicious Tale, Bulletin of the Center for Children's Books,* July-August, 1992, p. 307.

Jenkinson, Dave, "Portraits: Paul Yee," *Emergency Librarian,* May-June, 1995, pp. 61-64.

Jobe, Ronald, review of *Breakaway, Journal of Adolescent and Adult Literacy,* February, 1996, pp. 431-32.

Mackey, Margaret, review of *Breakaway, CM: A Reviewing Journal of Canadian Materials for Young People,* September, 1994, p. 139.

Wilms, Denise, review of *Tales from Gold Mountain: Stories of the Chinese in the New World, Booklist,* March 15, 1990, p. 1464.

Wishinsky, Frieda, review of *Teach Me to Fly, Skyfighter!, Quill and Quire,* October, 1983, p. 16.

Yee, Paul, *Saltwater City: An Illustrated History of the Chinese in Vancouver,* Douglas and McIntyre (Vancouver), 1988, University of Washington, 1989.

Yee, Paul, *Tales from Gold Mountain: Stories of the Chinese in the New World,* Groundwood Books (Toronto), 1989, Macmillan, 1990.

Yee, Paul, telephone interview with Jordan Richman for *Junior DISCovering Authors,* August 11, 1993.

Zeiger, Hanna B., review of *Tales from Gold Mountain: Stories of the Chinese in the New World, Horn Book,* July-August, 1990, pp. 459-60.

■ For More Information See

BOOKS

Children's Literature Review, Volume 44, Gale, 1997.
Seventh Book of Junior Authors and Illustrators, edited by Sally Holmes Holtze, H. W. Wilson, 1996, pp. 352-54.

PERIODICALS

Booklist, March 1, 1992, p. 1288.
Books in Canada, December, 1983, p. 17; December, 1986, p. 18; May, 1989, p. 5.
Canadian Children's Literature, Volume 22, number 3; Summer, 1990, pp. 93-94.
Canadian Literature, Spring, 1988, p. 168; Autumn, 1991, pp. 142-43.
Children's Book News, September, 1983.
Horn Book, March-April, 1992, p. 196.
Quill and Quire, December, 1989, p. 23; April, 1994, p. 39.
School Librarian, May, 1997, p. 91.*

—Sketch by Jordan Richman and Thomas McMahon

Acknowledgments

Acknowledgments

Grateful acknowledgment is made to the following publishers, authors, and artists for their kind permission to reproduce copyrighted material.

TIM ALLEN. Cast of *Home Improvement,* photograph. Archive Photos, Inc. Reproduced by permission. / Allen, Tim, with Kirstie Alley in film *For Richer or Poorer,* photograph. Courtesy of the Kobal Collection. Reproduced by permission. / Allen, Tim, with Eric Lloyd in film *The Santa Clause,* photograph. Fotos International/Archive Photos, Inc. Reproduced by permission. / Allen, Tim, photograph. AP/Wide World Photos, Inc. Reproduced by permission.

GREG BEAR. Miller, Ron, illustrator. From a cover of **Eon,** by Greg Bear. Tor Books, 1986. Cover art © 1985 by Ron Miller. Reproduced by permission. / Miller, Ron, illustrator. From a jacket of **Eternity,** by Greg Bear. Warner Books, 1988. Reproduced by permission. / Barlowe, Wayne, illustrator. From a cover of **Moving Mars,** by Greg Bear. Tor Books, 1993. Reproduced by permission. / Puckey, Don, illustrator. From a cover of **Queen of Angels,** by Greg Bear. Warner Books, 1994. Reproduced by permission. / Bear, Greg, photograph by Jerry Bauer. © Jerry Bauer. Reproduced by permission.

WILLA CATHER. "A Breezy Day," painting by Charles C. Curran. From a cover of **My Ántonia,** by Willa Cather. Bantam Books, 1994. Reproduced by permission of Bantam Books, a division of Bantam Doubleday Dell Publishing Group, Inc. / Cather, Willa, photograph by Carl Van Vechten. The Library of Congress.

MARC CHAGALL. Chagall, Marc, painter. "I and the Village." 1911. Oil on canvas, 6' 3 5/8" x 59 5/8" (192.1 x. 151.4 cm.) The Museum of Modern Art, New York. Mrs. Simon Guggenheim Fund. Photograph © 1998 The Museum of Modern Art, New York. Reproduced by permission. / "Self Portrait with Seven Fingers," painting by Marc Chagall. 1912/13. Foto Marburg/Art Resource, NY. Reproduced by permission. / Chagall, Marc, photograph. AP/ Wide World Photos, Inc. Reproduced by permission. / Chagall, Marc, photograph by Carl Van Vechten. The Library of Congress.

C. J. CHERRYH. Andrews, Martin, illustrator. From a cover of **The Faded Sun: Shon'Jir,** by C. J. Cherryh. DAW Books, Inc., 1979. Reproduced by permission. / Whelan, Michael, illustrator. From a cover of **Chanur's Venture,** by C. J. Cherryh. DAW Books, Inc., 1985. Reproduced by permission. / Whelan, Michael, illustrator. From a cover of **Cuckoo's Egg,** by C. J. Cherryh. DAW Books, Inc., 1985. Reproduced by permission. / Maitz, Don, illustrator. From a cover of **Cyteen: The Rebirth,** by C. J. Cherryh. Popular Library, 1989. Reproduced by permission. / Whelan, Michael, illustrator. From a cover of **Foreigner: A Novel of First Contact,** by C. J. Cherryh. DAW Books, Inc., 1994. Reproduced by permission. / Puckey, Don, illustrator. From a cover of **Tripoint,** by C. J. Cherryh. Warner Books, 1995. Reproduced by permission. / Cherryh, C. J., photograph by David A. Cherry. Reproduced by permission of C. J. Cherryh.

BARBARA COHEN. Hyman, Trina Schart, illustrator. From a cover of **Seven Daughters and Seven Sons,** by Barbara Cohen and Bahija Lovejoy. Beech Tree Books, 1994. Reproduced by permission of Beech Tree Books, an imprint of William Morrow & Company, Inc. / Cohen, Barbara, photograph.

GILLIAN CROSS. Cover of **Wolf,** by Gillian Cross. Scholastic, Inc., 1990. Illustration copyright © 1993 by Scholastic Inc. POINT is a registered trademark of Scholastic Inc. Reproduced by permission. / Cover of **Pictures in the Dark,** by Gillian Cross. Holiday House, Inc., 1996. Reproduced by permission. / Cross, Gillian, photograph by Bob Jesson. Bob Jesson Photography. Reproduced by permission of Gillian Cross and Bob Jesson.

SAMUEL R. DELANY. Lynch, Brian, illustrator. From a cover of **The Motion of Light in Water: Sex and Science Fiction Writing in the East Village, 1960-1965,** by Samuel R. Delany. Masquerade Books, 1993. Reproduced by permission. / Fox, Jon Gilbert, photographer. From a cover of **Flight from Neveryon,** by Samuel R. Delany. Wesleyan University Press, 1994. © 1994 by Samuel R. Delany. Reproduced by permission of University Press of New England. / Canty, Thomas, illustrator. From a cover of **They Fly at Ciron,** by Samuel R. Delany. Tor Books, 1995. Reproduced with permission of St. Martin's Press, Incorporated. / Delany, Samuel R., photograph. Masquerade Books. Reproduced by permission.

FARRUKH DHONDY. Jacket of **Black Swan,** by Farrukh Dhondy. Houghton Mifflin, 1993. Reproduced by permission of Houghton Mifflin Company. / Dhondy, Farrukh, photograph. Channel Four Television (London).

PHILIP K. DICK. Colmer, Roy, illustrator. Author portrait from a cover of **Time Out of Joint,** by Philip K. Dick. Carroll & Graf Publishers, Inc., 1987. Reproduced by permission. / Cover of **The Three Stigmata of Palmer Eldritch,** by Philip K. Dick. Vintage Books, 1991. Reproduced by permission of Random House, Inc. / Cover of **The Man in**

the High Castle, by Philip K. Dick. Vintage Books, 1992. Cover photograph © Digital Art/Westlight. Reproduced by permission of Random House, Inc. / Scene from *Blade Runner,* photograph. © Archive Photos, Inc. Reproduced by permission.

F. SCOTT FITZGERALD. Cugat, Francis, illustrator. From a cover of *The Great Gatsby,* by F. Scott Fitzgerald. Scribner Paperback Fiction, 1995. Reproduced by permission of Scribner, a division of Simon & Schuster, Inc. / Clark, Bradley, illustrator. From a cover of *Tender Is the Night,* by F. Scott Fitzgerald. Scribner Paperback Fiction, 1995. Reproduced by permission of Bradley Clark. / "Jean Cocteau," painting by Jacques Emile Blanche. From a cover of *This Side of Paradise,* by F. Scott Fitzgerald. Bantam Books, 1996. Reproduced by permission of Bantam Books, a division of Bantam Doubleday Dell Publishing Group, Inc. / Fitzgerald, F. Scott, photograph by Carl Van Vechten. The Library of Congress.

JODIE FOSTER. Foster, Jodie, in the film *The Accused,* 1988, photograph. AP/Wide World Photos, Inc. Reproduced by permission. / Foster, Jodie, with Dianne Wiest and Adam Hann-Byrd standing by door in film *Little Man Tate,* photograph. Courtesy of The Kobal Collection. Reproduced by permission. / Foster, Jodie with Anthony Hopkins, seated at table, in film *The Silence of the Lambs,* photograph. Ken Regan/Fotos International/Archive Photos, Inc. Reproduced by permission. / Jodie Foster and Robert DeNiro walking down sidewalk in film *Taxi Driver,* photograph. Columbia Pictures/Archive Photos, Inc. Reproduced by permission. / Foster, Jodie, photograph. AP/Wide World Photos, Inc. Reproduced by permission.

RUSSELL FREEDMAN. Jacket of *Cowboys of the Wild West,* by Russell Freedman. Clarion Books, 1985. Jacket © 1985 by Houghton Mifflin Company. Reproduced by permission. / Cover of *Lincoln: A Photobiography,* by Russell Freedman. Clarion Books, 1987. Reproduced by permission of Houghton Mifflin Company. / Cover of *Franklin Delano Roosevelt,* by Russell Freedman. Clarion Books, 1990. Reproduced by permission of Houghton Mifflin Company. / Freedman, Russell, photograph. © 1988 Charles Osgood/Chicago Tribune Co. Reproduced by permission of Houghton Mifflin Company.

JOSEPH HELLER. Cover of *Catch-22,* by Joseph Heller. Scribner Paperback Fiction, 1996. Copyright © 1955, 1961, renewed 1989 by Joseph Heller. Reproduced by permission of Scribner Paperback Fiction, a division of Simon & Schuster, Inc. / Heller, Joseph, photograph. AP/Wide World Photos, Inc. Reproduced by permission.

JON KRAKAUER. Cover of *Into the Wild,* by Jon Krakauer. Anchor Books, 1997. Reproduced by permission of Doubleday, a division of Bantam Doubleday Dell Publishing Group, Inc. / Krakauer, Jon, photographer. From a cover of his *Into Thin Air.* Villard Books, 1997. Copyright © 1997 by Jon Krakauer. All rights reserved under International and Pan-American Copyright Conventions. Reproduced by permission of Villard Books, a division of Random House, Inc. / Krakauer, Jon, photograph by Linda M. Moore. Reproduced by permission of the publicity department for Villard Books, a division of Random House, Inc.

BARBARA MERTZ. Mann, David, illustrator. From a cover of *Die for Love,* by Elizabeth Peters. Tor Books, 1987. Reproduced by permission. / Cover of *The Wizard's Daughter,* by Barbara Michaels. Berkley Books, 1995. Reproduced by arrangement with The Berkley Publishing Group, a member of Penguin Putnam Inc. All rights reserved. / Mertz, Barbara, photograph by Sigrid Estrada. Reproduced by permission of Sigrid Estrada.

RICHARD PECK. Cover of *Remembering the Good Times,* by Richard Peck. Dell Books, 1986. Reproduced by permission of Dell Books, a division of Bantam Doubleday Dell Publishing Group, Inc. / Boyer, Gene, illustrator. From a jacket of *Those Summer Girls I Never Met,* by Richard Peck. Delacorte Press, 1988. Jacket illustration © 1988 by Gene Boyer. Reproduced by permission of Delacorte Press, a division of Bantam Doubleday Dell Publishing Group, Inc. / Cover of *Are You in the House Alone?* by Richard Peck. Dell Books, 1989. Reproduced by permission of Dell Books, a division of Bantam Doubleday Dell Publishing Group, Inc. / Cover of *Anonymously Yours,* by Richard Peck. Beech Tree Books, 1995. Reproduced by permission of Beech Tree Books, an imprint of William Morrow & Company, Inc. / Pickerell, J., photographer. From a cover of *The Last Safe Place on Earth,* by Richard Peck. Laurel-Leaf, 1996. Cover photograph © 1994 by J. Pickerell. Reproduced by permission of Bantam Doubleday Dell Books for Young Readers. / Peck, Richard, photograph by Don Gallo. Reproduced by permission of Richard Peck.

FREDERICK POHL. Vallejo, Boris, illustrator. From a cover of *Gateway,* by Frederick Pohl. Del Rey Books, 1978. Reproduced by permission of Random House, Inc. / Sternbach, Rick, illustrator. From a cover of *Pohlstars,* by Frederick Pohl. Del Rey Books, 1984. Reproduced by permission of Random House, Inc. / Gutierrez, Alan, illustrator. From a cover of *The Starchild Trilogy,* by Frederick Pohl and Jack Williamson. Baen Books, 1986. Reproduced by permission of Baen Publishing Enterprises. / Cover of *The Space Merchants,* by Frederick Pohl and C. M. Kornbluth. St. Martin's Press, 1987. Reproduced by permission. / Mattingly, David, illustrator. From a cover of *Jem,* by Frederick Pohl. Baen Books, 1994. Reproduced by permission of Baen Publishing Enterprises. / Pohl, Frederick, photograph. AP/Wide World Photos, Inc. Reproduced by permission.

CARL SANDBURG. Hague, Michael, illustrator. From a cover of *Rootabaga Stories: Part Two,* by Carl Sandburg. Harcourt Brace, 1990. Copyright © 1989 by Michael Hague. Reproduced by permission of Harcourt Brace & Company. / Cover of *Carl Sandburg: Selected Poems,* by Carl Sandburg. Gramercy Books, 1992. Reproduced by permission of Corbis-Bettmann. / Cover of *Chicago Poems,* by Carl Sandburg. Dover Publications, 1994. Reproduced by permission. / Sandburg, Carl, photograph. AP/Wide World Photos, Inc. Reproduced by permission.

ROBERT SILVERBERG. Burns, Jim, illustrator. From a cover of *World of a Thousand Colors,* by Robert Silverberg. Bantam Books, 1984. Cover art © 1984 by Jim Burns. Reproduced by permission of Bantam Books, a division of Bantam Doubleday Dell Publishing Group, Inc. / Burns, Jim, illustrator. From a cover of *The Conglomeroid Cocktail Party,* by Robert Silverberg. Bantam Books, 1985. Cover art © 1985 by Jim Burns. Reproduced by permission of Bantam Books, a division of Bantam Doubleday Dell Publishing Group, Inc. / Whelan, Michael, illustrator. From a cover of *Hot Sky at Midnight,* by Robert Silverberg. Bantam Books, 1995. Cover art copyright © 1995 by Michael Whelan. Reproduced by permission of Bantam Books, a division of Bantam Doubleday Dell Publishing Group, Inc. / Burns, Jim, illustrator. From a cover of *The Mountains of Majipoor,* by Robert Silverberg. Cover illustration copyright © 1995 by Jim Burns. Reproduced by permission of Bantam Books, a division of Bantam Doubleday Dell Publishing Group, Inc. / Silverberg, Robert, photograph by Jerry Bauer. © Jerry Bauer. Reproduced by permission.

STEVEN SPIELBERG. McConaughey, Matthew with Morgan Freeman and others in film *Amistad,* photograph. AP/Wide World Photos, Inc. Reproduced by permission. / UFO hovering above group of people in film *Close Encounters of the Third Kind,* photograph. Fotos International/Archive Photos, Inc. Reproduced by permission. / Thomas, Henry (as Elliott) with E.T., in the film *E.T.: The Extra-Terrestrial,* photograph. AP/Wide World Photos, Inc. Reproduced by permission. / Men looking down at shark in the film *Jaws,* photograph. Archive Photos, Inc. Reproduced by permission. / Finnes, Ralph, as Amon Goeth, selecting Helen Hirsch (portrayed by Embeth Davitdz) as housemaid, in the film *Schindler's List,* photograph. AP/Wide World Photos, Inc. Reproduced by permission. / Spielberg, Steven, photograph. Archive Photos, Inc. Reproduced by permission.

STEVENSON, ROBERT LOUIS. Hobart, Rose, and Frederic March at piano in the film *Dr. Jekyll and Mr. Hyde,* photograph. Archive Photos, Inc. Reproduced by permission. / Craft, Kinuko, illustrator. From an illustration in *Treasure Island,* by Robert Louis Stevenson, adapted by June Edwards. Raintree Publishers, 1980. Reproduced by permission of Steck-Vaughn Co. / Scene from *Treasure Island,* photograph. Archive Photos, Inc. Reproduced by permission. / Fraser, Alan, illustrator. From a cover of *Kidnapped,* by Robert Louis Stevenson. Puffin Books, 1994. Copyright © Alan Fraser, 1994. Reproduced by permission of Penguin Books Ltd. / Stevenson, Robert Louis, photograph. AP/Wide World Photos, Inc. Reproduced by permission.

ROBERT TOWNSEND. Wright, Michael, with Leon, Robert Townsend, Harry J. Lennix, and Tico Wells in *The Five Heartbeats,* photograph. Courtesy of The Kobal Collection. Reproduced by permission. / Cast of *The Parent 'Hood,* photograph. Archive Photos, Inc. Reproduced by permission. / Townsend, Robert, photograph. AP/Wide World Photos, Inc. Reproduced by permission.

PAUL YEE. McGaw, Laurie, illustrator. From a cover of *Breakaway,* by Paul Yee. Groundwood Books, 1997. Reproduced by permission of Groundwood Books/Douglas & McIntyre. / Yee, Paul, photograph by James Ho Lim. Reproduced by permission of Paul Yee.

Cumulative Index

Author/Artist Index

The following index gives the number of the volume in which an author/artist's biographical sketch appears.